MANAGING HUMAN RESOURCE
Text, Perspectives and Challenges

MANAGING HUMAN RESOURCE
Text, Perspectives and Challenges

Prof. Lallan Prasad
& A. M. Banerjee

STERLING PUBLISHERS PRIVATE LIMITED
A-59, Okhla Industrial Area, Phase-II, New Delhi-110020.
Tel: 26387070, 26386209 Fax: 91-11-26383788
e-mail: mail@sterlingpublishers.com
www.sterlingpublishers.com

Managing Human Resource: Text, Perspectives and Challenges
© 2012, Prof. Lallan Prasad & A. M. Banerjee
ISBN 978 81 207 7434 6

All rights are reserved. No part of this publication may be reproduced, stored in a retrieval system or transmitted, in any form or by any means, mechanical, photocopying, recording or otherwise, without prior written permission of the original publisher.

PRINTED IN INDIA

Printed and Published by Sterling Publishers Pvt. Ltd., New Delhi-110 020.

Preface

There is a constant need to manage people whether they work in farms, factories, banking, finance, insurance, marketing, sales, construction, tourism, education, health, computer operations, public administration or the corporate sector to ensure smooth running of the organisation and achievement of goals. HR managers act as the facilitators who assist top management in policy formulation on HR – planning, procuring, training and developing, evaluating performance, motivating people and maintaining healthy industrial relations.

HRM is not an entirely new discipline. Studies on ancient civilisations of Indus Valley, Egypt, Greece and South America amply demonstrate that these civilisations were built by conscious human effort, planning and organisation. Kautilya, the famous ancient Indian philosopher, emphasised on selecting the right type of people for governing, motivating and giving fair treatment to all. In modern times, HRM assumed importance after Industrial Revolution in the late nineteenth and early twentieth centuries because of the widening gap between ownership and workmanship, rise of trade unionism and strained labour-management relations.

Managing Human Resource: Text, Perspectives and Challenges (enlarged and revised 5th edition) covers various important aspects of modern corporate structure with detailed chapters on concepts like HR environment, management philosophy, role and responsibilities of HR managers, emotional and social intelligence, personality development, motivation, communication, leadership, change and conflict management, dealing with unions, collective bargaining, social security, labour laws, grievance settlement, worker's participation in management, outsourcing, downsizing and restructuring, employee empowerment and HRM issues in TNCs, specially cross-cultural management. Each of these chapters contains sections like perspective, which highlights best industrial practices, and situation analysis to encourage innovative thinking and problem-solving skills in managers.

The book is designed to cater to the curriculum of HRM and HRD in MBA, MBE, M Com, MSW, PG Programs in Personnel

Management and Industrial Relations, BBA and BBE. Students in professional courses like CA, ICWA and B Tech will also find the book useful. Practicing managers can also benefit by refreshing their knowledge, understanding latest company practices and sharpening their skills of managing people at work.

The authors are grateful to the management scholars and professionals who have enriched the HRM discipline and are quoted in this book. They also appreciate the help of company executives in the private and public sectors, MNCs, and Dr U.D. Choubey, Director General and Shri K.N. Dhawan, Advisor Corporate Communications of SCOPE for providing useful material for the text. Other sources of information that have enriched the contents include websites, published reports of companies, chambers of commerce and various research organisations.

Contents

Preface   v

Part I
HR Environment and Management

Chapter 1. HR Environment   **3**

Introduction • Socio-psychological Factors • Cultural Factors • Work Culture in India • Work Culture in the West • Japanese Work Culture • Demographic Factors • Economic Factors • Technological Factors • Ecological and Environmental Factors • Political Factors • Legal and Administrative Factors • Situation Analysis • Review Questions • Further Readings

Chapter 2. Corporate Management and HRM   **32**

Functions of Management • *Planning* • *Organisation* • *Coordination* • *Control* • *Motivation* • Evolution of Management • *Management as a Psychological Process* • *Management as an Art* • *Management as Systematised Practice* • *Management as a Science* • F.W. Taylor • Henri Fayol • Parker Follett • Prof. Elton Mayo • Douglas McGregor • Management Hexagon • Management Hierarchy • *Top Management* • *Middle Management* • *Specialists* • *Front-line Supervisors* • *Management as an Economic Resource* • *Management as a System of Authority* • *Management as a Class or Elite* • Classification of Organisations • Bureaucracy • Open-System • Corporate Objectives and Policy Formulation • Management by Objectives • Managing Human Resource • HRM Defined • HRM and HRD • HR Manager's Role • Strategic HRM • HR Vision, Mission, Goals and Objectives • Aligning HRM Goals With Company Goals • Situation Analysis • Review Questions • Further Readings

Chapter 3. Organisation Structure and HR Division   **73**

Relationships • Types of Organisation • Types of Relationships • *Direct* • *Lateral* • *Functional* • *Staff* • *Matrix Organisation*

• Board of Directors • Decentralisation of Authority • Informal Organisation • Group Dynamics • Situation Analysis • Review Questions • Further Readings

Part II
Understanding People

Chapter 4. Emotional and Social Intelligence   93

Emotional Intelligence • Emotional Competence • Social Intelligence • IQ and EQ • EQ and Women • EQ and Age • Emotional Intelligence and Management • Situation Analysis • Review Questions • Further Readings

Chapter 5. Personality Traits and The Job   103

Heredity vs. Environment • Role of Learning • Personality Traits • Healthy Personality • Personality and the Job • Situation Analysis • Review Questions • Further Readings

Chapter 6. Motivation, Communication and Leadership   117

Sources of Authority • *The Formal Authority Theory* • *The Acceptance Theory* • *The Competence Theory* • *Persuasion* • *Supervision* • *Motivation* • *Maslow Model* • ERG Theory • Porter and Lawler Model • Motivation-Maintenance Model • Delegation of Authority • Communication • Communication Models • Means of Communication • Written *vs.* Oral Message • Noting Systems • Barriers to Communication • Management Committees • Leadership • Developing O.K. Feeling in Subordinates • Managerial Grid • Grid Styles • Paternalism • Opportunism • Facadist • Situation Analysis • Review Questions • Further Readings

Chapter 7. Resistance to Change   151

Resistance to Change • Individual Change Model • Organisational Resistance • Organisation Change Model • Change Process and Productivity • Participative Attitude • Situation Analysis • Review Questions • Further Readings

Chapter 8. Conflict Situations and Management Systems   162

Necessity of Conflict • Discovery of Conflict • Coping with Differences • Management System • Social Systems • Win or Lose Strategy • Win-win Strategy • Meeting Hostile Situations in Practice • Patient Hearing • Controlled Reaction • Diffusion • Alertness for a Catch • Right Atmosphere • Situation Analysis • Review Questions • Further Readings

Part III
Managing People

Chapter 9. Manpower Planning and Selection   **177**

Manpower Planning • *Bases of Manpower Planning* • The Annual Manpower Plan • Medium and Long Range Plans • Manpower Planning Models • Recruitment and Selection • Application Form • Interview • References • Medical Test • Appointment Order • Personnel Research • Personnel Statistics • Situation Analysis • Review Questions • Further Readings

Chapter 10 Job Evaluation and Enrichment   **202**

Definition • Job Analysis • Methods of Job Evaluation • *Non-analytical Methods* • *Analytical Methods* • Factor Comparison Method • *Steps in Factor Comparison* • Patterson's Approach • Job Enrichment • Situation Analysis • Review Questions • Further Readings

Chapter 11 Performance Appraisal and Promotion   **219**

Appraisal Objectives • Merit-rating Systems • Designing of Appraisal Forms • Promotion • Merit vs. Seniority • Performance Appraisal in Indian Companies • 360 Degree Appraisal • Situation Analysis • Review Questions • Further Readings

Chapter 12 Training and Development   **241**

Induction • Training the Workmen • Methods of Training • Training in the Workroom • Learning Curves • Training the Office Staff • Company Policy • Training of Management Trainees • Green Stamps for Shelf-sitters • Training the Executives • Social Changes • Identification of Training Needs • Role of the Training Division • Seminars and Outside Courses • Situation Analysis • Review Questions • Further Readings

Chapter 13 Compensation and Incentives   **262**

Wage Theories • Fair Wage Concept • Methods of Wage Payment • Dearness Allowance • Changes in Wage Structure • Earning Progression Analysis • Incentives • Incentive Scheme in a Steel

Plant • Executive Compensation • Work Content • Bonus Rate (Rupees/Day) • Situation Analysis • Review Questions • Further Readings

Part IV
Managing Industrial Relations

Chapter 14. Industrial Disputes and Collective Bargaining 283

Psychological Causes • Social Changes • Exploitation and Class Conflict • Role of the State • Systems Approach • *Technological Context* • *Market Context* • *Power Context* • *Influence of Industrialising Elite* • *Present Context* • Role of the Management • Responsibility of the State • The Role of Unions • Collective Bargaining • Theories on Collective Bargaining • Giri's View • Steps in Bargaining • Basis of Negotiation • Preparation • Background Data • Outside Counsel • Negotiating Committee • Conducting Negotiations • Finalising the Contract • Administration of the Contract • Adjudication Machinery • Authorities under the Industrial Disputes Act, 1947 • Situation Analysis • Review Questions • Further Readings

Chapter 15. Working Conditions and Social Security   320

Safety • Lighting and Ventilation • Distractions • Sanitation • Fatigue • *Symptoms* • *Causes* • *Effects* • *Measurement* • *Preventive Steps* • Accident Proneness • *Age and Experience* • *Monotony at Work* • Discipline and Attitude • *Safety Motivation* • Indian Factories Act, 1948 • Health • Safety • Welfare • Working Hours • Employment of Young Persons • Annual Leave With Wages • Flexible Working Hours • *German Experiment* • *British Experience* • *U.S. Practice* • *Employees' Outlook* • *Managerial Problems* • Social Security • Social Security Legislations • The Workmen's Compensation Act, 1923 • The Payment of Wages Act, 1936 • The Minimum Wages Act, 1948 • The Employees State Insurance Act, 1948 • Payment of Bonus Act, 1965 • Payment of Gratuity Act, 1972 • Situation Analysis • Review Questions • Further Readings

Chapter 16. Morale and Participative Management   335

Building up of Morale • High Morale • Satisfactory Morale • Low Morale • Removal of Grievance • Disposal of Grievance • Tier-I • Tier-II • Tier-III • The Constitution of the Grievance Committee • Revision Petition • Counselling • Suggestion System • Workers'

Participation in Management • Labour Union's View • Manager's Perception • Workers' Share in Capital • ESOPs in India • Profit Sharing Schemes • Situation Analysis • Review Questions • Further Readings

Part V
Technology and HR

Chapter 17. Technology and HR   373

Technology and Man • Productivity Improvement • *Factors of Productivity* • *Measures of Productivity* • *Why Low Productivity* • *Role of the Management in Increasing Productivity* • *Organising For Productivity* • *Motivation For Productivity* • *Productivity Centres and Coordinators* • Quality Circles • Sharing Productivity Gains • Situation Analysis • Review Questions • Further Readings

Part VI
Contemporary Issues in HRM

Chapter 18. HR Outsourcing   405

Reasons for Outsourcing • Outsourcing Models • Intelligent Outsourcing • BPO Portal • HR Outsourcing Decisions • Scope of HR BPO • Selecting the Service Provider • Offshore Outsourcing • Review Questions • Further Readings

Chapter 19. Downsizing and Restructuring   414

Defining Downsizing • Impact on Employees • Legal Protection • Restructuring Plan • Downsizing With Golden Handshake • Situation Analysis • Review Questions • Further Readings

Chapter 20. Employee Empowerment   421

Levels of Empowerment • Empowerment of Women • Kaizen To Empower • Five 'S' Approach to Empowerment at Work Place • Situation Analysis • You And Microsoft • Review Questions • Further Readings

Chapter 21. HRM in Transnational Corporations   429

Global Managers • Country Managers • Functional Managers • Qualities of Overseas Managers • Career Opportunities and

Threats • Employment Policy • Approaches to HRM in TNCs • Supply Constraints • Japanese TNCs' Practices • *Training and Career Planning* • *Executive Transfers* • *Team Work* • *Managerial Remuneration* • Situation Analysis • Review Questions • Further Readings

Part I

HR Environment and Management

Chapter Structure

Chapter 1.   HR Environment

Chapter 2.   Corporate Management and HRM

Chapter 3.   Organisation Structure and HR Division

Chapter 1

HR Environment

"Believe not because some old manuscripts are produced, believe not because it is your national belief, believe not because you have been made to believe it from your childhood; but reason it all out, and after you have analysed it, then if you find that it will do good to one and all, believe it, live up to it and help others to live up to it."

— **Buddha**

Learning Objectives

After reading this chapter you will be able to:

1. Understand the need for a supportive environment at work.
2. Classify environmental factors.
3. Examine HRM practices in different cultures.

Introduction

Human Resource Management aims at developing head, hands and heart of every individual working in an organisation. The objectives of any organisation can be met only by people who are competent and motivated. It is the job of the management to select the right type of people for the right jobs and at the right time, sharpen their skills and abilities, and motivate them to give their best to the jobs and the roles assigned. Since every organisation requires coordinated effort, management has to create an environment in which people can decide and act jointly and share the responsibilities and rewards as a team. An organisation is well-managed if its people strive willingly to achieve its goals and the management looks after their welfare, without being asked to do so.

An employee, whether he is working at the lowest ladder or directing from the highest seat, is a human being first and anything else later. As an individual, he is a separate entity. In the words of Swami Vivekanand, "Individuals have each their own peculiarities and each man has his own method of growth, his own life marked out for him by the infinite past life... Everyone born into this world has a bent, a direction towards which he must go, through which he must live..." Man has his own needs, aspirations, affiliations and egos and his own way of looking and judging events and people around him. He wants to do something and be something in an environment which is only partly in his control. He brings with him certain traits and characteristics and vast potentialities. Family, neighbourhood, society, culture and religion influence his life pattern and way of thinking. The economy of the country, the cost of living, income level, availability of goods and services, geographical factors and climate, the form of government, political and legal systems, and overall work culture constitute his environment. Man is not a passive observer of his environment. When he joins an organisation, he is not a raw material like cotton or iron ore, but a living human being. His reaction to management's policies and programmes, work environment and people around is influenced by multiple factors related to his own self, society, organisation and environment. His behaviour is not easily predictable. Managing man, therefore, requires knowing why and how he behaves in different situations the way he does, and what will or what will not motivate him at the job.

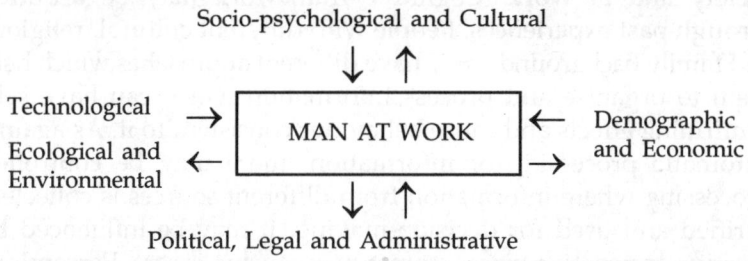

Fig. 1.1: Factors Affecting Man at Work

Socio-psychological Factors

Socio-psychological factors greatly influence people's thoughts, feelings, perceptions, attitudes and behaviour. Customs, traditions, cultural norms and value-systems to which a society is wedded are some of the decisive factors in people's attitude towards life and work. In India, for instance, the two most widely-read books are *Ramayan* and *Bhagavad Gita*, both highlighting the 'Law of Karma' as the supreme law. One should, therefore, perform his duties without longing for fruits, which will be there according to one's Karma – actions. The scriptures also emphasise on the purity of means. The dos and don'ts are prescribed even for the forces fighting on the battlefields. Achieving goals through undesirable means is considered a sin. It is in this context that one may realise why truth and non-violence have been the hallmarks of India's culture. In remote past, India had a flourishing economy and civilisation, but it never attacked other countries or forced others to accept its philosophy. There have been civilisations in the world which, on the contrary, expanded their frontiers by force, that is, militarily, as well as by forcing their religious and social beliefs on others. India has been a victim of such attacks in the past and has suffered heavily. British rulers partitioned India in 1947. It had a long-term impact on the social fabric and the mindset of people. The Constitution of India guarantees equal rights to all citizens, nonetheless differences exist in perception on vital national and social issues between communities adhering to different religious practices and faiths.

Socio-psychology helps in understanding how and why individuals behave, think and feel as they do in a given situation. Social cognition, perceptions, attitudes, stereotyping, prejudices, group norms and influences all affect people's interactions in society and at work. Cognitive framework may be acquired through past experiences. People with different cultural, religious and family backgrounds may have different approaches which help them to organise and process information which can have self-confirming effects and cause behaviour consistent to it. As against automatic processing of information, there may be controlled processing where information from different sources is collected, verified and used for decision-making. It may be influenced by positive or negative biases, sometimes causing errors. Perceptions help in identifying the causes of others' behaviour. Body language, gestures, postures and movements of people in different cultures and societies account for differing perceptions. The way in which people meet and greet each other, keep distance, address and get feedback, show group feelings and self-presentation are not the same everywhere.

Attitude reflects people's evaluation of social world and may colour their experience and opinion. When attitudes are strong, behaviour is strongly affected. Attitudes are formed through learning which may be the result of conditioned or unconditioned stimulus. A favourable attitude among workmen, for instance, may be created by employee benefit programmes and participative approach to management.

There are prejudices and stereotypes in all societies influencing people's behaviour in many ways. Age, marital status, occupation, gender, language, religion, caste and community, etc. may form the basis of prejudices. Behaviour based on prejudices is perceived as legitimate by the perpetrators. Women, for instance, are considered weak and emotional in many societies and discriminated against men. Even today, there are only a few women in large business houses who are able to make it to the top.

Family ties and relationships exert great influence on social and work life. In India, for instance, joint-family system has been popular since ages providing social security to old and weak, promoting brotherly feelings and joy of living together with parents, brothers, sisters and close relations. Members of the family do not feel the kind of loneliness as is widespread in the West.

Social groups influence people through norms to guide behaviour in certain situations which makes it easy to predict the behaviour of members. Behaviour of men and women, parents and children, husband and wife, managers and workers, all may be examined in this light.

A classification of social behaviour puts people in two broad categories:

Type A Behaviour	Type B Behaviour
* Extremely competitive	* Not always competitive
* Always in hurry	* Not always fighting the clock
* Especially irritable and aggressive	* Remain calm even when provoked

Organisations world over consist of both types with differing emphasis in different cultures. Japanese management style gives premium to group performance while American system promotes competitive behaviour based on individual capability and self esteem. Indian management style is influenced by joint-family system and old ethos as given in the Rigveda – *Vasudhev Kutumbakam* (world is a family) – emphasising living and working together.

Cultural Factors

Culture is the learnt behaviour transmitted by one member of the society to another. In the words of G.C. Schneider, "It is the glue that holds an organisation together". Hofstede analyses culture in five dimensions from one extreme to the other: individualism – collectivism, power respect – power tolerance, uncertainty acceptance – uncertainty avoidance, aggressive goal behaviour – passive goal behaviour and long-term outlook – short-term outlook. Not all people in society have similar orientations, but a broad categorisation on this basis is possible and helpful in understanding major orientations of a given society.

Organisations develop their own culture which is reflected in promoters' vision, values and beliefs, management philosophy, organisation design and hierarchical structure, leadership style, communication process, work environment and HR systems, and policies with regard to recruitment, promotion, compensation, training and employee empowerment, etc. Some organisations have open culture emphasising informal relations, cordial work environment, decentralised decision-making, opportunities for personal growth within organisation, while some are more bureaucratic with formal relations, rules, regulations, procedures, centralised decision-making and few opportunities for the personal growth of employees. Organisational culture in Western countries is different in some respects compared to countries in the East such as Japan, India, China and others.

Work Culture in India

One of the greatest philosophies which has direct bearing on HRD was given by Lord Krishna in the battlefield of Mahabharata. When Arjun became emotional and lost his sense of responsibilities, Lord Krishna explained to him the law of Karma and asked him to fight the enemy forces which was his only duty at that time. Who would live and who would die, who would win and who would lose were not to be his concern. He should fight like a true warrior. If he loses, he would get the heaven and if he wins, he would rule over the earth.

हतो वा प्राप्यसि स्वर्ग जित्वा वा मोक्ष्यसे महीम वा।
तस्मादुतिष्ठ कौन्तेय युद्धाय कृतनिश्चयः!

Lord Krishna also said, doing one's job efficiently was yoga.

'योगः कर्मसु कौशलम्।'

Encouraging people to work and work well is expected from all the rulers, administrators and managers. Success of management lies in creating a work culture in the organisation where people take their jobs seriously considering it as a moral responsibility and not just a way of earning or making money. The importance of discipline has been recognised in Indian ethos since long. Manu and Chanakya talked about *Dandaneeti* - policy to punish - applicable to everyone acting against established norms, be they holding very high positions or working at the lowest ladder, though the quantum of punishment may differ. "If the guilty was not punished," said Manu, "the guilt of the crime falls on the king who himself would have to go to hell."

तं राजा प्रणयन्सम्यक् त्रिवोणाभिवर्धते
कामात्मा विषमः शूद्रो दण्डे नैव निहन्यते।

Manu asked for impartial judgement and right punishment which would need consideration of motive, time, place and circumstances in which the offence is committed, nature of the offence and the offender. Welfare of the people, according to Chanakya, depends on *dandaneeti*. It is called *neeti* as it leads people to rightful conduct. Management in all types of organisations is concerned with the rightful conduct at all levels, and is responsible for maintaining discipline.

People everywhere need love and recognition. This fundamental truth was recognised by our saints and philosophers who considered kindness as one of the greatest virtues of man.

Buddha, Mahavir and Gandhi represent Indian ethos, not the barbaric rulers and dictators as in the case of many other countries. They emphasised on the purity of means in achieving the ends. Winning hearts of the people was considered more important by them rather than winning by the sword. Angulimar yielded before Buddha and British empire crumbled before Gandhi.

The lesson for management is obvious: give love to your people and you will be loved, be kind to them, they will be sensitive to the needs of the organisation, adopt right means to achieve organisation goals if you want people to do the right things.

Leadership matters in all types of organisations. Lord Ram is called मर्यादापुरुषोत्तम as he created ideals by his own deeds and sacrifices. Ashok and Akbar were regarded in high esteem by the people because of their great qualities as rulers. Nehru and Patel showed outstanding abilities in establishing a democratic and stable nation after partition of the subcontinent.

The value-systems which our saints, philosophers and nation builders gave have been forgotten by most of us. Western philosophy of materialism and stress on individualism have influenced people in all walks of life in the recent years. The bureaucrats in government and the managers in industry, trade and services are more westernised than the common people. Self-fulfilment has become more important for many of them than the wide-ranging social goals. The emphasis is not on the purity of means but the achievement of goals. Values are being sacrificed for getting quick results. It is not surprising in a situation like this that a scam in the banking sector could result into the loss of several thousand crores of rupees to the treasury. The growing managerial turnover – seeking greener pastures by leaving one organisation for another – and the rising demands of pay and perquisites by a section of highly-paid people in a society, where more than one third of population is living below poverty line, are the symptoms of deterioration in the value-system of our industrial life. This erosion can be stopped if our administrative and managerial systems are based on our culture and traditions and our way of thinking and living. There have been and there are still many enlightened industrialists and managers in India who have practised Indian ethos and brought glory to the industrial sector. Jamshedji Tata and Ghanshyamdas Birla, for instance, placed moral and spiritual values at the top. Jamshedji's concern for his employees is well-known. The philanthropic work done by the Birlas made them a household name in India.

> **Four Pillars of HR – NTPC**
>
> NTPC's human resource policy is aligned to its corporate vision of becoming one of the world's best power utilities. Its HR vision was formulated with the aim of "enabling the employee to become a family of committed world class professionals thus making the company a learning organisation."
>
> The company identified:
> - Competency
> - Commitment
> - Culture
> - System
>
> as the four pillars of its human resource strategy. In relation to its HR management, the company's corporate plan aims at creating a culture of teamwork, empowerment and responsibility to convert knowledge into productive action with speed, creativity and flexibility and thereby gain a knowledge-based competitive edge. People before plant load factor (PLF) is the guiding philosophy of the Company. Under its 'Grow your own Timber' philosophy the company hires fresh graduates, and grooms them from within to occupy leadership positions in the future. HR systems are designed to foster a culture of participation and innovation leading to organisation and employee growth. A comprehensive IT based knowledge management system has been introduced to converge multiple systems of learning with a view to further trigger innovation.

Following are some management practices in selected enterprises showing the changed attitude of managers towards their workers, trust and confidence they bestow in them, and the efforts they are making to develop people at work, and meet their obligations to the society:

— Management-employee meetings at regular intervals, officers to give reply on the spot, employee comments welcome.

— Cash your ideas scheme – suggestions invited and scrutinised by a committee; prizes awarded for good suggestions.

— Nationwide search for recruitment of right people, carefully drawn screening process, scientific methods of selection, induction and training, rotation after placement in different divisions and departments including field work, long-term career blueprint of each employee.

— Celebration of birthdays of all employees in the boardroom with the top executive present to felicitate the employee and offer token gifts from the company.

— Develop mentoring capacity of seniors, rapport-building, joint exploration of problems/issues and action planning to encourage the officer for self discovery, initiative and action.

— Celebration of festivals by managers and workers together, festival gifts to all employees, joint cultural and social programmes.

- Adopt villages and socially-backward areas, provide education to children and adults, build roads, hospitals and community centres, and give employment to socially backward communities and tribes.
- Promote sports, organise tournaments at company cost, sponsor players for national and international sports meet, assist sportsmen and athletes to achieve excellence.
- Live in harmony with the natural environment by following an environment-friendly policy, tree plantation, installation of anti-pollution devices, zero off project (no discharge of any liquid effluent), reuse/recycle waste, conserve energy, maintain pollution-free vehicles, work in natural light and use energy-efficient lights.

These examples show the growing concern among Indian companies for their people and environment, but a system of management which may be called truly Indian is yet to develop in this country. Same is the case with the People's Republic of China. The management practices followed are basically those prevailing in the West. Some research studies show the dominant role of hierarchy, particularly in high-tech enterprises, stress on observing rules and regulations, penalising for deviations from policies laid down by the seniors, centralised decision-making and bossism, etc.

> **PERSPECTIVE**
>
> **HR Transformation: RIL**
>
> Reliance Industries Ltd. (RIL) is focused on building what would be the best "To Be" organisation over the next few months. In order to achieve this objective, RIL is focusing on the following initiatives:
>
> - People energising and engaging the existing work force, building a pipeline for the future and creating an exciting workplace.
> - HR Process: To ensure that RIL continues to have the world's best practices and processes, existing processes are being re-engineered and new processes are being introduced.
> - Policies: The focus in FY-11 is to make policies employee-friendly, keeping in view specific employee needs. The HR policies are being reviewed and benchmarked with world-class organisations.
> - HR shared service centre: The Centre has been established to ensure efficient and effective delivery of HR services to employees.
>
>   RIL has launched Accelerated Leadership Programme in order to hire high-calibre young talent for the company. It was the youth in their 20s and 30s who put RIL on a high pedestal over the last three decades. The company intends to pass the baton onto the young leaders in next few years to further accelerate the success story of RIL for the next three decades.

Work Culture in the West

The West is known for its materialistic philosophy. Management has been viewed in the West primarily as a result-oriented activity. The stress has been on achieving the goals and not so much on the means. A hierarchical system with boss-subordinate relationship has been the core of the Western management thought. A pyramidical structure with concentration of power at the top, division of labour based on specialisation, defined relationships resulting into a chain of authority, accountability and responsibility, pay, perks and privileges based upon the position/status in hierarchy, rules regulating employment, service conditions and discipline are some of the specific features of management system in the West. Workers could be hired and fired depending upon the demand and supply conditions and wages could be determined on the basis of bargaining strength. The human side of enterprise developed quite late in the West. The father of Scientific Management, F.W. Taylor, asked managers to innovate better methods and techniques of work by scientifically analysing the components of each job and employing people who could match the requirements of the job. He was against following the rule of thumb. The system of wage and incentive payments suggested by him were targeted to gain maximum effort out of the workmen. Henry Fayol, a French executive, gave a set of principles of management which include division of work, authority and responsibility, unity of command, centralisation, scalar chain, esprit de corps, etc. A fair system of wage payment, and stability of tenure of employees were suggested by him, but he strongly advocated that group interest should prevail over individual interest. Oliver Sheldon, a British consultant, formulated a broad-based theory which includes determination of policy, coordination of functions, execution of policies and the process of combining the work of individuals or groups with the faculties necessary for its execution. The human relations approach began in the West with the pioneering work of professor Elton Mayo and Roethelsberger at the Hawthorne Plant of the Western Electric Company, Chicago. They established that workers respond to their work situation as a whole which includes conditions at work like heating, ventilation, lighting, work-posture, pay and perks as well as the social groups to which they belong. Men at work are guided by group norms, group standards and group behaviour patterns. Their attitude to work is determined by the total environment. Mary Parker Follet, a pioneer of Human Relations Era in the West, expounded that classical management principles, in terms of human factors such as groups, should be considered something more than a mere aggregation of individuals comprising it; authority should be depersonalised; conflict should be resolved through a process of integration rather than domination; and the leader should be a part of the group. In post-World War II era, new theories of motivation (discussed in detail in the book) were evolved by behavioural scientists, noteworthy among them were Douglas McGregor, Abraham Maslow, Fredrick Herzberg, David McCelland, Porter, Lawler, etc.

Management of business enterprises in most countries of the world today are based on Western management principles and techniques. Japan is the only country in the Eastern hemisphere which has developed a unique management system based upon its tradition and culture. A nation destroyed in the Second World War has risen to the heights of glory surpassing economic giants like the USA and Germany in less than four decades. This miracle has happened because Japan as a nation realised its inner strength. It did not follow the West blindly rather it made the West to follow. In late 1980s, Times reported that out of 1000 British companies surveyed, two thirds were using JIT production and 95 per cent were using or planning to use quality circles.

The core values of Japanese culture may be summed up as:

Japanese Work Culture

(a) '*Amae*' (dependence) – a desire to be passively loved and protected from the world of objective reality.

(b) '*On*' (duty) – Obligations passively incurred, one receives an 'on', one wears an 'on'.

(c) '*Giri*' (obligation) – a bond of moral obligations and debt that must be repaid. 'Giri' is mutual and reciprocal.

(d) '*Ninjo*' (feeling) – human feelings which spontaneously occur and include all natural impulses and inclinations.

The Japanese management system based upon decision-making by consensus and strong group loyalty is influenced by *Amae, On, Giri,* and *Ninjo*. Inter-personal relationships, internal harmony, owning responsibility as a group rather than pinpointing an individual for failure and respect for feelings of others are the hallmarks of this system. The Japanese culture is greatly influenced by Shintoism, Buddhism and Confucianism. The essence of Shintoism lies in taking an integrated view of individual and nation. A Japanese is called '*Kuni-Hito*' or nation man, where nation means a spot where man is providentially placed. Salvation of individual and nation is not separate, it is linked together. Absolute loyalty to Tenno or Emperor, deep emotional attachment with parents, respect for ancestors and love for children are the four major concepts of the great universal way – the way of the Gods. Shintoism has a powerful influence on Japanese mind till date. Buddha's message of love for all, respect for feelings and emotions of all living beings and kindness has been a guiding force to the Japanese way of life. Among the many principles of Confucianism, *Li*, for example, has had a great impact on Japanese people. It refers to the rules of propriety which structure interpersonal relationships into hierarchical dualities, such as father-son, old-young, sovereign-minister, etc. The social equity which Japanese management provides in terms of common uniform, common canteen, common social status, small disparity in the pay of managers and workers, regard for old age, etc. are in contrast to the Western pattern of bossism, superior lifestyle for managers, social distance and stress on individual competition rather than group loyalty.

The essential features of Japanese management system as characterised by most management thinkers are: lifelong employment, seniority wage, promotion systems, and decision-making by consensus. The associated features are: group-oriented loyalty and collective responsibility, restricting union to company affairs and management ideology based on the sense of community bound together by common fate, welfare paternalism and welfare corporation.

PERSPECTIVE

Kakushin: Revolutionary Change – Japanese Style

Change can be produced by *Kaizen*, but Japanese industry has gone a step ahead by adapting to *Kakushin*.

When the rate of change is too slow, organisations may resort to drastic changes or reform: *Kaikaku* through people. Too much movement of parts may be restricted to avoid scratches or damage in other forms which destroy value. People at work should ensure that things move as little as possible – close to the theoretical limit of zero. Doing that requires radical thinking – making the processes simple, keeping factory slim and having people closeby to observe the process. Simple and slim systems make it easier for people to notice abnormalities immediately. *Kakushin* is cost-effective and takes less time to complete a job. For instance, the biggest car factory in Japan has developed a process which enables it to apply three coats of paint at the same time without having to wait for each coat to dry.

Kakushin thus prepares people to make the leap from incremental improvement to radical improvement whenever possible.

Normally, when an employee joins a regular job in a company in Japan, he makes a lifetime commitment reciprocated by the employer's commitment to retain him. A written contract may or may not be entered, but moral commitment is there. If an employee shows interest in going through the clauses of undertakings to abide by employment seriously, he may be considered a potential troublemaker. Those joining temporary jobs can be discharged at will and get less favourable terms. Job hunting and job-hopping are not as popular in Japan as in the West. Legal action to settle employment dispute by management is considered as a failure, and even shameful. Companies retain people by offering them alternate jobs in case of closure of a unit. Mitsubishi, for instance, redeployed workers from Nagasaki shipyard to their automobile plant at Kyoto in the 1970s, and from their car manufacturing unit for Chryster in the U.S. to another location in the 1980s. Women are excluded from lifetime employment. If an employee does not perform well, he may be persuaded to retire or transferred to a lower-status job. Large companies have a vigorous selection procedure to recruit right type of people. Ideologically, a total man and not merely the productive capacity of a man is hired. Companies maintain a close link with schools and colleges. The institutions are ranked and leading companies recruit from the best institutions. Candidate's personality, attitude, life, philosophy and knowledge are given higher weightage than his family background, expression and other factors during the interview. Previous history of the candidate is normally investigated through an investigating agency. Specific skills are developed on the job and during in-house training programmes.

The determinants of pay in major companies are: educational achievement, length of service, age, sex, merit, family responsibilities and nature of the job. The salary curve rises slowly up to the expected age of marriage, reaches its peak when family responsibilities are high and declines when children become financially independent. The decline in salary may not take place in the case of directors. The components of the pay are basic (annual increment negotiable with the union), adjustment (according to rank), incentive (mostly group basis), attendance allowance, family, regional, travel and housing allowances, overtime (legal minimum 12.5%) and extra work, sick leave, etc. Bonus is paid twice a year: at the new year and during summer. It may amount to three months' additional pay. The major criteria for promotion are: ability, attendance, attitude or personality and the length of service. Each of the factors get equal weight in most cases. The pay and promotion based upon 'nenko joretsu' (ranking by years of experience) enable a man to predict with fair degree of accuracy the pay and status he will enjoy at a particular age.

'Nemawashi' (binding up the roots) is the most significant part of the decision-making process 'ringi' (consulting a superior and obtaining his consent) in Japanese companies operating at a large scale whether located in Japan or outside. The 'ringi' process institutionalised in the form of quality circles has been a great success. QC is a small group (five to fifteen persons) that performs quality control activities voluntarily within the same workshop. The basic idea behind QC is to encourage improvement and development of the enterprise, respect humanity and build a happy bright workplace worthy of living, display human capabilities fully, and eventually, draw out infinite possibilities. Unlike the Western management style of hierarchical control and inspection from above to maintain quality, the QC movement emphasised the bottom-up approach. The job of quality control is given to production department and not to the inspection department. Members of QC are prepared by considerable training in problem solving and statistical quality control. Approval or disapproval of circle recommendations rests with the higher management. By early 1980s it was estimated that one out of every eight Japanese employees was participating in QCS.

The success of Japanese style can be attributed to the following factors:

1. The technical problem of quality was attacked by improving work techniques. Workers were prepared through training, group participation and decentralisation. An interesting case in point is of Sanyo when it took over a television plant (which produced TVs for Sears). Quality was so bad that bankruptcy was close and only 500 workers were left. Michi Solume, the Vice-President for administration opened his door to union leaders and talked to them as friends. He told them, "I cannot do everything you ask, but I will openly tell you whatever we decide and why." The Japanese technicians were brought over to work side by side with American workers. They were there to act as role models and not teachers. At first, the Americans felt that the Japanese were only concerned with details like putting the labels on perfectly straight, but their attention to details showed their greater dedication to quality, compared to what Americans had experienced previously.

The reject rate dropped from 10 per cent to below 2 per cent and morale improved and the Americans developed an affection for the Japanese technicians.

2. High trust relations between managers and labour unions are fostered and industrial relations system, which operates on the assumption that interests are shared, is achieved. Most Japanese firms have single company unions. It is estimated that 20 per cent of the Presidents of Japanese companies formerly headed company unions. The Japanese companies have shown that the conflict between management and workers can be considerably reduced if managers are able to create team spirit and a sense of equality. The Nissan plant at Smyrna, Tennessee, tried in 1984 to put some Japanese-style commitment to work. Bosses wore the same uniforms as the workers, parked in the same lot and ate in the same cafeteria. Employees were given extensive training in welding, hydraulics, pneumatics, electronics on their own time with no extra pay. They were asked to maintain their own equipment and organise their work teams of 18-26 people. Job-rotation and cross-training in many jobs were arranged. They learnt new skills and got pay increases. The United Auto-Workers tried to organise plant employees, but workers insisted that they did not need a union.

3. A strong sense of loyalty to the nation, *Nihonjin ron* (the theory of being Japanese), among Japanese people has enabled management to get voluntary commitment of people to their job and the organisation. Morning prayers and exercises are common features in many companies. The song of a company (*matsuhita*), for instance, calls its workers to put their strength and mind together to build a new Japan, promote production and send Japanese goods to the people of the world, develop their industry continuously and endlessly, like water gushing from the fountain, and work in harmony with full devotion and sincerity.

4. Total employee involvement has paid rich dividend. The classic case in point is Toyota. In 1950s, Toyota was a mediocre company, manufacturing shabby imitations of the Western cars. Industrial relations were very bad. But by 1991, the same company had toppled General Motors to become the leading car manufacturing company in

the world. It is said that the Vice-President of Toyota introduced the Total Employee Involvement Scheme in 1962. The company never looked back.

Both the Western as well as the Japanese management philosophies and practices are deeply rooted in their soils. The art of administration which developed in the Roman empire became the basis of management thought in the West when Industrial Revolution took place. Japanese management style is greatly influenced by Buddhism, Shintoism and Confucianism. India, with a very rich tradition and culture, can be the home of a truly Indian management style based on principles such as:

- संगच्छद्ध्म् (joint together): Committees at different levels: *Shram Samitis* – committees of workers and supervisors at shop floor to advise on day-to-day operations, workers' problems, quality improvements and matters connected with employees and their welfare; *Prabandha Samitis* – management committees for interdepartmental and functional coordination; and *Panchayat* – an apex council with company chairman and senior representatives from workers and management sides to be the final arbitrator on major issues.
- न्याय (justice): Recruitment based on merit without discrimination on the basis of caste, community and family background, promotion based on scientific appraisal with due respect for age and performance, education and training for all keeping in view the work requirements and personal growth, uniform simple dress for all employees (specific work requirements to be taken care of), common canteen to be managed, preferably, by ladies, communication in mother tongue/local language in local and regional offices, common leave rules and joint celebration of festivals and occasions of national importance.
- सर्वेभवन्तु सुखिन: (happiness for all): Participating in development programmes for villages, *adivasis* and backward areas; health, education and welfare services for people; creating environment-friendly atmosphere with plantation of long-living trees like neem, peepal, banyan, etc. around factories and offices instead of promoting 'cactus culture' and showpiece environment.
- कर्मसु कौशलम् (Excellence at work): Achievement of organisation's goals by putting maximum effort.

Demographic Factors

Human resource is growing while other natural resources are depleting. The world population is nearing 7 billion, adding 83 million people every year. It has doubled during the last fifty years. Population had never grown at this rate in the past 200,000 years. The extreme growth of population is heavily taxing the earth and its resources. WWF has already warned that if the ecosystem continued degrading at the present rate, humans will need at least two planets worth of natural resources by 2050. Biodiversity has already been damaged with terrestrial species declining by 31%, fresh water species by 28% and marine species by 27% during the last few decades only. Ninety percent of human population growth is occuring in countries already struggling with poverty, illiteracy and civil unrest. Asia accounts for 61% population of the world, Europe for 12%, Africa for 13% and the western hemisphere for the remaining 14%.

India with 1.21 billion people, as per the census report of 2011, is the second most-populous country in the world. China is at number one. India's population has more than tripled since 1947. The fertility rate is 2.8%, one of the highest in the world. Population projection for India is around 1.5 to 1.8 billion by 2050 and is expected to cross 2 billion mark by the end of the century. High population growth has resulted into increasingly impoverished and substandard living conditions for a large section of the population. People below poverty line constitute almost one third of the total population. Situation in most developing countries is no better. The world is sharply divided between haves and have-nots.

India's population is labelled by some as the 'demographic dividend' as half of its population is below 25 years of age. The country faces an immense task of feeding, educating, housing, and employing its youthful population. To avoid a 'demographic liability', India must grow in double digits per year to provide jobs for the expanding working population. Almost 70% of Indians live in rural areas, although in recent decades migration to larger cities has led to a dramatic increase in the country's urban population which has led to mega slums and challenges to quality of life, social harmony and environmental impacts. Despite its youthful population, India's size has made it home to the second largest number of older people in the world in absolute terms (after China). With around 18% of world population, India has only 2.4% of world land area. Population control measures have been largely unsuccessful due to political and social reasons. The country thus faces a great challenge on the demographic front.

The literacy rate has risen in India in the last decade from 64% to 74% with a notable surge in female literacy for the first time in the post-independence era. But the male-female divide in education is still there. While male literacy is around 82%, female literacy is at 65%. Higher education in India is growing. The country has third largest education system in the world after the US and China. IIMs, IITs and some other universities in India are centres of world-class learning, education and research. But the number and size of educational institutions and facilities are grossly inadequate for a rising population. There is mismatch between demand and supply.

Economic Factors

Globalisation has created opportunities for global movement of talents despite immigration restriction and controls. It is no surprise that one third of Silicon Valley's software experts come from India and other countries in Asia which also provide call centre facilities and promote BPOs. MNCs today are not only employing local labour from host countries but also technical and managerial personnel. The movement of talent is no longer restricted from developed to underdeveloped countries. Universities and centres of higher education in the West have a large number of qualified faculty in different disciplines who have been trained in India, China and some other countries. Most universities in the US, UK, Australia and other developed countries are opening their doors for students from Asia, Africa and Latin America.

Liberalisation of economies since early 1990s have enabled MNCs to expand their manufacturing and trading operations at a large-scale in the less developed world. Flow of capital and transfer of technology have substantially increased resulting into the high growth rate of the GDP of many developing countries. China, India, Russia and Brazil are among the fastest growing economies in the world. While China has enjoyed double digit growth rate in the recent years, India had it between 7% to 9%. Business operations of Indian companies had impressive growth. In 2011, Forbes listed 57 Indian companies amongst the 2000 most powerful companies of the world.

The biggest economic depression in recent history which originated in the US has shaken faith on market economy. The silver lining was provided by the developing countries which gave MNCs the much-needed access to markets, in the absence of which economic recession would have been a disaster for many developed countries of the West with shrinking population, high rate of unemployment and poor growth rate. While developing countries provided a cushion to developed countries in the times of crisis, all sorts of restrictions are still continuing against them when it comes to the export of skilled manpower. Asian, African and Latin American countries continue to be the targets of economic imperialism. Restrictive trade practices of economic powers in the West, in some measures, defeat the very objectives of WTO and other such organisations to promote free trade, flow of capital and skilled manpower.

The rate of growth has been impressive in developing countries as a consequence of economic liberalisation but the benefits have not percolated to a large section of people who are poor. Income inequality has grown dramatically as reported by ILO in recent studies. Share of wages in national income has declined in majority of these countries. The largest decline in the share of wages in GDP took place in Latin America and the Caribbean followed by Asia. The cost of financial indiscipline and over-consumption by people in the West is in effect transferred to the developing East through market economy mechanism. The cost of primary products and labour has been deliberately controlled to be low and manufactured value added products much higher, resulting into economic exploitation and perpetuation of imperialism.

Technological Factors

Since Industrial Revolution in the early 20th century, machines have been replacing man with increased automation at work. Last few decades have witnessed computers as a powerful tool in the hands of managers. E-HR, as Ulrich puts it, is "a matrix with two columns: transactions – doing administrative things faster and better, enabling employees to be self-sufficient and self-reliant, building employee portals, etc., and transformation – becoming more strategic and building sustainable competitive advantage." Payroll system was the first to be computerised followed by employee recruitment, training, performance evaluation, promotions, incentives and rewards, and feedback systems. Job portals, online screening, testing, interviewing, skill matching on computers have not only facilitated transactions, but reduced cost and time. E-HR is most helpful in manpower planning, storing and disseminating information, sharing knowledge, empowering people and formulating future strategies. It has resulted in improving performance and employee morale. Higher-level management in most companies have fully integrated organisation-wide network of HR-related data and information services available at any time, enabling timely and effective decision-making.

Technological changes have further changed the skill requirements. The demand for knowledge and skill-intensive occupations have increased. There is a marked reduction in conventional office jobs and increase in services like BPO, call centres, security, catering, etc.

E-HR is interactive in nature enabling instant feedback, helping decision-making in ever-changing environment with vast amount of data and information available, communicating quickly, expanding geographical and time horizons.

IT-HRD companies have emerged as a big support to business operations all over the world. Indian IT companies have made their mark in providing financial and other services by their innovative skills in developing softwares. They are in the forefront of exporting software products and skills both. Infosys, TCS, Wipro, HCL, etc. are among the world-class IT service providers to most of MNCs and TNCs.

IT education in India has developed with the joint efforts of private sector corporations and the government. Most companies have their own training institutes with highly qualified expert staff. Government on its part has allowed banks and financial institutions in public sector to float special bonds to raise capital for IT education for providing loan to IT-HRD companies and institutions at a low-rate of interest. Entrepreneurs, including NRIs, are offered special financial packages including venture capital to set up IT education. IT companies are encouraged to set aside a certain percentage of value-added revenue to support IT-HRD sector.

Professionally qualified women in IT are provided telecommunicating facilities to operate from home when they are not in a position to attend to the job in office on a regular basis due to family constraints. They are also offered special loan/financial grants to set-up infrastructure at home to be able to telecommunicate. Job prospects for women have increased with the growth of IT sector.

Ecological and Environmental Factors

Ecosystems provide goods and services that sustain human societies and general well-being. Biodiversity sustains ecosystems. Environment includes the physical world; the social world of human relations and the built world of human creations. WWF's 2010 report points out the alarming rate of loss of biodiversity particularly in low-income countries. Rich nations are far ahead of poor countries in consuming resources of the earth. Rapid economic growth has fuelled an ever-growing demand for resources for food and drink, energy, transport, electronic products, living space and space to dispose waste. The ecological footprint shows a doubling of our demands on the natural world since 1960s, while the living planet index tracks a fall of 30% in the health of species that are the foundation of our ecosystem services on which we all depend. Even with modest projections for population growth, consumption and climate change by 2030, humanity will need the capacity of two earths to absorb waste and keep up with the natural resource consumption.

Ecosystems with plants, animals and microorganisms provide myriad of services upon which all life depends. These services are:

Provisioning: Food, medicines, timber, biofuel, etc.

Regulating: Water filtration, waste decomposition, climate regulation, crop pollution, etc.

Supporting: Nutrient cycling, photosynthesis, soil formation, etc.

Cultural: Enriching recreational, aesthetic and spiritual experiences.

Human activities which cause damage to ecosystems are:
- Conversion of land for agriculture, aquaculture, industrial and urban use; river water for irrigation, hydropower generation.
- Harvesting plants and animals for food, materials and medicines at a higher rate than the reproductive capacity of the population.
- Climate change due to the rising levels of greenhouse gases in atmosphere, caused mainly by the burning of fossil fuels, deforestation and industrial processes.
- Invasive species introduced deliberately or inadvertently to one part of the world from another becoming competitors, predators or parasites of native species.

The impact of loss of biodiversity and environmental degradation is felt most profoundly by the world's poorest and most vulnerable people living in the underdeveloped and developing regions of Asia, Africa and South America. Natural resources of poor countries are bought by rich nations at a price much lower than the price of manufactured products which they provide. The gulf between rich and poor nations is widening. Without access to clean water, land and adequate food, fuel and materials, vulnerable people cannot break out of the poverty trap and prosper. Ending ecological overshoot by rich nations is essential to ensure the continued supply of ecosystem services as referred above for future human health, wealth and well-being.

Political Factors

A functional democracy with a government genuinely concerned with the welfare of people by promoting literacy, healthcare, social security and welfare, guarding fundamental rights of freedom of speech, expression and information, equality of opportunity, no discrimination on the basis of religion, caste, creed and faith, providing employment opportunities and food security and a people-friendly administrative machinery and effective legal system may be ideal for the development of human resource of the country. Experience world over has shown that development of human resource leads to all other developments.

Democracies, even with inadequacies, are preferable over dictatorship in the long run. The collapse of totalitarian regimes in many countries in recent years including Soviet Russia confirms the belief that people should be the master of their own fate. This needs empowerment of the people. In many developing countries, governments, though elected, have not been able to eradicate poverty, illiteracy, unemployment, inequality of income and opportunities for their people. Government policy of liberalisation has resulted into impressive economic growth, but human resource growth has been slow as reported by UNDP in its reports from time to time. Lack of infrastructure, inadequate allocation of funds for education, health and social security, administrative inefficiency and corruption in high offices are the main reasons of failure in most developing nations. Most countries ruled by dictators, except the oil-rich, have poor records on HRD front.

Legal and Administrative Factors

Legal framework of a country directly influences HR management in several ways. The Factories Act in India, for instance, regulates working hours, health, welfare and safety measures at work place, leave with wages, overtime allowance, etc. The Minimum Wages Act authorises appropriate government to fix minimum rates of wages of employees in scheduled employment. The Payment of Wages Act aims at ensuring wage payment in prescribed time. The Workmen's Compensation Act helps in providing compensation for injuries/death of employees during the course of employment. Social security legislation like the Employee State Insurance Act provides for maternity benefit, disablement benefit, and medical benefits to the workers. Industrial Disputes Act provides machinery to settle disputes through conciliation and adjudication when parties fail to resolve a matter mutually.

General laws of the country have a huge impact on HR management and development. Constitutional guarantees of freedom of speech and expression, for instance, go a long way in raising voice against any type of exploitation of the weaker section of society to which workers in many countries belong to. Laws to promote economy increase employment opportunities, wages, working and service conditions of workers, control prices specially of necessities of life and improve public distribution system. Legislative and administrative measures on education, health, drinking water, sanitation, food security, employment guarantee promote welfare of people.

Legal system must cope with changing times. In India, there are many acts which are more than 100 years old. Economic, social and political systems and environment have since changed drastically, but laws remain the same. In recent years, however, higher judiciary has shown sensitivity to people's aspirations and needs of reform on such issues as environment protection, farmers' rights, civil rights, corruption and black money. Laws passed by the Parliament, like the Right to Information Act, have been welcomed by the people.

Good governance is a major challenge in developed as well as developing countries. The 2010 corruption perception index shows that nearly three quarters of 178 countries have the index score below 5 on a scale from 10 (highly clean) to 0 (highly corrupt). The problem is more acute in fast developing and underdeveloped economies and also in some developed economies, seriously hit by recession and unable to manage their financial system effectively. The case of bribery of public officials, embezzlement of public funds, frauds committed by big corporations, involvement of politicians and ministers in big scams and transfer of black money to some banks in the developed countries known to be haven for it, have been widely reported in recent years. Scams by giant MNCs have been eroding public confidence in the functioning of market economy. The Pongi, Maddott, Enron and Satyam scams in recent years show lack of accountability and disregard for laws by such corporations. Many stock market scams have hit small investors below the belt. Ethic-deficit at the highest levels of government and corporate sector seriously affects morale of the people.

Situation Analysis

Indian Oil is India's flagship national oil company with business interests straddling the entire hydrocarbon value chain. It is the leading Indian corporate in the Fortune's prestigious 'Global 500' listing (ranked 125) and the largest commercial enterprise with a turnover of more than Rs. 2.71 lakh crores (USD 60 billion). Indian Oil has 48% market-share in petroleum products market, 35% of refining capacity and 71% of downstream pipelines capacity in India. Indian Oil now has a new vision to be the 'Energy of India' and a 'Globally Admired Company'. Government of India has recently conferred the status of '*Maharatna*' on Indian Oil.

Indian Oil recreated its vision focusing on areas like ethics, people, innovation, environment, technology and customers. The vision-development process was based on Aspiration Driven Transformation philosophy and it involved employees at every stage so that the new vision becomes a 'shared vision' rather than a 'vision shared'.

The company realised very early that human resources are the only sustainable source of competitive advantage for the enterprises. With less than 1% attrition rate, most of Indian Oil employees consider their association with Indian Oil as a 'career' and not as a 'job'. Hence, attraction and retention of right talent becomes crucial. In view of this, the recruitment process has been revamped – Indian Oil became the first organisation to use Graduate Aptitude Test in Engineering (GATE) for recruitment of Engineers, which received kudos from other organisations. The company is now using Common Law Admission Test (CLAT), conducted by National Law Universities, for the recruitment of legal professionals.

Indian Oil quickly realised the importance of a strong 'Employer Brand' to attract and retain talent. Its employee value proposition (EVP) is based on the core values of Care, Innovation, Passion and Trust. In the selection process, a lot of emphasis is placed on 3 Cs – Courage, Conviction and Character of the prospective candidates.

The onboarding of all the new executives is directly supervised by the Human Resources Development (HRD) department at their corporate office. New executives are assigned mentors, who play the role of friend, philosopher and guide for the smooth transition of new officers from the bonhomie of academics to the rigours of professional life.

Since Indian Oil believes in growing its own timber – all executives are considered as potential board members and emphasis is given to their overall development through job rotations in different verticals. They also get exposure to different functional and developmental programmes throughout their career. Indian Oil Institute of Petroleum Management (IIPM) and a network of 20 other training institutes work tirelessly to develop new programmes based on training need identification (TNI). Indian Oil has tied up with leading global institutes like Universitas 21 Global, Singapore, and IFP, France, for programmes on strategic and project management and refinery technology, etc. Indian Oil is also pursuing a strong industry-academia interaction, and recently created a chair professorship in chemical engineering at the Indian Institute of Technology (IIT), Kanpur. It also provides support for self-development by sponsoring employees to pursue part-time MBA programmes.

Indian Oil was one of the first PSUs to implement an online performance management system (e-PMS). Based on well-defined KRAs and KPIs, Indian Oil started rewarding employees according to individual/small team performance, suitably differentiating high performers.

Indian Oil believes in open communication and uses multiple information channels to keep the employees informed about the nuances of business. Senior officials regularly meet the collectives to share performance highlights, future plan outlay, status of project implementation, steps taken on new business frontiers and key challenges. Chairman directly interacts with the employees and communicates through 'Straight Talk'. There are other forums like 'Personnel Touch', 'Discussion Forum', etc. through which employees can raise their concerns to the senior-most officials like the Director (HR). Total Productivity Management (TPM) tools are implemented at different production and administrative offices to enhance overall efficiency. To show appreciation to employees, different divisions have recognition programmes, like 'Reward for Key Positions', 'Best Field Officer', 'Best location', 'Pratibha Samman', 'Sammukh Uplabdhi Samman', etc.

Indian Oil takes care of its employees from 'cradle to grave'. Competitive remuneration and a plethora of other benefits are offered to the employees to keep them engaged. Medical facilities for Indian Oil employees are one of the best offered by any organisation in India. It also offers holiday home, nominated hotel facilities, etc. to the employees, club membership to senior officials to achieve a good work-life integration.

(Source: Best Practices in HR)
Scope: Comment on HR practices of Indian Oil as reported above.

Review Questions

1. 'HRM aims at developing head, hands and heart of every man and woman at work'. Comment.
2. 'Socio-psychological factors greatly influence people's thoughts, feelings, perceptions and attitude.' Elaborate.
3. Differentiate between type A and type B behaviour.
4. Do you believe that the 'Law of Karma' directly influences HR philosophy and practices?
5. What are the major differences in the HR philosophy of Western countries and Japan?
6. Do you subscribe to the view that a sharp rise in India's population in recent years is a demographic dividend?
7. What are the opportunities and threats of globalisation on the HR front?
8. 'Computer is a powerful tool in the hands of HR managers.' Discuss.
9. How have Indian IT companies helped global business in recent years?
10. What human activities are detrimental to environment?
11. 'Experience world over has shown that the development of human resource leads to all other developments.' Elaborate.
12. Comment on the HR philosophy and practices of the company as expressed in the Chairman's letter to the shareholders given below:

> **Extracts from the Aditya Birla Group Chairman's letter to Shareholders**
>
> I believe, your Company is well-poised to emerge as "Global Metal Business" comprising India Centric Upstream business and Global Value Added Downstream business. As I mentioned earlier, your Company has embarked on an ambitious growth path with an announced investment plan of over US $ 6.5 billion in India and globally in the next three years. In my view, your Company is all set for a quantum growth leap.
>
> *To our teams*
>
> I would like to say a big thank you to all of our teams for their consistent high performance. I take great pride in the performance of our people.

The Aditya Birla Group in Perspective

Today, we are a multi-ethnic, multi-dimensional group with a bench strength of 1,33,000 passionate and committed people, belonging to 42 nationalities across 6 continents. For the year 2010-11, our consolidated revenues stand at US$ 35 billion, compared to US$ 29 billion in the preceding year, recording a 22% growth. Our leadership, regardless of levels, has a penchant for collaborative and innovative solutions, for new ways of working that keep our companies and our products on our clients' and customers' radar all the time. This is what drives our performance.

I believe that purposive actions in the people area can be huge differentiators to our growth plans. For us, it is very important to know what our people think of us. So we recourse to a biannual Organisational Health Survey (OHS) conducted by Gallup as the barometer of the Engagement at Work index in our Group. Over 28,000 executives spanning 31 countries participated in OHS 7 (2010). The participation level at 97%, in Gallup's opinion, sets a new benchmark. Given its objectivity and the rigour of process, there is immense value in its findings.

It is a matter of great satisfaction for me that the key strength of the Group, as identified in the OHS, continues to be the great sense of pride that our employees experience and express in working for the Aditya Birla Group. More importantly, this pride stems from our employees' belief and conviction that we are a good corporate citizen. Given the decline in ethics we see in business today, that is a huge validation of our insistence on value-based leadership. Pride, in turn, is a great driver of positive energy and performance.

To capitalise on this positivity and to grow and hone the talent resident in the Group, we have launched several initiatives that further our *Employee Value Proposition* – a *World of Opportunities*. We have launched 'Career Management Services' – a pioneering effort which is an integrated end-to-end career service aimed at all employees. This is already afoot in the cement business. Over the coming years, it will be extended across other businesses in the Group.

On the issue of grooming talent, collectively our Business Directors and Business Heads, along with me, have invested over 500 man-hours in discussing, reviewing and working through the development plans for each of our talent pool members at the Group level. Their development plans include engagement with special projects, coaching and mentoring by the top leadership team, besides attending cutting-edge functional and behavioural programmes globally that open the frontiers of their mind and goad them to defy limitations. That 60% of total leadership positions were filled in from our existing talent in 2010-11 validates the talent honing processes which have laid a robust leadership pipleline within our Group.

Our commitment to employee learning and development at all levels is unrelenting. In 2010-11, there were 30,000 touch points with our learners through multiple formats of learning. More than 25,000 employees enlisted in e-learning programmes at Gyanodaya, our Institute of Management Learning. This year at Gyanodaya 200 colleagues at very senior levels attended specially designed programmes. They had the opportunity to interact with professors from leading universities and B-Schools. They were a great faculty drawn from universities such as Stanford, RICE, Michigan and Duke at the global level along with professors from the IIMs and ISB (Hyderabad). Our senior managers also derived immense value from the training and learning sessions conducted by leading consultancies such as the Centre for Creativity Leadership (CCL), The Hay Group and The Works Partnership (TWP), among others.

Finally, I am delighted to share with you that our employees have given a thumping vote of confidence to our Group as the 'best employers' in India and in Asia-Pacific. Aditya Birla Group, of which your company is an integral member, has been declared as one of the 'Best Employers' in India in the Aon Hewitt Survey conducted recently. We ranked 2nd from among 200 other Indian organisations who participated in the survey. In Asia-Pacific, we have been ranked among the top companies as well. Soon we hope to attain this stature in the rest of the world too – wherever we operate.

Our people are our future. With them and the wind in our sails, we feel buoyant about achieving our stretch goal of becoming a 65 billion dollar Group by 2015. Your company will play an important role in reaching this destination.

(Source: Hindalco Annual Report 2010-11)

Further Readings

1. Robert A. Baron, Nyla R. Branscombe, Donn R. Byrne and Gopa Bharadwaj: *Social Psychology* (Pearson, New Delhi, 2010).
2. Jagdish Bhagwati: *Economic and World Order from the 1970s to 1990s* (Orient Longman, Bombay, 1992).
3. Jean Dreze and Amartya Sen: *India's Economic Development and Social Opportunity* (Oxford University Press, New Delhi, 1995).
4. Himanshu Sekhar Rout and S. Bhyrava Murthy: *Human Development in India* (New Century Publications, New Delhi, 2010).
5. Michael J. Marquardt and Dean W. Engel: *Global Human Resource Development* (Prentice Hall, 1993).
6. I.G. Patel: *Economic Reform and Global Change* (Macmillan India, New Delhi).
7. M.E. Porter: *The Competitive Advantage of Nations* (Free Press, New York, 1990).
8. Rosalie L. Tung: *Human Resource Planning in Japanese Multinationals: A Model for U.S. Firms* (Journal of International Business Studies, Fall, pp. 139-149, 1984).
9. UNDP: *Human Development Report*.

Chapter 2

Corporate Management and HRM

"Traditionally, business has been held responsible for quantities, for the supply of goods and of jobs, for costs, prices, hours of work, and standards of living. Now business increasingly is being asked to take on responsibility for the quality of life in our society... It is a demand that the quality of life become the business of business."

– **Peter F. Drucker**
(Preparing Tomorrow's Business Leaders Today)

Learning Objectives

After reading this chapter you will be able to:
1. Define management and elaborate the functions managers perform.
2. Understand how modern management has evolved.
3. Define HRM and strategies to align HRM goals with organisational goals.

The term management has been defined by different people in different ways – some have defined it in a simple way and some in a complex way.

Management means the manner in which a given task is executed and supervised. It also implies accomplishing a task using the available limited resources and the skill in the manipulation of these resources.

Management is often viewed according to one's way of thinking. To a design engineer it may mean a matter of designing products, utilities and equipment. To a techno-economist or a cost accountant it may appear to be a matter of figures that can spell either loss or gain in monetary terms. To a research chemist it may mean formulae, chemical reactions and processes.

The fault lies not with these individuals but with the environment in which they have grown up and with the organisations that keep them in isolation and do not acquaint them with the various aspects of management. Unconsciously, a technical bias of the work being done by them sets into their sub-conscious mind. This is primarily due to the fact that no one has guided them as to what management actually means. Such people, when they rise to high positions by virtue of their long years of experience, find themselves in a difficult situation because of their technological bias and little understanding of professional standards. Owing to their lack of farsightedness and initiative, they fail to grasp the essentials of other disciplines around them.

Management Defined

Since management is responsible for getting the assigned task done within the given time, the given resources and in a particular manner, an acceptable definition, to our way of things, could be: *"Management is getting things done through people by effective utilisation of resources, time and environment"*. Environment includes government policies, legal framework, economic and social factors, competition, etc.

We shall try to reason out and assess as to what management does rather than quote some readily available definitions to make the meaning of the term 'management' explicit.

For example, let us determine the work that is involved in the construction of a mini-steel plant. What are the major elements of work involved in it? Broadly, these are:
 (i) Preparation of a feasibility report
 (ii) working out a detailed project report

(iii) projection of time schedule or PERT network for completion of project
(iv) arrangement and allocation of funds;
(v) selection of personnel and procurement of equipment
(vi) erection
(vii) commissioning
(viii) despatch, marketing finance and other commercial aspects

Functions of Management

If we break these broad categories into finer elements and analyse the nature of work involved in each of them, the process will reveal five basic elements which go into management. These are:

(1) Planning the course of action to be adopted to attain predetermined objectives;
(2) setting up an organisational structure and assigning specific responsibilities to different individuals;
(3) directing and coordinating the efforts of all members working for the organisation;
(4) controlling the activities of the members by setting up standards for their performance;
(5) motivating the members to cooperate with one another for the achievement of objectives.

Planning

Planning aims at achieving the desired results. It entails advance thinking of events to come, such as organisation, allocation of resources, framing of policies, setting of objectives, purchase of raw materials, and other items; storage, marketing; fixing of time schedules for construction, provisioning of matching facilities, etc. It would naturally include preparation of broad guidelines that would help in the execution of work within the available resources, in time, and subject to the existing restraints, the industrial policies of the State, and the social responsibilities of business.

Organisation

The second fundamental element may be defined as determining the activities necessary for executing a plan of action and assigning such activities to groups of individuals. The organisational structure so set up is the framework within which the total proceeds of executive control are carried on. This fact emphasises the importance of a sound organisational structure.

Coordination

Coordination seeks to blend the available factors into a relationship so that the plan can be put into effect. Modern business has a multitude of interdependent operations. Balancing the work and efforts of individuals into those of a group, and allocation and adjustment of resources are delicate functions. Efforts of many disciplines have to be harmonised for synchronised action. The task of blending the activities of different individuals, groups, machineries, processes, and maintaining the interdependence of operations as well as reconciling their differences is done by coordination.

Control

It ensures that activities are executed according to the plan. It includes follow-up. Determining a plan of action is not the end. Constant follow-up has to be maintained to see the job through. For this, it is necessary to provide an organisation or establishment with a formal line of authority which would be responsible for organisation, follow-up and control; outlining strategies to make up for loss either in units of time or quantum of production; checking the plans as projected against the actual status at a point of time; measuring performance against the norms laid; recording necessary statistical details for comparison and as basis for realistic planning for future; and taking corrective measures necessary to make the plan operative. Control is thus a continuous process of decision-making and embodying those decisions in the form of specific set of instructions on the behalf of management.

Motivation

Directions or orders alone cannot deliver the goods. The human mind has to be motivated to think and give its best. Instilling team spirit in the group and motivating them to be loyal and obedient; making them aware of their sense of responsibility; and making them put their best efforts, are necessary steps for the achievement of targets. Motivation is thus a process of inspiration that enables the members of the group to pull their weight effectively, to share group loyalty and to jointly meet the challenges that the group has accepted.

These are called fundamental elements because the correctness and successful execution of managerial decisions depend upon the extent to which these elements have gone into the making and execution of these decisions.

In case all the above mentioned functions are carried out smoothly, the task is accomplished within the time schedule,

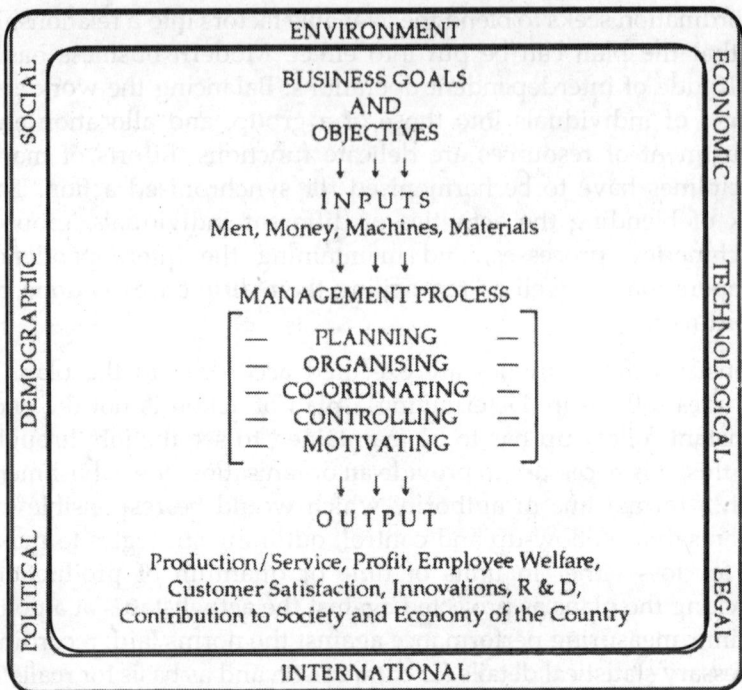

Fig. 2.1: Task of Management

resources available and in the manner desired. However, in actual practice, this is not the case. Mistakes, wrong directives, lack of coordination, loss of opportunity, defective planning, communication gap, group frictions, misunderstanding, professional jealousy, etc., which are common to any organised activity, keep the task from being accomplished. These factors are also described as the forces of misdirection and activity trap in management terminology. External forces, which are outside the control of organisation, also limit managerial effectiveness.

Management as such is an amalgamation of the broad functions outlined above and many other sub-functions or specialised functions that are associated with them. Each aspect or each function is a part of the management and everyone has a contribution to make towards the total process.

Of the five principal functions of management discussed above, all are not technical, some are social functions as well. Management, therefore, is not only technical but also involves human factors and relations. Since it is chiefly the activities of the people that have to be coordinated and regulated by the management, it is also called a social or socio-technical process.

We may, therefore, deduce that management is a social process entailing responsibility for realistic planning, organisation, coordination; effective follow-up (control) and group motivation for the fulfilment of a given task or purpose.

To fully understand the intricacies of management, so far explained, it is necessary to briefly discuss the history and evolution of management.

Evolution of Management

Management has been of some concern to organised society throughout civilised history. Initially, contributions came from practitioners and later from theorists.

Necessity and awareness of the need of management skills date back to the period before the beginning of recorded history. In the villages of the Euphrates Valley, priests, who were worshipped by people as representatives of God, had evolved a system of management. Those priests had laid down rules for organising trade, the work of labourers, societies, soldiers, etc. They employed men to keep records and prepare reports. The Indus Valley civilisation was an excellent example of planning and administration of township.

Similar records exist in the case of ancient China. Confucius' parables include practical suggestions for public administration to choose honest, sincere and dynamic officers. Records of early Greece do not give much insight into the principle of management. But the Athenian system of courts, administrative councils and board of generals indicate the existence of a system of managerial functions.

History of the Roman Empire also gives much evidence of managerial knowledge in the fields of army operations and civilian/government administration. The Roman Catholic church also made notable contributions to organisation and management.

These principles of organisation and management were, somehow, lost sight of during the Dark Ages which continued up to the sixteenth century. They were gradually rediscovered between the sixteenth and twentieth centuries. The history of this rediscovery can be studied through four different mediums, viz.:

(i) as a psychological process
(ii) as an art
(iii) as a systematic practice
(iv) as a science

Management as a Psychological Process

Entrepreneurs had neither any experience of their own nor of others to guide them in their work in the early days of the Industrial Revolution. They, therefore, had to depend entirely on their inborn abilities and skills in the performance of their job. This gave rise to the belief that management was basically a psychological process. Importance of qualities such as intuition and foresight gave further support to the belief that management flowed from certain inner impulses of individual managers. In short, it gave rise to a strong and universal belief that managers, poets and artists were born and could not be made.

Management as an Art

There was, however, another school of thought which did not recognise or accept this view. They argued that if this view was correct then superior managers could be developed simply by a strict adherence to the principles of the science of Eugenics. But actual experience had frequently shown that the successors of some distinguished founders and managers of industries were not so capable and, occasionally, utter failures. This gave rise to the doubt that abilities to manage were not inborn. Acceptance of this theory helped to raise the status of management from a psychological process to that of an art.

Management as Systematised Practice

Management was regarded as an art as long as practising managers were greatly engrossed in their day-to-day activities and had to depend on their personal abilities and skills to tackle their problems. In course of time, however, managers were able to observe some of their colleagues at work with whom they exchanged their views on mutual problems. Such exchanges enabled them to discard their old hit-or-miss methods/practices and adopt those which had proved to be successful.

For quite some time, the practising managers did not consider it necessary to analyse the cause and effect relationship underlying such practices. They were content to adhere to them as long as they got satisfactory results. In this way, a large number of useful practices, dos and don'ts came to be accumulated and the later generations of managers had no difficulty in adopting them. Management at this stage took to systematised practices of the past. However, this frequently resulted in a rigid and conservative attitude, since many managers who had found these practices successful refused to abandon them later when they had become redundant due to change in conditions.

Management as a Science

This last and most important phase in the evolution of management was brought about by the operation of two forces: one was the effort of practising managers to establish standard practices and, the other, the effort of scientists to demonstrate the application of the scientific methods of observation, experimentation and verification in the field of management.

The first scientist to attempt this was Charles Babbage, a British mathematician. Having studied industry from the outside, he came to the conclusion that the methods of science could be applied to the operations of factories. He, therefore, recommended "accurate observation, exact measurement and precise knowledge of the cause and effect relationship as a substitute for guess work, intuition, and opinion".

It was, however, left to Frederik Winslow Taylor to synthesise these ideas, which had been germinating in Great Britain and the United States during the last few decades of the nineteenth century, and present them as a reasonably coherent whole. He gave a title and a philosophy to a disconcerted series of initiatives and experiments. It was he who, for the first time, asserted that the study of management required adequate intelligence, an orderly habit of mind and the ability to see a subject as a whole while keeping track of the parts. Since then, many others, notable among them being Henri Fayol, Mary Parker Follett, Elton Mayo, Chester I. Barnard, Lyndall Urwick, Douglas McGregor, etc. have made very significant contributions to the theory of management and have helped to raise its status to that of a science.

For about twenty years Taylor's book on scientific management was confined to applications in machine shops and factories. Simultaneously, his ideas were being developed and refined by Gilbreth, Emerson, Gantt and others. Still, it essentially dealt with the technical aspects of management. It was Henri Fayol who applied the same methods and techniques to the analysis of the work of a chief executive in a factory and, thereby, extended the scope of scientific management.

He was followed by Mooney, Reiley, Chester I. Barnard, L. Urwick, and E.F.L. Brech who developed and refined the principles of administration formulated by Fayol. In spite of these developments, there were many who were sceptical about scientific management, because they felt that some important segment of management was missing from it.

It was left to Prof. Elton Mayo and Prof. Roethlisberger to discover this missing segment of human relations in management and to prove conclusively that attitudes of individuals and groups towards their work and towards one another have as much influence on the quantity and quality of their output as material and technical factors. This discovery opened a new vista to sociologists, research workers and thinkers, among whom Mary Parker Follett, L. Urwick and Douglas McGregor have received worldwide recognition for their valuable contributions.

F.W. Taylor

The honour of being the first to establish the claim of management as a science has been unanimously given to F.W. Taylor. His two important books on management are *Shop Management* published in 1903 and *Principles of Scientific Management* published in 1911. According to him, if a machine shop or a factory is to work with a reasonable degree of efficiency, it must have the following features:

(i) It must be organised on a functional basis so that the work of planning and supervision is taken away from the departmental foreman and entrusted to those who are specialists in their own fields.

(ii) All the jobs must be carefully analysed with the help of the techniques of motion study, time study and fatigue study.

(iii) Machines and tools must be standardised.

(iv) The method of wage payment must be such so as to provide adequate incentive to more efficient workers and penalty to the less efficient ones.

(v) There must be a complete mental revolution on the part of both the employers and the employees towards their work and towards each other.

The basics of Taylor's scheme of scientific management lie in functional organisation. Its central idea is division of the work of management in a workshop in such a way that each executive, from an assistant superintendent to a supervisor, has as few functions as possible to perform. Taylor sought to achieve this by setting up a planning department which would be responsible for planning all the work, including work of a routine nature connected with planning.

Henri Fayol

Henri Fayol's book *The General and Industrial Administration* was, in a large measure, complementary to Taylor's work. Fayol's book is divided into two parts: the first is concerned with the theory of administration and the second with the training of administration. In the first part, he gives a classification of the main groups of operations to be found in any business.

He distinguishes six such groups, viz., technical, commercial, financial, security, accounting and administrative. The administrative group of operations is further classified into five sub-groups concerned with organisation, coordination, command, control, and forecasting and planning.

He then points out that administration is not something set above the other operations, but is merely a specialised function which occurs in a greater or lesser degree in relation to all other business activities. As one goes higher up on the ladder of hierarchy, administrative knowledge and skill become relatively more important than technical skill.

According to him, it is the inability or unwillingness on the part of the top executive to recognise this fact that is often responsible for the failure of a business.

Having analysed the nature of administration, Fayol listed fourteen principles which formed the core of his theory of administration. These are:

(i) authority and responsibility
(ii) discipline
(iii) unity of command
(iv) unity of direction
(v) subordination of individual interest to general interest
(vi) division of work
(vii) remuneration of personnel
(viii) centralisation
(ix) scalar chain
(x) order
(xi) equity
(xii) initiative
(xiii) stability of tenure
(xiv) *Esprit de corps*

These principles of administration were also accepted by Lyndall Urwick and others as quite complete and comprehensive.

Having enumerated the principles of administration, Fayol went on to discuss the five elements of management, viz. planning, organisation, coordination, motivation and control which we have already discussed in the earlier part of this chapter.

Parker Follett

Miss Mary Parker Follett was the first to make managers and management thinkers of her time aware of the realities of human behaviour through her writings. Being intensely conscious of man's group life, she saw that a person's association with his fellowmen gives rise to powerful emotions which colour his every action as the member of a group. He ceases to be the sole creator of his thoughts and actions and comes to be moulded by the influence that the group exerts. A human group, therefore, has a life that is something more than the sum of the individual lives composing it. This philosophy of dominance of emotions in human behaviour underlines her analysis of the industrial organisation and its problems.

According to her, conflict in an organisation arises not out of difference of opinion between individuals but out of the failure of the individuals to make their differences contribute to the common cause. Another important concept in her analysis is the concept of authority which, as generally thought of in terms of status, is of one man having power over another. From her intimate study of human behaviour, Miss Follett pointed out that personal subordination is offensive to human emotions and if it is made the foundation of an organisation, it may cause resentment and friction. To avoid these undesired reactions, she suggested that orders and authority must be depersonalised.

Prof. Elton Mayo

Prof. Mayo was the first to get the opportunity to analyse the behaviour of work groups. His experiments clearly demonstrated the tremendous influence of emotions on group behaviour. Through these experiments it was discovered that the rapid rise in the output of the test group was largely in response to an emotional stimulus. Many management thinkers tried to reassess the prevailing management techniques in the light of the conclusions that were arrived at by Elton Mayo and his followers; among these, Chester I. Barnard and L. Urwick are the most well-known. Chester I. Barnard published his book *The Functions of the Executive* in 1939 and it has been said that this book made as deep an impression as Taylor's *Shop Management* had done on the thinking of serious-minded business leaders about the nature of their work.

As a result of all these developments, it is now being clearly realised by an increasing number of executives in business that, in addition to the problems of the task, of adjustment of the individual to the task, and of arranging and correcting the tasks, there is an equally important problem of motivating the members of the group. This has naturally led to an increasing emphasis on such concepts as leadership, informal organisation and morale in the theory and practice of management today.

Douglas McGregor

Douglas McGregor challenged some of the prevailing concepts about the attitude of people towards work, and the system of reward and punishment to get things done. He described the traditional concept of management as theory X and the modern concept as theory Y. The traditional managers, according to him, emphasise on directing and controlling the efforts of others. They believe that man does not want to work, he shirks responsibility, resists change, lacks ambition and is not very bright. Unless a system of reward and punishment is introduced, which would create fear in his mind, he would remain inactive. The traditional approach thus rests upon the distrust of basic human nature.

The new theory of management, according to McGregor, looks upon man as a social being who likes work as much as rest or play. He wants to share the responsibility of and grow with the organisation. If people do not give their best in an organisation it is not because of dislike for work or irresponsibility on their part, but because of the environment of the organisation in which they work. If management creates opportunities and permits people to be creative and responsible, they feel motivated. The carrot and stick policy, according to this theory, does not work. Instead, the principle of self-direction and self-control works better. Management, in McGregor's view, is thus "a process, primarily, of creating opportunities, releasing potential, removing obstacles, encouraging growth, providing guidance."

The application of new approach requires decentralisation and delegation of authority, job enlargement, participative and consultative management, and self-evaluation in place of conventional performance appraisal by the supervisors. McGregor believes that only the management that has confidence in human capacities and is itself directed towards organisational objectives rather than towards the preservation of personal power, can grasp the implications of this emerging theory.

Management Hexagon

The following functions, in actual practice, are varied in nature and depend on the type of enterprise one is working in. These can be further divided into short-term or current functions and long-term or future functions.

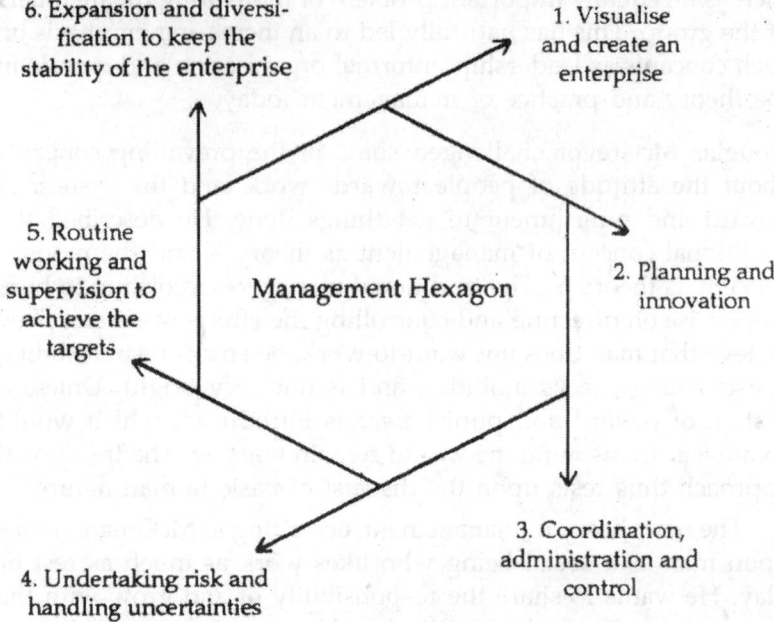

Fig. 2.2: Management Hexagon

The major short-term or day-to-day functions are:
- Production
- Quality Control
- Maintenance
- Personnel
- Finance and Accounting
- Marketing and Commercial Aspects
- Material Management
- Operations Research
- Stores and Purchase
- Public Relations
- and other allied aspects

Functions which come under long-term or future field of activities are:

(i) Long-term policy decisions like whether to diversify the activities of the business or to specialise in a particular field; share of total market to be controlled.

(ii) Centralisation or decentralisation of management.

(iii) Long-term planning and action needed for business operations. For instance, a steel plant of capacity of 2.0 million tonnes per annum wants to attain the capacity of 10 million tonnes over a period of 15 years, it has to have a detailed plan to locate raw materials, machinery, spares, energy, finance, personnel and other infrastructure.

(iv) Research and development to consider the changes continually taking place in processes, products, usage, technology, pricing, etc.

A contemporary manager has to face many problems which managers in the past did not consider important. Such problems arise because of changes like:

* Bigger business
* Individualism
* Less managerial authority
* Stronger unions
* Differential incentives
* Higher levels of education and specialisation
* Larger population
* Possible shorter shift durations
* Rapid technological changes
* Fewer operatives and more managers
* Community participations
* Government interference in favour of workers
* and many other allied factors.

A unified and integrated concept of management is, therefore, of prime importance. This would enable the manager to plan, organise his work and delegate authority to appropriate hands/levels. Since the role of a manager is not to do each job himself but to get it done in a proper manner by inspiring, leading, driving, coordinating and directing the workers/executives to achieve the objectives of the management, he has to analyse his job, determine the interdependence of different jobs and find out the extent to which he should do his work and distribute the work to be done by others. A manager will thus become more successful and effective if he successfully adopts the use of the unified concept of management.

Management Hierarchy

The form of management hierarchy varies from country to country, depending upon social outlook, political culture and a number of other factors. However, the most common form of management hierarchy is:
- Top management
- Middle management and specialists (engineers, technologists, statisticians, etc.)
- Front-line supervisors

Top Management

Top management is the keystone in the arch of management. The top manager may be an owner, promoter or a professional manager. His function is to establish the conditions under which other members of the management can achieve their goals by performing the tasks assigned to them. The success of an organisation would depend upon the extent to which he can infuse the whole hierarchy of the organisation with energy, drive and vision, and to the extent of effective communication between the members of the team.

Middle Management

Middle management plays a vital role in communicating the objectives and policies of the top management to the line supervisors. The middle managers are also responsible for providing feedback from line supervisors to the top management.

Specialists

Specialists are those organisational pillars on which rests the responsibility of maintenance of various professional skills and disciplines. They transform ideas into practice, analyse, suggest and improve technology, innovate, devise logistics and strategies for the growth/welfare of the organisation. By virtue of their skill and mental prowess they can be placed in any of the management cadres depending upon their educational background as well as achievements.

Front-line Supervisors

The line supervisors are responsible for conducting day-to-day operations of a company as per predetermined schedules, and also for achieving targets set by the management. They maintain a close contact with the workers and thus form an important link between the workers and the middle management.

Management is often viewed as:
(a) an economic resource
(b) a system of authority
(c) a class or elite

Managerial Pyramid

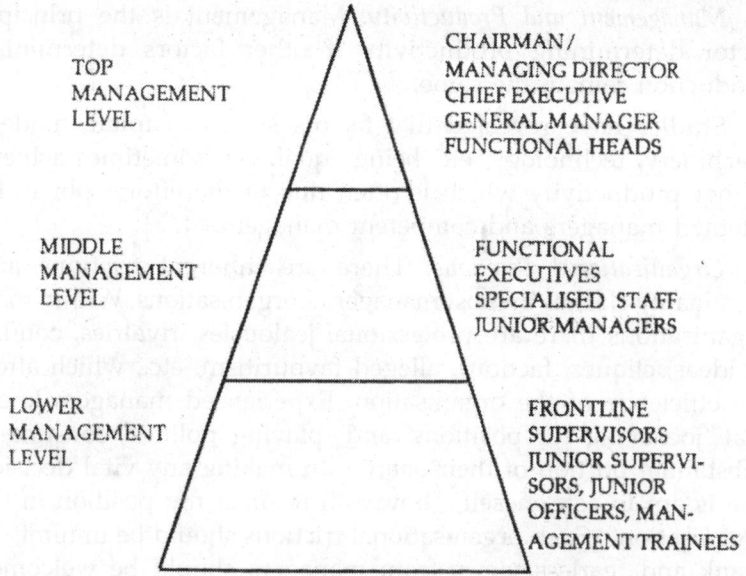

Fig. 2.3: Managerial Pyramid

The theory of management as an economic resource views management as a factor of production along with land, labour, capital and natural resources. The basic propositions which are fundamental to the understanding of management as an economic resource are:

Complexity of Business: Adequate managerial resources are needed for complex business organisations like steel plants, heavy industries, etc. These cannot be run only with land, labour, capital and natural resources; highly capable managers are a must to design, direct and control various activities like marketing, selling, production, profit planning, industrial relations, etc.

Management and Marketing: The larger the market and more complicated the market structure, the greater is the use of managerial resources. For competitive pricing, packaging, distribution and advertising, highly competent management is required.

Capital Investment: The higher the capital investment in an enterprise, the greater the need for managerial talent, to ensure a profitable return on investments.

Innovation and Resources: Innovations, diversifications and modernisation of any kind often require heavy investment, and call for high-level managerial resources. The individual inventor is being replaced by large industrial research and control laboratories and research and development departments in major industries.

Management as an Economic Resource

Management and Productivity: Management is the principal factor determining productivity if other factors determining production remain the same.

Studies have revealed that factors such as capital, modern machinery, technology, etc. being equal, can sometimes achieve higher productivity which is often due to the efforts put in by talented managers and competent management.

Organisational Frictions: There are inherent frictions and personality clashes in most managerial organisations. Within most organisations there are professional jealousies, rivalries, conflict of ideas, cliques, factions, alleged favouritism, etc., which affect the efficiency of the organisation. Experienced managers know that 'jockeying for positions' and 'playing politics' consume a substantial portion of their energy. In making any vital decision one is apt to ask oneself, "how will it affect my position in the organisation". Such organisational frictions should be minimised. Frank and fearless views from managers should be welcomed rather than encouraging 'yes sir' officers.

Management as a System of Authority

Management is a system of authority which is evident from the fact that for successful implementation of policies, plans and objectives of the organisation, the management has to exercise its authority over its employees:

(i) within management group
(ii) over workers

Authority within groups: The most primitive system of management is sovereign rule by a single person or a single family without delegating authority to the middle management. It works only at the top, and when the top disappears, the organisation either collapses or necessitates re-building.

The modern theory of management lays emphasis on objectivity and self-control. Here the job of the top manager is to assist and develop managers under him by delegating authority and responsibility. The powers of top management are no doubt decentralised among various divisional managers but the ultimate policy decision, cooperation and control is normally left to the top boss.

Authority over Workers: While exercising control over workers, management expects the following response from the workers:

(i) discipline
(ii) loyalty to the management

(iii) team work and collective efforts
(iv) higher productivity and profits

Various theories or philosophies of management for exercising control over workers have been put forward. Prominent among them are:

(i) Dictatorial or authoritarian
(ii) Paternalistic
(iii) Constitutional
(iv) Democratic or participative

Leadership Qualities
Henry Mintzberg's Categorisation

* Peer Skills
  – Ability to establish and maintain a network of contacts with equals
* Leadership Skills
  – Ability to deal with subordinates, and the complications that are created by power, authority and dependence
* Conflict Resolution Skills
  – Ability to resolve conflict to handle disturbance under psychological stress
* Information Processing Skills
  – Ability to build networks, extract and validate information and disseminate information effectively
* Skills In Unstructured Decision-making
  – Ability to find problems and solutions when alternatives, information and objectives are ambiguous
* Resource Allocation Skills
  – Ability to decide among alternative uses of time and other scarce organisation resources
* Entrepreneurial Skills
  – Ability to take sensible risks and implement innovations
* Skills of Introspection
  – Ability to understand the position of a leader and his impact on the organisation

---

Dictatorial or Authoritarian: According to this theory, the management should control the workers ruthlessly, i.e. in a dictatorial way. It is felt that then alone will workers work more and be loyal. This philosophy, commonly found in private contractors, is primitive and considered inadequate in modern industrial atmosphere. Modern management researchers often stress that management should be inspiring and not driving; it should be firm but at the same time fair.

Paternalistic: Industrialisation of Japan is attributed to the paternalistic philosophy of its industrial management. According to this philosophy, the needs of the workers and their welfare are well taken care of by the management and in return the management expects that the workers would be loyal, disciplined and productive. Here the role of the manager is that of a benevolent autocrat.

Constitutional: Under constitutional philosophy, while exercising control over workers, the management has to be aware of government legislations and pressures from various labour unions. Government forms legislations to regulate conditions of employment and also to protect the growth of labour organisations, ensure proper working environments, welfare needs, etc. Yet workers/unions often challenge the authority of the management. In such cases, both the workers and the management are bound to settle their disputes within the framework of prescribed rules. No side can take the law in its own hands and act in whatever manner it likes.

Democratic or Participative: The theory behind democratic or participative philosophy is that people respond best to an organisation when they can participate in the process of decision-making on matters that directly concern them. As per this system, workers should be encouraged to participate in management decision-making process and shoulder equal responsibility. Representatives of workers or workers' unions are inducted at various levels of decision-making, including up to the level of Board of Directors in some industrial undertakings/organisations.

Management as a Class or Elite

Management as a class is, essentially, a group of people, small in number, but aggressive in nature, who enjoy very high positions and privileges in the organisation. They can be classified as:

Patrimonial Managers: These managers are members of the family which owns the enterprise or their chosen representatives.

Political Managers: These managers are found where ownership, major policy-making positions and key administrative posts are held by persons on the basis of their political affiliations and loyalties. It is generally practised or found in communist countries.

Professional Managers: These managers are selected on the basis of their managerial and technical competence obtained by experience, qualifications or training rather than by family or political affiliations. The present trend is mostly towards engaging professional, talented and competent managers, specially in large and technologically complex industries.

Classification of Organisations

Katz and Kahn have given a classification of the types of organisations based on the functions performed by them. These are:

(1) *Production or Economic Organisations*

Such an organisation is concerned with creation of wealth, manufacturing of goods and providing services to the general public or the specific segments of it. Manufacturing organisations come under this category.

(2) *Maintenance Organisations*

These kind of organisations are devoted to the socialisation of people for their roles in other organisations and in the society, at large. Schools, social and cultural organisations come under this category.

(3) *Adaptive Organisations*

The object of such an organisation is to create knowledge, develop and test theories and, to some extent, apply those theories to existing problems. Universities, research institutes, arts and science academies come under this category.

(4) *Managerial or Political Organisations*

Managerial or political organisations deal with the adjudication, coordination and control of resources, people and sub-systems. The State, labour unions and the professional bodies of doctors, lawyers, technicians, etc., are examples of this type of organisation.

The above differentiations are, however, not clear-cut. A single organisation may engage itself in more than one function. An economic organisation may take up the adaptive function also. Research divisions, for instance, form an important part of many manufacturing organisations. Katz and Kahn have considered major organisational characteristics as they interact with these major functions while employing the above classification.

Organisations can also be considered from a closed or open system perspective. Traditionally, an organisation was considered sufficiently independent so that its formal structure and the relationships among its members could be established without reference to external situations. This is the closed-system model. The machine-model or the bureaucratic form of organisation is identified with the closed system. The open-system model looks at an organisation not only from the viewpoint of its goals, objectives and formal structure, but also from its response to external environment and internal pressures. This refers to the contingency model which modern theorists advocate.

Bureaucracy

The bureaucratic or the closed-system of organisation can be dimensionalised in the following ways :

    (i)   division of labour based on functional specification;

    (ii) well-defined hierarchy of authority;

    (iii) system of rules covering the rights and duties of employees;

    (iv) system of procedures for dealing with work situations;

    (v) impersonality of internal personal relations; and

    (vi) promotion and selection of employees based on qualifications and competence.

The closed-system developed as a reaction against the personal subjugation, nepotism and subjective judgements of the administrators. It aimed at developing a rational structure of the organisation, based on 'tradition rather than the cult of personality' and 'technical competence' rather than whims. But when the rules, regulations and procedures become ends in themselves rather than becoming the means to achieve the ends, the organisations become rigid and inflexible.

Open-System

The open-system view recognises that the biological or social system is in a dynamic relationship with its environment and receives various inputs, transforms these inputs in some way and exports output.

Input → Transformation System → Output

The open-system consists of a number of sub-systems. These are:

    (i)   Internal organisation (organisational goals, values, etc.)

    (ii) Technical sub-system (knowledge and techniques required to transform inputs into output).

    (iii) Psychological sub-system (individual behaviour, motivation, status and role relationships, group dynamism, etc.)

(iv) Structure (organisation chart, job description, authority, communication, etc.)

(v) Managerial sub-systems (developing strategies, plans, controls, etc.)

(vi) Environmental sub-systems (legal framework, government policies, economic and social environment, etc.)

The managerial decisions in the open-system are contingent to the circumstances: different organisations, with different tasks and different competitive environments, require different plans. The system, therefore, regards managers as a dynamic and life-giving force of the organisation.

Various factors such as the social, cultural or economic set-up of the country also influence the organisation or management of an enterprise. We, therefore, observe many instances of lack of uniformity in the pattern or philosophy of management. One has to choose an organisation that provides cordial employer-employee relationship, higher productivity, lower cost, security and welfare of workers, discipline, industrial safety, technological advancement, professional growth, etc.

Corporate Objectives and Policy Formulation

The objectives of management specify the goal towards which management aims, whereas policies provide guidelines which help attain that goal. The top management of successful enterprises defines the company's objectives so that the management knows what the company stands for and the goals it has to achieve. A clear definition of the scope, responsibility and authority within which the company has to operate is a must.

Based on the framework of corporate objectives, departmental policy manuals are drawn which likewise define and elucidate departmental functions to help achieve the corporate objectives of the company. Drawing up of or laying down of corporate objectives appears simple, but is a very difficult task in actual practice. It requires long deliberations at the top management level to clear the concepts before they can be defined and projected.

We shall discuss in detail the objectives laid down by one of the Government of India undertakings to form an idea as to how that undertaking proposes to conduct its business. The said company operates large integrated steel plants in the country and being a government undertaking, is morally bound to the national goal of ensuring rapid economic growth through efficient production and supply of high quality iron, steel and allied products at reasonable rates.

The objectives of the company stem from the following major premises:

- As a public sector undertaking accountable to the people of India, the company will strive to maintain a sense of national interest in discharging its responsibilities and will constantly seek to deserve and enjoy the highest measure of public trust and esteem.
- In conducting its business with honesty and integrity, the company will also endeavour to function as a profitable enterprise striving towards the achievement of a self-reliant and self-generating economy.
- The company will operate in the highly specialised fields of iron and steel manufacture, and pioneer in the new fields of applied science through the pooling of the best scientific and engineering talent in an environment which will facilitate the proper utilisation of their knowledge, interest and skill.
- The operations of the company will be led by a management group which will enjoy the respect of the whole organisation for its ability, integrity, fairness and human approach to problems.
- As a high rate of economic growth sustained over a long period is the essential prerequisite for achieving a higher standard of living for the people, the company will seek to increase investment in basic production capacities and economic and social overheads, within the limits of resources it can generate, so as to yield benefits now and in the future.
- The company will ensure good corporate health by adopting sound management practices, including the establishment and maintenance of a dynamic organisational structure suited to meet present and future company needs; long-range planning; product diversification; strong financial control and comprehensive research, development, engineering and consultancy services.

Objectives

Towards the People of India

- As an autonomous body, the company will be accountable to the people of India through the Parliament and the government, for running a highly competent, business-minded, technically-oriented enterprise, engaging in

manufacture, research and development to meet the needs of the country as well as the world markets for iron, steel and allied products.
- The company will endeavour to earn a fair return on investments, maximise production, institute adequate cost control, so managed as to inspire confidence and a sense of pride in the minds of the people.

Towards Employees

The company will seek to be a model employer by:

- Attracting competent personnel with growth potential and by developing their maximum capabilities in a working environment through the provision of opportunities for advancement and incentives;
- Developing and sustaining a favourable employee attitude and obtaining maximum contribution of employees through stable employment; providing adequate wages commensurate with the company's capacity to pay, good and safe working conditions, and job satisfaction;
- Establishing a system for redressal of employees' grievances in the shortest possible time with the smallest possible step;
- Providing training facilities and other opportunities for self-development in their current jobs as well as for further advancement;
- Fostering fellowship and a sense of belonging to the company by means of closer association of employees with management; by way of participation in various joint bodies and, through this machinery, inculcating in them respect for their occupation and the tools of production;
- Dealing fairly with recognised representatives of the workers, and encouraging in them healthy trade union practices.

Towards Customers

The company will serve its customers by:

- Providing prompt, courteous, dependable and competitive services;
- Selling products of the right quality at prices determined by the best interests of the nation; and

— Establishing confidence in the customers that it will supply the required products and services backed by modern production and research facilities manned by the most competent men available.

Towards Suppliers

The company recognises the important role of its suppliers in providing various materials and services for its operations by:

— Ensuring prompt dealings based on integrity, impartiality and courtesy; making available to them the benefits of research, skills and information in order to promote indigenous growth, reduce drain on foreign exchange and improve the quality of indigenous products and services.

Towards Community

The company accepts its social obligations to the community in which it operates by:

— Promoting the concept of national integration in the broadest sense; by providing community services, developing and assisting democratic institutions and generally ensuring that the company, as a whole, and its employees act on the ideals of social justice without discrimination;

— Providing know-how and assistance, and encouraging talent and growth among members of the community by establishing cooperative institutions.

The company endeavours to be one of the most enlightened, progressive and efficient producers of iron and steel and allied products in India and abroad, by making the most effective use of capital, personnel and management skills.

While it is important to set the goals in as detailed and specific a manner as possible, it would be wrong to assume that corporate objectives will be all-inclusive and do the job alone. The respective departments of the company have to have their own policy manuals further elucidating the action to be taken by them to help achieve the overall objectives.

For example, if the top management declares in its corporate objectives that, wherever practicable, the deliveries of the items have to be made on the stipulated dates and that no extension of dates would generally be granted, the production planning and control department, in that case, has to study each order in detail and give a delivery schedule only after a very careful study of the various factors involved. The production planning and control department will then be obliged to set up a system of follow-up and corrective action to meet this requirement. The system is to be so designed and controlled for reliability as to see that this objective is honoured.

Large companies often employ systems and procedures managers who help the departmental heads in preparing policy manuals for their departments. Depending on the circumstances, such as political changes, change of government/board of directors controlling the company, declaration of war, declaration of national emergency, etc., the objectives of a company may undergo changes or show signs of changes or drifts. The top executives should keep themselves up-to-date in this respect but use their discretion and judgement in communicating a part or the whole of this change down the line to specified positions in the hierarchy.

Management by Objectives

While speaking of objectives, it may be useful to know about a style in management known as MBO or management by objectives. It is a dynamic system which seeks to integrate the needs of the enterprise along with the growth of its managers. It is a demanding but rewarding style of management.

Peter F. Drucker in his book *Practice of Management* has described in a very lucid manner as to:

— What are the needs of *team spirit*
— Why *objectives* are a must
— What are the forces of *misdirection*
— How can these be *coordinated*
— When management by *drive* develops
— Who should set *objectives*
— What are the advantages of MBO

Team Spirit

Business enterprises must build a team, and for this, efforts must be put in the same direction; contributions must fit together to produce a worthwhile team – without cracks or friction, without unnecessary duplication of efforts. Business performance, therefore, requires that each job be directed towards the objective of the whole business. The collective spirit is the essence that matters.

Misdirection

The managers must know and understand what business goals demand of them in terms of performance, and their superiors must know what contributions to demand and expect of them. They must be judged on that scale. Managers are not automatically directed towards a common goal. The directions have to come from the top and have to be carefully explained to the hierarchy below in a simple and understandable manner. Unless a man knows his goals precisely, his efforts maybe misdirected and may lead to infructuous activity.

There are generally three powerful forces of misdirection:
  (i) specialised work of most managers
  (ii) hierarchical structure of management
  (iii) difference in vision and work

The functional manager's legitimate desire for workmanship (unless counterbalanced) produces a centrifugal force which tears the enterprise apart and converts it into a loose confederation of functional empires, each concerned only with its own craft, jealously guarding its own secrets, bent on enlarging its own domain rather than on expanding the business.

The future technologies will need both the drive for excellence in workmanship and the consistent direction of managers at all levels to achieve common goals.

The hierarchical system of dictatorial management often creates speculations. What the boss does and says, his most casual remarks, his habits, even his mannerisms, tend to appear to his subordinates as calculated, planned and meaningful. This happens when the hierarchy believes in and suffers from the 'yes sir' complex and undervalues the logic or logistics of the situation.

Coordination

The solution to this problem requires a structure of management which focuses both the manager's as well as his boss's eyes on what the *job* is rather than what the boss demands.

Each level of management sees the same elephant – the business – from a different angle of vision. The production foreman sees only the immediate production problems. The quality foreman is interested only in his quality specifications. The top management only tends to see the enterprise as a whole. An effective management must direct the vision and coordinate the efforts of all managers towards a common goal.

Drive

Drive without a proper goal or guidance misleads the management. During a misdirected 'economy drive', for instance, a few people may be fired. But this hardly offers any solution. Similarly, for unplanned and abrupt 'inventory cut drive', there may be four weeks of cost cutting followed by four months of production and human relations problems.

Management by *drive* or *crisis* is an admission of incompetence. It is a sign that management does not know how to plan. Above all, it is a sign that company does not know what to expect of its managers.

Each manager should develop and set objectives of his unit himself. Higher management must, of course, reserve the power to approve or disapprove these objectives. The objectives of a district sales manager, for example, should be defined by the contribution he and his district sales force make towards the sales department.

Some people advocate that each subordinate should write to his senior about the objectives he feels are expected of him and the objectives of his superior. Further, he should list his own responsibilities and the difficulties he may encounter. His expectations and the help he expects from his superiors for fulfilling his task should also be outlined.

Each manager from the 'big boss' down to the production foreman or the chief clerk needs clearly defined objectives. These objectives should specify:

(i) the performance he and his unit are supposed to make;

(ii) the contribution he and his unit are expected to make to help other units attain their objectives;

(ii) the contribution the manager expects from other units towards the attainment of his objectives.

Right from the start the emphasis should be on *team work* and *team spirit* and *team result*. It is the proper synchronisation and tuning of collective efforts that produces the results.

Advantages of MBO

Some of the specific advantages of Management by Objectives (MBO) are:

1. It makes it possible for a manager to control his own performance. Self-control means stronger motivation – a desire to do the best rather than just enough to get by. It means higher performance and broader vision.

2. It enables us to substitute management by self-control for management by domination.
3. It enables complete rethinking on our use of reports, procedures and forms. Procedures should not be a substitute for judgement. They should, at best, be regarded as tools and an aid to decision-making.
4. MBO rests on the concept of human action, human behaviour and human motivation.

Story of Ford and MBO

In the early twenties, Ford's market share in the automobiles had climbed to over 60%. Fifteen years later it went down by 20%. Ford's only son died during World War II. Survival of the company seemed impossible. There were even plans to nationalise it to give loans to Studebaker Company, the fourth largest automobile producer of the US which was less than one-sixth of the size of the Ford, to buy up Ford Motors.

What was the cause? The fundamental mistake of Henry Ford was that he had made a systematic, deliberate and conscious attempt to run the billion dollar business without managers. The secret police that spied on all Ford executives served to inform Henry Ford of any attempt on the part of any of his executives to make a decision. When they seemed to have acquired managerial authority or responsibility of their own, their services were generally dispensed with.

Henry Ford wanted only technicians and reserved management for himself as the owner. He did not like sharing either ownership or management with others. It was thus the absence of management which was responsible for the fall of Ford Motors.

Later, it was Henry Ford II (the grandson of Ford) who reversed the old policies. He appointed Ernest R. Breech as the Vice-President of the Company and gave him full operating authority. MBO was achieved by setting up different managerial cadres with defined objectives throughout the organisation.

Management came to be governed by the concept of management by objectives. Whereas Ford executives under the old regime were never told anything, the new Henry regime tried to provide every manager with the information he needed to do his job. The company was decentralised into various autonomous divisions, each operating with its own complete management. Ford II borrowed most of these ideas from his competitors (General Motors) and thus saved Ford Motors from closure.

When a system of management by objectives is operating in an enterprise, there is a continuous process of:

(a) reviewing critically and re-specifying the enterprise's *strategic and tactical plans;*

(b) specifying the *key results* and *performance standards* which each manager must achieve so as to fulfil the objectives of the enterprise and gain his share from it;

(c) inspiring and driving each manager to carry out *a job improvement plan* which makes a measurable and realistic contribution to the units and company's plan for better performance; and

(d) providing and maintaining conditions in which it is possible to achieve key results and improvement plans like *an organisation structure* which gives a manager maximum freedom and flexibility in decision-making and execution.

Managing Human Resource

Managing people has been one of the greatest challenges of Industrial Revolution. Henry Ford II said in a talk before the American Society of Engineers, shortly after he was made President of the Ford Motor Company:

> "Machines alone do not give us mass production. Mass production is achieved by both machines and men. And while we have gone a long way toward perfecting our mechanical operations, we have not successfully written into our equations, whatever complex factors represent men, the human element."

The success of an industrial enterprise depends ultimately upon its people and if they can be made to give the best out of them, the greatest obstacles in other fields can be overcome. When scientific management was developed by F.W. Taylor, Gilbreth and others, it was the man who figured in all principles and practices that evolved. When Taylor, as a consulting engineer, increased the capacity of people to load and unload pig iron from 12.5 tonnes to 47.5 tonnes per day in Bethlehem Steel Co., and when Gilbreth found a way in his studies to increase the capacity of people to lay 300 bricks per hour instead of the old practice of laying 120 bricks, different aspects of manpower management were closely scrutinised and principles evolved. The importance of selecting the right man, proper method of training, effective utilisation of manpower were thus recognised. Researches by social scientists also highlighted the importance of human element. Elton Mayo's researches in the Western Electric Company, Chicago, where productivity rose because of the feelings of "We mattered" and declined because of "We do not matter" due to the depression in 1930s, fear of unemployment of fellow workers, showed the importance of social set-up and mental conditions influencing people's morale and productivity. The play of the group mind and its impact over individuals comprising the groups was revealed in the Ahmedabad experiment when reorganisation of the groups in multiple loomsheds resulted into an increase in efficiency from 80% to 93% and a decrease in damage to the cloth from 30% to 11%. The span of manpower management has been widening from the routine of selection, training, promotion, wage and salary administration to boosting the morale of the employees and developing healthy relations between management and labour.

Technological innovations, greater automation, changes in skill requirements, growth of computer technology and softwares, dominance of services sector in economies all over the world, especially tourism, transport, banking and finance, media and entertainment in the last few decades have made human resource management more crucial to the success of enterprises. Google's Vice President of People Operations, Laszlo Bock, has rightly remarked:

"It's not the company provided lunch that keeps people here. Googlers tell us that there are three reasons they stay: the mission, the quality of the people, and the chance to build the skill set of a better leader or entrepreneur. And all our analysis are built around these reasons." (HBR, Oct 2010).

PERSPECTIVE

HR Policy: ECC

The Basic principles of Engineering Construction and Contract division of Larsen & Tubro's human resource are:

* Recruitment based solely on merit following well-defined and systematic selection process without discrimination.

* Identification of training needs within the organisation, designing and implementing need-based training programmes resulting in the continuous upgradation of knowledge skills and attitude of workers.

* Maintaining a quality management system to meet international standards as per ISO 9001 and planning, designing, training and motivating the staff to meet those standards.

Company's message to the prospective employees is: "If you feel like a seagull in the sky, if you feel you belong to the top and want to go higher, you are ready for ECC – India's largest construction organisation."

Experience of organisation world over reveals that operating units with highly satisfied employees have higher revenue, lower costs, greater employee retention and superior customer loyalty. A 'high-tech/hightouch' phenomenon, as described by John Naisbitt, is occuring which necessitates more personal and human touch in management as work environment gets more technical. More qualified people seek more meaning in their jobs. Employees today have to operate in an environment which is changing fast, demanding of them to understand expanding geographical and time horizons, capacity to deal with concrete and abstract work processes and ability to make decisions and assume more responsibilities than ever before.

HRM Defined

Human Resource Management, today, is more complex and challenging than in the 19th and 20th centuries. Its nature has changed from transactional to transformational. Office automation and computerisation have taken over a good deal of manual operations involved in recruitment and selection, training and development, performance evaluation, wage and salary administration, maintenance of records and other routine activities. We would like to define HRM as:

"Managerial activities related to integrating HR goals with organisational objectives, evolving and operating policies, procedures and systems for efficient operation of manpower planning, recruiting, training, promotion, performance evaluation, compensation, employee welfare and industrial relations, and promoting environment for higher productivity with employee satisfaction."

Managerial activities of planning, organising, supervising and leading are performed by all departments in most organisations in some measure or the other. HR department has to plan for manpower, analyse and evaluate jobs, recruit and place people at work, coordinate with all line departments in matters relating to employees, help management in formulating policies on all personal and industrial relations issues, develop and administer compensation system which motivates people, develops employees at different levels including managers to acquire new skills and leadership qualities.

Staffing is one of the basic functions of HR department along with training and compensation systems. In most organisations, these fall within the exclusive control of HR division. For its own division, line functions are also performed by the HR department, e.g. recruiting, training, division of work, coordinating, motivating, supervising and leading its own staff.

Some of the aspects of HR management, which scholars on the subject have emphasised in attempting to define HRM include mutuality between employers and employees, employment systems, open channels of communications, and building of trust and collaboration. Walton stressed on mutuality – mutual goals, mutual influence, mutual respect, mutual rewards and mutual responsibility to elicit commitment which in turn would yield both better economic performance and greater human development.* Hendry and Pettigrew see HRM as a perspective on employment systems, characterised by their closer alignment with business strategy.** Beer and Spector emphasised on a new set of assumptions in shaping the meaning of HRM, which includes linking HRM with strategic planning and cultural change. Coincidence of interest between stakeholders, open channels of communication and goal orientation, etc.*** Gary Dessler stresses on HR's role being that of a protector and screener as well as a strategic partner and change agent. According to him, the metamorphosis of personnel into human resources reflects that.****

HRM and HRD

HRM and HRD are two sides of the same coin. The former includes all managerial functions related to HR while the latter is normally understood as the development aspect of HR such as training, employee empowerment, career development and organisation development. We have defined HRD in the beginning of this book as the "development of head, hands and heart of every man and woman working in an organisation." Werner and DeSimone have defined HRD "as a set of systematic and planned activities designed by an organisation to provide its members with the opportunities to learn necessary skills to meet current and future job demands." This definition emphasises the learning aspect at work. In majority organisations, HRM divisions look after HRD functions also.

---

* Walton: *From Control to Commitment* (HBR, Vol. 63, Issue 2, 1985).
** Hendry and Pettigrew: *HRM Agenda for 1990s* (HRM, Dec. 1990).
*** Beer and Spector: *Managing Human Assets* (Free Press, New York, 1984).
**** Gary Dessler: *Human Resource Management* (Pearson Education, Singapore, 2003).

American Society for Training and Development (ASTD) has identified the major development roles of HRM as given under:

HR Manager's Role

* NEED ANALYST

    Identifies gaps between ideal and actual performance as well as causes for their discrepancies.

* PROGRAMME DESIGNER

    Prepares objectives, defines content and selects sequences for specific HRD activities.

* RESEARCHER

    Identifies, develops and tests new information for HRD utilisation.

* MATERIALS DEVELOPER

    Produces and adapts written or electronically mediated instructional material.

* INSTRUCTOR/FACILITATOR

    Identifies, directs structured learning experiences and manages group discussions and group processes.

* EVALUATOR

    Identifies the impact of HRD intervention on individual or organisational effectiveness.

* ORGANISATION CHANGE AGENT (CONSULTANT)

    Influences and supports changes in organisation behaviour

* ADMINISTRATOR

    Provides coordination and support services for the delivery of HRD programmes and services.

* MARKETEER

    Markets and contracts for HRD programmes and services.

* HRD MANAGER

    Plans, staffs, leads and supports the HRD functions and links that work with the whole organisation.

* CAREER DEVELOPMENT ADVISOR

    Helps individuals to assess personal competencies, values and goals to identity, plan and implement career and personal development action.

Strategic HRM

The word 'strategy' is derived from the Greek term 'generalship' originally applied to the deployment of forces by the commander. Its now a widely used term in business in the context of long term objectives and policies to achieve them. It includes situation analysis, assessment of environment – internal and external, formulating company vision, mission, objectives and goals, schemes to give practical shape to the desired goals, efficiently and effectively. Business world over has become highly competitive throwing challenges before management on all fronts – production, finance, marketing and manpower. Human talent is the key to success and needs to be managed in alignment with company's business goals. Cost-effectiveness, for example, is one goal with which HR managers are concerned everywhere. Restructuring organisation by eliminating certain layers which are not needed, downsizing, outsourcing, replacing most manual operations by computerising all routine office work, developing communication network for speedy and effective flow of information, building a knowledge-based department by promoting learning activities to empower employees with skills, concepts and techniques needed by the company not only today but also in the years ahead to avoid any mismatch between the needs of the people and their availability, supporting change process, formulating performance assessment procedures based on objective criteria and incentive schemes to boost people's morale in the organisation.

HR Vision, Mission, Goals and Objectives

Objectives have different layers. At the top comes the vision which is like a dream, a position which the organisation intends to acquire in future. A company, for instance, may desire to be known as the best employer in the country. Mission refers to the purpose for which the organisation exists, e.g. shareholders, customers and employee's satisfaction. Goals are the targets organisation intends to fulfil like empowering all employees by continuous training, performance evaluation and feedback. Objectives show the course of actions company would take to fulfil its vision, mission and goals. Objectives may be framed in each functional area of HRM – recruitment, training, promotion, compensation, etc.

> **PERSPECTIVE**
>
> ### HR Vision, Mission and Objectives – ONGC
>
> **HR Vision**
>
> To build and nurture world-class human capital for leadership in energy business.
>
> **HR Mission**
>
> To adopt and continuously innovate best-in-class HR practices to support business leaders through engaged, empowered and enthusiastic employees.
>
> **HR Objectives**
>
> * Enrich and sustain the culture of integrity, belongingness, team work, accountability and innovation.
> * Attract, nurture, engage and retain talent for competitive advantage.
> * Enhance employees' competencies continuously.
> * Build a joyous work place.
> * Promote high-performance work systems.
> * Upgrade and innovate HR practices, systems and procedures according to global benchmarks.
> * Promote work-life balance.
> * Measure and audit HR performance.
> * Integrate employee family into the organisational fabric.
> * Inculcate a sense of corporate responsibility among employees.

Aligning HRM Goals With Company Goals

HR division plays a crucial supporting role in achieving company goals by providing manpower according to the requirements of the organisation. But its role does not end here. It needs to be a change agent to develop professional attitude, competency and potentialities of people for higher productivity. It has to be a strategic partner with other divisions of the company to build an environment conducive to the growth of organisation, quality culture, learning spirit and benchmarking with the best employers. Restructuring, re-energising, golden handshake when overstaffed, attractive incentives for retaining the best, and other such strategies which meet organisational goals are implemented by the HR division. Peter F. Drucker has suggested these stages to achieve company goals: setting objectives, developing action plans, conducting periodic reviews and appraising performance. All these apply to HRM as well. HR goals integrated with company goals, planned and monitored effectively, benefit the organisation as well as its people.

> **PERSPECTIVE**
>
> ### HR INITIATIVES: INDIAN OIL
>
> The Vision Statement of Indian Oil, seeking to emerge as "The Energy of India," is sought to be achieved by adhering to six cornerstones – Ethics, People, Innovation, Environment, Technology and Customers. In the fulfilment of the Vision, human resource plays a crucial role.
>
> **HR initiatives include:**
>
> * Inducting quality manpower in the organisation.
> * Honing talent in a way that the inducted personnel are not only retained for their respective skills, but are trained for future leadership roles.
> * Making direct recruitment for middle level management when new business needs are felt.
> * Continuing assessment of capabilities of manpower through surveys and periodic reviews and reframing the pivotal roles of executives and non-executives.
> * Organising long duration training programmes at the Indian Oil Institute of Petroleum Management with emphasis on enhancing business perspective, leadership and strategic skills.
> * Using a 'Cafeteria Approach' to allow executives to choose from a set of perks and allowances as per their wish rather than fixed remuneration.

Situation Analysis

A steel plant which is situated about 800 km away from the source of coal supply normally consumes about 10,000 tonnes of coal daily. The coal stock was observed to be going down from the then existing level of 180,000 tonnes owing to lower receipts of coal as compared to the consumption.

The prescribed stock limit of the company was as under:

Description	No. of days Consumption	Tonnes in stock
Normal	15 days	150,000
High	20 days	200,000
Low	10 days	100,000
Critical	7 days	70,000

The superintendent in charge of the raw materials at the plant took it casually till it reached the level of normal or 150,000 tonnes. Then he took up the matter with the area superintendent of the Railways but before any effective measures could be taken, the stock of coal had slumped down to the level of 100,000 tonnes. The superintendent had been complaining of low receipts and pressing the Railways for an increased supply of wagons as sufficient coal was reported at the pitheads of the collieries. Railways, on the other hand, were complaining about higher detention of coal wagons in the plant in the wake of nationwide shortage of wagons.

By the time the matter was brought to the notice of the company's General Manager for taking it up with the general manager/chairman of the Railways, the coal stock had slumped down to the critical level of 70,000 tonnes, and the superintendent of Coke Ovens expressed his inability to carry on the blending operation and supply of the right blend of coal to coke oven batteries owing to low stocks.

By the time the matter was discussed at the level of the Steel and Railway ministries and measures considered for the emergency lift-off, the following developments had taken place:

(i) Owing to a severe drought and lower rainfall, the hydro-electric power generation was drastically reduced and the supply of power to the collieries was affected.

(ii) This affected the rate of production at the collieries and the stock of coal at the pitheads was completely wiped off.

(iii) Owing to the takeover of the foodgrains trade by the government, there were artificial shortages in some parts of the country resulting in alleged starvation and incidence of high price rise.

(iv) The Government ordered massive movement of foodgrains to deficit areas on a *war footing*. The Railways diverted the increased number of wagons for foodgrain movement resulting in depletion of wagons for the movement of coal. This further depleted the coal stock to 2 days or 20,000 tonnes at the steel plant.

The General Manager of the company was eventually compelled to order a 30% reduction in the production of coke for a period of 3-6 months because coke oven batteries cannot be subjected to frequent temperature fluctuations on technological grounds. An overall assessment of the situation at the corporate level indicated that, even with the best possible arrangements and with support from the highest levels, it may take around 6 months to bring the stock back up to the low level of 100,000 tonnes with the production level of coke ovens remaining at 70%.

Lower production of coke and consequently, hot metal (pig iron), resulted in an overall shortage of gaseous fuels, and there was a marked reduction in production in all the major units.

Because of lower production, incentive earnings of the workers went down and financial losses of the company increased.

The bonus earnings are linked with the volume of production. So, workers started agitating for normal incentive earnings ignoring the rules for bonus and threatened to go on strike if bonus equivalent to rated capacity production was not paid to them. Stray cases of threats of damaging the equipment were also being voiced by the workers.

The General Manager found it difficult to get the support of the union because of the multiplicity of unions and inter-union and intra-union rivalries.

After a lot of thinking, the General Manager addressed the following open letter to the workers:

Dear Colleagues,

I would like to share with you some of my thoughts with regard to the current production problems and our future hopes for growth and development. The last financial year brought us to the pinnacle of glory in terms of new records of production and magnificent performance. Based on this, we planned for a still higher production of steel ingot in current year.

In achievement of the objectives which we have set before us, we are now facing some problems which I would like to share with you so that we work hand-in-hand in tiding over the crisis, and redeem our pledge to maintain the tempo of production.

We are in the grip of a very serious problem of coal shortage as a consequence of power shortage in the collieries. This is the outcome of the national calamity of monsoon failure which has affected all segments of production from food and power generation to coal production. We have made all possible efforts to keep our production at optimum level and efforts are afoot at the highest level to improve the prospects of coal supplies. The present position, however, is rather disturbing and taking this into account and low stock of only 16,000 tonnes as it exists today, the management had to take the decision of reducing the pushing rate to 350 ovens as against 500-525 ovens per day in the interest of safety and security of the plant. This will naturally affect all other shops in terms of coke and gas supplies and resultant production performance.

Normally, in such circumstances the management resorts to lay off, as is legally permissible. However, this we shall not do, keeping the spirit of mutual goodwill and harmony alive, to which the collective endeavour of this plant is committed. I am sure the reduction in incentive earnings will be taken as a measure of sacrifice, in view of the national problems which beset us.

During the past few months, the industrial relations climate has also been affected due to inter-union and intra-union rivalries; demands for upgradation not justified on evaluation, revision of pay and decrease in the working hours, etc. I am confident that during this period of crisis we shall forget the differences to build a better future.

Let us keep our obligations to the economic development of the country foremost in our minds by putting up with stress and strain, with fortitude and courage. We shall face the challenge as one man and one soul.

With best wishes.

Yours sincerely,
General Manager

However, to guard against any untoward incident, the General Manager called for a meeting of the departmental heads to discuss the gravity of the situation and find out ways and means to resolve it. If you were one of the departmental heads what would you suggest to get over the situation? If you are the HR chief, what role will you play?

Review Questions

1. Define management and discuss the functions managers perform.
2. Discuss 4 Ps approach to management.
3. Give a brief historical perspective of the development of management thought.
4. Who is the Father of Scientific Management? Discuss his contributions.
5. What are the general Principles of Management?
6. Discuss the contribution of social scientists in developing the Human Relations approach.
7. Explain the system of authority in an organisation and the need to delegate authority.

8. What is MBO? What are the steps involved in it?
9. "Managing people has been one of the greatest challenges of Industrial Revolution." Comment.
10. Define HRM and the functions HR managers perform.
11. How will you define HRD? What are the roles of HR managers in developing people in an organisation.
12. Define vision, mission, goals and objectives with suitable illustrations.
13. Discuss the process of aligning HR goals with company goals in the light of GE's practice as given below:

At the beginning of each year, GE's management and HR teams sit down to review the template of common goals and objectives for the HR function. The discussion then turns to what are the key elements that the HR strategy should drive, relative to business objectives and both internal and external customers.

The aim is to have everybody driving in the same direction with a clear vision of what that business is looking to deliver in that year. There is continuous monitoring to ensure the results that are required.

HR is very much a partner to the business leaders, and looks at its role from many dimensions.

Further Readings

1. Gary Dessler: *Human Resource Management* (Pearson Education, New Delhi, 2005).
2. Peter F. Drucker: *Management's New Paradigms* (Forbes, pp. 152-177, Oct 5, 1998).
3. C.D. Fisher, L.F. Schoenfeldt and J.B. Shaw: *Human Resource Management* (Cengage Learning, New Delhi, 2006).
4. R. Harrison: *Human Resource Management: Issues and Strategies* (Addison-Wesley, Wokingham, 1993).
5. H. Koontz and C. O'Donnell: *Principles of Management: An Analysis of Managerial Functions* (McGraw-Hill, New York, 1972).
6. Douglas McGregor: *The Human Side of Enterprise* (McGraw-Hill, New York, 1960).
7. C. Mabey and G. Salomon: *Strategic Human Resource Management* (Blackwill, Oxford, 1995).
8. Thomas J. Peters and Robert H. Waterman: *In Search of Excellence* (Harper and Row, New York, 1982).
9. Lallan Prasad and S.S. Gulshan: *Management Principles and Practices* (Excel Books, New Delhi, 2010).

Chapter 3

Organisation Structure and HR Division

"We need managers who can operate as capably in an open door, free flow style as in hierarchical mode, who can work in an organisation structured like an Egyptian pyramid as well as in one that looks like a Calder mobile, with a few thin managerial strands holding a complex set of nearly autonomous modules that move in response to the gentlest breeze."

– Alvin Toffler
(The Third Wave)

Learning Objectives

After reading this chapter you will be able to:

1. Understand the need of a formal structure and drawing an organisation chart.
2. Learn the status of HR Division in the company structure.
3. Analyse the functioning of informal groups and relationships in an organisation.

The foundation of organisation structure is the descriptive definition of the responsibilities that are to be undertaken.

Although every business manager will affirm that a sound organisation is a must for business prosperity, there is a difference of opinion regarding what an organisation is. Whether the organisation is concerned with finding, placing and developing the people within its structure or is only concerned with procedural aspects which guide its day-to-day activities, are some of the questions which are always mooted in the context of an organisation. We can hardly employ a manager for establishing the business on a sound footing until we have a precise concept of organisation.

Drawing an organisation chart is not sufficient in itself. Organisation does not mean only the grouping of responsibilities and functions. This may be helpful only in showing the facts in an organisation pictorially. To make it useful, it has to codify the responsibilities and functional relationships vis-a-vis other departments. It is essential for the various groups within an organisation to cooperate with one another in the pursuit of a common task and the fulfilment of determined policies.

Organisation can, therefore, be defined as the process of identifying, defining and delegating responsibility and authority, and establishing relationships for the purpose of enabling people to work effectively together in accomplishing its objectives.

A wide variety of organisations exist in our society. These may be classified according to the purpose or functions, inter-relationships of people and the systems being followed. The aim of classification should be to indicate a meaningful difference between the types or classes identified and not to oversimplify them.

The two main principles on which organisational structure is based are:

1. Division of Labour

There must be division of labour to enable every group to contribute its measure towards the achievement of objectives so that the work of one group does not duplicate or overlap that of another.

2. Source of Authority

There must be some means of securing compliance of individual members of the group in contributing towards the common goal. Whether such an authority emerges from instinct, culture, consent of the governed, or intelligence of the superiors, it must exist. Unless this happens, everyone would do what as they want and integrated efforts would be impossible.

Relationships

How are individuals to work together in an organised group? In teamwork, someone takes a decision and the others follow it. Individuals in different groups, at various levels of authority, have to establish contact with one another and work together. They ought to know the channels they must follow for this is necessary to establish standing procedures in the form of relationships between individuals and groups. These relationships in reality are the rules for work.

Types of Organisation

Line Organisation

The simplest type of organisation is line organisation in which lines of authority are direct with no advisory activities. Such an organisation is commonly found in small business enterprises.

Line and Staff Organisation

Most organisations are more complex than the simple line organisations. The line and staff organisation provides for advisory staff positions as indicated in fig. 3.1.

Whatever be the size, character and aims of an organisation, it has to fulfil the principle of unity of management and the organisational structure from the top to the bottom has to be the framework of a single process.

Types of Relationships

The types of relationships within an enterprise that give meaning to the organisational structure are:

(i) direct
(ii) lateral
(iii) functional
(iv) staff
(v) matrix

A very clear understanding of these relationships is essential for the proper application of the working of management. These are explained below in brief:

Direct

It is the relationship that exists between a senior and a direct subordinate and vice-versa. It may be between a chief engineer and a deputy chief engineer or between a foreman and his chargeman. In principle, the relationship is that of a direct authority with his immediate subordinate.

76 Managing Human Resource

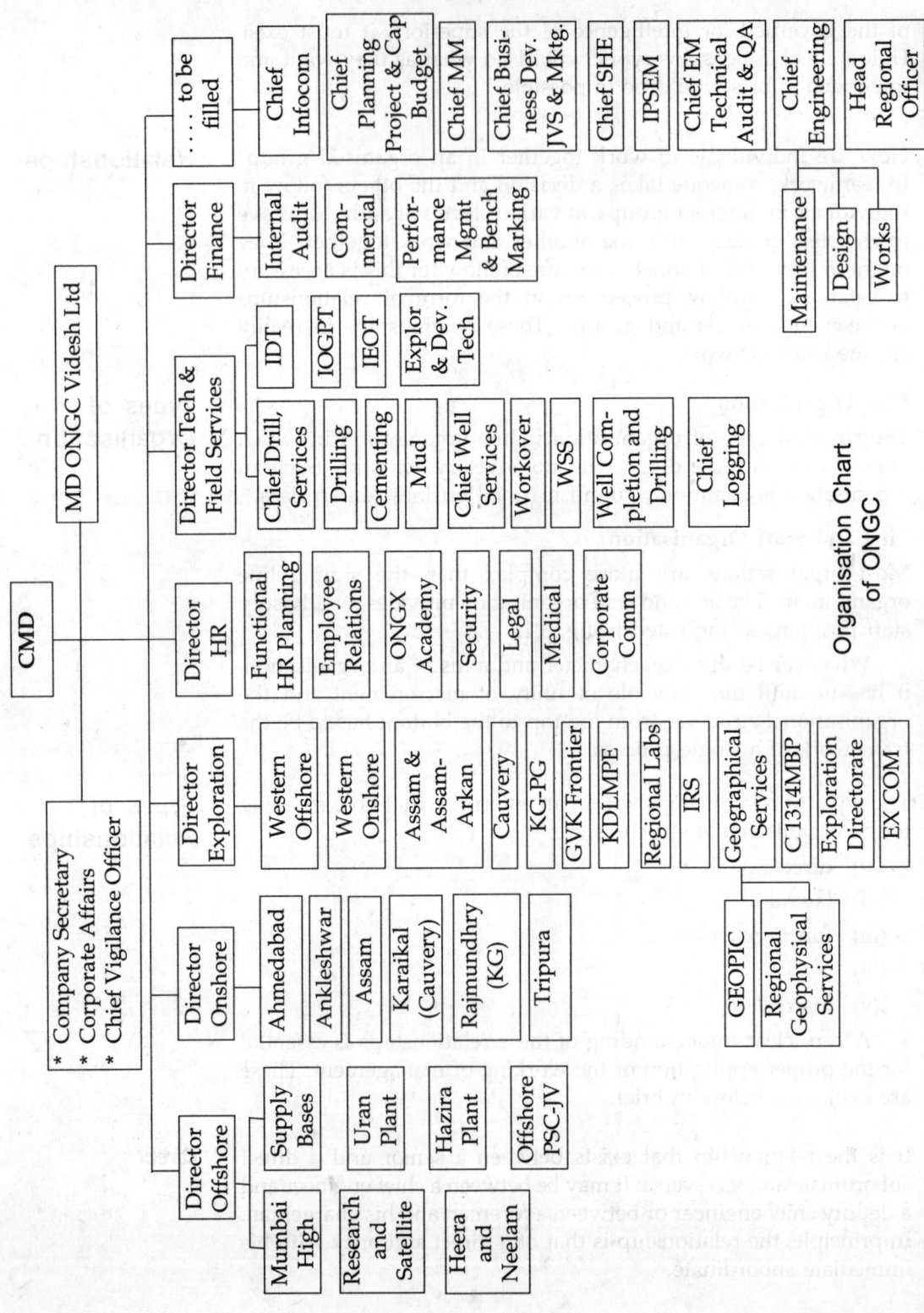

Organisation Chart of ONGC

Lateral

This represents the working relationship between executives at the same level of responsibility, i.e. say between two departmental or sectional heads in the same organisation. Even though they may be linked with a common senior in the organisation chart, a dialogue or collaboration between them is necessary with regard to mutual interest. This is necessary for discharging their day-to-day responsibilities without referring back to the common senior. Such type of functional relationship between two executives is termed as a lateral relationship.

Functional

Large industrial and commercial organisations, owing to the vastness of their operations, often departmentalise certain groups of functions under a specialist. This specialist has the expertise which he exercises for the effectiveness of management in the organisation as a whole. The HR department is responsible for such specialised functions as selection, recruitment, transfers, development of human skill, performance evaluation and promotion, wage and salary administration, incentives and compensation schemes, personnel records, industrial relations, welfare, retirement, pension and security, etc. The major role of the HR department is long-term planning and strategy formulation for human resource procurement and development.

Staff

It normally involves organisation at the top level. Examples are the technical secretary to the general manager, the personal assistant to departmental heads, etc. where the nature of responsibility can be clearly defined as assisting an executive to whom one is attached or allocated. In his own right, he may not carry any authority to direct others. At best, he may be regarded as an extension of the personality for whom he works.

Matrix Organisation

When the conventional functional organisation is combined with a 'project team' organisation, it results into a matrix organisation. For instance, an HR manager incharge of project manpower, may have to report to the project manager as well as the chief of the division. This type of organisation first began in the defence and aerospace industries and later became popular in industrial firms, service organisations and even in governmental agencies.

The matrix structure helps in the flow of needed information and expertise to places where it is needed, minimising red tape and the danger of important decisions being hung up in the limited channels of the pyramid. It provides the flexibility needed in the organisation: experts attached to a project may be moved back to the parent department once the project is over or when their services are not required. Task forces may be formed or disbanded as per the situation. The problem with matrix organisation is that it may create tension between functional heads and the project head over exercising authority and controlling the staff.

Most expanding organisations tend to become matrix. The structure of a matrix organisation is shown in Fig. 3.2.

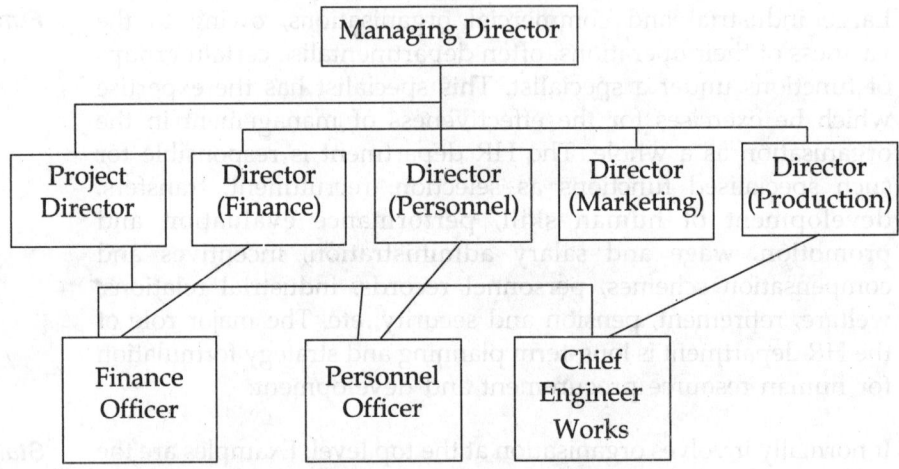

Fig. 3.2: Matrix Organisation.

Board of Directors

In the corporate form of business organisation, the board of directors is elected or selected by the shareholders. The members of the board represent shareholders in the conduct of the business of the corporation. The board exercises such rights, on behalf of the shareholders, as are delegated to it by the charter of incorporation and by-laws, subject to overall government regulations. The acts of the board of directors are subject to approval by the shareholders. The right to plan, organise and control the use of corporation's property rests with the directors for all practical purposes. The board of directors of any company is concerned with the ultimate objectives and with general policies underlying long-range planning. Its participation in organising involves the approval of general organisational plans and the appointment of principal executives. Its scope of activities is, as such, broad. Concerned with the administrative control of basic programmes of the corporation, it is generally interested in the evaluation and follow-up of policies in the attainment of corporate objectives.

The board members have little direct contact with the day-to-day operations that are carried on by the managing director and functional managers. However, the directors may be working directors as well who are charged with the specific responsibility of executive policies of the corporation, who may also function as liaison officers between the board and the subsidiaries of the corporation. In this capacity, a director is obligated to maintain a thorough understanding of the areas under his responsibility. In the case of subsidiaries, this includes all kinds of problems in the field of management, not only those of any particular subsidiary. This requires constant touch with the management of the subsidiary with which he works but such authority rests with the board as a whole. The board is in a position to appoint officers in the subsidiaries in consultation with the managing directors concerned.

The board is not a staff organisation. It is the source of delegation of functions, responsibilities and authority within the ambit of corporate organisation. It is concerned with the objectives and formulation of overall policies and plans. The board can exercise leadership of ideas in some way by evaluating the corporation's general course of activities over the years.

The major functions of the board can be outlined as:
(i) trusteeships
(ii) determination of objectives
(iii) selection of executives
(iv) checking on plans and results
(v) approval of the budget
(vi) securing long-range stability
(vii) distribution of earnings
(viii) examining company's programmes and policies

The board is the apex of the pyramid of corporate organisation. Its functional success depends upon:
(i) well-defined authority and scope
(ii) determining size
(iii) selecting members
(iv) selecting subject matters
(v) importance of the chairman
(vi) checking conclusion

An example as to how, at times, reality becomes invisible to the board is indicated below as narrated by a renowned member of a board of directors:

"When I was first invited to join a board of directors, I was pleased to be asked to sit at the top level of a company, and looked forward to the experience. I pitched into learning about the company, I asked questions at the meetings and darned good ones. I often called on the president between board meetings with suggestions and ideas. Much to my surprise, I was not selected at the next annual meeting, and all they told me was some kind of a vague story about reorganising to make place for a customer at their banker's suggestion. I know now that was not the reason. I was too active. Presidents do not want people on the board to try to run the company or be too assertive. I am on several boards now, and generally I attend meetings, give my opinion where it is asked for, and the rest of the time keep my mouth shut. I am now convinced that the board of directors does not direct but only endorses the recommendations put up. The board of directors is generally not in touch with the realities. Going deeply into the details of business is particularly frowned upon. If any member of the board is troublesome, he may not be selected again. The only way to become a member of a board and to last as such is to avoid most of the realities of the firm – to be in touch with reality entails responsibility for failure."

There are often many fallacies in a board's decision-making process. Some of these are:

— Preconceptions instead of information: biases, prejudices.
— False polarisation: polarising of opinion–extreme logic.
— Contradiction compromise: posing the problem as a contradiction to allow statements.
— Needless parallelisms: to justify inaction and continuation of old practices.
— Global issue swamp: turning the most simple proposals into metaphysical questions of deeply intellectual character.
— Converting facts into hypothetical questions: if we had done this, what would have been the effect?
— Erroneous authoritative statement taken as gospel by the management; exercise of power becomes an end in itself.
— The role of devils advocate – seeing its role as a critic and a judge.
— Time will tell delusion – statements like time will be on our side, etc.

The situation demands that the board behaves like a group of reasonable adventurers so that they:

(i) conserve the assets entrusted to them and retain the best features

(ii) introduce change

(iii) set an example

Policy formulation is the joint responsibility of the board. However, many organisations have functional directors on the board whose expertise in their respective areas is useful. When a company has an HR director, policy initiatives on HR matters are his responsibility even though final decisions are made by the board of which he is a part. HR issues which the board may consider include broad policy measures on recruitment, training, promotion, compensation, disciplinary matters, sanction of new posts at the senior level, and heavy expenditures (e.g. setting up of a training institute, pay revision, decision of managerial remuneration, etc.)

Some organisations also have a labour director on the board. As a Board member, he participates in the deliberations, but his role is normally limited to matters connected with the workers. He represents the workers and is supposed to look after their interest.

Decentralisation of Authority

Decentralisation of authority may be defined as a situation in which ultimate authority to command and ultimate responsibility for results is localised in as many channels in the organisation as the efficient management permits. It is carried out by creating, under the central organisation, a number of autonomous units.

Decentralisation takes place when some higher and central source of authority delegates certain functions and duties to subordinate individuals or groups. The extent of decentralisation is generally governed by the attitude of the top leadership as it involves delegation.

Why is the present trend in industry/business favourably disposed towards decentralisation of function, responsibility and authority? This may be because of one to two centuries of experience – mostly in politics, where centralisation is generally associated with the loss of liberty. Believers in democracy generally oppose centralisation of authority.

Centralised control tends to become a disadvantage when an organisation grows bigger in size. Factual data, complete knowledge of the background, and hold on the situation decrease as the organisation grows larger. This makes correct and timely decisions difficult under centralised control. At the same time, compensation by way of having a large number of secretaries, the system of maintaining files, records and communication devices tend to increase overhead costs. Also, the decisions of the top executive tend to become dictatorial even if they sincerely desire to be fair. Other common disadvantages of centralisation are:

— increasing pressure of work at the top
— decrease in the generation of new ideas
— tendency for organisational instability
— lack of opportunity at subordinate levels to make local decisions, thereby slowing managerial growth
— loss of flexibility and of speed in decision-making under emergency situations
— morale of the organisation tends to be lower

However, large-scale decentralisation should also not be done without thinking properly about the size and complexity of the operations. Some situations may not require it. Losses in policy uniformity and other costs of decentralisation may not make it that advantageous. When an authority is decentralised, the manager becomes a more independent operator of his business. He may set up his own empire by acquiring his own personnel officer, accountants, statisticians, technical assistants, secretariat, etc., thus duplicating the specialised services of the top management with an associated increase in cost but not acquiring the same quality of proficiency that the central authority had.

What is the primary change in decentralisation? Control is passed on from very few to many hands. But this has to match with the financial capabilities of the company. Therefore, if financial imbalance of the company has to be avoided, decentralisation must be conditioned by:

— the quality of managers in important units/departments
— selective centralisation of vital and major policy areas

Planning and organising for executive centralisation must, therefore, be based on sound business policies. Also, the degree of emergency that the management may have to face is an important consideration that determines the degree of centralisation. Time is of the essence in handling an emergency situation and, therefore, it should be handled at such lower organisational levels where the executives have sufficient authority, competence and maturity. Otherwise, an emergency situation may spread and engulf larger areas of the organisation.

The extent of decentralisation may be governed by the attitude of the top leadership, since it involves the delegation of leadership responsibilities as well as operative activities. Either the conditions created by the growth of the organisation will force decentralisation or the growth itself may be stopped.

It is very difficult to precisely lay down the principles of decentralisation of authority because it is interdependent on so many other factors and normally associated with many pitfalls. In the opinion of the authors, the most comprehensive list of guidelines was compiled by the researchers of the General Electric Company around 1950. These are:

- Decentralisation places authority to make decisions at points as near as possible to where the actions take place.
- Decentralisation is likely to get the best overall results by getting the most directly applicable knowledge and the most timely understanding into play on the maximum number of decisions.
- Decentralisation will work if real authority is delegated, and not if the details then have to be reported, or worse still, if they have to be 'checked' first.
- Decentralisation requires confidence that associates in the decentralised positions will have the capacity to make sound decisions in the majority of cases, and such confidence starts at the executive level. Unless the president and all the other officers have a deep personal conviction and an active desire to decentralise full decision-making authority and responsibility, actual decentralisation will remain a dream. The officers must set an example in the art of full delegation.
- Decentralisation requires an understanding of the fact that the main role of the staff or services is the rendering of assistance and advice to line operators through relatively few experienced people, so that those making decisions can themselves make them correctly.
- Decentralisation requires the realisation that the natural aggregate of many individually sound decisions will be

better for the business and for the public than the centrally planned and controlled decisions.
- Decentralisation rests on the need to have general business objectives, organisational structure, relationships, policies and measurements known, understood, and followed, but realising that policies do not necessarily mean uniformity of methods in executing such policies in decentralised operations.
- Decentralisation can be achieved only when higher executives realise that authority genuinely delegated to the lower echelons cannot, in fact, also be retained by them.
- Decentralisation will work only if responsibility commensurate with the decision-making authority is truly exercised at all levels.
- Decentralisation requires personnel policies based on measured performance, enforced standards, rewards for good performance, and removal for incapacity and poor performance.

Two techniques of effecting decentralisation are often seen in practice. One is to promote a manager only when his subordinate has been trained and made capable to shoulder the responsibility of his superior. This often forces the manager to delegate responsibility to his subordinate so that he learns decision-making. This is a sort of "on the job" training. Moreover, this helps in the major cause of hoarding of authority which is often guided by the desire of a manager to prove his indispensability by making sure that his responsibilities cannot be handled by his junior in his absence. The second is to give the manager a good number of assistants, and at the same time making sure that each is loaded with sufficient work and each one is held responsible for a high degree of performance. When the span of management is stretched, it results in the delegation of authority and leads to decentralisation.

HRM functions are centralised when the size of an organisation is small. As the organisation grows, the need for decentralisation starts. When a company has many plants/branches, policies on HR matters are framed at the head office and operational autonomy is given to the other units so that they can have the staffing pattern, training and compensation systems according to their needs and the prevailing practices in the region of their location. Units operating in different states of the same country and in countries other than where the headquarter is situated may have to follow laws, rules and regulations as applicable to them. In such events, a centralised structure may create problems and may not be sustainable. However, coordination between the headquarter and the units is a must. Uniformity is needed on matters like service conditions, discipline, rewards and recognitions, performance evaluation, promotions and transfers. HR division at the head office needs to be on the lookout for the happenings and disputes and dissatisfaction amongst employees in the units. However, a friendly headquarter and not a dictatorial one is preferable.

Informal Organisation

The formal organisation structure shows prescribed roles and relationships. The informal groups, which are the result of the interaction of people at work, are never shown in an organisational chart. These groups consist of members knit together by common interest, beliefs, faiths and objectives. Such a group may cut across the formal structure and the lines of communication. It may have its own leader, customs and norms. Normally, the number of members is limited to make face to face communication and interaction possible.

Informal groups come into existence due to several reasons. With the growth in the size of an organisation, the personal touch between the leader and the led is lost. Life at the workplace becomes monotonous. Small groups are formed to make life pleasant through informal chats, gossips, get-togethers, sharing of news and ideas, etc. Regional affinities, threat from the supervisors, existence of other groups and a lack of sense of security are some of the other reasons that unite people in small numbers. Sometimes, informal groups create problems for the management by developing their own norms regarding productivity, quality and cost, going on leave, implementing organisational plans and policies, etc. Such groups also create their own channel of communication, the grapevine, which serves as a speedy means of circulating news and views, rumours and gossips, etc.

The informal groups can be classified as under:
— Friendship group: Such a group is marked by a close relationship between its members. They may be relatives or close friends. The affinity may be the result of education at the same place or belonging to the same area, caste or community, etc.
— Cliques: A small number of people living or working together, following a common strategy to meet certain situations and having effective communication among themselves may form the clique.

— Sub-clique: When one or more persons are admitted to a clique only partially, the sub-clique is formed. Such members may be from outside the department or the organisation.

Managers should not ignore informal groups. They may take advantage of using these groups for speedy communication of certain policies or plans and knowing the reaction of the people. These groups may be taken into confidence by understanding their problems and meeting their genuine aspirations. Informal groups with which supervisors have good relations may help them in overcoming difficult situations at the workplace. Informal groupings at the managerial level are also not uncommon. Much of the organisational politics is directed through such groups.

Group Dynamics

Group dynamics refer to the adjustive changes that take place in the group structure as a result of changes in any part of it. As Kurt Lewin puts it, "a change in a part brings change throughout the entire system analogous to the change witnessed in an electrical or magnetic field." The adjustive changes may take place in the process of interpersonal behaviour or intergroup behaviour.

Interpersonal behaviour is governed by interpersonal needs. What a member wants to contribute, what he can contribute to the group cause and the extent to which he will interact with the other members of the group will depend upon factors such as his physique, mental abilities and intelligence, aptitude, interest and personality.

Intergroup behaviour consists of interactions between the various groups and depends upon factors like the knowledge of the task, objectives and interdependence. When the groups know their job and the objectives behind it, they are likely to perform better. The interdependence amongst the groups may be of three types:

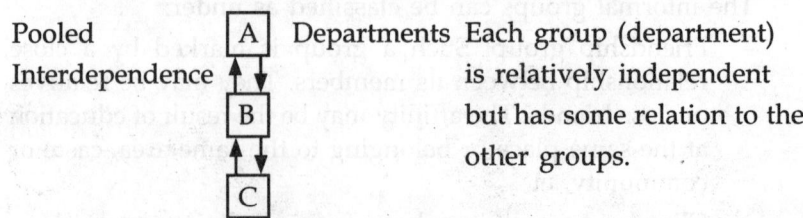

Pooled Interdependence — Departments — Each group (department) is relatively independent but has some relation to the other groups.

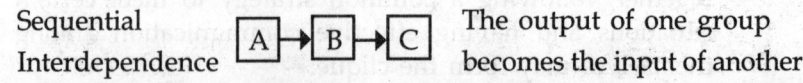

Sequential Interdependence — The output of one group becomes the input of another.

Reciprocal 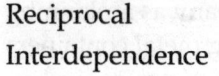 The output of each group
Interdependence 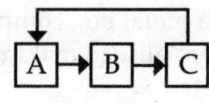 becomes the input for other groups.

The intergroup relationships in any organisation are further regulated by the rule of division of labour, regulations and procedures. Some departments may have functional authority while others may have advisory status. One department may have full control over finances, while another may look after the human resources. The power of the group is defined in many cases. For instance, the board of directors makes the policy while the management team is responsible for its implementation. The groups may also drive power through negotiation and contracts, absorbing or joining hands with other groups.

Informal organisation and groups put additional responsibilities on the HR division which is considered to be the eyes and ears of top management. It has to keep them informed about what is going undercurrent without losing the trust and confidence of people in the organisation.

The structure and role of the HR division varies from organisation to organisation. In labour-intensive plants, manpower problems necessitate early formation of the HR department to develop sound procedures for different personal and industrial relations functions with separate units to deal with the two. Adherence to labour laws, rules and regulations formulated by authorities and collective bargaining and union relations are on the priority list. In capital-intensive plants, where most operations are mechanised and fewer people are required to manage, the HR division may be small in size and labour problems may be less acute. Again, in organisations with a horizontal structure, staffed mostly by technical and specialised personnel, the size of the HR division may be small. Most routine functions may be operated by a few persons with the help of computers which are a must in organisations of all sizes – big, medium or small. In retail organisations also, like malls and departmental stores, the size of the HR department is small as operations are mechanised and fewer people are employed.

In large organisations with multiple plants and offices, the HR division at the head office looks after policy formulation and coordination with units. The HR chief at the head office may hold as powerful a position and status in the hierarchy as the chief of finance, production or marketing. Authority wielded by the HR chief in most organisations depends upon company policy and the proximity he has to the MD/CEO of the company.

Situation Analysis

Swaminathan was working in a metal box company as a planning officer. The company used to specialise in making metal containers for vanaspati oil, toothpaste, etc.

For making vanaspati tins, the process involved was cutting sheets to sizes, enamelling them after acid cleaning, printing trademark, the name of the product, rolling metals to cylindrical shape and soldering ends. One of the vanaspati manufacturers used to take about 5 lakhs containers of specific type and size each month. The cost for setting up of the equipment was about Rs. 10,000 each time.

The planning officer used to plan a run of 10 lakh containers each time. He used to despatch half of the quantity immediately and the rest in the next month. Sufficient storage space was available in the factory to store 5 lakh containers at a time and saving of Rs. 10,000 for a set up was considered a valuable saving.

The customer was getting prompt delivery and was benefited. However, he had told the planning officer that though he does not guarantee, he would give a notice of one month before he discontinues placing orders to this firm for any reason whatsoever.

The arrangement was going on smoothly for years. When Swaminathan, planning officer, proceeded on three month's leave, Singh took over the position. He was in great hurry to show some improvement and gain quick recognition as a planning officer. He thought why to spend Rs. 60,000 on set-up alone. Besides, he could save the set-up time itself if he plans a long term arrangement.

Without consulting his superiors or thinking in great depth, he planned a single run of 60 lakh containers to be sufficient enough for a year's supply since the storage space was no problem and was available at cheaper rates nearby.

The first month went well. He was busy preparing a report to the general manager about the savings effected when the customer announced that from next month onwards a new large economy size product in rectangular containers would be marketed.

This came as a bolt from the blue for Singh who was in a hurry to show his ability as planning officer. He ran to his customer after reading the announcement in the newspaper and went on arguing and requesting; he even pledged his support to the customer on future deals which was against the conduct rules of the company he was serving – in case the customer agrees to keep his plans in abeyance for another 10 months by which time all the containers would be used up. This would save him from embarrassment and predicament in which he had put himself.

He went further to the extent of suggesting that he would try for a reduction in the cost of containers if he is allowed to step out of the tight corners where he has been placed.

However, the customer could not agree to such a proposal for he had spent large sums on advertisement of the new product; also going back at this advanced stage would mean spoiling the public image of his company.

Finally, the matter reached the level of the general manager of the company and he called for a meeting to discuss the situation.

What changes in organisational set up do you recommend to avoid recurrence of such incidents in future?

Review Questions

1. 'A sound organisation structure is a must for smooth running of an organisation.' Comment.
2. What are the main principles on which an organisation structure is built?
3. Explain line, staff and line-and-staff organisation.
4. What is a matrix organisation? What purpose does it serve?
5. Draw an organisation chart and show the place of HR division in it.
6. What are the major responsibilities of the Board of Directors in any company?
7. Distinguish between centralisation and decentralisation.
8. What is informal organisation? Why such an organisation comes into existence within the formal structure?
9. What is group dynamics? Discuss the communications network in the group.

Further Readings

1. R. Daft: *Organisation Theory and Design* (Thomson Learning, Missouri, 2000).
2. Earnest Dale: *Planning and Developing the Company Organisation Structure* (American Management Association, New York, 1952).
3. Henry Mintzberg: *The Structuring of Organisations* (Prentice Hall, Englewood Cliffs, New Jersey, 1979).
4. M.H. Overholt: *Flexible Organisation: Using Organisational Design as a Competitive Advantage* (Human Resource Planning, Vol. 20, pp. 22-32, 1997).
5. Lallan Prasad: *Personnel Management and Industrial Relations in Public Sector* (Progressive Corporation, Bombay, 1973).

6. Paul Pigors and Charles A. Myers: *Personnel Administration: A Point of View and a Method* (McGraw-Hill, New York, 1961).
7. W.R. Scot: *Organizations: Rational, Natural, and Open Systems* (Prentice Hall, New Jersey, 1997).

Part II
Understanding People

Chapter Structure

Chapter 4. Emotional and Social Intelligence

Chapter 5. Personality Traits and The Job

Chapter 6. Motivation, Communication and Leadership

Chapter 7. Resistance to Change

Chapter 8. Conflict Situations and Management Systems

Chapter 4

Emotional and Social Intelligence

"It is very important to understand that emotional intelligence is not the opposite of intelligence, it is not the triumph of heart over head – it is the unique intersection of both."

– **David Caruso**

(Emotional What?)

Learning Objectives

After reading this chapter you will be able to:

1. Understand how do our senses perceive the external world and direct our behaviour.
2. Learn about EQ and IQ.
3. Analyse others' behaviour objectively.

Behaviour is directed by our senses. In *Kathopanishad*, senses are likened to the horses yoked to a chariot. If horses are well trained and disciplined, they will pull the chariot efficiently and reach the destination, otherwise the *sarathi* (driver) will be in trouble. When we let our senses control us, we lose the ability to judge situations correctly, we fail to manage. Acharya Shankar warns that if one wants to have lasting happiness by letting one's senses uncontrolled, he is only trying to cross an ocean on the back of a crocodile[s].

The five senses – sight, hearing, smell, taste and touch – are designed to perceive the external world on the basis of which we decide and act. Senses are faithful when we are true to ourselves, when we adhere to moral values and honest practices. The three monkeys of Gandhi – see no evil, hear no evil, do no evil – constantly remind us to use our senses rationally. Senses have a weakness of being drawn towards anything which is pleasant, which gives instant gains. While in most animals only one or two senses are strong, in human beings all senses are powerful and any one of them can influence our thoughts and deeds. One may see rightly but ignore what he hears or touches and he may fail to act rightly. Sometimes senses may fail to gather data correctly or read others correctly and this may result into uncalled for behaviour.

The strength of emotions depends upon two factors: how strongly the information is reported by our senses and how soon we give in and act. In similar situations there might be people who lose all hope and get depressed, and also those who stand firmly and win. In an experiment, which gave rise to many studies afterwards, four year old children were offered marshmallows with an option to take either one piece each immediately or wait for some time to get two or more. Some children could not resist and took a piece immediately while some waited till they were given two or more. Both the groups were kept under observation for a number of years. It was found that the children who waited life than those who could not resist and gave in easily to the temptation.

Emotional Intelligence

The word 'Emotional Intelligence' was coined by Mayer and Salovey in the early 1990s. They developed a four branch model which defines emotional intelligence as the ability to:

(a) accurately perceive emotions in oneself and others

(b) use emotions to facilitate thinking

(i) Vedant Kesari: *The Lion of Vedant*, a cultural and spiritual monthly of the Ramkrishna Order, Ramkrishna Math, Myalapore, Chennai, May 2006, pp. 16-170.

(c) understand emotional meanings, and

(d) manage emotions.

The ability to recognise one's own feelings and emotions and expressing them, perceiving others' emotions in face or voice or activity, using emotional input in thought process and creativity, analysing messages received and their possible outcome, and regulation of ones own and others' emotions are crucial in understanding human behaviour and dealing with situations.

The credit for popularising emotional intelligence as a concept in behavioural sciences goes to Daniel Goleman. His work *Emotional Intelligence: Why It Can Matter More Than IQ*, published in 1995, became one of the best-sellers of his time. Passions, according to Goleman, overwhelm reason time and again. It is the result of the basic architecture of mental life. Man has been trying to control passions since ages. The first laws and proclamation of ethics – the code of Hammurabi, the Ten Commandments of Hebrews, the Edicts of Emperor Ashoka – can be seen as attempts to harness, subdue and domesticate emotional life.

Emotions, according to Goleman, play a unique role as revealed by their distinctive biological signatures. For instance, when a man is angry, blood flows to his hands, making it easier to grasp a weapon, or when one is in the grip of fear, blood goes to the large skeletal muscles, such as in legs, making it easier to flee, or tender feelings and sexual satisfaction entail parasympathetic arousal – the psychological opposite of 'fight or flight' mobilisation shared by fear and anger. The biological propensities are shaped further by life experiences, customs, traditions and culture which guide one to act rationally. The two minds in us – emotional and rational – operate in harmony for the most part. But when the passions surge, the balance is disturbed. We are taken over by emotions. At times, this may result in losing control over oneself and doing something which one would regret for the rest of life.

The emotions which are crucial in intrapersonal and interpersonal relations include worry, anxiety, melancholy, anger, fear, hope, joy, love, etc. Sometimes one worries about something which may never happen but the person continues to live in a state of anxiety which may affect his mental as well as physical health. There is a famous saying that funeral pyre burns the dead body but worry destroys the living man. Melancholy is another such killer. It shakes the person and diverts energy to

---

(ii) Daniel Goleman, *Emotional Intelligence: Why It Can Matter More Than IQ* (Bantam Books, New York, 1993, p. 5).

the things already lost. Anger hijacks an individual's capacity to behave rationally. It gives birth to hostility which if transacted from both the sides may result into physical conflict as well. The dialogue between Lakshman and Parashuram in the *Ramayan* is an excellent example of behaviour in a state of anger. Fear makes a person avoid confrontation and run away from the situation. It may block initiative. Hope is the sunny view which brings optimism, makes the person accept challenges and provides strength to stand in situations which may otherwise make life miserable. There is a famous Greek story of the Pandora's box. A princess was given a gift, a mysterious box, by gods jealous of her beauty. She was told not to open that box but one day, out of curiosity, she lifted the lid to peep in. It resulted in letting loose diseases, malaise, madness, etc. into the world. Fortunately, she was advised by a compassionate god to close the box in time and capture an antidote which will make life's misery bearable – hope. Hope serves as a buffer against falling into helplessness and depression when the going is tough. Joy is a big motivator. It energises the body as well as the mind. Love is the source of our tender feelings and passion. It generates feelings of pleasure and sexual desire. It cements the bond between mother and child, husband and wife and, at times, may prompt the greatest sacrifice.

Emotional Competence

The ability to handle emotions and use them rationally is crucial to success in life. Emotional management is as important for managers as for the common man and professionals in other walks of life. The components of emotional management include emotional self-awareness, emotional self-management, social awareness and social skills or relations management.

Emotional Intelligence Competency Framework

Recognition	SELF AWARENESS Emotional Self Awareness, Accurate Self-Assessment, Self-Confident	SOCIAL AWARENESS Empathy, Organisational Awareness, Service Orientation
Regulation	SELF-MANAGEMENT Self-Control Transparency Achievement Drive, Initiative	RELATIONSHIP MANAGEMENT Inspirational Leadership Developing Others, Influence Change Catalyst, Conflict management, Building bonds, team work

Source: McBare Report on Emotional Intelligence (2000)

Fig: 4.1

Self-awareness means being aware of both our mood and our thoughts about that mood. It may help in recognising one's own boundaries, developing independent thinking and positive outlook.

Managing feelings requires monitoring, 'self talk' to catch negative messages, realising what is behind such feelings and finding ways to handle our anxieties, fear, anger and sadness. Talking about feelings effectively, openness in dealings and building an atmosphere of trust, recognising one's strength and weaknesses, and commitment to values may help in managing the self.

Social Intelligence

Social awareness grows with sensitivity to other's feelings, proactive behaviour and better understanding of consequences of behaviour. The failure to read another's feelings is considered to be a major deficit in emotional intelligence. People who are empathetic are more attuned to subtle social signals that indicate what others want or desire. The ability to read non-verbal channels like tone of voice, gestures, facial expressions is considered important in this regard. As against empathy, psychopathy is the incapacity to feel compassion. The serial killers, for example, are not moved by the pain of their victims.

Social skills or relations management requires ripeness of the first three components – self-awareness, self-management and social awareness (people's skills). Gardner has identified four components of such skills – organising groups, negotiating solutions, personal connection and social analysis.

Components of Interpersonal Skills

ORGANISING GROUPS	NEGOTIATING SOLUTIONS
Essential skill of leader coordinating efforts of the network	Talent of mediator, preventing conflicts
PERSONAL CONNECTION	SOCIAL ANALYSIS
Recognise and respond to people's feelings and concerns	Being able to detect and have insights about people's feelings, motives and concerns

Fig: 4.2: Gardner's Four Components of People's Skills

Gardner summarised interpersonal skills as the ability to understand other people, what motivates them, how they work, and how to work cooperatively with them. Successful people in all walks of life are likely to be individuals with a high degree of interpersonal intelligence.

IQ and EQ

IQ theorists have tried to bring emotional/social skills within the purview of a person's intelligence. E.L Thorndike considered social intelligence – the ability to understand others and act wisely in human relations – as an aspect of a person's IQ. Some thinkers in favour of IQ went to the extent of describing social intelligence as a 'useless concept'. Many psychologists and researchers in social sciences have, however, challenged IQ as the sole determinant of success in life. In practical life, men with very high scores in college are not necessarily more successful than their peers with low IQ scores. In his famous work *Frames of Mind*, Howard Gardner talked about seven frames of mind in place of the monolithic concept of one frame propagated by the IQ theorists.

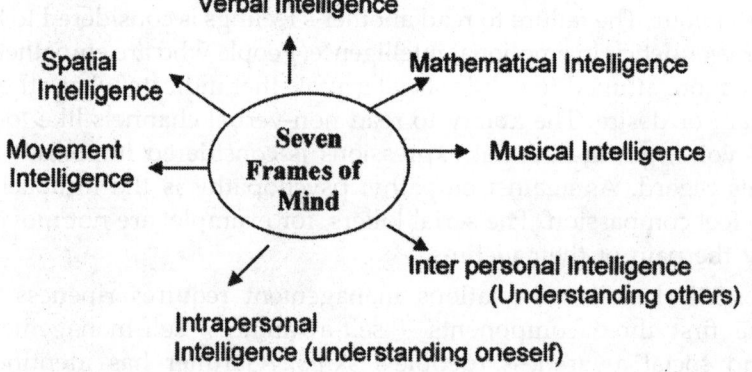

Fig: 4.3: Seven Frames of Mind

Stephen R. Covey in his book *The 8th Habit* classified skills into four types: Body or Physical Intelligence (PQ), Mental Intelligence (IQ), Emotional Intelligence (EQ) and Spiritual Intelligence (SQ). He describes these four intelligences as our third birth gift.

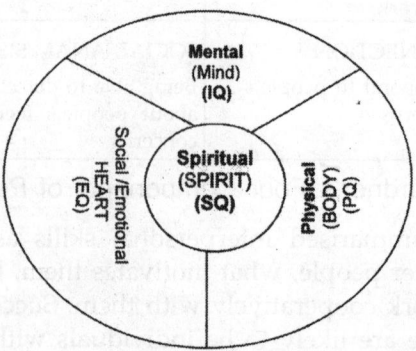

Fig: 4.4: Four Human Intelligence Capacities

(iii) Stephen R. Covey: *The 8th Habit: From Effectiveness to Greatness* (Simon & Schuster Ltd. London, 2004).

He has placed PQ and SQ over the popular two – IQ and EQ. PQ refers to the respiratory, circulatory, nervous and other systems which go on unconsciously every moment we live. Spiritual intelligence represents man's quest for eternal truth and connection with the infinite. Indian philosophy and religions have emphasised on this for ages. Ethical and moral values are the key to SQ.

Thorndike considered social intelligence to be distinct from academic abilities. At workplace, it is the sensitivity which allows effective managers to pick up tacit messages.

Studies on emotional intelligence in recent years have started a virtual revolution – the revolution of emotional awareness. Dr. Tony Alexander, an authority on marketing tactics, has formulated the platinum rule in place of the golden rule of social relationships. The golden rule is 'Do unto others as you would have them do unto you'. It assumes all human beings are alike and that others would like to be treated the way one would like to be treated by the others. The platinum rule goes a step further: 'Treat others the way they want to be treated'. This implies understanding what people want and treating them accordingly. This rule accommodates feelings of others.

EQ and Women

Women are better empowered than men when it comes to empathy. In general, they are more sensitive and prone to be swayed by emotions. It is their strength as well as weakness. In their different roles – mother, daughter, sister, wife, friend and relative – they use love and compassion more than logic and calculation. However, at times, their ability to withstand adverse events is also weakened by emotions. They may show less stress-tolerance than men.

EQ and Age

Age has its influence on IQ and EQ. Some research findings reveal EQ scores peaking in the late forties and early fifties while IQ has been found to peak in the late teens and level off by the late fifties, slowly declining afterwards in most cases.

Theorists have been emphasising one or the other – IQ or EQ – based on their researches but the fact remains that the two are complementary to each other rather than opposites. We all are a mix of IQ and EQ in varying degrees. Aristotle once said that anyone could become angry, that is easy, but to be angry with the right person, to the right degree, at the right time, for the right purpose and in the right way is not easy. Balancing wisdom and emotions is difficult at times, but it pays in life.

Emotional Intelligence and Management

Management is getting things done through and with people. Unlike resources – money, machine and materials – which can be used the way management likes, human beings are governed by emotions and feelings. There is no fixed law governing their behaviour. In a similar situation different people may react differently. Human behaviour is very complicated, discovering human mind is very difficult. What motivates one man may not motivate another in the same work environment, what may be music to one's ears may be an unpleasant noise to others, what may look reasonable to one may be unacceptable to others. Managers as leaders, motivators and communicators can be successful only when they understand people and develop a relationship which creates trust and confidence and encourages them to give their best. Anticipating people's reaction to any course of action is crucial for managers as decision-makers. Making people to accept a plan and work on it and achieve the goals needs their involvement, their participation not only technically but also emotionally. Among all the factors which motivate people, personal involvement is the most crucial. Money as a motivator does not have the same weightage for everyone.

Motivating factors like challenges at work, opportunities to rise, policies of equity and justice, physical environment, etc. are all linked with feelings and emotions and their weightage is not the same for everyone. Some people are more calculative while others are more emotional. In many cases, managers have to deal people as individuals rather than as a hoard of workers.

Communication in different forms and through different means influences people at work. Gestures and other non-verbal communications may be as important, at times, as verbal or written communication. Leadership style of the boss is reflected in communication. An autocratic leader's way of communicating with employees is different than that of a participative one. The former relies on authority while the latter on personal relationships. EQ plays an important role in managing change. People feel emotionally disturbed when they are asked to do something other than what they are accustomed to do and which they find easy to perform. The desired new practice may appear unpleasant for reasons which may be based on problems, real or imaginary, anticipated by the employees. The change agents are successful when they are able to convince people not only about the desirability of change, but also removing fear from the minds of those who have to carry the change, and arousing enthusiasm and optimism.

The play of emotions may be at peak when people work in a group. For instance, emotions of employees on strike are easily swayed by the trade union leaders. Workers resort to *gherao* of officers, violence, slogan-shouting, damaging factory premises and equipment when passions are running high. Managing people during such times requires more EQ than IQ.

Situation Analysis

Virendra Singh, a young, energetic and highly qualified executive, joined the branch office of a big company as GM a few months back. He was seen as a 'terror' by the staff who were mostly in the age group of 40 to 50, qualified and highly paid. His entry in the office was greeted with pin drop silence with everyone on seats doing their job. Even a whisper, at times, could be intolerable.

Within a few days of joining, he had terminated the services of a senior officer who was a popular figure in the office addressed as 'hero' by his colleagues, a jolly fellow with a pleasant personality, mixing freely with all and helping others with their problems. Virendra didn't like him from day one and decided to show him the door.

One day on a minor issue, which Virendra considered as insubordination, Millind was issued an office memo to explain. Virendra informed the head office that the environment of the branch office was being polluted by Millind and it would not be in the best interest of the organisation to let him continue at his job. Head office agreed, Virendra had his way, and Millind had to go.

Comment on Virendra's leadership style.

Review Questions

1. 'We lose ability to judge people and situations correctly when we let our senses control us.' Comment.
2. Discuss Goleman's theory of emotional intelligence.
3. 'Fear makes a person avoid the situation and run away while hope is the sunny view which brings optimism.' Comment with illustrations.
4. Explain Emotional Intelligence Competency framework.
5. 'Social awareness grows with sensitivity to others' feelings.' Comment.
6. What are the seven frames of mind according to Gardner.
7. How would you behave with others?
    (i) 'Behave with others as you would like others to behave with you.'
    (ii) 'Behave with others as they want you to behave.'

Further Readings

1. J.R. Averill and E.P. Nunley: *Voyages of the Heart: Living an Emotionally Creative Life* (Free Press, New York, 1992).
2. Reuven Bar-On and James D.A. Parker *The Handbook of Emotional Intelligence: Theory, Development, Assessment, and Application at Home, School, and in the Workplace* (Jossey-Bass, San Fransisco, 2000).
3. T. Butler and J. Waldroop: *Understanding 'People' People* (Harvard Business Review, pp. 78-84, June 2004).
4. R.K. Cooper and A. Sawaf: *Executive EQ: Emotional Intelligence in Leadership and Organizations* (Grosset/Putnam, New York, 1997).
5. Frank Shipper, Joel Kincaid, Denise M. Rotondo, and Richard C. Hoffman: *A Cross-cultural Study of Linkages Between Emotional Intelligence and Managerial Effectiveness* (Salisbury University, 2003).
6. S.J. Stain and H.E. Book: *The EQ Edge: Emotional Intelligence and Your Success* (MacMillan, New Delhi, 2000).
7. Frances Wilks: *Intelligent Emotion: How to Succeed Through Transforming your Feelings* (Arrow Books, London, 1998).

Chapter 5

Personality Traits and The Job

A famous cinestar was asked in a television interview: Who are you? A proud father, a good husband or a renowned actor? The reply was: I am all the three in one.

Learning Objectives

After reading this chapter you will be able to:
1. Define personality and the role of heredity and environment in shaping human personality.
2. Analyse factors influencing personality including learning.
3. Discuss personality traits and match them with the job.

Personality is the sum total of an individual's qualities reflected in his or her behaviour. The early definitions of personality emphasised manifest aspects of it as observed by others. The word personality is derived from the Latin term 'persona' which means 'mask'. The viewers could see the mask, not the real person behind it. The modern concept of personality, therefore, includes individual's own evaluation of himself along with others' perceptions.

Gordon Allport defines personality as the 'dynamic organisation within the individual of those psychological systems that determine his characteristic behaviour and thought'. The word 'organisation' in this definition points out that personality is not just a sum of traits, but rather that the different traits or manifest aspects of personality pattern are held together and influenced by a central core, called the concept of life (person's inner world – his thoughts and feelings, fears and fantasies, etc.) and an integrated system of learned responses. A normal healthy personality is a highly correlative structured person. The abnormal personality, in contrast, shows disorganisation. The constantly evolving or changing nature of personality makes it 'dynamic'. The 'psychological systems' are composed of habits, attitudes, emotional states, sentiments, motives and beliefs, all of which are psychological but have a physical basis in the individuals' neural, glandular or general bodily states – making personality a function of both mind and body. Psychological systems are not a product of heredity although they do have hereditary foundations. They are the products of learning derived from the life experiences of the individual. The 'characteristic behaviour' refers to the uniqueness of a person's behaviour which distinguishes him from others.

Heredity vs. Environment

Personality is formed as a result of interaction between significant figures (first the mother, later the father and siblings, then the extra-familial figures) and the child. The child brings to this action certain needs, drives and intellectual capacities which determine his response to the way in which he is acted upon by these significant figures. In the interaction between heredity and environment the individual selects from his environment what fits his needs and wants and rejects what does not.

There has been a dispute over the relative importance of heredity and environment. Some claim heredity to be a more weighty determinant of an individual's behaviour while others belittle it in the favour of environment. Francis Galton in his pioneering work, *Heredity Genius* (published in 1889), showed that while there is a seeming chance of the appearance of genius, the probability of the occurrence of greatly gifted children is vastly higher when the fathers are of a superior intelligence. Karl Pearson, who carried out Galton's work further, applied his method of correlation to the problem and concluded that the influence of environment was far less than that of heredity in the determination of human differences. He produced evidence to prove that for people of the same race within a given community, heredity is seven times more important than environment. On the basis of an empirical study conducted in early twentieth century, F.A. Woods concluded that the American men of science emanated in the largest numbers from the professional classes and in the smallest numbers from the agricultural class.

The advocates of the supremacy of environment over heredity claim that the specific groups that were studied had specific environments. The members of royal families were brought up in a different environment than that of the ordinary families. Similarly, the children born in professional class families have a far superior environment than those in simple agricultural families. Races are discriminated on the basis of colour, religion, faith, etc. on the basis of which equality of opportunity has been denied to some for centuries. Children belonging to deprived classes suffer, even their stature as well as weight is affected. When a botanist takes the seeds of a plant and grows them in varying soils and climatic conditions, the differences in plant size, colour and strength are attributed to the environment. Similarly, children brought up in different environments show attributes greatly influenced by their respective environment. Even twins brought up in different environmental conditions develop different attributes – physical as well as mental.

Most researches in recent times have confirmed Professor H.S. Jenning's view that what heredity can do, environment can also do. Every phenomena of life is a product of both. Each is as necessary to the result as the other. Both have been operative to produce every particular situation through unimaginable time. Heredity – the germ cells – contains all the potentialities of life, but all its actualities are evoked within and under the conditions of environment. MacIver and Page have rightly concluded that the potential of heredity is made actual within an environment. All qualities of life are in heredity, all the evocations of quality depend upon environment. The higher the potentiality of an individual, the greater will be the demand on environment.

The evolving or changing nature of personality offers opportunities for the development of each individual. For instance, better care of one's body, better use of one's intellect, improved conditions at home and improved relations at workplace may increase one's potentialities and personality.

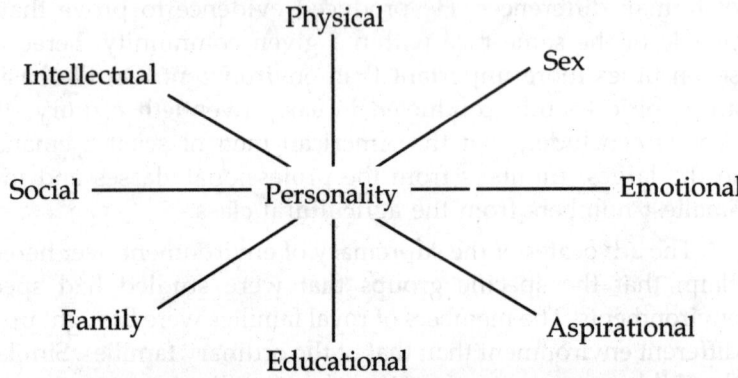

Fig. 5.1: Factors Influencing Personality

Physical: An object which is ever present in one's personal world is his body. It determines personality directly by deciding what a person can and cannot do. Indirectly, it influences his physical abilities and disabilities. A favourable attitude of others also indirectly influences one's perception of his own physical attractiveness. Physical defects and poor health affect personality directly by placing limitation on what one can do.

Intellectual: Intelligence provides a person with the capacity to meet and solve the problems one faces while making adjustments to life. How he uses his intellectual capacities determine how successful his adjustments will be.

Intellectual capacities directly influence the kind of adjustments a person makes to his environment, to people and to himself. Indirectly, it also influences the judgements other people make of him which further determine his self-judgement. One who is considered bright by the society is more influential than the one regarded as dull.

Emotional:	Emotions, whether fleeing or persisting, colour an individual's perception of himself and his environment. A person who feels habitually frustrated will be hostile and impulsive. One who is habitually jealous will be suspicious of whatever others say or do. Company of a cheerful person is liked more than that of a sad and depressed one. Emotions directly affect an individual's physical and mental functioning and his attitude. They are indirectly affected by the judgements others make. The predominance of a particular kind of emotional reaction is called temperament. Mood is a temporary emotional reaction.
Social:	Every social group expects its members to do two things: to be sociable and to play an approved social role. Living up to group expectations increases self-esteem of the individual. Being deprived of opportunities for social contacts can play havoc with the personality pattern of the individual. Social isolation, whether from neglect or rejection, is very likely to deflate his ego.
Aspirations and Achievements:	A person is judged by his goals, achievements and how early in life he is able to make these accomplishments. Aspiration means a longing for and striving after something higher. Behind all aspirations is the fundamental need for achievement. Factors that influence aspirations include intelligence, sex, interests, family pressures, group expectations, competition with others, past experiences, mass media and personal characteristics. Feelings of achievement make a person happy and satisfied.
Sex:	Sex hormones influence the growth of the individual, body formation and functioning and the quality of behaviour. Sex organs function most actively between the ages of 13 to 45 in females and 14 to 55 in males. The attitude towards sexuality, sexual behaviour, sexual differences is a product of the culture which also prescribes sexual roles for men and women.

Educational: Next to family, schools and colleges are the chief determinants of what a person thinks of himself and what his habitual patterns of behaviour will be. Children attend school during the early years of their life when the personality pattern is being framed.

Family: The home is person's primary environment from the time he is born until the day he dies. Glasher says that personality is formed in the first instance within the womb of family relationships. Home climate, family size, composition of family, its roles – all affect personality.

Role of Learning

Learning in its various forms plays a pivotal role in the development of personality pattern. It is defined as the relatively permanent changes in response tendencies due to the effects of experience.

Learning may be divided into two types: classical and operant. Classical conditioning creates association between unconditioned and conditioned stimulus. It refers to a strong stimulus-response (S-R) relationship. Operant conditioning, also called instrumental learning or respondent reinforcement (R-R), refers to increasing the frequency or probability of a response by following the occurrence of a response with reinforcement. People will most likely engage in desired behaviour if they are positively reinforced for doing it.

Classical conditioning is associated with Russian psychologist Ivan Pavlov's experiment in which in the first state a hungry dog is shown some food. Its mouth waters. It is allowed to eat the food. In the second stage, a bell is also rung when the food is shown. But in the third stage, food is not shown, only the bell is rung. The dog's mouth waters at the sound of the bell. In this experiment hunger is the drive, showing food is the stimulus, watering of the mouth is the response and allowing to eat is the reinforcement. Ringing of the bell is the new stimulus to which the dog becomes accustomed when its repeated over times. Since response is a reflex action, i.e., not consciously controlled, it is called conditioned reflex.

Operant conditioning is associated with American psychologist B.F. Skinner's experiment in which a rat is kept in a box with a bar that can be pressed to receive a reward (corn) and avoid punishment (electric shock). By manipulating the reward, the experimenter can change the rate of pressing the bar. The animal is active and its behaviour is consciously controlled. Here, behaviour

is shaped by operant conditioning which is different from classical conditioning in the following respects:
 (i) The animal is not passive but active (hence, operant).
 (ii) Its behaviour is instrumental in obtaining a reward or reinforcement, whereas in classical conditioning the reward is not operant.
 (iii) It learns new behaviour instead of providing an existing response to a new stimulus.
 (iv) Its behaviour is consciously controlled, not a reflex action.

Operant conditioning is considered more relevant to human learning than classical conditioning which does not deal with consciously determined responses. Certain fears and superstitions in human beings may be ascribed to classical conditioning, but its application in personality development is limited. On the other hand, operant conditioning has very specific human applications. For example, when training people for skilled jobs, trainers have to motivate them to complete the programme successfully. This may be done through various methods such as dividing the tasks into small units with a given standard of performance, promoting competition among trainees, giving tangible rewards for good performance in the course of training, etc. A pat on the back by the trainer is a good reinforcement in most cases, but too much of criticism may be a deterrent in the learning process.

Operant conditioning is criticised by the Action Learning School which considers learning to be essentially a participative process. In operant conditioning the learner has little or no say regarding what should be learned or which method should be adopted. The action learning advocates do not depend upon stimulus-response factors. People, according to them, learn about time, space and logic not through the means connected with operant conditioning, but through adjustment of their attitudes and perceptions in consequence of their attempts to relate to the outside world.

The Social Learning Model is another approach to learning which is based on the assumption that the individual possesses intellect which he starts using from the first day of his life to understand events and surroundings, and react. When placed in a similar environment, the feelings and perceptions of two individuals may be similar. Individuals learn in life by interacting.

The Cognitive Model is yet another alternative to operant conditioning. Cognition governs the acquisition of knowledge and it involves institution, perception, imagination and reasoning. The advocates of this model believe that the learning process cannot be dismembered into simple stimulus-response components because cognition is derived from the complex interactions between thoughts, emotions, observations and experiences.

Learning is important to personality development for obvious reasons. Attitude towards self, characteristic modes of responding to people and situations, assumptions of socially approved roles and methods of personal and social adjustments are all learned through repetition and reinforcement by the satisfaction they bring. It is through learning that the concept of self is built up in each individual and his learned responses become habitual, constituting the traits of his or her personality.

Personality Traits

Psychologists have identified a number of traits which are steady and constant sources of behaviour. More specifically, a trait is defined as any distinguishable, relatively enduring way in which one individual differs from another. The basic assumptions of trait approach are:

(a) Traits are common to many individuals and vary in absolute amounts between individuals,

(b) Traits are relatively stable and exert fairly universal effects on behaviour regardless of environmental situations, and

(c) Traits can be inferred from the measurement of behavioural indicators.

Some major traits identified by psychologists are as under:

Reserved	—	Outgoing
Less intelligent	—	More intelligent
Affected by feelings	—	Emotionally stable
Submissive	—	Dominant
Serious	—	Happy go lucky
Expedient	—	Conscientious
Timid	—	Venturesome
Tough-minded	—	Sensitive
Trusting	—	Suspicious
Practical	—	Imaginative
Forthright	—	Shrewd
Self-assured	—	Apprehensive

Conservative	— Experimentative
Group-dependent	— Self-sufficient
Uncontrolled	— Controlled
Tense	— Relaxed

The criticism of trait approach is that the terms are not easy to define, there are contradictions and the inferences about personality based on these may be questionable in many cases. An extension of this approach is the Swiss psychologist Carl Jung's work on introversion and extroversion. Most people, according to him, are either predominantly introverted or extroverted. Introverts look inwards at themselves while extroverts are oriented towards the outside world. Introverts avoid social contacts and tend to be withdrawn and quiet. Extroverts are friendly, they enjoy company, dislike solitude, are aggressive and express their feelings openly.

	High Anxiety	Low Anxiety
Extrovert	Tense, Excitable, Unstable, Warm, Sociable and Dependent	Composed, Confident, Truthful, Adaptable, Warm, Sociable and Dependent
Introvert	Tense, Excitable, Unstable, Cold and Shy	Composed, Confident, Truthful, Adaptable, Calm, Cold and Shy

Fig. 5.2: Personality Types

The four-type thesis is criticised on the ground that in practice most people tend to be ambiverts, i.e. they alternate between introversion and extroversion.

Mavis Klein has given a classification of personality as discussed below:

Personality Type	Characteristics
Be Perfect	Too great or too rigid structuring of life
Be Strong	Conditioned, emotional withdrawal, manifestly cold, aloof, self-contained, unemotional
Please	Over adaptation par excellence, cutting both ways: 'I will please you and when it is my turn, you will please me.'
Try Hard	Believes in luck, puts all eggs in one basket, expects big time, starts a dozen projects, completes none.

Hurry Up   On the run all through the life, frowning upon others, deeply anti-life.

The five elements – Be Perfect, Be Strong, Please, Try Hard and Hurry Up – together make up the substance of human nature. In practice, these elements are mixed and matched in a large variety of ways such as Be Perfect/Be Strong, Be Strong/Please, Please/Hurry Up, etc. in individual human beings. Some people have one element dominantly and overwhelmingly present in most of their everyday transactions, while others seem to make use of the all five elements in quick succession. But generally, most people seem to concentrate on two mini scripts to confirm the core existential position whose continual reaffirmation is the chief motivator throughout their life.

Healthy Personality

Individuals pass through different stages in life while trying to adjust with the environment. Chris Argyris has postulated a 'Maturation Theory', according to which healthy individuals move from immaturity to maturity:

Passive	— Increasing Activity
Dependence	— Independence
Few ways to behave	— Many alternatives
Shallow interests	— Deeper interests
Short-term perspective	— Long-term perspective
Subordinate	— Superior position
Lack of awareness of oneself	— Awareness of oneself

Healthy individuals tend to show maturity while unhealthy ones demonstrate childishness.

Gail Sheehy has proposed another theory in this regard. She says that all adults progress through five crises:

Pulling Up Roots : Occurs between 18-22 years of age when individuals exit from home and incur physical, financial and emotional separation. They cover fears and uncertainties with acts of defiance.

The Trying Twenties : Period to grab hold of who we are and where do we want to go. All things seem possible, period of opportunity and also fear, period to build and explore.

The Catch Thirties : Life commitments are made, broken or renewed in the thirties. This is a period of change, turmoil and an urge to burst out.

The Deadline Decade : The age of thirty-five to forty-five years is the period of being at the crossroads, youth becomes history, time is running out, reexamination of purpose and method of spending is needed.

Renewal or Resignation : The mid-forties bring a period of stability. It may bring staleness or resignation. But for individuals working with determination for a goal, it may be the best period.

Individuals face crisis during different periods of life. During teenage, the nature of crisis may be different from what one may experience in the mid-thirties. The behaviour pattern changes through different phases of crisis.

One feels motivated and satisfied when he gets the job of his choice – the job which matches his personality. John L. Holland has developed six personality types to fit with different types of occupations:

Personality and the Job

Personality Type	Characteristics	Suitable Occupations
Realistic	Aggressive behaviour, physical activities requiring skill, strength and coordination	Forestry, Farming, Architecture
Investigative	Activities requiring thinking, organisation and understanding rather than feeling or emotion	Biology, Mathematics, News Reporting
Social	Interpersonal rather than intellectual or physical activities	Foreign Service, Social Work, Clinical Psychology
Conventional	Rule-regulated activities and sublimation of personal needs to the organisation or person in power	Accounting, Finance, Corporate Management

Enterprising	Verbal activities to influence others, to attain power and status	Law, Public Relations, Management of Small Business
Artistic	Self-expression, artistic creation or emotional activities	Art, Music, Writing

The empirical findings of Holland support a hexagonal diagram which shows that the closer two fields or orientations are in the hexagon, the more compatible they are. Adjacent categories are quite similar while those diagonally opposite are highly dissimilar. This would mean that satisfaction is the highest and turnover the lowest when personality and occupation are in agreement. Thus, the best occupation for social individuals will be social jobs, conventional individuals, conventional jobs and so on. Similarly, a social person may be a misfit in a realistic job or a conventional personal may be misfit in an enterprising job.

The jobs fit theory of John L. Holland recognises the intrinsic differences in personality among individuals, differences in requirement of jobs and the need to match personality with the job. What is debatable in the categorisation of personality and jobs is the issue of specific types. For instance, an investigative person may also be enterprising. Similarly, the jobs in corporate sector may need personality types like enterprising, social, etc. at management levels. It is difficult to place either personality or job in well-defined compartments. Nonetheless, the model is practical and highly useful in identifying and matching people with jobs.

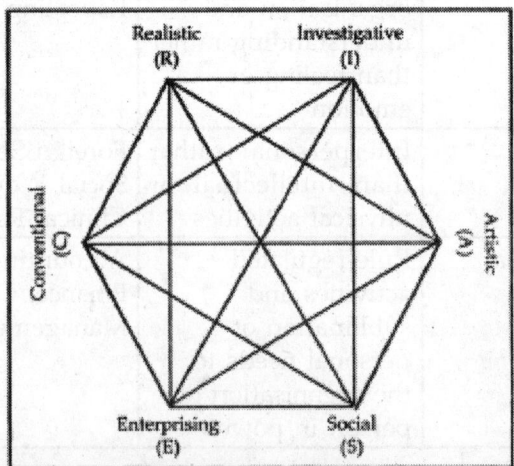

Fig. 5.3: Hexagonal representation of the relationships among occupational personality types.

Situation Analysis

Brin and Page, the founders of Google, first met during a student orientation at Stanford. They had common ambitions though their personality traits were different.

Brin was a brash young man, very ambitious and a problem-solver engineer while Page was basically a thinker, working hard to apply his knowledge for results. Professor Rajeev Motwani was the mentor of Brin. He worked with him to extract information from large chunks of data. Page was engaged in search engines and how they analysed data. The two teamed together and brought out the first version of their search engine – BackRub. They continued refining it and thus was born Google. They had limited financial resources but succeeded and never looked back. They strongly believed that search would be the key to navigate the ever-expanding world wide web.

The first CEO who was appointed by Brin and Page for Google was a man with a cool temper and good credentials. He was made responsible for running the business, and the duo continued focusing on the search engine and formulating strategies to compete successfully with other players in the field and take Google to the heights where it is now.

Comment on the personality traits leading to success as you have seen in this case.

Review Questions

1. 'Personality is the sum total of an individual's qualities reflected in his or her behaviour'. Comment.
2. How do you look upon the dispute regarding the relative importance of heredity and environment in shaping personality?
3. Discuss the factors which influence personality.
4. Distinguish between classical and operant conditioning.
5. Give a classification of personality traits and types.
6. 'Healthy individuals move from immaturity to maturity'. Comment.
7. Relate personality types with occupational suitability.
8. 'Best occupation for social individuals will be social jobs'. Discuss.
9. Comment on the following:

   Boss wants everything to be perfect, even a simple mistake by an employee, for instance, in putting comma or full stop in the report, irritates him. He talks nicely when the employee comes to him with the report, but begins to look for inadequacies and mistakes, and starts lecturing. Old employees are habituated to listen, but young and new employees are disheartened every time they meet him.

Further Readings

1. G.W. Allport: *Pattern and Growth in Personality* (Holt, Rinehart & Winston, New York, 1961).
2. J.M. Digman: *Personality Structure: Emergence of a Five Factor Model* (Annual Review of Psychology, Vol. 41, pp. 417-440, 1990).
3. Sigmund Freud: *An Outline of Psychoanalysis* (Norton, New York, 1949).
4. T.A. Judge, J.J. Martocchio and C.J. Thoresen: *Five Factor Model of Personality and Employee Absence* (Journal of Applied Psychology, Vol. 82, pp. 745-755, 1997).
5. Carl Jung: *Psychological Types* (Harcourt Brace, New York, 1923).
6. V. Locke and L. Johnson: *Stereotyping and Prejudices: A Social Cognitive Approach* (M. Augoustinos and K.J. Reynolds (Ed.) Understanding Prejudice, Racism and Social Conflict, London, 2001).
7. C.K. Stevens and A.L. Kristof: *Making the Right Impression: A Field Study of Applicant Impressions Management During Job Interviews* (Journal of Applied Psychology, Vol. 80, pp. 587-606, 1995).
8. H.C. Triandis: *Cultural Influences on Personality* (Annual Review of Psychology, Vol. 53, pp. 133-160, 2002).
9. C.L. Walck: *Training for Participative Management: Implications for Psychological Type* (Journal of Psychological Type, Vol. 21, pp. 3-12, 1991).

Chapter 6

Motivation, Communication and Leadership

Every manager makes assumptions about people. Whether he is aware of these assumptions or not, they operate as a theory in terms of which he decides how to deal with his superiors, peers and subordinates. His effectiveness as a manager will depend on the degree to which his assumptions fit empirical reality.

– **Edgar H. Schein**
(Organisational Psychology)

Learning Objectives

After reading this chapter you will be able to:

1. Understand basic theories of motivation, communication and leadership.
2. Explain the significance of motivating people at work through financial and non-financial incentives.
3. Analyse situations arising due to lack of motivation and communication.
4. Discuss the role of leaders in organisation, qualities required of them and situational factors creating challenges for them.

In practice, managers perform mostly the same functions as they are all concerned with getting the work done through people irrespective of the type of organisation in which they are working.

A manager need not be an expert in all the skills which he is directing. However, he should have an idea about the work, acquired either by reading or through experience. A manager can successfully use the technical skills of others but he need not possess all the skills himself. Managers should know what type of skill is necessary for a particular job so that they can enlist the help of that skill or the department engaged in that skill. Also, a manager should know the interrelationship between skills. This is particularly important when a number of departments are involved in a project.

The task of management becomes easier if people at different levels of hierarchy understand in general terms how others are engaged. This is because at times people at operative levels feel that it is they who do all the work and the executives/managers do nothing. Such misconceptions are not conducive to the proper understanding of working relationships. An understanding of men and human relations is an important aspect of managing them and, therefore, proper attention should be paid to it.

Various techniques and practices by which human resources can be *organised, disciplined, motivated* and *gainfully channelised* in a *collective* manner for *constructive* work are discussed hereafter.

Sources of Authority

Authority to managers means the right to command others. Since managers are primarily engaged in getting work done through people, a superior-subordinate relationship develops. It cannot be avoided. It is this authority which becomes the force behind compliance of many vital instructions even though they may not be to the liking of others. Authority becomes the basis for responsibility, and the binding force in an organisation.

There are a few schools of thought in matters relating to the source of authority. These are:

The Formal Authority Theory

According to this, managers inherit or have authority of command delegated to them from the top management so as to achieve compliance of duties assigned to them. This is apart from the authority they possess as a consequence of statutory laws, government controls, etc.

The Acceptance Theory

It stresses that the real authority of a superior comes through the acceptance by subordinates of the powers that the manager holds. It leans towards democratic ways of acceptance but at times has more disadvantages than advantages. In actual practice it has been seen that subordinates are guided, on many occasions, by the threat of 'hire and fire' powers of the executives. A soldier's action to attack the enemy, in many cases, stems not out of genuine self-acceptance but out of the fear of the firing squad and court-martial. It is the fear of law and the damage one can do that brings about acceptance in many situations.

The Competence Theory

This emphasises that authority should be commanded by the manager. It should come to him as a result of his competence, acceptability as a leader, sound performance and winning the hearts of the subordinates with his competence and personality. According to Urwick, authority is generated by personal qualities of technical competence. However, he does not undermine the importance of formal authority with its institutional foundations.

Persuasion

It has been observed on many occasions that persuasion has succeeded where authority failed. Experienced managers, while aware of the importance of authority or order, often avoid using it openly and keep it as a last resort. While commanding or giving verbal orders one may mention it as responsibility being delegated to the subordinate to ensure that the work is done. A manager should have faith in his people because then his subordinates would not let him down.

There are social, biological, technological and many other complex limitations to executive authority which should be borne in mind before issuing any orders. A shift supervisor should never be asked to produce more than the rated capacity without examining the inherent process limitations or other operating problems. One should not be asked to walk barefoot on fire.

Discussions with subordinates enable the manager to know the limitations of an order. If the limitations are known or explained and a persuasive encouragement is given to a capable subordinate, he may surpass the limits of the order in achieving results.

Supervision

Efficient supervision is an important task and immediate supervisors of the working force are the key men of any industry. Whether aims and objectives can be achieved or not depends upon the calibre of the supervisor or the foreman supervising the job.

Experience shows that a mature supervisor should have the following characteristics:

(i) delegate authority as and when needed.

(ii) rise to the occasion when the situation demands and make decisions whenever needed.

(iii) concern himself with what is right and good for his men.

(iv) give specific tasks and attainable challenges to workers.

(v) check performance daily or at the end of the work programme.

(vi) show how to handle difficult situations (knowledge of work is extremely important to the immediate supervisor of a group of workers).

(vii) pull up his men when they are in the wrong and also admit his own errors when he has faltered (reprimanding, when properly done, is a fine art which every supervisor should know how to use).

In short, a good supervisor should be more of a leader than a driver of his men. He should always be near his workmen and thereby get to know and learn the methods of solving human factor problems.

Motivation

To understand the need of motivation, one has to know human behaviour with respect to one's needs. Motivation outside the realm of the needs of employees has little meaning. Blindly making efforts not related to the needs of the employees may not bring about any results. An experienced manager, therefore, has to understand the needs of his subordinates. Thereafter, he can create a need for motivation by either providing or withholding fulfilment of that need in his own subtle way.

A man always desires something and his needs increase progressively. First the basic need may be only food, then clothing, then shelter, good company and so on. Once these are satisfied, he looks for recognition and respect from his fellow men. When this is fulfilled he seeks higher and higher modes of adjustment and adaptation.

A classic analysis of needs was done by A. H. Maslow who developed the need hierarchy theory of motivation. He classified needs as under:

Maslow Model

Physical needs : These relate to the survival and physiological maintenance of the body. Man's requirement for food, shelter, rest, etc. are included in this category. Until reasonably satisfied, these needs are a strong driving force.

Security needs : Next to physiological needs are security needs. These include both economic (steady employment, provision for old age, etc.) as well as psychological security (e.g. person's confidence in dealing with the problems that confront him, his ability to meet future requirements of the job, etc.).

Social needs : These relate to the desire for sociability (e.g. informal contacts, friendly greetings, conversations, etc.), a sense of belonging to a group, and a position (status) in the organisational hierarchy.

Self-expression needs : The personal aspirations of a man such as opportunity of self-assertion, exercise of power, personal achievement and growth are included in this category. As an individual grows from childhood to adulthood, he works towards achieving independence, self-reliance, development of his physical and mental faculties and achieving as much as possible in his chosen field.

As one set of needs is satisfied, man moves to the next most important one. When an individual's physical needs are reasonably met, he looks for job security. When he is reasonably assured of a future, he works for social acceptability and status. Self-expression needs increase when other needs are reasonably satisfied.

> **PERSPECTIVE**
>
> **Motivational Incentives: PNB**
>
> Punjab National Bank offers the following motivational incentives to its employees:
> * The Bank has put in place a performance-linked cash incentive scheme to offer cash awards to employees based upon key performance indicators. Under the scheme, the bank has earmarked payment of a percentage of PAT as incentive amount to cover 20 to 25 percent of the staff strength of the bank.
> * The Bank offers incentives to its employees for acquiring higher/professional qualification in banking, finance and related fields.
> * The Bank offers cash incentives to the top 3 (in merit list) promoted officers in JMG scale I.
> * The Bank has in place an Employee Suggestion Scheme wherein cash rewards are considered for employees offering suggestions for improving/simplifying systems/procedures of products.
> * The Bank has a well-established grievance redressal system in the form of PNB Samadhan wherein the CMD is accessible to the staff members.

ERG Theory

Alderfer, who disagreed with Maslow on the question of lower needs being satisfied before the next higher need can become dominant, divides needs into three categories:

(1) *Existence needs*: They include various forms of material and physical desires, e.g. food, water, good working conditions, salary, etc.

(2) *Relatedness needs*: They include need for relationships with other significant people – superiors, colleagues, subordinates, etc.

(3) *Growth needs*: They include all needs which involve a person making creative or productive efforts on himself and the environment.

Alderfer and Maslow agree that the need categories tend to form a hierarchy. But Alderfer does not agree that lower needs must be satisfied before the next higher category can become dominant. Any category of needs may become dominant if it lacks satisfaction itself or because the next higher category is dissatisfied. For example, relatedness needs may become dominant if the individual is starved of affection or because he cannot find a way to satisfy his growth needs. Further, a person can never get "too much" satisfaction of growth needs. In fact, Alderfer argues that satisfaction of growth needs simply leads to a higher level of aspiration requiring more satisfaction.

The dominance of need is not a static phenomenon. A person's relatedness need may tend to be dominant but at any given moment that person might experience a dominant need for food. Thus, we can speak of tendency of a particular category of needs to be dominant over a period of time.

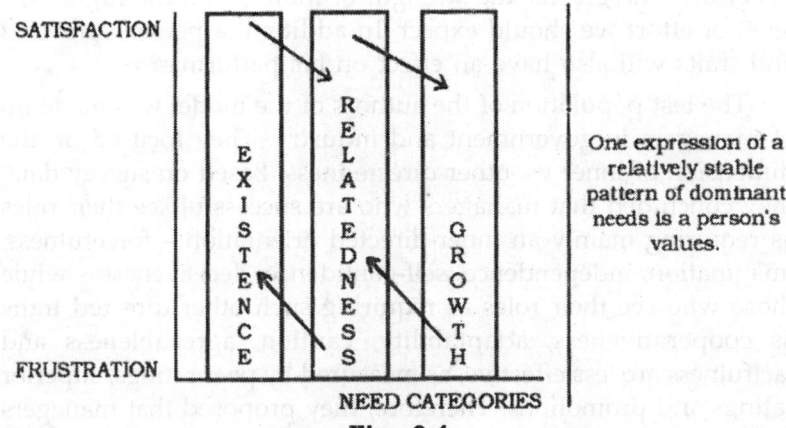

One expression of a relatively stable pattern of dominant needs is a person's values.

Fig. 6.1

The strength of motivation to behave in a certain way depends on one's perceived probability that it will lead to the outcomes that one desires. Porter and Lawler trace out the logical implications of this relationship, combined with other factors that affect performance, in a model as given below:

Porter and Lawler Model

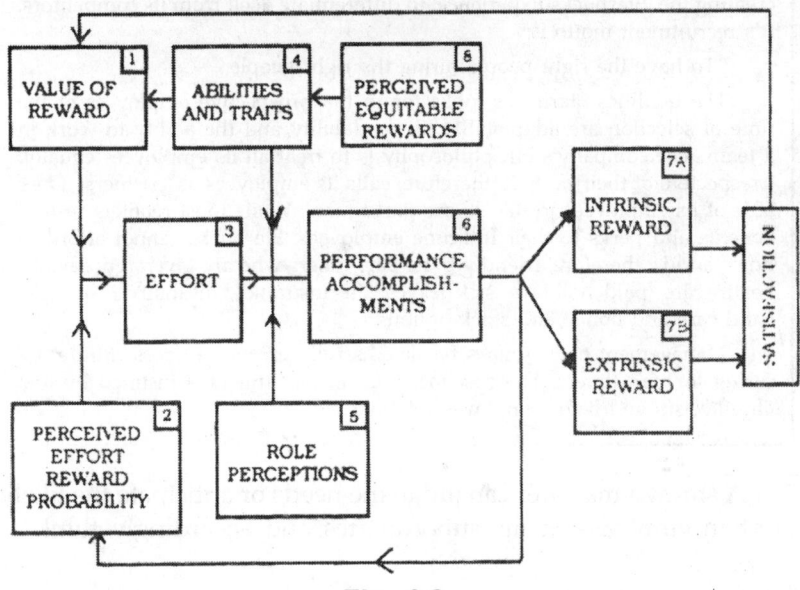

Fig. 6.2

The model works as follows: Two factors are assumed to affect the amount of effort a worker will put into his work. The first is the value a person places on the reward that he hopes to receive as a result of first putting effort in his work; the second is the probability that he will, in fact, receive the reward, given his effort. The greater the strength of motivation, the higher the level of effort we should expect. In addition, a person's abilities and traits will also have an effect on his performance.

The test population of the authors of the model was made up of managers in government and industry. They focused on the dimension of inner vs. other directedness. Based on survey data, they concluded that managers who are successful see their roles as requiring mainly an inner-directed orientation – forcefulness, imagination, independence, self-confidence, decisiveness – while those who see their roles as requiring such other directed traits as cooperativeness, adaptability, caution, agreeableness and tactfulness are less effective, as measured by peer ratings, superior ratings and promotions. Therefore, they proposed that managers who see their roles as requiring an inner-directed orientation would, other things being equal, perform better.

PERSPECTIVE

Caring For Part-Time Employees: Starbucks

Starbucks relies on its baristas and other frontline staff to a great extent in creating the 'Starbucks Experience' to differentiate itself from its competitors. It's recruitment motto is:

"To have the right people hiring the right people."

The qualities Starbucks looks for in the prospective employees at the time of selection are adaptability, dependability and the ability to work in a team. The company's HR philosophy is to treat all its employees equally, irrespective of their rank. It, therefore, calls its employees as 'partners'. Over 60% of its employees in the US are part-timers. While most retailers restrict benefits and perks to their full-time employees, Starbucks cannot afford to do so and is, therefore, friendly to its part-timers who are given retirements, health care, paid holidays, sick leaves, life insurance, disability insurance, child care and bonus and stock options.

Management of Starbucks has successfully created a 'cross-culture' by caring for part-timers. The cost incurred on part-timers is justified by low absenteeism and better employee relations.

A shrewd manager can judge the needs or anticipate the likely shift in emphasis of his subordinates and accordingly think of the motivating factor which would satisfy them. Managers must attempt to understand the needs of subordinates in order to select effective motivational factors to be tried on individuals.

Motivation - Maintenance Model

Herzberg developed a motivation-maintenance model on the basis of interviews with engineers and accountants. He found that there is a set of factors which when present tend to result in higher levels of motivation. These maybe called 'motivational factors'. If these factors are present in a job, they operate to build high levels of motivation. However, if they are not present, they do not necessarily cause dissatisfaction. These factors are:

(i) Achievement – successful accomplishment of task
(ii) Recognition for achievement
(iii) The work itself – interesting, challenging work
(iv) Advancement or growth, and
(v) Responsibility

Dissatisfaction is caused by the absence of a set of factors which are called 'hygiene' or maintenance factors. They are not the factors which motivate when present. But when absent, make the employee unhappy and dissatisfied. These factors are:

(a) Supervision
(b) Interpersonal relations with peers, superiors and subordinates
(c) Working conditions
(d) Salary
(e) Status, and
(f) Job security

Managers have been giving more attention to the hygiene or maintenance factors considering them to be the source of motivation. Herzberg emphasised that the existence of the duality of needs should be recognised and the job should be designed in such a way as to meet both hygiene and motivational needs. Minute division of work takes the challenge out of work. A solution to design challenge back into work is the job of enrichment.

The jobs are enriched by removing unnecessary controls, increasing accountability for individual's own work, granting more freedom, giving new and difficult tasks, and enabling the employee to achieve excellence in his work.

Delegation of Authority

Delegation of authority is the key to effective functioning of an organisation. As one person cannot do all the tasks necessary for the accomplishment of group purpose, similarly it is impossible for a growing organisation to invest all the authority in one person for making decisions.

Thus, delegation of authority is a primary art of management. Yet many management studies indicate that the principal reason for the failure of managers lies in their inability to delegate authority.

Authority is delegated when power is vested in a subordinate by a superior. The process of delegation involves:
— assignment of tasks
— delegation of authority for accomplishing the tasks
— exaction of responsibility for accomplishment of the tasks

Delegation of authority, wherever possible, should be clearly documented as it then becomes extremely useful both to the one who receives it and the superior who delegates it. It enables the superior to isolate those decisions for which he can hold his subordinate responsible. However, there are occasions when it is difficult to make delegation of authority specific. This happens particularly in the case of new and developing jobs at top management cadres – at least in the beginning and till the work fully evolves. A minor argument against specific delegation is that it does not allow the subordinate the flexibility which could help him to develop in the best way.

There are situations where what we call splintered authority exists, where a problem cannot be solved alone and pooling of authority of one or more managers is necessary. For example, the superintendent of a steel melting shop thinks that he can reduce his cost by making minor changes in logistics of operations or modification in the procedures of the blast furnace department (where hot iron is produced for conversion to steel), where his authority cannot encompass the change. However, the superintendents of both the steel melting shop and the blast furnace shop can agree upon the change if it does not affect any other equal or superior superintendent. Most of the present day managerial conferences are held because of the necessity of pooling authority to make decisions, and interdependence of working.

Delegation of authority is always subject to withdrawal by the grantor. Even though the right to cover authority is unquestionable, it is generally not resorted to unless the need arises to modify enterprise objective, policies, organisation structure, etc. Reorganisation inevitably involves recovery and re-delegation of authority. Delegation of authority is generally extensive in decentralised organisations and limited in centralised organisations. Little or no delegation restricts the growth of the organisation and the number of managers.

Certain kinds of personal traits and attitude of the superior govern the extent of delegation. Personal attitudes that favour delegation are:

(a) Receptiveness – to give others' ideas a chance
(b) Willingness – to allow the subordinate to develop
(c) Willingness – to let others make occasional mistakes
(d) Willingness – to trust subordinates
(e) Willingness – to establish and use broad controls

Hazy or partial delegation, pseudo-delegation, delegation inconsistent with expected results, expectation that the subordinate must come to the superior for each decision – these are widely looked upon as weaknesses of delegation of authority by superior managers. On the other hand, subordinates who are weak in decision-making, who place too much reliance on spoon-feeding by superiors, untrained officers lacking in planning abilities or officers with lack of confidence in them seem to add to the problem of weak delegation.

The following are some of the practical guidelines for making delegation real and effective:

(i) Define assignments and delegate authority in the light of the results to be achieved.
(ii) Maintain open lines of communication.
(iii) Select the right man in view of the responsibility to be delegated.
(iv) Reward effective delegation and successful consumption of authority.
(v) Establish proper control for occasional checks to ensure that the authority delegated is not being misused and is being properly used.

Proper delegation helps in evolving a system. It is this system that works and personalities only assist the system.

Communication

Communication can be termed as an exchange of thoughts, information, facts, ideas, opinions or emotions between two or more persons with the objective of bringing about mutual understanding, confidence or good human relations. Its purpose is generally to effect change or influence action.

Very often we say that employees should be persuaded:
(i) to be loyal to the firm
(ii) to work diligently
(iii) to have good productivity

Analysing each one of the above mentioned activities, one realises the need for proper communication at every level of the organisation. One of the greatest attributes of a successful manager is the ability to communicate effectively. The frequently mentioned qualification 'to work with people' requires ability to pass information to various channels and to make ideas known. The manner in which this is accomplished is through communication.

Knowledge alone is not adequate for managerial success; it requires knowledge plus ability to communicate clearly and accurately. The popular saying 'knowledge is power' should be modified to 'applied knowledge is power'. And it requires effective communication to apply it.

Sharing of information generates cooperation and involvement in all levels of the organisation. Such a programme is not merely about giving facts and figures. It should be viewed as an activity that increases confidence in managerial members, stimulates interest and influences attitudes.

Managerial action is necessary to assist the employees in creating an interest in their work, understanding the company, and promoting confidence in the managers. To this end, sincere efforts to maintain the communication system are especially helpful. There is no place for fear in a good communication system. Fear is negative and destructive in its effects.

All members of an enterprise wish to be kept informed. It is the responsibility of the manager to receive and to answer the questions of the employees in an understandable manner and to let his group know what he is trying to accomplish, how, where and why.

> **P**
> **E**
> **R**
> **S** **Open Communication: Indian Oil**
> **P**
> **E** Indian Oil believes in open communication and uses simple information
> **C** channels to keep the employees informed about nuances of the business.
> **T** Senior officials regularly meet the collectives to share performance highlights,
> **I** future plan outlay, status of project implementation, steps taken on new
> **V** business frontiers and key challenges.
> **E**
>   The Chairman directly interacts with the employees and communicates
> through 'Straight Talk'. There are other forums like 'Personnel Touch',
> 'Discussion Forums', etc. through which employees can raise their concerns
> with the senior most officials like the Director (HR).
>
>   To show appreciation to employees, various divisions have recognition
> programmes, like reward for key positions, 'Best Field Officer', 'Pratibha
> Samman', 'Sanmukh Uplabhdi Samman', etc.

Communication Models

Communication models help management in better utilisation of human potential by keeping people informed and by sustaining their interest in their jobs. Social scientists, psychologists and technologists have contributed to the growth of better systems of communication. Aristotle emphasised on the form of communication which was persuasive in nature. The speaker, in his view, influences the listeners by logical, emotional and ethical proofs. The speaker being more important in his view, his approach to communication is described as speaker-oriented 'persuasion model.'

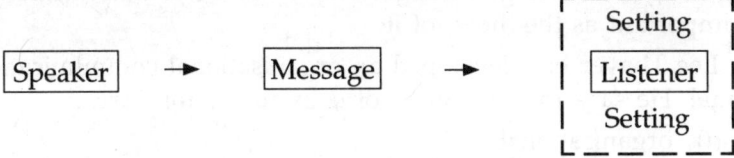

Fig. 6.3: Speaker-oriented Persuasion Model

The weakness of this model lies in its emphasis on one-way flow of information from the speaker to the listener.

Newcomb developed an interpersonal communication model. He assumed that when person A communicates to person B about something X, the orientation of both A and B towards X will be determined not only by X itself, but also by the relationship of the other person to X. The interaction between A and B would also depend upon the perceived symmetry in relationship.

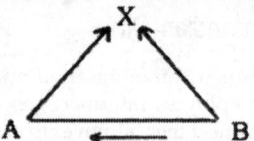

Fig. 6.4: Interpersonal Communication Model

A worker may like to develop good relations with a supervisor, but the fear that this may affect his relations with fellow workers comes in his way and does not allow him to do so.

The information theorists have developed a model of communication which deals with information devoid of meaning. They are concerned with communication of the content rather than the content itself or the listener's reaction to it. The problem of communication, according to them, may arise at any one of the following three levels:

(i) technical

(ii) semantic

(iii) effectiveness

For information theorists, problems at the technical level are the most important. However, communication problems at the semantic and effectiveness levels are also significant, and any communication model which ignores them may not be very helpful in getting the message through. The 'what' of communication is as important as the 'how' of it.

Lee Thayer has developed an organisational communication model. He says that the levels of communications are:

(i) organisational

(ii) interpersonal

(iii) intrapersonal

(iv) technical

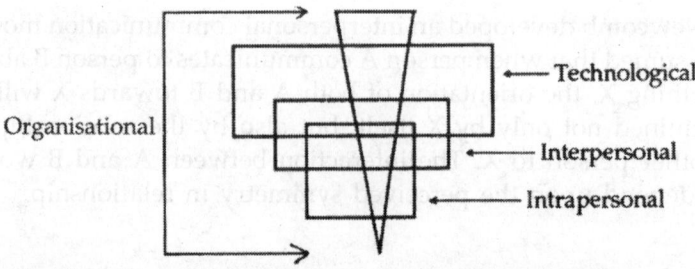

Fig. 6.5: Organisational Communication Model

At the intrapersonal level, it is necessary to distinguish between that which really exists and that which is perceived to exist.

The basic information systems, according to Thayer, are: operational, regulatory and maintenance.

The operational information system maps the flow of messages relevant to the enterprise's daily work, e.g. production, inventory, etc. The regulatory information system deals with messages concerning the setting of objectives, defining the task, framing decisions, etc. The maintenance and development of information systems deals with messages on matters such as grievances, training, evaluation, etc.

Managers in every organisation are responsible for developing an appropriate system of transferring information to make communication effective. It is their job to ensure that the right messages reach the right person at the right time.

Means of Communication

A variety of media is available for communication. Notwithstanding certain modifications, the important means of communication are:

  (i) letters, memos, notices, circulars
 (ii) special interviews, counselling sessions
(iii) departmental meetings
 (iv) mass meetings
  (v) conferences, seminars and workshops
 (vi) telephone calls, telex and fax messages
(vii) company magazines/hand books, brochures
(viii) other publications, posters, etc.
 (ix) computers

When something goes wrong in the main office or factory because of lack of communication between the employee and his superior, it is seldom due to lack of technical knowledge on the part of the superior. Instead, it is mostly due to his inability to impart knowledge to the employee.

Special phraseology, if employed in communication, may be more helpful because it permits those who know the particular field to communicate with one another with conciseness and clarity. Effective communication basically depends upon understanding the other party and speaking and writing in their language. To realise this, some practices have to be followed. These are:

- (i) Establish mutual trust in one another
- (ii) Find a common ground of experience
- (iii) Use mutually known words
- (iv) Practise delaying reaction
- (v) Have regard for content
- (vi) Secure and hold the receiver's attention
- (vii) Employ examples and visual aids.

These points are discussed below:

- (i) Acceptance of any statement needs a proper climate of mutual trust and confidence. Without these, no communication system will work.
- (ii) It is necessary to reach the individual to communicate with him perfectly. The communication must be sensible to both the communicator and the receiver.
- (iii) The best way to communicate is to use words and language known to both parties for the sake of convenience.
- (iv) While communicating it is best not to be wholly governed by immediate reaction or by the first impression gained. Hasty reaction often results in saying what one does not intend to say.
- (v) Gestures, tone of voice and the choice of words influence the meaning conveyed by a communicator. A word spoken in anger may convey a different meaning from one that is spoken in a friendly manner.
- (vi) Both spoken and written words must be carefully selected so as to secure complete attention where desired. Distracting gestures and mannerisms should be avoided.
- (vii) Stories and word pictures help fix the attention of the listener. Visual aids can be used to stress important points.

Written vs. Oral Message

Written and oral messages have their own advantages and disadvantages. Some of which are as follows:

Advantages	Disadvantages
Oral	
It is more dynamic and makes a direct impact.	It cannot be quoted or made use of later as no records are maintained.

Questions can be asked and replied to clear misunderstandings.	Records, even maintained, of conversations are not considered as legal records.
Written	
Can be retained as legal record and as a source of reference.	Often couched in a complicated language so as to reduce understandability.
Can be more carefully worded than oral communication.	Too much paper work and energy spent in distribution, etc.
Can depict a picture methodically with graphs, charts, etc.	People's response is not prompt as it becomes a one-sided communication.
	People generally do not ask questions to clarify doubts.
	Can be one-sided and can highlight only favourable points.

Movement of files and notings is yet another form of communication needed for decision-making. Great care is necessary to lay down a system of noting which does not add to the volume of a file or make it move unnecessarily from one table to another or give twists to the issue involved or confuse a situation. Much of red-tapism can be reduced with an effective system of noting.

Some guidelines prepared by a large undertaking on the noting system are given below:

Noting Systems

I. *Objective*

To evolve a noting system commensurate with the needs of the organisation and economy of paper work, prompt action and effective record.

II. *Scope*

The procedure extends to all the departments of the organisation.

III. *Principles*

Noting should be resorted to only when absolutely necessary.

Only a limited number of staff members should be empowered to initiate or comment on notes.

Multiple noting should be avoided.

IV. *Procedure*

1. *Initiation of a note is not necessary*
    - where a line of action on a receipt is obvious or is based on a clear precedent or practice or where the course of action has been indicated by the officer-in-charge.
    - on reference which is simply to be forwarded and on which no further communication is likely to be received.

    Explanation: It follows that a draft or final reply, wherever required, should be put up for consideration, without a note, in the above mentioned circumstances.

    It is necessary where it is advisable
    - to point out mistakes or misstatement of facts in a PUC (paper under consideration).
    - to refer to statutory or customary procedure in the light of company's rule or labour laws.
    - to refer to precedents or papers containing previous policy decisions.

    Or

    - to underline, for emphasis, a particular point covered in the draft letter.
    - when a new subject is to be opened for consideration or fresh issues are involved.
    - when heavy financial commitments are involved.
    - when policies are involved or a departure from an existing enunciation of policy is called for.

2. *Who may initiate a note*

    Generally speaking, a note may be initiated by only one of the following two:
    - a person in a non-executive scale directly reporting to an officer (referred to as staff member/office staff hereinafter).
    - by an officer.

    However, comments on a running note should always be by an officer.

3. *Guiding circumstances*
    - A note will be initiated by a staff member only when his officer desires a note. The officer may indicate this by endorsing 'with a note please' on PUC.

In all other cases the officer will merely connect with old and/or quoted references and files and put up the case.

Naturally, in an officer-oriented organisation, the 'with a note please' instruction will be kept to the minimum and may be confined to such cases as:
- summing up a complicated case agreed over quite a long time.
- acquainting a new officer about the history of a case.
- the note will be taken by the head of the department of higher authorities.

4. *Role of office staff*

Whether a note is initiated/commented on by an officer or initiated by a staff member, the latter will be responsible for:
- Connecting with old and/or quoted references/files.
- Flagging of all references quoted in the note.
- Pointing out any mistake or misstatement of facts.
- Drawing attention, where necessary, to the statutory or customary procedure and to point out the law and rules and where these are to be found.
- Supplying other relevant facts and figures quoting precedents or papers containing previous decisions of policy.

If before reaching the chief executive, a note has become a point of controversy and/or multiple notings, the last officer who submits the case to the chief executive should summarise the entire proceedings and put up a self-contained note.

5. *Framework of a note*
- The subject of the file should be mentioned at the top of each note sheet, preceded by the remark 'from pre-page' wherever applicable.
- A note should be self-contained, yet brief and to the point.
- The points for discussion should be clearly spelt out and summarised, preferably at the end of the note.
- The note should be broken up into short paragraphs, each dealing with a single point.

- Long sentences and unnecessary expressions such as 'in this connection', 'it may be observed that', 'it maybe stated that', etc. should be avoided.
- The paragraphs of the note should always be numbered in sequence and when a note or a series of notes extends beyond two pages, the pages should also be numbered.
- The note should be free from personal remarks.
- In case of notes which are to be submitted to senior heads of departments for seeking orders, they should be written so as to finish within three-fourths of the sheet leaving space for the officer to write his remarks.
- If the note is lengthy and occupies almost the whole sheet, it should be so adjusted that the concluding words of the note are written on a fresh note sheet. This will leave the officer concerned enough space for his noting/order.
- Notes should be initialled and dated by the official concerned.
- A blank note sheet should always be attached to all the case files.
- Notes should be properly flagged to help in locating the references, especially to rules, instructions, etc. made in them.
- Only stiff, printed flags should be used for the purpose of reference and the number of flags used should be kept to the minimum. Also no two flags should overlap.
- Cross-referencing should be done properly so that no time is wasted in tracing relevant papers.

6. *Feedback*

Any suggestion on the improvement of the proposed system is welcome. The system should be reviewed periodically to ensure that it is in line with the dynamics of the prevailing situation.

A committee may be considered a limited membership/staff group which meets for specific purposes for effecting an integration of ideas concerning the solution of a problem or a matter of importance in a collective way.

There are situations where a committee may perform some functions more effectively than an individual. However, it should not be regarded as a substitute for individual action.

PERSPECTIVE	**Communication Gap**

* In an interview, an American member of a U.S.-Japanese team that was assessing the potential expansion of a U.S. retail chain in Japan was seen as 'not interested in Japanese consultants' feedback' and felt that 'because they weren't as fluent as Americans were, they weren't intelligent enough and, therefore, could add no value'. Without input from Japanese experts, he risked overestimating opportunities and underestimating challenges.

* In a Korean-U.S. negotiation, the American members were having difficulty getting information from their Korean counterparts, so they complained directly to higher level Korean management, nearly wrecking the deal. Korean members were mortified that their bosses had been involved before they themselves could brief them. The crisis was resolved only when high level U.S. managers made a trip to Korea, conveying appropriate respect for their Korean counterparts.

Barriers to Communication

In large organisations where face to face communication becomes difficult, the possibility of messages being distorted, misinterpreted and wrongly communicated increases both down the line and upward in the hierarchy. The persons involved may withhold, stop or absorb part of the message, pass on the information which suits them and colour or twist the information, thus depriving the person concerned to get all the facts correctly. The communication may be delayed deliberately to stop the person concerned from acting in time. The communicators themselves may thus become barriers to adequate and timely communication.

The persons who are supposed to receive the message may also act as barriers. By adopting a confrontationist attitude, by refusing to listen to others or understanding their viewpoints, one may stop the flow of ideas and information correctly to himself or herself. Getting prejudiced in any situation may result in closing the doors of understanding. Lack of knowledge of the subject matter or the language may also result in poor communication.

The social and economic factors which act as barriers to communication may be listed as under:

— Status in hierarchy
— Differences in income and standard of living
— Caste, community and religion
— Attachment to customs, tradition and other cultural values

All organisations are part of the social structure. Business enterprises are no exception to it. Social harmony and social tension both are reflected in an organisation's life.

The communication may also fail due to mechanical barriers. The telephone, telex or fax lines may be off or the instrument might break down causing unavoidable delay in the transmission of information.

Management Committees

A committee could be any of the following types:
- Review Committee
- Action Committee
- Advisory Committee
- Consultative Committee
- Committee for exchanging views and ideas
- Investigational, judicial, integrative committees and so on

The major objective in the formation of committees, in most cases, is effectiveness of control by providing services, advice, control, etc. which further the achievement of organisational objectives. A committee can also be termed as a device by which knowledge and experience of various departments or individuals can be pooled to bear on a problem of importance.

A committee may or may not be vested with authority. Some high-powered committees include chief executives or similar members of high rank. Their advice is often accepted by top executives as a matter of practice. At times, committees have limited functional authority within their specialised functional areas. Sometimes, committees may give guidelines and advice or investigate or act as recommendatory authority. There are certain types of committees which have no authority whatsoever and function merely as recreational, educational or communication tools of an organisation.

Generally large organisations, because of coordination difficulties, make greater use of committees than smaller companies. However, there is no hard and fast rule in this regard. What is more important is the number and calibre of the members constituting a committee as well as how to put it to best use. Practice shows that the acceptable size of a committee is five members. Beyond seven or so, the committee becomes too large and it is seen that only a few members take initiative, others playing the role of silent partners. With smaller committees, there is sharp difference of opinion at times and it is difficult to arrive at a consensus. In a three-member committee two members may oppose the third. These difficulties can be avoided if the committee chairman effectively controls its proceedings.

Some of the situations indicating the advantages and disadvantages of a committee are indicated below:

Committee is advantageous		Committee is disadvantageous
1. Where group ideas and judgements are considered the best.	1.	Where the manager is considered to be a better judge.
2. Where fear of bias or improper use of status or one-line thinking exists.	2.	Where responsibility may be diffused but fixing accountability is necessary.
3. Where exchange of ideas is considered necessary before making definite recommendations.	3.	Where fast decision-making is involved.
	4.	Where unanimous opinion is required.
4. Where group interest is involved like major policy decisions.	5.	Where work is to be performed and group interest is not involved.
5. Where training and developmental or educational needs are to be developed as a policy.	6.	Where group thinking is likely to be influenced by emotions.
6. Where suggestions, innovations, interaction of ideas are made.	7.	Where technical reports which can be printed or circulated are available.

A list of committees functioning in a large public sector undertaking which is known for its high production rate and trouble-free labour-management relations is given below:

Top Level Committees
— Central Production Committee
— Joint Coordination Committee
— Central Safety Committee
— Inspection Committee
— Sports and Recreational Council

Zonal Level Committees
— Grievance Committee
— Suggestions Committee
— Sports Committee
— Technical Training Committee
— Welfare Advisory Committee

- House Allotment Advisory Committee
- Medical and Public Health Advisory Committee

Departmental Level Committees
- Production Committee
- Education Committee
- School Welfare Advisory Committee
- Canteen Committee
- Safety and Welfare Committee
- Reconciliation and Coordination Committee
- Security Committee
- House-keeping Committee.

The above list is indicative of the diversified nature and the manner in which matters of common interest can be delegated by the management to various elected/nominated collectives to manage or advise the management as to how they can or should be handled. It helps in avoiding conflicts between the management and the employees.

Leadership

Leadership is the art of influencing people to attain group objectives willingly. What a minister does in his State, a captain does on the playground, the manager has to do in his organisation. Leaders in all walks of life should have some basic qualities. They should be able to establish contact with their equals, deal with their subordinates and guide them, mediate in conflicts, resolve issues by weighing various alternatives, allocate scarce resources properly and take risks and initiatives.

The environment in which a leader is placed is important. The organisational culture, the economic and social set-up, the extent of unionisation and other factors may demand different types of leaders in different situations. A task-oriented leader, for instance, may be more successful in situations which are either very favourable or very unfavourable to him, while a relations-oriented leader may be more effective in intermediate situations.

Some managers believe that they can get things done only by the exercise of authority and power while others believe in persuasion, consultation and willing cooperation of the subordinates. Rensis Likert has analysed the characteristics of different management systems in his book *The Human Organisation*, where he has divided these systems into four types:

- Exploitative authoritative
- Benevolent authoritative
- Consultative
- Participative

As management moves from the authoritative to the participative system, an atmosphere of mutual trust and confidence is created. And this results in better cooperation, higher productivity and improved morale. The operating characteristics of the four systems are described on page 143.

PERSPECTIVE

Leadership Concept: Motorola

Leadership in Motorola refers to four different aspects:

* At the top of the rung is the basic philosophy on which the organisation exists, i.e. the core value, which is that whatever we do, we will keep in mind our respect for people, and the highest integrity, which is the fundamental and non-negotiable foundation.

* Then comes the leadership of individual dignity which talks of six points in a person's career:

    (a) Real job

    (b) Meaningful job

    (c) Performance factors

    (d) Training needs and implementation of training aspirations

    (e) Career plans

    (f) Getting feedback in a bias-free organisation

* The third part is that of implementation i.e. are you delivering, and if you are delivering, what are your goals, are they achievable, are they stretchable, do they add value to the organisation and what are the key initiatives regarding how we will go in the future.

* And the last pillar, not necessarily in that order, is what we call leadership renewal. It is easy to start some process and get lost in implementing it or sitting on our past laurels and saying we have arrived. Or doing something good and then being complacent. That part is the leadership of challenge – challenging the status quo, calling for something that has not been tried before, having the courage to experiment, having the gumption to fall within the boundaries. This is not recklessness but calculated environment building for people to take new risks and come up with new ideas.

It has been made mandatory for managers at Motorola to cross a TOML Score (Totality of Motorola Leadership Score) prescribed by the company to be promoted.

Dr. Eric Berne's concept of 'Transactional Analysis', which is described as a blueprint of the mind, is of great help in understanding people and improving relations. This concept was

Developing O.K. Feeling in Subordinates

popularised by Thomas A. Harris in his book entitled *I'm OK, You're OK*.

According to this theory, three states exist in all the people:
- the parent
- the child
- the adult.

The parent is a "huge collection of recordings in the brain of unquestioned or imposed external events", perceived by a person in his early years. What his father, mother, and elderly people in the family say and do are recorded in the parent. The recording is permanent.

Another recording which takes place in the early years is of internal events: "the responses of the little person to what he sees and hears". When a person is in the grip of feelings, it is said that his child has taken over.

The adult is the 'data processing computer'. The adult accumulates data when the child is able to find out for himself what all is different from the things that were taught to him.

The recorded experiences and the feelings, good and bad, are available for replay and determine the nature of today's transaction. Based upon the recorded experience, one of the following life-positions develops in each individual:
- I am not OK, you are OK
- I am not OK, you are not OK
- I am OK, you are not OK
- I am OK, you are OK

Transactional analysis aims at enabling a person "to have freedom of choice, the freedom to change at will, to change the responses to recurring and new stimuli". It helps in getting the freedom back which was lost in early childhood. The freedom grows from "knowing the truth about what is in the parent, what is in the child and how this data is fed in the present day transactions". The words used, tone of voice, body gestures and facial expressions, etc. offer clues to discover which part of the person – parent, adult or child – is generating each stimulus and response.

Motivation, Communication and Leadership

Likert's Classification of Managing Systems

Operating Characteristics	Authoritative		Consultative	Participative
	Exploitative	Benevolent	Consultative	Participating group
1. Characteristics of motivational forces	Fear, threat, punishment, occasional reward	Occasional reward and actual or potential punishment	Rewards, occasional punishment, some involvement	Rewards on cooperation: system based on participation
2. Characteristics of the communication process	Downward	Mostly downward	Down and up	Down, up and with peers
3. Characteristics of the interaction process	Little and along with fear	Little with some fear and caution	Moderate with fear and caution	Extensive, friendly and confident
4. Characteristics of the decision-making process	Decision by top management	Policy at top even though matters may be at different levels	Broad policy at top, specific decisions at lower levels	Decision-making widely dispersed throughout the organisation although well integrated
5. Characteristics of goal-setting	Orders issued	Orders issued, opportunity to comment may be	Orders issued after discussion	Except in emergencies, goals established by participation
6. Characteristics of control process	Strong forces to distort and falsify	Fairly strong forces to distort, meaning incomplete	Some persons to distort and some to protect	Strong pressure to obtain complete and correct information
7. *Performance* characteristics	Mediocre productivity	Fair to good productivity	Good productivity	Excellent productivity

The 'I am OK you are OK' feeling can be developed by making the adult strong. This can be done by:

— Learning to recognise one's own 'child' – its vulnerabilities, its fears, its principal methods of expressing feelings.
— Learning to recognise one's own 'parent' – its admonitions, injunctions, fixed positions and principal ways of expressing.

PARENT   (P)   unquestioned or imposed
"The taught concept"   external events perceived by a person in his early years

ADULT   (A)   findings: what is different
"The taught concept"   from the things taught

CHILD   (C)   internal events – the response of the little person to
"The felt concept"   what he sees and hears

Fig. 6.6: PAC Analysis

— Becoming sensitive to the 'child' in others – talk to that child, protect that child, stroke it and appreciate it.
— Using the 'adult' to process data to sort out parent and child from reality.
— Working out a system of value.

A manager who tries to understand the feelings of his subordinates and circumstances which provoke them, appreciates their efforts when required, avoids using coercive and directive methods and promotes their participation in decision-making process, decides things on merit and gives them just and fair treatment makes better use of the 'adult'. He generates the OK feeling in his people which is vital for better human relations.

Managerial Grid

The leadership behaviour in any situation can be a mix of two dimensions: concern for people and concern for task. Some business leaders are highly people-oriented while some are hard taskmasters. In between the two styles there are many permutations and combinations possible. Robert R. Blake and Jane S. Mouton have developed Managerial Grid to show different styles of management practised by businesses. These are shown in the figure given below.

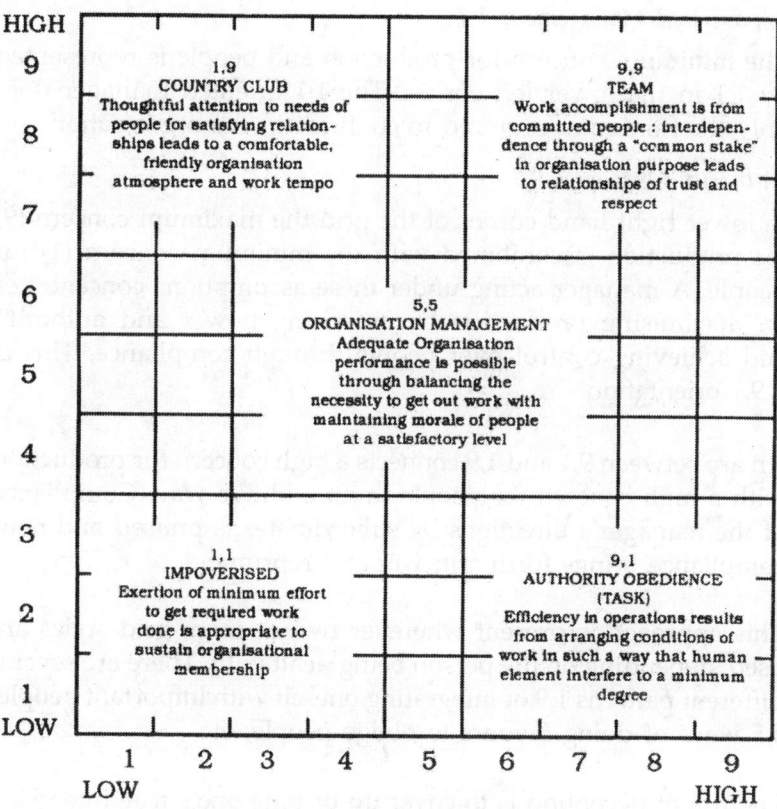

Fig. 6.7: The Managerial Grid

Country Club Management 1,9

The 1, 9 leadership style is in the top left corner. Here the minimum concern (1) for production is coupled with the maximum concern (9) for people. Primary attention is given to promoting good feelings among colleagues and friends.

Team Management 9,9

Production and people concerns are integrated at a high level in the upper right corner representing the 9,9 style of managing. This is the team approach and seeks to gain results of high quality and quantity through participation, involvement, commitment and conflict resolution.

Grid Styles

Organisation Management 5,5

The 5,5 style is in the centre. This is the middle of the road theory or the 'go along to get along' assumptions which are revealed in conformity to the status quo.

Impoverised Management 1,1

The minimum concern for production and people is represented by 1,1 in the lower left corner. The 1,1 oriented manager does only the minimum required to continue in the organisation.

Authority Obedience 9,1

In lower right hand corner of the grid the maximum concern (9) for production is combined with the minimum concern (1) for people. A manager acting under these assumptions concentrates on maximising production by exercising power and authority and achieving control over people through compliance. This is a 9,1 orientation.

Paternalism

An arc between 9,1 and 1,9 connects a high concern for production with a high concern for people in an additive way. Compliance of the manager's directions by subordinates is praised and non-compliance brings forth criticism and reprimand.

Opportunism

This approach is present wherever two or more grid styles are used, depending on the person being dealt with. There are several different patterns 1,9 of integrating oneself with important people, 5,5 ways of doing favours to oblige people, etc.

Facadist

The use of deception is to cover up or hide one's true intentions from view in order to achieve something believed unattainable if one's true grid style were evident. The 'front' is usually a 9,9 orientation to hide 9,1 paternalism or opportunism.

Blake and Mouton have analysed the leadership styles of some eminent American industrialists on the basis of the grid technique developed by them. Alfred P. Sloan of General Motors, a true organisational genius of the 20th century, according to them, managed in 9,9 style, while Henry Ford, a great entrepreneur of his time, had paternalistic orientation. At the outset, Ford was the stronger of the two giants, but General Motors overtook Ford during the aegis of Sloan, which shows the superiority of 9,9 style. Henry Ford II, who believed in 'never explain, never complain', managed in 9,1 style. Shapiro of DuPont had 5,5 style while Geneen managed ITT in a style approaching 9,1.

Robert K. Murray and Tim H. Blessings have used grid technique to analyse leadership styles of 14 twentieth century American presidents. The 9,9 grid style is assigned to T Roosevelt, F. Roosevelt and Truman, 1,9 to Taft and Harding, 1,1 to Coolidge and 5,5 to Eisenhower. Wilson and Carter had a paternalistic approach while Nixon's leadership included facadist strategies. Kennedy and Johnson were placed in the grid style opportunism. Murray and Blessings' analysis confirm the view that it is the individual who makes the office rather than the other way round.

Leadership effectiveness is associated with the grid style that an individual adopts. The human resource managers can use the grid technique to train people to be more effective in their jobs. They can do so by developing six process elements in trainees: initiative, enquiry, advocacy, conflict resolution, decision-making and critique.

Situation Analysis

(A) Laroia has been appointed assistant superintendent to Kundu, superintendent of the assembly department. Kundu has six foremen working under him. Two of them do not accept Laroia and feel that he does not have the experience and expertise to guide them in their work. They are bypassing Laroia and going to Kundu directly knowing his weaknesses too. They do not pay much attention to Kundu's advice of not short-circuiting Laroia. Kundu is reluctant to issue directives to those two foremen for they are excelling in their work. He is further afraid that these two may lose interest in their work if forced to route their papers through Laroia. Laroia, on the other hand, is unhappy with Kundu for not reprimanding those two foremen for bypassing him.

How would you resolve the situation?

(B) Islam, Mandal and Ram are working as foremen in the maintenance, heavy repair and construction departments. Each has a different section under him independently. Each maintains about 50 persons on the regular strength and another 50-60 persons on NMR on daily wage basis as the workload is not steady. Of the daily wage workers, some are men (young and old) and others women (single and married).

Owing to bad financial position, the company instructed its foremen to reduce the daily wage staff by 50%.

The foremen effected the reduction in the following manner:
- Islam laid off all the old men and old women. He allowed the young men and women to continue to work.
- Mandal laid off all those who in his opinion were inefficient and troublemakers, irrespective of their age or sex.
- Ram laid off men according to seniority and the financial condition of his employees, i.e., who would best be able to stand the loss of pay for a few days till they got some other work.

In your opinion which foreman acted in the best interest of his company and the employees?

Review Questions

1. 'A manager need not be an expert in all the skills which he is directing'. Comment.
2. What are the sources of authority in an organisation?
3. Explain Maslow's model of motivation and compare it with Herzberg's model.
4. Discuss ERG theory of Alderfer. In what respects Alderfer differs from Maslow?
5. Elaborate the Porter and Lawler model. Do you agree with the view that managers who see their role as requiring an inner directed orientation would, other things being equal, perform better?
6. Why do some managers hesitate in delegating power? What suggestions will you give to make delegation real?
7. Discuss communication models and the objectives behind such models.
8. What are the different means of communication in an organisation?
9. Discuss the significance of electronic media as the lifeline of modern communication system.
10. What are the barriers to communication? What suggestions would you like to give to make communication effective?
11. What are the different types of committees formed in large organisations? Explain the merits and demerits of the committee form of organisation.
12. Explain Likert's classification of leadership styles and the characterstic features of different styles.
13. What is PAC? How will you relate 4 life positions with leadership styles?

14. Explain the concept of Managerial Grid. Does it provide any management style applicable to all situations?
15. What inspiration do you get from the following success stories:
    (i) A native leader: Dr. Verghese Kurien
    (ii) Success Mantra: Indra K. Nooyi

A Native Leader: Dr Verghese Kurien

Dr. Verghese Kurien once stormed out of a Nestle board meeting in Switzerland. The multinational dairy officials refused to take technological help from India as they could not let "natives handle a sensitive commodity like milk." Two years later the same Nestle officials came down to a dusty town called Anand to do business on Indian terms after they were impressed with the world-class facilities in the Gujarat town.

This was in 1956. Dr Kurien, who gave it back to the MNC, created India's largest food brand 'Amul'. He is best known as India's Milk Man – the architect of the largest dairy cooperative in the world. An ardent supporter of farmer's cause, he believes that farmer's power is useless without right management. Good management gives this power the right direction and thrust. Nothing can stop them then, least of all an MNC. When he started, there were Cadbury, Horlicks, Nestle and Polson. They are nowhere near Amul now. Dr. Kurien was given charge of Amul by its founder Tribhuvandas Patel, a visionary Gujarati entrepreneur, who wanted the cooperative to be run by a professional manager. His dream came true.

Success Mantra: Indra K. Nooyi

Indra Krishnamurthy Nooyi's long journey began decades ago, when her mother would hold a contest to test her children. Every night after dinner the children were asked to make speeches on what they wanted to do when they grew up. The winner was given a piece of chocolate. Heading Pepsi Co. after that must have been just a logical progression.

Tales abound on Nooyi's achievements: of how she worked as a receptionist to pay for her studies in the U.S. where she went to Yale after graduating from IIM Calcutta and earlier the Madras Christian College, how she won hearts, how she had the guts to take strong decisions.

> The success mantra of Nooyi, who shares her birthday with Bill Gates, is fascinating: focus on strengths, strong communication, work-life balance and plan well. But what is really significant is that she knows how to mix things that do not at face value seem mixable. She is hard on numbers but thinks people and relationships are important, she prays a lot but puts reasons above emotions.
>
> In U.S., Nooyi worked at Motorola and Asea Brown Boveri before joining Pepsi Co. in 1994. She was elected director, president and CFO of Pepsi Co. in 2001 after negotiating Pepsi's 14 billion deal for Quaker Oats. Pepsi's stock reached a five year high after her promotion, making it one of the five largest consumer product companies in the world.

Further Readings

1. R.F. Baumeister and M.R. Leary: *The Need to Belong: Desire for Interpersonal Attachments as a Fundamental Human Motivation* (Psychological Bulletin, Vol. 117, pp. 497-529, 1995).
2. D.M. Bersoff: *Why Good People Sometimes Do Bad Things: Motivated Reasoning and Unethical Behaviour* (Social Psychology Bulletin, Vol. 25, pp. 28-39, 1999).
3. Robert R. Blake and Jave S. Mouton: *The Managerial Grid* (Gulf Publishing, Houston, 1954).
4. William F. Dowling, Jr. and Leonard R. Sayles: *How Managers Motivate: The Imperatives of Supervision* (McGraw-Hill Book Co., New York, 1971).
5. Thomas A Harris: *I am OK - You are OK* (Harper & Row, New York, 1961).
6. J. Koehler, K. Anatol and R. Applbaum: *Organisational Communication: Behavioural Perspectives* (Holt, Rinehart & Winston, New York, 1976).
7. Abraham H. Maslow: *Motivation and Personality* (Harper and Bros, New York, 1954).
8. David McClelland, et al: *The Achievement Motive* (Appleton-Century-Crofts, New York, 1953).
9. Lallan Prasad and S.S. Gulshan: *Management Principles and Practices* (Excel Books, New Delhi, 2011).
10. Charles E. Redfield: *Communication in Management* (University of Chicago, Chicago, 1958).
11. Arnold E. Schneider, et al: *Organisational Communication* (McGraw-Hill, New York).
12. G.A. Yuld: *Leadership in Organisations* (Prentice Hall, New Jersey, 2006).

Chapter 7

Resistance to Change

"Like people and plants, organisations have a life cycle. They have a green and supple youth, a time of flourishing strength, and a gnarled old age.... An organisation may go from youth to old age in two or three decades, or it may last for centuries."

– *John Gardner*

Learning Objectives

After reading this chapter you will be able to:

1. Understand why no individual or organisation can escape change.
2. Analyse causes for resistance to change by individuals and organisations.
3. Explain change models and corporate practices to manage change.

Change is defined as planned or unplanned alteration in the *status quo* of an organisation's situation or process. It affects the structure, technology and human resources of the whole organisation.

Change is the law of nature. No individual or organisation can escape change. During the last few decades, there have been among others, a knowledge explosion, a technological explosion, a communication explosion and an economic explosion. Science has unfolded new frontiers of knowledge. New processes, new techniques and new methods have been developed in all spheres that enable humans to talk, report and get feedback from people sitting at far-off places, including space, in a matter of seconds. Economic values and social systems are also changing fast. Organisations have to adjust continuously to the changing environment and the managers of today are responsible for preparing their people and organisations to face the tomorrow, the future.

The areas in which planned change is required include the knowledge framework (conceptual understanding of new objects, processes), the skill framework (new ways of doing things through practice), the attitude framework (adoption of new feelings), and the value framework (adoption of new beliefs, ideas).

Resistance to Change

Very often change is not accepted easily by the people. There are reasons for it.

From a micro viewpoint, it has been seen that individuals resist change because it scares them and poses a threat to them. Such resistance is not to be taken lightly as it may lead to conflicts, slowdown, drop in productivity and quality of workmanship and strikes.

From a macro viewpoint, organisations may resist change because of the effects it can have on the stability greatly needed for higher productivity and efficiency. Organisations operate at the optimum level in a predictable environment for that has shown what the future holds in store for them.

The most common reasons for resistance to change by individuals are:

— Perception
— Habits
— Security

Individuals see reality in a particular set-up that is created over a period of time by their own attitudes, experiences and beliefs. This is no doubt a biased interpretation of reality. It is known as selective perception and is the root cause of individual resistance to change. Unionised workers often do not look upon the management as trustworthy (again, a biased perception). Even managers use selective perception to resist change.

Habit makes a work repetitive with little strain on the thinking faculties of a person and serves as a source of personal satisfaction. Any proposed change, since it may bring a change in habits, is often resisted.

Individuals tend to find security in their past behaviour and methods of working. In government offices, a great deal of faith is placed on established procedures or proven precedents. It is felt that action or decisions taken on the basis of precedents are safe and secure. Therefore, doing things in the old way gets priority over trying new methods.

The situations in which resistance to change usually occurs are:

— There is satisfaction with the *status quo.*
— The purpose of change is not made clear – lack of understanding.
— There is poor communication regarding the change.
— When the persons involved in the change or affected by the change are not involved while planning the change.
— Anxiety over personal security is not relieved or autonomy is not preserved.
— Excessive pressure is exerted or undue hurry is shown for the change.
— The effort or cost is too high as compared to the expected rewards or gains.
— There is a fear of failure and anxiety of punishment arising out of failures.
— When the existing habit patterns are ignored.
— The need for change comes because of personal reasons.
— The initiator of change is not trusted and respected.

Most of these are human aspects and can be solved or prevailed upon if the human aspect is kept in mind and not neglected or brushed aside.

Individual Change Model

Warren Bennis has developed a model to understand individual response to change. An individual may express different levels of response to change: oppose, resist, tolerate, accept, support or embrace. His response will be affected by factors such as:

- ambiguity of the meaning of change
- control of environment
- trust in change initiators
- intensity of search behaviour
- impact of change as seen by the individual, e.g. threatening, uncertain, positive, etc.

The individual perceptions and reactions to the change will also be affected by the extent of information he gets about the change, his involvement in the change process, his past experiences, etc. The model is helpful in understanding and examining various forces at work in the change situation.

PERSPECTIVE — Capability Maturity Model

Wipro is the first Capability Maturity Model (CMM) certified IT Company globally. Its people processes are based on the current best practices in human resources, knowledge management and organisation development, giving a great focus to match changing business needs with the development of employee competencies.

People Capability Maturity Model was developed by SEI and introduced in 1995 to bring a focus to workforce process efficiencies and productivity to enhance organisational capabilities and effectiveness. The model consists of five maturity levels that establish successive foundations for continuously improving individual competencies, developing effective teams, motivating improved performance and shaping the workforce the organisation needs to accomplish future business plans. Each maturity level is a well-defined evolutionary plateau that institutionalises new capabilities for developing the organisation's workforce. By following the maturity framework, an organisation can avoid introducing workforce practices that its employees are not prepared to implement effectively. This model introduces best practices in phases with each progressive level providing a unique transformation in organisational culture by equipping it with more powerful practices. Continuous workforce innovation, coaching personnel and improving work environment are the hallmarks of this model.

Organisational Resistance

Like individuals, organisations also resist change; reasons being:
- stability
- prior investment
- past obligations

Acquainted with the art of shipbuilding, one of the authors has seen the captain's insistence on proven systems even though the new systems being offered are advanced and more reliable. The statutory authorities have a preference for age-old systems and show resistance to alter even for a better system and gauge. Their primary aim is to see that a ship should be able to carry men and material safely and smoothly through the high seas in a proven way. For them, safe arrival and stability are of prime importance and matters like higher efficiency, technological innovations, cutting short the cycle time of production, indigenisation, etc. are of secondary importance.

Many organisations resist changes because of heavy investment of their resources in a given project or location or a particular strategy or commitment. At times, economic and legal constraints too discourage change.

Every organisation makes commitments and enters into contract with others. Some sort of interdependence develops and this comes in the way of unplanned change. Some such examples are agreements with the union, the local state administration, suppliers, competitors, customers, etc.

Organisation Change Model

G.L. Lippitt has suggested an organisation change model which is also referred to as 'confrontation model', i.e. appropriate response to the situations that arise in an organisation. The principal elements of the model are:

Situations : This is the focal point of the model. It includes such terms as 'confrontation', 'crisis', 'problem solving' and 'everyday decisions'. Thus, a strike, financial crisis, accident in factory, change in top leadership, etc. are all covered by situations. A situation may not always be a problem. The situations test whether individuals and groups are able to face and meet the challenges.

Model for Understanding an Individual's Response to Change

		1	2	3	4	5
I		A major change is proposed	The individual's perception of the change	The individual initiates search	The individual's evaluation of the impact of change on him	The individual's response to the change
II	Dimensions	High ambiguity of meaning of change	Low control of environment and change	High intensity of search behaviour	Self-destructive, threatening, negative uncertainty, does not know, positive uncertainty, self-enhancing	Oppose, Resist, Tolerate, Accept, Support, Embrace
			Low trust in the change initiator			
		Low — High	High — Low			

As affected by

III

a. Extent of information about change

Zero ————————————————— High

| A little information | Some information | Quite a bit of information | Full information |

b. Extent of psychological participation in change

Zero ————————————————— High

| A little influence | Some influence | Quite a bit of influence | A great deal of influence |

c. Other factors such as the individual's acceptance of organisational folklore and his past experience with change

Zero ————————————————— High

| A little acceptance and experience | Some acceptance and experience | Quite a bit of acceptance and experience | A great deal of acceptance and experience |

Source: Warren Bennis, *The Planning of Change* (Holt, Rinehart and Winston Inc., New York, 1969).

Renewal stimulator	:	This shows the ability to respond appropriately to the situations. The appropriateness of response will depend upon the adequacy of the action, e.g. whether the action optimised the effective utilisation and development of human resources in the organisation, whether it is responsive to the environment in which organisation exists, etc.
Human resources	:	Individuals, pairs, groups and large units of people in the organisation constitute the human resource. The multiple goals of an organisation are achieved through them.
Interfacing	:	This is the process through which human beings confront common areas of concern, engage in meaningful dialogues, actively search for solutions to mutual problems and purposefully implement them.
Organisational growth	:	This refers to the idea that organisations are complex organisms that have a life cycle with stages of development commencing with birth and progressing through survival to the later stages of maturity. In its various stages, this resembles the mental and psychological growth of an individual from childhood to adulthood.

The process of change and growth of an organisation depends upon the way situations are handled by the management. The human resources are the essential element in the change process. The circular model of organisational functioning emphasises the need for organisational system to re-examine its goals, evaluate its performance and renew its spirit; and it demonstrates that the ability of the socio-technical system to cope is an essential element. Renewal stimulation, e.g. a qualified trainer, may add to the quality of situational coping.

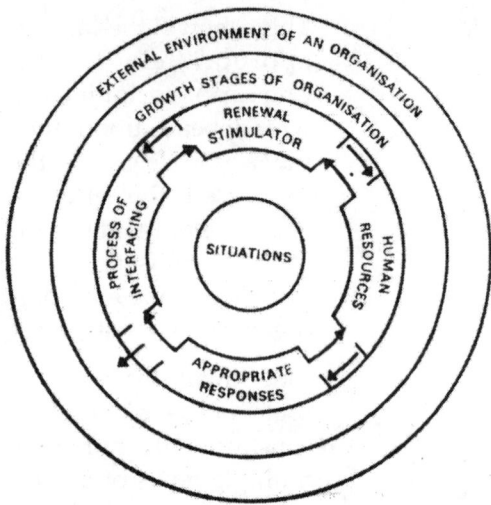

Fig. 7.1

Source: G.L. Lippitt, Organisation Renewal (Appleton-Century-Crofts, New York, 1969, p. 18).

The model looks upon an organisation as a living organism and describes the informal and external forces influencing it in the growth stages.

Change Process and Productivity

A general phenomenon often seen while introducing change for better methods of work or while introducing new processes or for improving technology is given below. The existing production level shows a temporary downward trend during the change period owing to resistance/non-cooperation/other related factors. The downward trend is arrested when people accept change, an upward trend is noticed and then it stabilises at a higher improved rate.

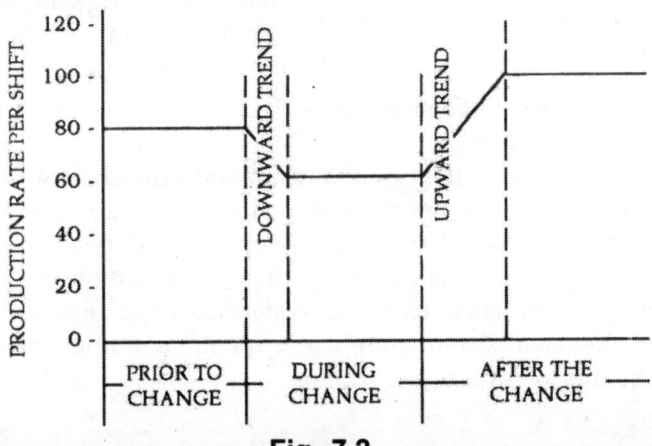

Fig. 7.2

Participative Attitude

Every effort should be made to reach a participative change whereby the individual/group/union can consider and select their new goals/objectives/methods and adopt them. Sometimes it is observed that a new or immature director lacking proper exposure to business problems tries to introduce change by a directive method or by court martial attitude which fails to achieve the desired objectives. The situation in such cases gets worse when such a director/manager has (what is called) wrong inner circle advisers, who misguide the management for their own gains rather than keeping the interest of the organisation in mind. Use of position to force any new thing on people may achieve little, but when people are involved in the change process, results may be excellent.

Situation Analysis

An industrial undertaking had appointed a consultant (without discussing the matter with the workers or the executives or the union) to develop a management information and costing system. The report had been passed on to the planning, finance and production managers for implementation with immediate effect.

The managers examined the report and found many conceptual faults in it. Rather than pointing those out and rejecting the report or deferring its implementation, they decided to take a positive stand. They decided to correct the changes in the report to correct the wrong concepts and implement them.

They first tried to find out the grounds or reasons on which the subordinates might resist the change or create a conflict, and then the favourable points by which they could influence others and pressurise them for the change. They exchanged their notes and came to the following agreement:

Resistance to Change

- The existing report is easy to fill out. This is so because data flows in easily as per the established practice of various departments.
- The existing report takes little time to think and compile. The subordinates can prepare the report without much running about and guidance from the superiors.
- The top management made little use of these reports in the past for exercising any control and therefore go in for all this botheration.
- The new report will be very comprehensive and time consuming. It would require more compiling and typing efforts.

Factors in Favour of Change

— Cost of production is going high and profits are coming down; hence, bonus will go down if this trend is not stopped or reversed.
— Organisational controls are getting out of control.
— Streamlining of organisational reporting formats is necessary.
— If at all a monthly report is to be made (which is being made right now also), why not make it a meaningful one for the benefit of all.
— The new report would now be examined by each departmental head and useful recommendations would be forwarded to cut down infructuous expenditure and plug wastages.

Within the parameters of two extreme variables, the managers attempted to unfreeze the situation by trying to convince and point out to the subordinates as to how the new system of reporting could be helpful. Then the officers themselves moved on to the change phase by filling out the reports themselves as a trial. Slowly, the subordinates fell in line and started filling the new reports. Thus, the new system of reporting became a part of their monthly routine.

Review Questions

1. Define change and discuss the need for change.
2. Why do individuals resist change? What are the situations in which resistance to change usually occurs?
3. Explain Warren Bennis's individual change model.
4. Why do organisations resist change? Is it desirable?
5. Critically examine G.L. Lippitt's model of organisational change.
6. What action management should take when employees in general oppose a change considered necessary by it to improve productivity?

Further Readings

1. S. Balachandran: *Managing Change: An Indian Experience* (Business Book, Bombay, 1987).
2. Michael Beer: *Organization Change and Development: A Systems View* (Goodyear Publishing, California, 1980).
3. W. Burke: *Organization Development: A Process of Learning and Change* (Addison Wesley, Massachusetts, 1994).
4. T.G. Cummings and C.G. Worley: *Organization Development and Change* (West Publishing Co., Minnesota, 1993).

5. M. Hammer: *Deep Change: How Operational Innovation can Change Your Company* (HBR, Vol. 4, pp. 84-93, 2004).
6. Gordon L. Lippitt: *Visualizing Change: Model Building and the Change Process* (University Associates Inc., California, 1973).

Chapter 8

Conflict Situations and Management Systems

A primitive society uses primitive procedures for coping with differences and conflicts; a feudal society employs feudal concepts and principles. A modern industrialised nation's approach to the management of disagreements and conflicts reflects its more sophisticated philosophy, values and social system as do all the other principles and procedures employed by organisations within that society.

– Rensis Likert and J. Gibson Likert

Learning Objectives

After reading this chapter you will be able to:

1. Define conflict and comprehend the typical situations resulting into conflict in different levels of the organisation.
2. Suggest ways to discover conflict in time and methods to cope with differences.
3. Analyse how conflicts are resolved in different management systems?
4. Explain 'Win-lose' and 'Win-win' strategies.

Conflict Situations and Management Systems

A conflict may be defined as an active effort by an individual or a group for its own preferred interests at the cost of others. Some conflict is inevitable in any organisation because of basic divergence of interests between the subordinates and management. Some typical conflict situations are given below:

(a) Production personnel feel that quite a few labour leaders have access to the personnel department, and information about any disciplinary action proposed to be taken by the department is leaked out to these leaders and it has its reactions at the shop floor.

(b) Quality control staff feel that they are unnecessarily pressurised for okaying defective components on grounds such as the components are functionally all right; production would be held up; or that such a practice was followed in the past, etc.

(c) Accounts people feel that the operative departments are not cost-conscious. In their opinion, some of the expenses which could be easily avoided are incurred on untenable grounds. When they object to such payments, they are pressurised from the top.

(d) Officers feel that they should go on strike while the 'iron is hot', but their leaders, who are in league with the management, adopt delaying tactics to cool down the tempers and thus render any action meaningless.

(e) Management seeks to rationalise costs by installing automatic plants and labour-saving devices. Workers look upon this as a potential threat to their jobs and earnings and refuse to accept any proposal aimed at rationalisation.

(f) Head of one department leaks some vital information about another head to one of his subordinates, who takes advantage of it and instigates other members of the department against his counterpart.

(g) A supervisor is alleged to have misbehaved with a worker. Shop floor employees in all departments stop work and demand his immediate dismissal. He may be in the good books of the management and his immediate boss may refuse to recommend any action against him.

(h) At the negotiating table, workers are promised certain benefits, which the management fails to honour. The workers lose faith in the management and give a strike call.

Necessity of Conflict

Despite best efforts and management practices, conflict between the management and workers will occur in one way or another. Reality demands that this fact should be accepted. A total absence of conflict would be an unbelievable statement. It does not mean good management either. On the other hand, it is a strong indication that something is wrong and perhaps conflicts are being suppressed by brutal and strong tactics. This is also an indication that an explosive situation is developing and violence could erupt any day.

It does not pay to seek to resolve conflict by either trying to defer it indefinitely or by denying the legitimate rights of the workers to express their independent views and participate in the decision-making process, etc. The highest levels of creativity are found in organisations which deliberately stimulate innovative minds by encouraging diversity and difference of opinion among persons engaged in tasks where imaginative thinking yields valuable results. Peltz calls this stimulation the 'dither effect'. This stimulation shakes people out of their comfortable ruts and makes them think anew.

It is also wrong to think or insist that conflict can be resolved somehow but its intensity can certainly be reduced and violence avoided.

Therefore, in order to avoid violence, a mature management should always be willing to discuss matters and bring suppressed conflict to the surface where it can be triggered off. If conflict cannot be totally eliminated, it can at least bring the suppressed facts to the surface, remove misunderstandings, prevent rumour spreading and lead to the re-examination of basic issues, assumptions and practices to bring about such adjustments which would help not only to resolve conflict but also improve upon organisational effectiveness.

At times conflict may even be engineered by some managements/unions to maintain the health of the organisation and weed out what is not desirable. Either side employs an extreme strategy and the attitude of win or lose. The occurrence of such a battle has many far-reaching effects. When such a situation is inevitable, a battleground of one's own choices is prepared by each party to inflict defeat on the opponent.

Discovery of Conflict

An important step towards the resolution of conflict is discovery and exposure of the possible source of conflict.

A usual method of discovery is receiving a complaint or a grievance or a suggestion. In a situation of conflict, it is immaterial whether the grievance is written or oral, valid or untrue, logical or illogical. It has to be assumed that once discontent has arisen, it must have something to do with the functioning of either the management, the labour or the union. Therefore, it should be properly looked into.

Managers, during their rounds, discussions, meetings or going through performance analysis reports get ample opportunities to discover if anything is going wrong anywhere. An experienced manager familiar with human psychology can visualise the trouble spots and can prevent a complaint from becoming a grievance.

A supervisor knows his workers to quite an extent. Whenever he observes any significant behavioural change in a worker or a group of workers, he should try to get to the facts and analyse the situation. Sometimes he might even know the reason which, for example, could be failure to get an expected promotion or denial of training overseas that was promised. In such cases, even if the individual does not say anything, his attitude to work changes temporarily. Dissatisfaction among workers comes to the surface in the shape of the charter of demands, union meetings and resolutions, representations, individual disputes, threat to direct action, etc.

Many a time disagreements lead to resignations. If an 'exit interview', as it is called, is tactfully organised, many facts may come to light. This may provide the individual with an excellent opportunity to discuss the nature of complaint or grievance that has been so strong as to compel him to resign or quit his job.

Coping with Differences

'Might is right' was the principle followed in primitive societies to resolve differences. The feudal society employed feudal means. Modern society which believes in individual freedom and dignity employs more sophisticated philosophy and means to resolve conflicts.

The philosophy associated with the activities within an organisation such as its leadership, decision-making, communication, motivation and control, determines the ways of meeting conflict situations. Every organisation in the operation of all its characteristics, including its customary procedures for resolving disagreements and conflicts, displays an orderly and internally consistent pattern.

Management System

In an organisation, the methods of resolving conflict depend upon the system of management being followed. Although the principles used by the managers are essentially the same in any industry, the specific methods of applying these principles usually differ, depending upon the situation. The basic principles used by the managers have been integrated into a general organisational system as indicated below:

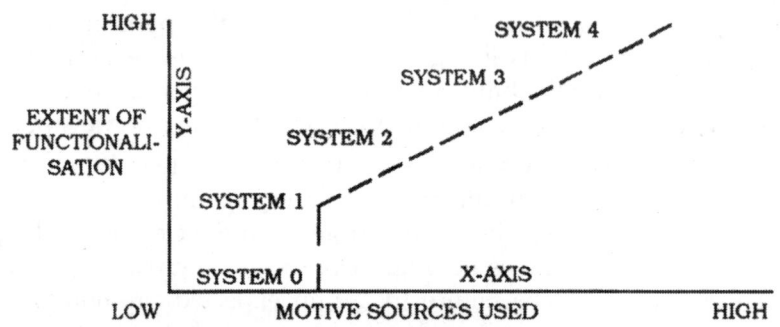

Fig. 8.1: Management Systems

The given figure shows schematic location of System 0 (little differentiation in function, excessive span of control, confusion about individual's role, etc.) to System 4 in relation to the degree of functionalisation and the motivational forces used (involving people in decision-making, recognition of achievements, providing opportunity for self-actualisation, etc.)

The Y-axis shows the extent to which the basic concepts of functionalisation are applied through appropriate structure; the X-axis shows the extent to which major innate motive sources are used in ways that reinforce rather than conflict with one another. The manner in which an organisation copes with conflict is governed by the operative characteristics of its interaction influence network and the management system upon which its interaction influence network is based. The more an organisation moves towards System 4, less will be the intensity and the harmful effects of the conflict.

Social Systems

Every conflict (other than that internal to a particular individual) involves an interaction among persons, groups, organisations or large entities and occurs within a social system. The higher the effectiveness of the social system, the greater is the probability of resolving the conflict constructively. Mature and effective social systems can be created and can be used in every conflict situation by those who wish to see the conflict resolved more constructively and successfully.

A period of time is required to build an effective social system and have its full potential ready to use in a difficult, emotion-laden conflict. For this reason, it is desirable to anticipate major crises and create a social system which can take care of them, before the conflict occurs.

The implication that changes are needed to improve management of conflict is clear. When inadequacies become evident in the existing interaction influence network, substantial improvement can be made in the management of conflict by strengthening the interaction influence network at the level which exposes weakness.

Win or Lose Strategy

Win-lose, in one form or another, appears to be the prevailing strategy for resolving conflict. Confrontation, non-negotiable demands and ultimatums have become the order of the day as a method to deal with deep-rooted differences. The party marshals all its forces in order to gain what it has already decided it wants.

The approach, according to Likerts, displays the following characteristics:

— When inter-group conflict occurs with the sole aim of winning, all other possible outcomes such as finding a mutually acceptable solution, are overlooked. Group loyalty and team spirit become more evident. Members close ranks, spirits go up and every one starts working hard towards their chosen objective.

— Leadership in a group extends to a few persons or to a single person but generally to extremists. A clear-cut power structure emerges quite rapidly.

— The dictatorial method of dealing with people lays the foundation of serious internal strife which often backfires after the pressures created by the inter-group conflict subside.

— Perceptual distortions occur. The members of each group develop and express hostile attitudes towards the members of the other group. Each group tends to select individuals seen as strong, aggressive and good orators or speakers for its solutions.

- The representative who wins becomes a group hero. The one who loses is looked upon as a traitor. Both (the hero in order to win, and the loser in order to avoid being seen as a traitor) discard objectivity in their role as representatives and never engage in unbiased problem solving and evaluation of solutions.
- The winning group glorifies its leader who becomes complacent and easygoing. There is little motivation to strive for improvement. The defeated group displays bitterness among its members. Internal fighting and splintering occurs.

In some cases, the outcome, whether it is a win or a loss, becomes hazardous. The losing party immediately begins to strengthen its forces, by ethical or unethical means, to prepare for a confrontation in future and deploys every opportunity to undermine its opponent. Thus, a process of retaliation is generated which aims at converting a defeat into a win. Such a process of retaliation prevents cooperation and collaboration which are so necessary for collective betterment.

Bargaining, negotiating, compromising and similar approaches to handle the conflict are essentially forms of win-lose confrontation. They all start with a relatively clear solution which each party of the conflict prefers and wishes to attain. They fail to create problem-solving orientations.

Win-win Strategy

A better approach to conflict resolution is the 'Win-Win Strategy'. It is based on coordinated fact-gathering coupled with group decision process. The factual information is analysed and interpreted by the group in terms of experience which is shared in the process of discussion. This leads to less diverse experience being focussed on decision-making processes. Alternative course of action is examined and ultimately narrowed down to a mutually acceptable solution. It becomes the solution reached by all and not by one party or person. The parties involved in the conflict feel motivated when they are fully involved in the process of gathering and analysing facts and figures, weighing alternative courses of action, and deciding in favour of the most acceptable one. It is the responsibility of the leadership to involve the parties in the process of conflict resolution.

Sometimes the parties in dispute agree to refer it to a third party for a possible solution. A third person or party may examine the facts more objectively and in an unbiased manner than the parties in dispute. But in most cases, it may be desirable that the parties themselves evolve some formula to resolve the conflict rather than depend upon a third party.

Meeting Hostile Situations in Practice

Very often supervisors have to face unpleasant situations, or a hostile employee or union representative; such hostile situations can arise out of anything. Some egoistic workers may not like being told by their supervisors how to do a particular job; some may resent or complain about frequent interference by the supervisors. At times union representatives may tend to be hostile or militant while losing ground during discussions or while failing to be logical in support of their arguments. A hostile atmosphere may suddenly arise out of nowhere owing to an unfortunate incident or accident. Sometimes such hostile situations may be real and at times just created with ulterior motives.

At times such confrontations take an exacting toll on either side. Therefore, the supervisor has to think and devise ways and means of changing hostile situations into manageable ones. There are many ways of doing this and some are discussed hereafter.

Patient Hearing

Supervisors should give an impression to the aggrieved individual or group that he/she or they are being listened to attentively and patiently. The aggrieved employee must feel that the supervisor has the same perception that he or she has.

When the employee explains a point or a situation, the supervisor should note those areas where possible agreement can be reached, and the minor demands that can be acceded to. When some mutual agreement is reached in limited areas, the core difficulties envisaged should be explained carefully and slowly and with clarity, at the same time watching the reaction of the employee.

The skill of effective listening in a tense situation can lead to an opportunity for constructive response. It may be noted that whatever be the controversy, it would help the supervisor if he attempts to emphasise the points and areas of agreement first and then talk about the areas of disagreement.

Controlled Reaction

A good supervisor resists reacting instantly to what the other person has to say. The supervisor who responds calmly and conserves emotional energy can contribute more towards problem solving. Controlled reaction also helps effective listening.

To react constructively, it is important to evaluate the ideas of the employee and not the attitude or the manner in which he is putting up his case. If the objective of the meeting is to solve a problem, the supervisor should not hasten to assert his position and try to prove that the employee is wrong or that he does not understand the situation. In a heated argument, a party is more likely to respond to the manner in which something has been said rather than to what has been said.

Diffusion

'Anger begets anger' is an old saying. Unless one party has a powerful personality, coupled with the authority to silence the other or make him surrender, such a situation should be avoided to the extent possible. The supervisor, while listening, should learn to contain himself and bear with the other side with as little interruption as possible. When it gets difficult to find an immediate solution to an otherwise explosive situation, he should try to diffuse the situation with a promise to investigate into the matter or even to form a committee to investigate into the matter.

Alertness for a Catch

Supervisors should always be alert to a catch or hidden traps specially during discussions with the union representative or groups. The real issues may be camouflaged by gestures, irrelevant examples, repetitions, angry comments, jokes, clouding of the issues, and other distractions. This happens very often when the group or the spokesman of the group starts losing the argument or logic of the case.

Right Atmosphere

A comfortable and quiet place should be selected for such discussions. The aggrieved should be made to feel at home. He should be assured that his supervisor/manager is paying full attention to the problem he is discussing. He should also feel that enough time and importance is being given to explore possible solutions to the problem. Sometimes, in order to give the employee the impression that his problem would be listened to without interruption and that the meeting would be as congenial as possible, a supervisor may have to direct his assistant or secretary (loudly) that no telephone calls should be connected and that no visitor be admitted to his office during the course of this important meeting. This satisfies the ego of the employee and creates a congenial atmosphere for mutual communication.

It must be understood that creating the right atmosphere, listening to learn, controlling reaction, reacting constructively, and diffusing the situation are some of the methods by which a hostile employee can be made to react in a positive manner.

Situation Analysis

Continental Products Private Ltd., is engaged in the production and marketing of cosmetics and beverages. For a number of years it has done a very good business. From a one-man company it grew into a professional and functionally-managed company. The production, marketing and product development departments work with a close understanding of one another. Their products, in spite of increasing costs (owing to higher research and development cost, marketing expenses, etc.), enjoy a national stature and sell well.

Two years back, they hired a new general manager – a very dynamic person, a hard worker himself and a go-getter. He does not believe in any excuses. His motto is that the set targets (sometimes unrealistic) must be met at any cost. He does not believe in democratic decisions or in the consensus of his senior managers. When he calls a meeting to arrive at some decisions, he generally gives his own ideas and expects other managers to blindly follow him as he believes that he is always right.

Last year the organisation saw a change in the union leadership. It went into the hands of a group more aggressive than the earlier one. Before this changeover, the general manager used to crush the moves of the then docile union and prevent the workers from either raising a grievance or protesting against any action of the management.

Within a year the industrial peace of the company has been disturbed to a great extent under the new union leader. The attitude of go-slow, work stoppage, wildcat strikes, absenteeism, and demands of overtime and wage increase has taken over. Union leaders have started to feel that the management has no effective machinery for negotiation and settlement of disputes. The management now wants to crush the rightful trade union activities by its brutal force.

Another disturbing factor that is greatly influencing the functioning of the company is the marketing of a similar product by another company, backed by effective publicity, at a lower price. The company under discussion is, therefore, finding it difficult to sell its so-called highly profitable items at a favourable price which can offset its high overhead costs and union demands.

The general manager has given a call to bring down the cost of the products. The union has been unresponsive owing to their basic conflict with the management and managerial attitudes. They have made it plain that any reduction in the overall strength of the workers would be resisted physically and there would be stoppage of work.

The marketing department could not achieve its sale targets. The stocks in the warehouses have started piling up. The company wants to decrease the selling prices of the products and introduce discount sales, and for this they want the manufacturing department to cut its production cost.

The manufacturing departments are finding it difficult even to maintain their production cost which is actually mounting due to low productivity, rise in cost of materials, increase in the dearness allowance, and increased downtime of equipment. The production manager is accusing the marketing department of setting high marketing and distribution costs. He wants that marketing and distribution costs should be cut down.

The Finance Manager blames the high research and development costs for lower profits. The production manager and the marketing manager have also joined the finance manager in raising their voice to press research and development to undertake a crash programme to come up with a new and superior product for the market at a cheaper price which could be sold at a profit.

The inter-departmental conflicts coupled with the management-union conflict have made a heavy dent into the financial capability of the company. The share prices of the company have started declining rapidly and it has become evident that the company would either become a sick unit or face closure.

The Board of Directors is becoming very worried. The chairman of the company and the Board of Directors had to call the General Manager to find out as to how the deteriorating conditions could be checked, financial stability maintained and market shares recaptured. They did not got a satisfactory answer. So they decided to call the managers. Each manager started blaming the other and the union.

Suppose, you have been invited as a consultant by the company. What would you suggest to tackle the prevailing situation and put back the company on track?

Review Questions

1. 'Some conflict is inevitable in any organisation.' Comment.
2. What steps are needed to discover conflict in an organisation?
3. What are the ways to cope with differences? Under what circumstances 'might is right' still works?

4. What motivating sources are employed under different management systems to resolve conflicts?
5. How does a social system help in the resolution of conflicts?
6. What are the characteristics of 'win or lose' strategy?
7. What are the merits of 'win-win' strategy? Discuss the role of management in creating a situation favourable to such a strategy?

Further Readings

1. R.A. Baron, S.P. Fortin, R.I. Frei. and M.L. Shack L: *Reducing Organisational Conflict and Effectiveness of Organisational Teams* (Journal of Organisational Behaviour, Vol. 22, pp. 309-328, 2001).
2. W.G. Bennis and J.M. Thomas: *Management of Change and Conflict* (Penguin, Harmondsworth 1973).
3. Debra L. Nelson and James C. Quick: *Organizational Behaviour: Foundations, Realities and Challenges* (Cengage Learning, New Delhi, 2008).
4. John R. Ogilvie and Mary L. Carsky: *Building Emotional Intelligence in Negotiations* (The International Journal of Conflict Management, Vol. 13 , pp. 381-400, 2002).
5. Stephen P. Robbins: *Organizational Behaviour: Concepts, Controversies and Applications* (Prentice Hall of India Pvt. Ltd. New Delhi, 1985).

Part III
Managing People

Chapter Structure

Chapter 9. Manpower Planning and Selection

Chapter 10. Job Evaluation and Enrichment

Chapter 11. Performance Appraisal and Promotion

Chapter 12. Training and Development

Chapter 13. Compensation and Incentives

Chapter 9

Manpower Planning and Selection

If people of poor calibre are hired, nothing much else can be accomplished – and Gresham's law will work: the bad people will drive out the good (or cause them to deteriorate).

– Robert Heller

(The Business of Winning)

Learning Objectives

After reading this chapter you will be able to:

1. Understand why manpower requirement needs to be assessed, located and harnessed.
2. Elaborate the steps to be taken for long-term and short-term manpower planning.
3. Develop a selection procedure which ensures appointment of the right people for the right job at the right time.
4. Focus on the need for personal research and records.

Though the organisation of men for managing a purpose is an age-old thing, the science of management is still in nascent stages.

Manpower is a primary resource without which other resources like money, material etc. cannot be put to use. Even a fully automatic unit such as an unmanned satellite requires manpower to execute it and plan further improvements/activities. That is why man learned the use of manpower much before he learned to use other resources.

Manpower Planning

In order to achieve a goal, manpower requirement needs to be assessed, located and harnessed. Manpower planning requires not only a simple assessment of the number of men required but also their categories and skills as well as their balanced allocation. Improper planning may lead to either over-staffing or under-staffing, both of which should be avoided. Over-staffing not only increases direct cost (salary) but adversely affects the cost of training, housing amenities etc., besides production cost. Under-staffing also affects production morale and, therefore, industrial relations.

Optimum manpower planning therefore assumes importance. It should aim at:

- avoiding imbalances in distribution or allocation of manpower
- controlling the cost aspect of human resources
- formulating transfer and succession policy

Manpower planning is needed wherever production of goods and services is involved. It is an important factor of labour productivity and profitability of the enterprise. In an industrial undertaking this is done very carefully by:

External agencies such as professional consultants and suppliers of plant and machinery for they have the knowledge of working of similar units. It is generally done in the initial stages or when internal agencies do not have the required expertise for manpower planning.

Internal agencies such as the personnel department, industrial engineering, plant manager and finance department as all these agencies are interested in production, productivity, industrial relations and other aspects of manpower planning.

Bases of Manpower Planning

Manpower planning is done on the basis of:

- Growth plans which provide information about expansion, modernisation, diversification of business and new projects to be commissioned with likely commissioning dates and details about manpower requirements.

- Separation data available from company records. Separation due to superannuation may be known easily, but those due to future resignations, transfers, terminations and voluntary retirements may be projected based upon past experience and the company policy in this regard.
- Manpower used, various grades offered, etc., in similar plants outside. These may give broad guidelines of the requirements. However, the guidelines may be modified to suit the process, layout, local conditions and other associated factors like the extent of mechanisation, climatic conditions, statutory requirements, social systems, etc.
- The experience of the manager based on direct and intimate knowledge of the working of similar shops. This can act as a guide to determine manpower requirement. However, *ad hoc* manpower decided on this basis should be subjected to 'work study' and 'activity sampling' techniques for containment, rectification of imbalances and manpower requirement.
- Job analysis and knowledge of work and historical records (if available) to determine manpower requirements, skills, responsibilities required of the job holder, type of position to be manned, etc.

PERSPECTIVE	"Grow Your Own Timber Philosophy" – NTPC
	NTPC follows its commitment that employees are individuals and not just employees under its "Grow Your Own Timber" philosophy to enable their growth. Its aim is to develop leaders at all levels of the organisation. Fresh graduates from colleges and university campuses are hired and groomed in-house for future leadership positions. The grooming programme includes: * Planned training interventions in career progression to instil competencies for progression to the next stage of their careers right from the level of junior Executive Directors. * Assessment centres and 360 degree feedback systems that have been set in place to assess leadership qualities of employees at the senior management level. * ED Programme at IIM-B, coupled with experimental learning and executive coaching, that has been initiated for middle management levels to suit the diversification and expansion plans. * Engineering graduates in specialised disciplines from IITs and NITs being inducted through campus recruitment programme. * A comprehensive IT-enabled Knowledge Management System that has been introduced to converge multiple streams of learning experiences into a readily accessible repository of information. HR systems are continuously renewed based upon employee feedback.

Time studies are used for setting up standard times which help to work out norms of manpower requirements.

Other factors which influence the determination of manpower requirements are:

Layout

If an equipment works in isolation (say a drill or lathe) but needs continuous supervision (say by excavators, etc.) then one man per machine is essential. If a group of machines works in unison, the whole group may be attended to by one or more persons. If equipment is not in continuous operation, one person may look after more than one equipment.

Requirements

There are certain positions in mines, electrical installations, hazardous places where welfare amenities have to be provided as per statutory regulations. First aid posts, creches, etc. fall under this category. For example, the Mines Creche Rules 1966 stipulate the number of categories of staff to be provided.

Shifts

Manpower requirements are determined by the number of shifts in which the work is to be carried out – whether in a general shift or in combined shifts. Once the number of persons per shift has been determined, this will be multiplied by the number of working shifts. When work goes on round the clock, manpower has to be provided for all the shifts.

Leave Reserve

Certain allowances have to be made for manpower requirements thus worked out as human beings cannot work on all days of the year. They have to be allowed regular leave for certain periods in a year depending on the legislation or mutual agreement between the unions and the management on the basis of leave availed of during the study period. A certain percentage towards leave reserves is added to arrive at the number of required manpower.

A simple example is give to illustrate this.

Problem

Calculate the number of crane drivers needed for working in a soaking pit where hot ingots are handled.

Data

    Number   : 5 nos
    Number of working shifts   : 3 per day

Working hours per shift fixed
in view of the working conditions : 6 hours

Allowance for weekly-off and
leave reserves determined by study : 20%

Calculation

Number of operators required : $\dfrac{5 \times 3 \times 8 \times 1.20}{6}$

or 20 × 1.20

or 24

The Annual Manpower Plan

An annual manpower plan for the next financial year may be worked out a few months in advance of the close of the current financial year.

The process followed would be:

— Preparing a detailed designation-wise inventory of retirements and separations.

— Carrying out an analysis of the criticality of jobs where separations were taking place and categorising them into jobs where full replacement was essential, partial replacement sufficed, and where no replacement was required, at least for the year under consideration.

— Working out a schedule of the additions/modifications to be made to the required manpower for the year on account of commissioning of the old units.

— Identifying people who could be redeployed for posts that need to be filled.

PERSPECTIVE	War For Talent
	Shortage of qualified personnel in pharma organisations in India is due to:
	Entry of New MNCs
	Experienced and qualified people are required for production, development, sales and product management. People working in existing medium and large pharma companies will be their target.
	Big Retail Groups
	Trained people are required by big retail groups setting pharmacies in India. They will look towards people working in Indian companies.
	Clinical Research
	Large pharma organisations are shifting clinical research to India. BSc graduates who were their prime source of supply will like to shift to clinical research as it offers better emoluments and career development opportunities.
	Growth of Pharma Sector
	Many pharma companies are expanding fast both in India as well as abroad. This will further affect the war for talent.

- Working out the balance that would have to be not through external recruitment.
- Checking whether the figure of recruitment thus arrived at fulfils the expectations of minimising external recruitment, and within the guidelines the corporate office may have laid down regarding the numbers to be recruited, fraction of separations to be recouped, or labour productivity targets.
- In case the recruitment figures worked out are too high, critically re-examining the previous assumptions so as to pare recruitment down to the required level.
- Fractionalising all data so as to have a one to one correspondence with recruitment categories.
- Making a separate plan for each specific recruitment category, considering the in-position manpower, additional requirements for new units, reductions due to closing down of old units, changes in manning patterns due to changes in technology/automation, and identified surpluses.
- Pinpointing not only the numbers to be redeployed but also the actual people to be redeployed. The attempt would be to match the existing skills with requirements as far as possible. Retraining plan would have to be evolved, if needed.

Medium and Long Range Plans

Manpower plans for the next 5 years and next 15 years (synchronised with the national 5-year plans) should also be drawn up periodically apart from the annual plans. This exercise should normally be undertaken every 5 years and be available one year ahead of the commencement of the next five-year plan. However, if major changes in the overall plans of the company in respect of expansion/modernisation, etc. take place at any point of time, the 5-year and 15-year plans should be revised to match the changed circumstances.

It is necessary to use a sound forecasting model for setting long-term policies and targets.

Manpower Planning Models

Models have been developed by Berry, Mason, Haire, etc. that illustrate the flow of people into and out of an organisation. The examination of such flows enables an organisation to predict its short-run human resources needs. One such model is shown here. Correlation and study of past data on managers leaving the organisation (for instance, twenty on an average quit, retire, are discharged or become ill in management level III) and managers being promoted (for instance, ten, on an average, will be promoted to level IV from level III) helps to predict how many new managers must be hired at each level to maintain a stable system. The model can also be used to predict the consequences of other contingencies such as the policy of promotion from within or the impact of increased or decreased recruitment and turnover. Such models aid in the analysis of career planning and human resource forecasting.

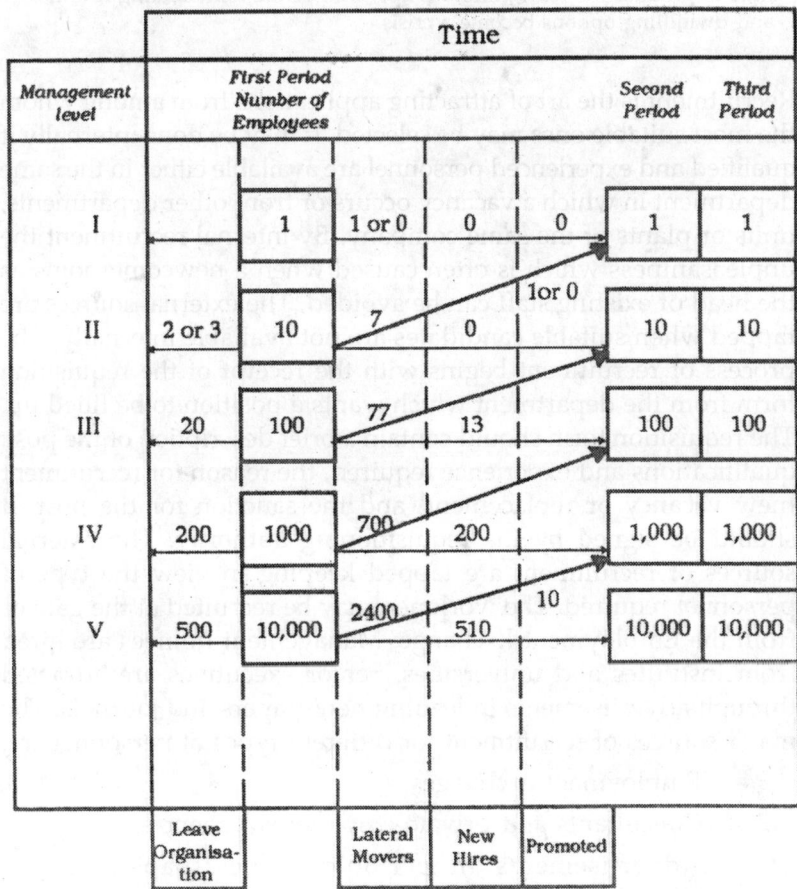

Fig. 9.1: A Model of Human Resource Career/Movements Overtime (Haire)

> **PERSPECTIVE**
>
> **Succession Planning: Intel**
>
> Simple continuity is not Intel's goal in making changes at the top, however, evolving the business is. For instance, when Grove stepped down from the top spot in 1998, he was still a highly effective leader. If continuity had been Intel's overwhelming concern, Grove might have stayed for another three years, until he reached the mandatory retirement age of 65 years. But instead, he handed the baton to Barrett, who then implemented a strategy for growing Intel's business through product extensions.
>
> Every Intel CEO has left his mark in a different way. Through structured succession planning, Intel ensures that it chooses the CEO who is right for the challenges the company is facing, and not simply the person next in line. And by changing CEOs early, the company gives its new leadership time to produce the reinvention needed, well before deteriorating revenues and dwindling options become a crisis.

Recruitment and Selection

Recruitment is the art of attracting applications from among whom the most suitable ones may be selected. It may be done internally if qualified and experienced personnel are available either in the same department in which a vacancy occurs or from other departments, units or plants of the same company. By internal recruitment the unpleasantness which is often caused when a newcomer joins as the head of existing staff can be avoided. The external sources are tapped when suitable candidates are not available internally. The process of recruitment begins with the receipt of the requisition form from the department which wants a position to be filled up. The requisition form should contain a brief description of the post, qualifications and experience required, the reason for recruitment (new vacancy or replacement) and the sanction for the post. It should be signed by the requisitioning authority. The external sources of recruitment are tapped keeping in view the type of personnel required. The workmen may be recruited at the gate or from the Employment Exchange. Management trainees are hired from institutes and universities. Senior executives are attracted through advertisements in leading newspapers and journals. The major sources of recruitment for different types of personnel are:

- Employment exchanges
- Consultants and private employment agencies
- Advertisements in periodicals, newspapers, radio, television and internet
- Deputation
- Universities, management institutes and colleges
- Word of mouth
- Trade unions

Employment exchanges register candidates seeking various types of jobs. Under the Compulsory Notification Act of 1959 the employers are required to notify certain types of vacancies to the nearest employment exchange and recruit the candidates from among the applicants registered with them. Skilled and unskilled workers and clerical staff are recruited mainly through employment exchanges.

Consultants and private agencies assist in locating technical and managerial staff. They charge for the services rendered.

Advertising in newspapers, magazines, radio, television and internet is one of the most effective sources of attracting prospective candidates. It also helps in building the image of the company. The advertisement should be informative and should have an attractive layout. Since advertising is a costly affair, the advertisement copy must be prepared carefully.

Factual information regarding the job; requirements of age, qualifications and experience; salary and perks attached to the position and important conditions of service; time limit and the mode of applying should be clearly indicated in the advertisement. There are agencies to help companies in drafting, publishing and releasing the advertisements. Executive officers, trainees and secretarial staff from different localities, regions and states are attracted to apply for company jobs through advertisements.

Deputationists are appointed mainly in public sector undertakings. Civil servants are deputed for manning senior and middle level positions for a specified period.

Universities, management institutes and professional and technical institutes are approached by business houses for the recruitment of management trainees and technical apprentices. Campus interviews provide the employer with an opportunity to meet a number of prospective candidates at one place on a short notice and also get acquainted with the course content, and the training programmes available at the institution.

The word of mouth method may be resorted to by inviting the company employees to recommend suitable candidates working elsewhere but known or related to them. The employees may approach the company on their own with recommendations in this regard. Some of the family managed undertakings in the private sector resort to this method of recruitment which does not involve any expenditure. But the number of candidates that such a process may attract is small.

The trade unions help in recruiting workers at the gate. In companies where the closed shop system is practised, workers are recruited on the recommendations of the recognised union.

When applications are received and the last date for receipt of applications is over, the personnel division is required to sort out the applications. The shortlisting may be done in three categories:
- Clearly unsuitable
- Possible
- Probable

Some applications may be put in the reserved category for jobs other than those advertised or likely to be advertised in view of the qualifications and experience of the candidates. Where the number of positions vacant is limited and the number of applicants is large, the criteria for choosing candidates for interview may be strict so as to eliminate the average and below average candidates from the selection process in the very beginning. The normal curve of distribution of applicants may be as under:

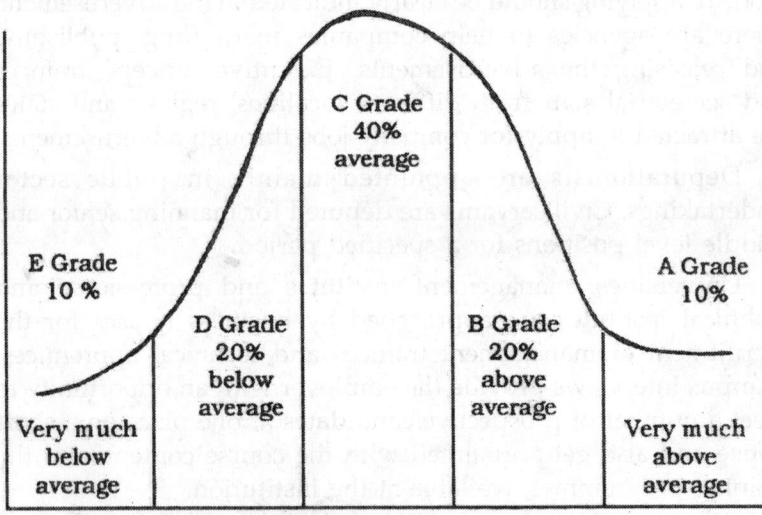

Fig. 9.2: Distribution of Applications

E-Grade 10% very much below average	D-Grade 20% below average	C-Grade 40% average	B-Grade 20% above average	A-Grade 10% very much above average
4	8	12	16	20

The candidates in categories A and B only may be considered for interview. Application forms may be mailed to them with a cover to collect their detailed bio-data.

Application Form

The application form is designed to contain detailed information about the candidates. It also helps in comparing the merits of the applicants. The information required in the application form will include some or all of the following:

(i) Post applied for.
(ii) Personal data: name, address, telephone number, age, sex, marital status, children, nationality, next of kin.
(iii) Education: school, college and university attended, degree/ diploma passed, year of passing, subjects offered, grade or division obtained.
(iv) Professional qualification(s).
(v) Languages known: ability to read, write and speak.
(vi) Employment history of all jobs since leaving college/ university, dates from and to, employer's name, address and nature of business, position and duties held, reasons for leaving.
(vii) Personal circumstances; when required, prepared to serve anywhere or not, etc.
(viii) Medical history; brief details of any serious illness, disability, major operation, etc.
(ix) Interest, hobbies, sports and other activities.
(x) Anything else which an applicant may like to add.
(xi) References

Space for the candidate's signature, date and place and for office use is given at the end. The printed forms generally contain too much printed matter leaving little space for the applicant to fill in his particulars. There should be at least four times as much space to write in the form as is covered by the print. Some companies have forms printed in different colours for different categories of posts. This facilitates the sorting out and handling of applications by the concerned officials. A specimen application form of a large organisation is given on the next page.

APPLICATION FORM

M/s. . . . . Ltd.

Please Use English
*Delete as Necessary

Please Print or Type

ATTACH TWO RECENT PHOTOGRAPHS (PASSPORT SIZE)

*MR./MRS./MISS	SURNAME	NAME	MAIDEN NAME (MARRIED WOMEN)
PRESENT			TEL. NO. HOME. . . . .
PERMANENT			BUSINESS. . . . .
POSITION APPLIED FOR (1) (2)	SALARY EXPECTED		WHEN ABLE TO COMMENCE
PASSPORT NO.	DATE OF ISSUE		PLACE OF ISSUE

DATE OF BIRTH	AGE	PLACE OF BIRTH	NATIONALITY	DIALECT

In case of Emergency whom shall we notify? Name. . . . .
Relationship . . . .
Address . . . . Telephone . . . .

EDUCATION	NAME AND ADDRESS OF INSTITUTION	FROM	TO	DEGREE/CERTIFICATE OBTAINED WITH DIVISION	AREA OF STUDY/SUBJECTS OFFERED
PROFESSIONAL TRAINING/HIGHER UNV. DEGREE					
UNIVERSITY DEGREE (POST GRADUATE)					
UNIVERSITY DEGREE (GRADUATE)					
SECONDARY SCHOOL					
MATRICULATION					

LANGUAGES	SPOKEN			WRITTEN			UNDERSTAND		
	EXCEL	WELL	FAIR	EXCEL	WELL	FAIR	EXCEL	WELL	FAIR

SKILLS (GIVE DETAILS)				
HEALTH STATUS	HEIGHT .... metres	WEIGHT .... kilos	COLOUR OF HAIR	COLOUR OF EYES
	Any Disabilities or Handicaps?			
	When did you last see a Physician? For what reason?			
	Any major illness in the recent past? If so, give details.			

EMPLOYMENT RECORDS

Start with your present position and work back. List all employment. (ATTACH CERTIFICATES)

COMPANY OR FIRM			ADDRESS	MONTHLY SALARY
NATURE OF BUSINESS			NATURE OF YOUR WORK	ADDITIONAL PERKS
NAME OF SUPERVISOR	FROM	TO	REASON FOR LEAVING	
				MONTHLY SALARY
NATURE OF BUSINESS			NATURE OF YOUR WORK	ADDITIONAL PERKS
NAME OF SUPERVISOR	FROM	TO	REASON FOR LEAVING	
COMPANY OR FIRM			ADDRESS	MONTHLY SALARY
NATURE OF BUSINESS			NATURE OF YOUR WORK	ADDITIONAL PERKS
NAME OF SUPERVISOR	FROM	TO	REASON FOR LEAVING	
COMPANY OR FIRM			ADDRESS	MONTHLY SALARY
NATURE OF BUSINESS			NATURE OF YOUR WORK	ADDITIONAL PERKS
NAME OF SUPERVISOR	FROM	TO	REASON FOR LEAVING	
COMPANY OR FIRM			ADDRESS	MONTHLY SALARY
NATURE OF BUSINESS			NATURE OF YOUR WORK	ADDITIONAL PERKS
NAME OF SUPERVISOR	FROM	TO	REASON FOR LEAVING	

If additional blocks are needed for stating previous employment, use another sheet of paper and attach to this application

CHARACTER REFERENCE LIST 3 OR MORE PERSONS, BUT EXCLUDE RELATIVE OR FORMER EMPLOYER

NAME	ADDRESS	OCCUPATION/ POSITION HELD	LENGTH OF ACQUAINTANCE

RELATIVE(S) OR FRIEND(S). IF ANY, EMPLOYED BY US	NAME	LOCATION	RELATION

FAMILY RECORD

Marital (Mark with an X)
Status   Single........ Married........ Widowed........ Separated........ Divorced........

If married, State
Name of Spouse _____   Occupation _____   Number of Children _____ Boys _____ Girls

RELATIVES : List father, mother, brothers and sisters. If married list names of children.

Name	Relationship	Age	Address	Occupation

Places outside of India you have lived in or visited :

From	To	City	Country

State name of Professional bodies, Club, Society or Organisation that you are a member of, or were a past member of.

State extra curricular activities participated in at School/College

Mark with an "X"	No	Yes	If so, give particulars
Have you ever been discharged from employment because your work or conduct was not satisfactory?			
Do you receive any other income such as retirement pay, compensation for injuries, etc.?			
Have you ever been charged in court?			

May enquiry be made from your present employer regarding your qualifications and character?		
Have you been interviewed for employment in our organisation before?		
Do you take part in politics?		
State reasons as to why you consider yourself suitable for the position applied for.		

DECLARATION

Information entered on this application is voluntarily given by me as a statement of fact and qualifications for the positions applied for and/or hired for.

I authorise the company to secure any information regarding myself and submit the said information to any person, firm, corporation body, bureau, department, police record for the purpose of any investigation which it may desire to make with reference thereto.

I further declare that the statements made by me in this application are true, complete and correct. A false statement or dishonest answer to any question may be grounds for my immediate discharge from employment with the company.

Date   Signature

Interview

An interview is the first face to face interaction between the candidate and the company representatives. It is a *sine qua non* for applicants who qualify in the first screening as probable ones having all the basic requirements. The objectives of selection interviews are to elicit information about the candidate's motives and behaviour, to assess personality, to check the factual information already given by him and to inform him about the job and the company. The interview may be held either in two stages – preliminary and final – or in one stage only. A preliminary interview could help in recruiting the most probable candidates who could be called for the final interview. It must be conducted by skilled interviewers, otherwise some potential candidates may be lost. In some cases companies organise successive interviews, i.e. the same candidate is interviewed by one or more interviewers separately one after another. The panel or the board interviews are, however, more common. The panel may consist of a small number of experts while a board may have a larger number.

The interview may be patterned or open. In a patterned interview a set of questions is already prepared. The interviewers are able to collect information about the candidate in a systematic and uniform manner. The candidate's basic characteristics and motivations should also be probed into by the interviewers to arrive at a judgement. In a non-patterned or open interview, interviewers put such questions as they feel would make the candidate reveal his mind and his strong and weak points.

For recruiting technical and highly skilled personnel, technical interviews may be arranged to assess the competence of the candidates in their own special fields. The technical expert on the selection board should properly assess the candidate's strengths and weaknesses. If he gives his judgement in such terms as a 'nice chap', or 'got rattled easily', or a 'bit glib', he does not take his job seriously.

Each candidate may be interviewed separately or a number of candidates may be interviewed in a group. Personal interview exposes the candidate only before the board, but group interview exposes him before the other applicants also. In a group interview, a candidate must get an opportunity to show his initiative and leadership qualities better than in a personal interview.

The interview aims at selecting the best out of the most probable candidates. It must be conducted in an objective manner. The interviewers should not permit their personal likes and dislikes and prejudices to come in the way of proper assessment of the candidates. They should not allow the filtering of information about the candidate through their own 'subjective screen of views, needs and prejudices'. They are supposed to pay the same degree of attention to all the candidates on similar aspects of performance. The very often committed errors by interviewers are:

- the halo error: giving high rating to the candidates whose liking and disliking seem similar to his own
- the logical error: judging on a wrong yardstick
- the errors of leniency: helping to come out for something which the candidate cannot cope with
- the contrast error: penalising the candidate for having opposite ideas or preferences.

An objective assessment of a candidate's performance would require an unbiased evaluation by the interviewer of the following qualities, as suggested by John Munro Fraser:

1. First impression and physical make-up
2. Qualifications
3. Brain and abilities
4. Motivations
5. Adjustments

The interviewer should keep an open mind till the end of the interview. Too much warming up to the candidate should also be avoided. The candidates should be given an opportunity to talk in a free atmosphere. There should be minimum stress in the beginning so that the candidate does not feel nervous. The room where the interview is conducted should be free from interruptions of telephone calls or visitors. The assessment of the interviews should be recorded immediately after the interviews are over. All members of the board/panel should give their rating on a defined scale such as: A = Outstanding, B = Good, C = Average and D = Poor. Final selection should be made on the basis of consensus as far as possible after discussing the relative merits and demerits of potential candidates who are on the top of the list. A specimen form of interviewer's report of a reputed company is given below:

Specimen Form of Interviewer's Report
For Office Use only

INTERVIEWER'S REPORT	NUMBER CODE		1. OUTSTANDING	2. EXCELLENT	3. GOOD	5. POOR
	CODE	REMARKS			REMARKS	
GENERAL APPEARANCE						
ATTITUDE						
ELOQUENCE						
MENTAL ALERTNESS						
INITIATIVE						
JOB KNOWLEDGE						
DECISION	FIRST INTERVIEW DATE.......... BY..........			SECOND INTERVIEW DATE.......... BY..........		
	JOB TITLE			DEPARTMENT		EMPLOYEES NO
	SALARY ON START		GRADE	SCALE		TO START WORK ON
	REMARKS					
REMARKS	ACCEPTED/NOT ACCEPTED			2. PERSONNEL MANAGER		
	1. DEPARTMENT HEAD			4. ORDER OF MANAGING. DIR./ VICE CHAIRMAN		
	3. GENERAL MANAGER					
	GENERAL REMARKS					
	REFERENCE CHECKS					
CERTIFICATES ATTACHED (FOR PERSONNEL USE ONLY)	NO.	NAME OF COMPANY	ISSUED BY	DATE OF ISSUE		CONTENTS
	1.					
	2.					
	3.					
	4.					

Employment Tests

As a method of selection, the employment tests are an exception rather than the rule. They may be used to supplement the information already collected through the application forms and interviews. The future performance of the candidate in a particular field may be predicted to some extent by the tests specially designed for the purpose. The disappointment which arises from failures and dropouts in training and later on the job can be avoided by the use of the tests of ability and potential of applicants.

The five main groups of psychological tests are:

— Intelligence tests
— Attainment tests
— Aptitude tests
— Interest tests
— Personality tests

Intelligence tests are particularly useful in selecting candidates for jobs which call for problem solving abilities or which involve extensive training. The score of intelligence tests is expressed as intelligent quotient (IQ), which is calculated by the formula:

$$IQ = \frac{\text{Mental age}}{\text{Actual age}} \times 100$$

Different forms of intelligence tests are used for candidates of different age groups.

Attainment tests measure the degree to which a person has acquired knowledge or skill. Tests of knowledge have been developed for spelling, vocabulary, arithmetic, mechanical information and a range of more specialised subjects.

Aptitude tests identify an individual's innate suitability for particular types of work and can indicate whether a man would be more suited to one type of work rather than another. Tests of 'sales aptitude', 'managerial aptitude', 'mechanical aptitude', etc. are used to identify the candidate's potentialities in a chosen area. The General Aptitude Test Battery identifies a candidate's abilities in such areas as verbal comprehension, numerical ability, motor coordination, manual dexterity, general intelligence, etc.

Interest tests help in predicting the areas in which the candidates are most likely to settle down and be satisfied. The candidate's preference for indoor or outdoor jobs, routine or creative work and individual or group responsibilities may be ascertained by administering interest tests.

Personality tests are designed to measure the degree to which an individual possesses such qualities as drive, persuasiveness, self-confidence, stability, etc. The most promising kind of test to throw light on the personality area is the situational test, e.g. the leaderless group discussion.

The psychological tests have some limitations. The predictions based upon these tests cannot be hundred percent correct. Further, the candidates brought up in poor families, and in the rural and backward regions may be put to a disadvantage as compared to those coming from affluent urban families when these tests are used as a primary measure for judging their abilities, levels of maturity, etc. The tests should be properly designed and administered by the experts. They should be used to supplement other methods.

References

References should be sought after the selection is finalised. These may be either in a written form or checked over the telephone. If references are sought before the interview, they may bias the thinking of the members of the selection board. The opinions of the previous employers and other persons referred to by the candidate are only as reliable as the judgement of the person giving them. References may help in checking certain facts given by the candidate in the application form.

Medical Test

The selected candidates are medically examined by the company's doctor or approved medical practitioners. Medical tests may vary from the comprehensive to the nominal, depending upon the nature of the job. The manual jobs may require comprehensive medical tests to prevent infection, detect ailments and complicated diseases.

PERSPECTIVE

Selection Process

Maruti Udyog Ltd

* Initial screening to weed out undesirable/unqualified candidates.
* Application form: traditional references to caste, religion, birth place be avoided as these may lead to discrimination.
* Selection tests are increasingly used to judge attitude, behaviour and performance when the number of candidates is large. Cut-off is decided.
* Employment interview aims at obtaining information about the background, education, training, work history and interests of the candidate and establishing a friendly relationship between the employer and the candidate.
* Medical examination of successful candidates.
* Reference checks.

Appointment Order

The selected candidates are issued letters of appointment after the recommendations of the selection board are approved by competent authority in the company. Appointments at senior positions such as the chief executives, general managers, financial advisors, etc. need the approval of the board of directors. The chief executive may be the approving authority in the case of other posts. An appointment order states the post offered, salary and perquisites, service conditions, duration of the post (permanent, temporary, contractual), reporting authority, time limit for communicating acceptance and joining the post, etc. It is duly signed by the employing authority and becomes the first basis of contractual relationship between the company and the candidate.

Personnel Research

The objective of recruitment these days is not only to select a good person but also to retain a motivated work force as this tends to keep the conflicts low. For this purpose a personnel manager has to fall back on reliable data maintained in his own organisation, researches carried out by other bodies/research institutions or appoint consultants to study a specific area and offer advice. An independent study by a consultant or a research body brings credibility to the findings and recommendations as:

(i) Generally, it is objective and devoid of subjectiveness and prejudices of individuals.

(ii) It is systematic and properly identifies the problem, its magnitude and draws a scientific plan of study.

(iii) It is purposive as the problem is clearly spelt out and the information collected serves the specific purpose of dissecting the problem and seeking answers to it.

(iv) It is scientific. By being systematic and purposive, it identifies methods, tools, approaches and techniques to understand/solve the problem.

(v) It can be generalised. As the study is controlled for specific purposes, extraneous factors and irrelevant matters are not allowed to influence it and clear conclusions which can be generalised are easy to draw.

Personnel research is the task of searching and analysing facts for solving personnel problems and arriving at principles/laws governing their solution. It is necessary for anticipating personnel problems likely to occur; evaluating current policies, changes in policies and practices; predicting employees' response to changes (be it machinery, change of work, promotion policies, staggering holidays, performance appraisals, welfare measures, etc).

Since research is selection of facts in specified areas and search for trends that will help in solving the problems, it can be of various types or an amalgamation of a few types such as: specific case studies, historical studies; opinion survey, exploratory studies, experimental studies. What is important is a sound knowledge of the process of research and various steps that are to be followed through the identification of problems, methods of data collection, analysis and conclusions.

The contents of research reports generally vary depending on the type of study but these should essentially include the following:

1. Title of the study
2. Purpose of the study
3. Statement of the problem clearly and precisely
4. Magnitude of the problem
5. Methods and procedures adopted for the study
6. Limitations of the study, if any
7. Discussions and analysis of the problem
8. How the inference and conclusion have been drawn
9. Area of extended studies and future research
10. References

Personnel Statistics

Depending on the size of the company, a statistical cell to collect and collate data may be helpful in analysing many problems and decision-making processes to reduce conflicts and confrontations. The areas of collection and maintenance of statistics on routine basis could be:

Employee's Record : Age; sex; length of service; region; occupation; size of the family; education; training; salary range; etc. compared occasionally with similar firms. Exchange of statistical reports with a similar industry is a healthy practice after taking due care of the confidential nature of the data.

Transfers : Reason for transfers; whether by request or by the management itself; relationship of expertise with the department; type of work; age; sex; length of service; earning; occupational hazards, etc.

Absenteeism	:	Causes of absenteeism. Correlation with season, age, sex, occupation, department, length of service, health, etc.
Health	:	Cause of illness and whether it is related to the working conditions, age, sex, size of family, etc.
Accident Proneness	:	Analyse accident rates according to department, working environment, age, sex, season/shift, type of accident. Compare the trend of accidents and severity rate.
Grievance and Resignation	:	Analyse cause, subject, department of work, frequency, education level, sex, rank, etc.
Manpower Productivity and Standards	:	Number of employees; time standards; output records; productivity and value added per person according to department, age, sex, qualifications, working environments, etc. compared with similar industries.
Personal Appraisal Reports	:	For purposes of promotion, transfer, training needs, changes before and after training, future development prospects, etc.
Recruitment and Training Expenses	:	Department-wise, trade-wise: qualifications, age and sex for comparison with similar firms.
Payroll Data and Control of Overtime	:	According to trade, department, age, sex, accident, health, etc.
Suggestion Records	:	Suggestions received, reviewed, accepted and rewarded, savings effected, classifying them according to qualifications, department, age, sex, salary, etc.
Service and Welfare Records	:	How the employees are making use of canteens, cafeterias, libraries, recreation and sports facilities to examine the trends.

The data collected, analysed and tabulated should not be merely for the sake of records. It should be periodically analysed and made use of for the good of the company. Data collected should be periodically examined with a similar industry with a view to:

Decreasing	:	absenteeism; resignation, accidents; health hazards; reprimands; grievances; conflicts; disparities; stoppages of work, etc.
Increasing	:	employee effectiveness; utilisation; output; productivity; value added per person; time standards; job security.
Improving	:	working conditions; welfare measures; morale and motivation; suggestion schemes; sense of belonging and pride of working for the company; community/labour relations; industrial peace and safety.

Situation Analysis

(A) An important post of the foreman is to be filled. Two persons, Misra and Lal, are available for the post.

— Misra is 45 and joined the company 25 years back after completing his matriculation. Thereafter, privately and through correspondence courses, he acquired further qualifications and now fulfils the requirements of the post. He has good relations with other departmental heads and is well spoken of. He is somewhat rigid in his ideas and mostly depends on his own experience while taking decisions but generally takes the right decisions.

— Lal is comparatively younger and is 35 years old. He joined the company after graduation and has now acquired 10 year's experience in the company. His working record is also good. He has an open mind and is a good listener. He is not very confident of himself and believes in discussing things with the juniors before taking a decision. His decisions, thus obtained, seldom fail him.

From the standpoint of company's interest and overall efficiency, which man will you prefer and why?

(B) Prasad and Swaminathan are heading two important units as general foremen. Both are qualified and experienced; both generally fulfil the targets assigned to them. However, there is a major behavioural difference between them.

- Prasad goes along excellently well with his superiors. He is a 'yes man' to his bosses. However, he has poor relations with his subordinates. His juniors do not like his attitude. He generally does what he is told to do by his superiors and at times goes out of his way to fulfil the desires of his superiors.
- Swaminathan does not get along with his superiors simply because he is not a 'yes man' and makes technical decisions mostly on merit rather than on hunches or feelings of his superiors. His behaviour with his juniors is excellent to the point that he is very much liked by them.

A post of manager is vacant. Considering the company's interest, whom would you prefer as manager and why?

Review Questions

1. 'In order to achieve organisational objectives, manpower requirements need to be assessed, located and harnessed.' Comment.
2. What steps will you take to assess the manpower requirements of a new plant?
3. What factors govern the demand and supply of manpower?
4. What should be the content of an advertisement for a job?
5. What purpose does an application blank fulfil?
6. Discuss various types of interviews and group tests for recruitment and selection.
7. Discuss the uses and limitations of employment tests.
8. Suggest a selection procedure for management personnel.
9. Discuss the need of personnel research and records in modern organisations.
10. 'Recruitment process is revolutionised with the use of information technology'. Comment.

Further Readings

1. J.C. Chambers, S.K. Mullick and D.D. Smith: *How to Choose the Right Forecasting Technique* (HBR, pp. 45-74, July-Aug. 1971).
2. D.H. Gray: *Manpower Planning* (Institute of Personnel Management, London, 1966).
3. Roger F. Holdsworth: *Selection Testing: A Guide for Managers* (British Institute of Management, 1972).
4. R. Meehan and B. Ahmed: *Forecasting Human Resource Requirement* (Human Resource Planning, Vol. 13, Issue 4, pp. 297-307, 1990).

5. W.J. Rothwell: *Effective Succession Planning* (AMACOM, New York, 2001).
6. Benjamin Schneider: *Staffing Organizations* (Goodyear Publishing, California, 1976).
7. Gareth Stainer: *Manpower Planning*
8. James W. Walker: *Human Resource Planning* (McGraw-Hill, New York, 1980).

Chapter 10

Job Evaluation and Enrichment

When I first reached the status a few years ago, I bought a book by a distinguished author called 'The Role of the Managing Director'. On the front page it said: "The Position of the Managing Director is essentially a precarious one." This statement, daily demonstrated as true, filled me with unease and I never read any further. But the book sat on my shelf as concrete evidence that I had taken my elevation seriously.

– **David Moreau**
(Look Behind You!)

Learning Objectives

After reading this chapter you will be able to:

1. Understand that a rational pay structure is based on an evaluation of all jobs in an organisation.
2. Analyse jobs on the basis of requirements of skill, efforts, responsibility, work conditions.
3. Compare jobs and determine their relative worth.
4. Prepare job enrichment programmes.

A job is created when accumulated tasks or work justify the employment of an individual or a group of individuals for accomplishing the task or purpose.

Jobs carry remunerations according to their worth. An engineer gets more than a technician, a supervisor gets more than the workmen and a manager gets more than the supervisors and office assistants. A rational pay structure is based on an evaluation of all the jobs in an organisation. Job evaluation is a process which helps in determining the worth of each job in relation to other jobs in an organisation and thus it helps in evolving a rational wage and salary structure.

The British Institute of Management has defined job evaluation as *"the process of analysis and assessment of jobs to ascertain reliably their relative worth, using the assessment as a basis for a balanced wage structure"*. In an ILO publication, *Payment by Results,* the term job evaluation has been referred to as *"describing and assessing the value of all jobs in the firm in terms of a number of factors, the relative importance of which varies from job to job"*. According to Prof Bryan Livy, job evaluation *"seeks to highlight significant disparities between units of work on a comparative basis and so produce a more equitable distribution of income within an organisation than might be obtained by more arbitrary methods"*.

Definition

Job evaluation is thus a scientific study of jobs in an organisation to ascertain the comparative worth of each job. It is a practice which seeks to provide a degree of objectivity in measuring the comparative value of a job within an organisation and among similar organisations. It lists the underlying factors in all jobs and creates scales or measures for each job. These factors include elements of responsibility; job knowledge or skill; mental application; dexterity and accuracy; physical requirements; working conditions; tools and equipment to be handled; hazards, etc. It seeks to quantify what each job constitutes in terms of money. It is the job that is evaluated and not the person doing the job. The person may change but the job will continue.

Different systems suit different types of work. An evaluation worked out for the factory workers may not be suitable if applied to clerical or ministerial staff. Systems applied should assist in determining the relative worth of the jobs. The absolute monetary value of the job would eventually depend upon many factors like:

— existing union-employer agreements

- prevailing wage rates in the region
- demand and supply position of workers
- minimum wages to the lowest rank of workers

and other associated factors. The objective of applying a system of evaluation is only to help remove guesswork, favouritism and expediency.

It may be remembered that job evaluation is not a shortcut to an equitable wage structure. It is a difficult science and a time-consuming procedure. It should be carried out with a high degree of integrity and fair-mindedness, otherwise it may adversely affect the morale of the organisation. It should evolve a fair method by which the wage structure of an organisation can be settled to the mutual satisfaction of the employer and employee.

Job Analysis

All job evaluation systems should start with job analysis. The analysis must be a comprehensive record of all that the job consists of. It is the foundation on which the structure is built and hence due attention is needed to ensure accuracy of date and relevant details. The jobs are therefore rated on the basis of job descriptions and specifications evolved. Rating is more a matter of judgement than of fact-finding and, therefore, calls for ability and integrity to compare jobs with one another.

Methods of Job Evaluation

The methods of job evaluation tend to fall into one of the two main categories and are referred to as either non-analytical or analytical. Each has two sub-divisions.

A – *Non-Analytical*
 (i) Job Ranking Method
 (ii) Job Classification Method

B – *Analytical*
 (i) Weighted Point Assessment Method
 (ii) Factor Comparison Method

The basic difference between the two is that the non-analytical methods, whilst establishing a grading hierarchy, are non-quantitative, and the analytical methods are quantitative and are expressed in some numerical form.

Comparison: When the number of jobs is few and the strength of employees is below 30 to 40, the non-quantitative methods may be used effectively. The quantitative methods are useful for big organisations where a large number of people are employed.

Non-Analytical Methods

Ranking Method

Ranking, the original method, is a direct system of comparing jobs together so that they are ranked in order of their importance, starting with the least important in the first rank and moving to the most important in the last. Jobs are not divided factor by factor, but are considered whole entities. This appears to be a simple method, but its application calls for a high degree of personal knowledge on the part of the evaluator of the jobs under review, especially when judging and comparing a job that requires considerable skill against another where the responsibility is high. The evaluator simply compares each job against the others by deciding whether it is:

- less demanding
- demanding
- more demanding.

Having compared jobs 'vertically', the evaluator will then, if more than one distinct area is under review, look at the situation horizontally in order to equate jobs of equal worth across the whole area. Thus, it is possible to draw up a complete schedule which will show the relative position of all the jobs. Job of the same ranking are allocated the same grade and a grading structure emerges. The final phase is the attachment of monetary values to the various grade levels.

The ranking of jobs is reliable when it is done systematically. To begin with, a benchmark job or a key job should be selected which may be compared. A comparison may be made by asking the question: Is this job more important than the benchmark job, or less important? The jobs are then placed in rank order above or below the key job according to the answer. When the number of jobs is large, the jobs may have to be grouped into job families, for e.g. accounts, engineering, administrative, etc. and key jobs for each family may have to be ascertained before ranking jobs in order of their importance. When the number of jobs is large, an organisation-wise ranking will not be simple.

Ranking is the simplest and oldest method of determining the economic value of a job. It can be executed quickly with a minimum expenditure of time, energy and resources. The jobs, under this system, are compared as 'wholes', they are not broken down into their component elements. The system is thus non-analytical and non-quantitative. It only produces the rank order of jobs. The most important job comes on the top and the least important one on the bottom.

Monetary values are assigned to each job after ranking. Although this does not form a part of job evaluation which is concerned with determining only the relative worth of each job, it is a useful device for the managers. Key jobs with known monetary value become the cornerstone for determining the monetary value of other jobs. The demand and supply position of personnel with different qualifications may, however, upset such calculations. Market conditions, an organisation's paying capacity, the existing salary structure, and past conventions may be other limiting factors in this regard. A simple ranking of an office job is given as follows:

Simple Ranking of Office Job

Rank Order	Job Title	Monthly Starting Salary (Rs)
1.	Peon	3000.00
2.	Jr. Clerk, Despatcher	5000.00
3.	Typist, Telephone Operator	6500.00
4.	Clerk	7500.00
5.	Assistant	9000.00
6.	Cashier	12000.00
7.	Sr. Assistant	15000.00
8.	Accountant	20000.00
9.	Office Superintendent	25000.00
10.	Administrative Officer	30000.00

The ranking system is marked by simplicity and easiness. But it is of a very limited use when the number of jobs is large as it fails to provide a satisfactory yardstick for comparison. The existing position of a job in the hierarchy of jobs and the rater's personal judgement are important factors which affect ranking more than the objective criteria like mental, physical and other requirements of a job.

Classification Method

As in job ranking, the classification method does not call for a detailed or quantitative analysis of individual parts of the job, but is based on the job as a whole. It differs from the job ranking method in that, before any evaluation of a job takes place, the number of grading levels and the criteria for determining the type of work or responsibility to meet those levels are defined.

It is usual in job classification to select one or two jobs from each of the levels in the grading structure and prepare descriptions of the duties, responsibilities and requirements necessary to fulfil them to an acceptable level of performance. These jobs are known as *benchmarks or key jobs* and indicate the type of work and level of responsibilities at each grade in the structure. Having selected the benchmark or key jobs, the other jobs in the area under review are compared against them to indicate their grade.

This method is basically a ranking operation as it ends in classifying jobs into various grades in the organisation. More important jobs are put into higher salary grades and jobs with lower ranking are assigned lower scales. This method has been a forte of the government organisations. Officials positions are ranked into grades I, II, III, etc., and different pay scales are provided for each grade.

The grades are selected on the basis of varying levels of duties and responsibilities. The nature of work is combined with the salary range to show that there is a direct relationship between the rating of the importance of the job and the salary paid. In the example given below, an organisational pyramid is divided into eight grades, indicating differential stages in levels of responsibility:

Grade		
I	Rs. 300,000-500,000/-	General Manager
II	Rs. 200,000-350,000/-	Departmental Heads
III	Rs. 150,000-250,000/-	Sr. Executives
IV	Rs. 100,000-150,000/-	Jr. Managers, Officers
V	Rs. 7,500-15,000/-	Technicians, Chemists, etc.
VI	Rs. 5,000-10,000/-	Supervisors, Foremen
VII	Rs. 4,000-9,000/-	Skilled Workers
VIII	Rs. 2,500-7,500/-	Unskilled Workers

The classification method helps in manpower budgeting. The manpower costs can be accurately computed and can be broken down to their respective levels. The future cost may be predicted with a degree of accuracy and career planning may be done for the existing employees according to projected assumptions about organisational structure and establishment. This system also helps in developing a uniform wage structure in an industry or a region as comparison becomes easy and a basis for negotiation between the employers and employees is prepared.

The classification system has some limitations. It enables subjective grading and rating of jobs by total content, which may create distrust among employees. The existing grades and past conventions also seriously affect the process of fixing new grades. The system thus suffers from inflexibility which may be harmful for jobs which change in their nature and have contents like scientific advances, discoveries, etc. When compared to ranking, classification is certainly more advanced, but when it is compared to quantitative techniques like the point method, its utility is challenged.

Analytical Methods

Weighted Points Assessment

This is the most commonly used system. It is an analytical technique. It involves breaking down the job into several compensable factors, giving each job a numerical score on each of these factors and summing these scores to obtain the value of the job. The same factors are used for each job. It is similar to the classification method in that a scale is set up against which jobs are measured. The difference between the two methods is that while a scale is developed for jobs in the case of the classification method, a scale for each compensable factor is developed in the points assessment method.

In this method, a carefully worded rating scale is constructed for each compensable method. This rating scale includes definition of each compensable factor, several divisions (called degrees) of each factor carefully outlined, and a point score for each such degree. These rating scales may be thought of as a set of rulers to be used to measure jobs. The so-called rulers must be constructed from words and the so-called measurements are still judgements. The same points assessment plan is not normally used to cover the entire range of jobs in an organisation, but the common practice is to have separate plans for manual, clerical and managerial jobs. This is because the different nature of work in these jobs calls for assessment by different factors and for giving different emphasis to them.

An early and very widely used points scheme was devised by Kress (1939) for the National Electrical Manufacturers Association in the USA in which he studied jobs under eleven characteristics, grouped under the generic headings of 'skill', 'effort', 'responsibility' and 'job condition'. Each generic group consisted of a number of specific sub-factors:

Skill	Education
	Experience
	Initiative and ingenuity
Effort	Physical demand
	Mental and/or visual demand
Responsibility	For equipment or process
	For materials or product
	For safety of others
	For work of others
Job conditions	Working conditions
	Hazards

Each characteristic was divided into five degrees and weighted according to its considered importance *vis-a-vis* other factors in the scheme.

The British Institute of Management has suggested the following factor complex:

Acquired skill and knowledge	: Training and previous experience
	Central responsibility
	Complexity of process
	Dexterity and motor accuracy
Responsibilities and mutual requirements	: Responsibility for material or equipment
	Effect on other operations
	Attention needed to orders
	Alertness to details
	Monotony
Physical requirements	: Abnormal position
	Abnormal effort
Conditions of work	: Disagreeableness
	Danger

In a public sector steel plant in India, a twelve-factor job evaluation plan has been adopted with a system of weightages as given in the following table:

Sl. No	Factors	Percentage	Base	I	II	III	IV	V
1.	Education	12	0	12	24	36	48	60
2.	Experience	14	0	14	28	42	56	70
3.	Mental skill	10	0	10	20	30	40	50
4.	Manual skill	5	0	5	10	15	20	25
5.	Responsibility for materials	10	0	10	20	30	40	50
6.	Responsibility for tools and equipment	10	0	10	20	30	40	50
7.	Responsibility for work of others	8	0	8	16	24	32	40
8.	Responsibility for safety of others	5	0	5	10	15	20	25
9.	Physical effort	8	0	8	16	24	32	40
10.	Mental/visual effort	6	0	6	12	18	24	30
11.	Surroundings	7	0	7	14	21	28	35
12.	Hazards	5	0	5	10	15	20	25

The contents of each job are analysed on the basis of point values involved, and on the basis of the total score, the job is assigned a specified grade. In the table given below, the jobs of melter and chargeman are assigned point values on different job evaluation factors and are assigned grades on the basis of total points scored.

Point Values Assigned To Melter And Chargeman's Job

Sl. No.	Factor	Job Title	
		Melter	Chargeman
1.	Education	48	24
2.	Experience	56	56
3.	Mental skill	40	30
4.	Manual skill	5	5
5.	Responsibility for materials	40	30
6.	Responsibility for tools and equipment	40	20
7.	Responsibility for work of others	24	24
8.	Responsibility for safety of others	10	10
9.	Physical effort	16	8
10.	Mental/visual effort	24	18
11.	Surroundings	28	14
12.	Hazards	5	5
	Total	336	244
	Grade	9000-12000	6000-8000

Usually, the weightages in the point system are assigned in arithmetic progression. In some organisations geometric progression is used for assigning weightages. But this may produce arbitrary and probably unwanted loadings in the higher degree range.

Factor Comparison Method

In this, jobs are examined using a predetermined monetary scale for each factor, and the total of the factor values so determined for each job represents its evaluated cash rate. Its significance lies in the fact that once the factors have been identified, the jobs are evaluated in cash terms rather than using a numerical points scale. The method embodies the principles of 'point rating' with the principles of ranking.

The initial stages are basically the same as in the points assessment method, and as a first step, job factors are selected. However, in points assessment method, sub-factors are not used.

Key jobs are then selected and job description prepared. It is, however, important that the key jobs should be considered to be adequately paid in relation to the local labour market.

The key jobs are then ranked under each of the factors. The next step is to decide the current rate for each job to be paid for each factor. A schedule can be built using this matrix.

Comparisons are then made between the ranking and the agreed factor rate. This serves as a useful check on the suitability of key jobs originally selected. It is recommended that a ranking/factor rate schedule be drawn up at this stage.

The final stage is to prepare a factor comparison schedule, which shows the piece rate value of all the key jobs under each of the factor headings. Using this as a matrix, other jobs can be compared against the key jobs under each factor heading, and a factor value assessed. The sum total of these factor values represents the cash rate of the job in question.

The factor comparison scheme described above is specific to shop-floor levels, but a number of adaptations have been used for managerial levels. This system is also known as the job comparison system. Eugene Buye originated this system in 1941. He divided jobs into five compensable factors, viz.:

– Mental requirements
– Skill requirements
– Physical requirements
– Responsibility and
– Working conditions

Steps in Factor Comparison

(1) A few key jobs that represent a cross-section of all the jobs to be evaluated are selected by an expert belonging to a committee representing the management and the employees.

(2) Key jobs are ranked according to five basic factors, one factor at a time, in order of their relative importance. The ranking is first arranged numerically.

(3) The average salary is established after ranking all key jobs, and money value for each job is divided among the five factors according to their relative importance to the key job.

(4) The rankings are pooled in a reference master table after monthly salaries have been assigned to the key jobs.

To illustrate the above steps, we take two key jobs, those of the cleaner and the receptionist. The factor ranking of these jobs may be done as follows:

Factor Rank Order	Cleaner	Receptionist
1.	Physical requirements	Skill requirements
2.	Working conditions	Responsibility
3.	Skill requirements	Mental requirements
4.	Responsibility	Physical requirements
5.	Mental requirements	Working conditions

The next step is to ascribe monetary value to each factor. If the composite wage is known then each factor must have a certain value. For the two benchmarks, we may ascribe the following monetary values:

Factor	Receptionist (Rs.)	Cleaner (Rs.)
Mental requirements	1200	200
Skill requirements	2000	600
Physical requirements	800	1000
Responsibility	1600	400
Working conditions	400	800
	6000	3000

The actual cash values are assigned according to the ranking. In the above analysis, the receptionist is ranked higher than the cleaner under mental requirements, hence she has been given higher monetary value for the factor. Since working conditions are not considered as important for her as for the cleaner, she gets less on that point. The ratio between the total emoluments of the receptionist and the cleaner is also reflected in the assignment of monetary values to individual factors as can be seen from the table given on the following page.

The weakness of the system lies in assigning monetary values to the factors on the basis of prevailing rates as standards. Inequities then creep into the factor comparison method.

Patterson's Approach

Professor Patterson criticises the conventional techniques of job evaluation referred to above, on the grounds of their subjectivity, arbitrary methods of analysis, frequent inappropriateness and the inability to compare dissimilar jobs with theoretical validity. Instead, he proposes a scheme which uses a single factor, viz. decision-making which, he says, is a common criterion for all jobs. "The common denominator from tea boy to Chairman is the quality of decision," he remarks. His approach to job evaluation involves four stages:

- Establishment of job bands according to decision type and structure.
- Job analysis – examining the content of jobs.
- Job grading and sub-grading – the ranking of jobs.
- Job assessment – ascribing monetary values.

Job bands are broad generic categories of work according to the type and level of decisions made. According to Patterson, every known job can be considered and compared against six basic levels of decision-making:

Band E: Policy-making decisions, made by the top management.

Band D: Programming decisions, made by the senior management in the execution of policies.

Band C: Interpretative decisions, made by the middle management within the limits set by Band D on what is to be done.

Band B: Routine decisions made by skilled operators concerning the execution of interpreted policy and the process involved.

Band A: Automatic decisions made by semi-skilled operators on the operational aspects of the process such as 'when', 'how' and 'where' to do something.

Band O: Defined decisions made by the unskilled workers.

Jobs are categorised into appropriate bands. The bands are broken down into grades. The grades may be divided into subgrades in order to provide differentials that indicate, in greater detail, differences in the value of jobs. The system thus provides a uniform classification system which can be applied universally. Its weakness lies mainly in the fact that it relies on the judgement of one man, the job analyst, who decides what jobs are to be put into which bands.

Matrix of Factor Ranking And Factor Evaluations

Rank order	Mental requirements	Skill requirements	Physical requirements	Responsibility	Working conditions
1.	Receptionist Rs. 2000/-	Cleaner Rs. 1000/-			
2.				Receptionist Rs. 1600/-	Cleaner Rs. 800/-
3.	Receptionist Rs. 1200/-	Cleaner Rs. 600/-			
4.			Receptionist Rs. 800/-	Cleaner Rs. 400/-	
5.		Cleaner Rs. 200/-			Receptionist Rs. 400/-

Prof Elliott Jaques and a few other authors have also criticised the conventional methods and suggested new ones. Whatever system of job evaluation is adopted by a company, the following points should be taken into consideration:

— The evaluation should be done by a committee consisting of the job analyst, representative of the management and the workers.

— The evaluation should be objective. Job evaluation factors should be selected keeping the nature and type of jobs in view and not the individuals holding different jobs.

— There should be a periodic review of the jobs evaluated. Improved technology, working conditions, R & D, training, etc., may bring important changes in job content from time to time.

— Job evaluation may not be considered as the sole criterion for fixing wages although it should be considered as an important criterion.

— The system should be uniformly applied to all the jobs to avoid discrimination and the resultant unpleasantness and grievances.

Job Enrichment

Job enrichment is an effort to add such attributes to a job as a variety of tasks, freedom to decide and operate, wholesomeness and completeness of the tasks performed, and performance feedback for the job. The man at work should feel motivated, and this can be done by making the job more interesting and challenging. Some of the situations which call for job enrichment are as follows:

- I get tired, it is boring and dull.
- It would be better if I could have a different type of job.
- I do not see anything good in this job.
- It is very simple, I do not get to learn anything on it.
- There is nothing to do in this job.
- I do not get to make any decisions as they are already made.
- It's all routine.
- I do not like to be treated as a child.
- I do not know what my bosses feel about my work.

Job enrichment is based upon the intrinsic reward theory – the reward should be built into the job. It is more effective and long-lasting than extrinsic rewards which are in the form of additional benefits like productivity bonus, better pay, perks, etc. Job enrichment makes the job more pleasant and gives a sense of accomplishment.

Job enrichment is done by adding or changing the contents of the job or by giving more discretion to the jobholder or both. Addition to the job content is also described as job enlargement. It may be done by loading the job horizontally or vertically or both ways. Loading the job horizontally would mean addition of more of the same kind of content as earlier, while in the case of vertical loading, the new content involves greater stimulation and variety. Loading, however, should not result into a perception on the part of employee that he has to exert more for the same amount of benefits as earlier. It must result into more job satisfaction. The other method of job enrichment is increase in the power – the discretion of the employee to enable him to act freely, make judgements independently and account for his performance. A judicious combination of content and discretion can result into higher productivity as the following graph shows:

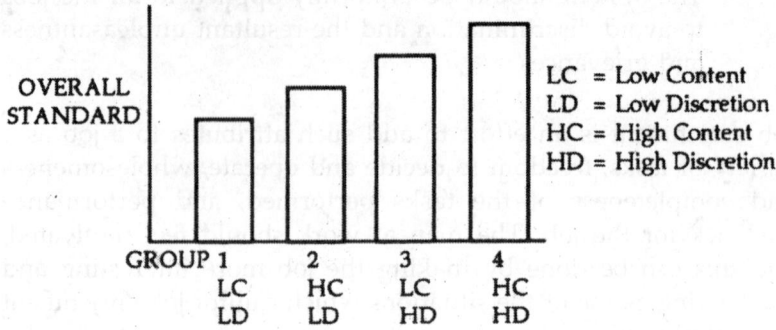

Fig. 10.1 Content/Discretion Hypothesis.

The test of job enrichment is employee satisfaction and the resultant improvement in productivity. If the employee begins to respond in the terms given below, it would be an indication of success:

— I enjoy my work though I have to work harder.
— My work is important.
— I have a really interesting job now. I would like to stick to the company.
— At last, my worth has been recognised.
— I wish the management would have given this job to me much earlier.

Some of the problems which arise while introducing job enrichment scheme may be related to the individual's own preferences and personal difficulties. Some people are happy with simple jobs and the existing pay and perquisites. They do not want any further responsibility, learn anything new or accept new challenges. A better job may sometimes require mobility, for which an individual may not be willing.

The factors on which the success of job enrichment programmes may depend are:

(i) Identification of the problem: What is lacking in the job? What are the expectations of the jobholder?

(ii) Training of the jobholder to enable him to cope with the challenges of the new job.

(iii) Assigning job responsibility with adequate discretion to decide and operate.

(iv) Adding content or changing it to make the job look more pleasant rather than burdensome.

(v) Providing opportunity for self-assessment.

(vi) Linking performance with the reward system.

Situation Analysis

An analysis of the turnover of the office staff of a company shows that the number of accounts assistants leaving their jobs has been the highest during the last three years. While not a single assistant from the purchase department resigned from service, five out of seven from the accounts department left during this period. Two assistants out of eight in the personnel department also resigned. The exit interviews indicated that the assistant's job in the accounts department required more technical knowledge and carried heavier responsibility than the jobs of the same rank in other departments. The employees leaving the personnel department had a grudge that their workload was very heavy. All office assistants are placed in one pay-scale in the company, irrespective of the jobs assigned to them. The union is firmly against any discrimination in the pay-structure of the employees of the same rank posted in different departments. It has asked for an upward revision in the salary of all office employees.

How will you solve this problem?

Review Questions

1. Define job analysis and job evaluation.
2. How does job evaluation help in evolving a payment system based on the merit of each job?
3. What are the non-analytical methods of job evaluation?
4. What is the factor comparison method? How is weightage assigned to each factor?
5. Explain the concept of job bands. Why is it said that job bands are broad generic categories of work according to the type and level of decisions made?
6. Define job enrichment. What is the content/discretion hypothesis in the context of job enrichment to ensure higher productivity?

Further Readings

1. S.A. Fine: *Functional Job Analysis: An Approach to a Technology for Manpower Planning* (Personnel Journal, pp. 813-818, Nov. 1971).
2. J.V. Ghorpade: *Job Analysis: A Handbook for the Human Resource Director* (Englewood Cliffs, New Jersey, 1988).

3. W.J. Paul and K.B. Robertson: *Job Enrichment and Employee Motivation* (Gower Press, London, 1970).
4. Lallan Prasad: *Personnel Management and Industrial Relations in the Public Sector* (Progressive Corporation, Bombay, 1973).
5. H.W. Risher: *Job Evaluation: Validity and Reliability* (Compensation and Benefits Review, Vol. 21, Issue 1, pp. 32-33, 1989).
6. Dale Yoder: *Personnel Management and Industrial Relations* (Prentice Hall of India, 1973).

Chapter 11

Performance Appraisal and Promotion

I am sorry to say that you are incompetent. How can I be so certain? Because everyone is. It is not just that I believe in Peter principle which ordains that everybody is promoted until they reach and pass their level of incompetence. It is that, if you give me half an hour of your time... I will find a blank area in you.

– David Moreau

(Look Behind You!)

Learning Objectives

After reading this chapter you will be able to:

1. Understand the objectives of performance appraisal.
2. Discuss merits and demerits of different methods of merit rating.
3. Develop an appraisal form to facilitate objective appraisal by boss, peers and self.
4. Critically examine the promotion policy of an enterprise.

Merit rating or appraisal of the performance is an important tool in the hands of superiors to assess their subordinates. It is a systematic evaluation of an employee by some other qualified person who is familiar with the employee's performance. It is also an important command in the hands of seniors which the subordinates respect. This makes many juniors obey reasonable orders of their superiors to avoid any unwanted or adverse entry. However, this authority should never be misused by the executives for personal reasons.

Appraisal Objectives

The purposes of rating could be many:

— Assessment of tasks assigned and fulfilled
— Suitability for promotion

Administrative use — Transfers, layoffs and termination
— Evaluation of training needs
— Personnel research

Self-improvement of the employee

— He should know where he stands
— He should make up for his deficiencies

> **PERSPECTIVE**
>
> ### Performance Management: TISCO's Initiatives
>
> TISCO initiated a management restructuring program for transforming into a high performing and growing organisation. On the HR front, the management focussed on providing career opportunities and building a team of high performing professionals for which they hired a reputed consultant who proposed a lean and flat business unit with enriched jobs, increased accountability and autonomy.
>
> A Performance Ethics Program (PEP) was also introduced for promoting young and dynamic professionals and this was a replacement of seniority based promotion. A new Performance Management System (PMS) was introduced for aligning the Key Resource Areas (KRAs) with business strategies and identifying superior performances in the organisation by defining clear career paths and accountabilities.
>
> The rewards and recognitions were linked with the PMS. New measures in the direction of performance management boosted employee motivation and performance. Job satisfaction also improved due to fair and transparent reward system.

The most obvious purposes of any rating system are to obtain such personal information which will be useful in assessing the potential of an employee, his good and weak points, and in designing management development programmes.

The objectives of the annual or periodical appraisal should therefore be:

(i) to evaluate results and plan for better performance;
(ii) to understand the gaps in knowledge, skill and training needs; and
(iii) to identify men with potential to man higher positions in the future.

Appraisal at each level may be done annually by the superior (known as the reporting officer) and the next superior manager (known as the reviewing officer). In the case of service department personnel who are attached to other departments, their performance can be assessed by the executive of that department. The responsibility of reporting generally rests with the reporting and reviewing officers. Higher authorities may also record their views on the performance and potential of an employee if they are aware of it.

The performance of the individual should be assessed on the success of the tasks assigned, and the causes of failure, if any, should also be recorded. The gaps in knowledge and skills should be properly ascertained so that these can be filled by planned guidance and training.

The potential for development should be judged by the reporting and reviewing officers on the basis of performance and results achieved on the present job. Promotion should be like climbing a mountain which requires effort, zeal and willingness to achieve distinction. It should not be like climbing a building by an escalator which requires little effort.

No personal bias should influence the filling up of merit rating forms. The reporting officer should:

(a) Discuss with the person concerned his achievements/failures in the performance, and ascertain his difficulties in managing the job, if any.
(b) Find out measures to overcome those difficulties.
(c) Work out action plans for better performance in future.

The discussion should be constructive rather than an inquest as the objective of appraisal is to help the individual in improving his performance. The estimate of potential for higher positions need not be disclosed during the discussions. While discussing performance, the criteria should be:

— objectives

- tasks assigned
- failures and reasons thereof
- suggestions to overcome obstacles
- help needed by the subordinate from the superior to improve his performance.

For a person to do his job to the best of his ability, it is presupposed that:

(i) he understands what is expected out of him in terms of output, quality, loss, etc.

(ii) he is given adequate resources, necessary freedom and authority to do his work.

(iii) he receives due backing and guidance.

(iv) he has job satisfaction.

That is why the ability to perform well and his understanding of the work assume importance. Common limitations of improperly designed performance appraisal/merit-rating system are:

(i) it is just a record of opinions;

(ii) there are zones of uncertainty;

(iii) rating seldom tells the whole story; and

(iv) rating depends upon the rater's ability and personal biases.

Merit-rating Systems

The different types of merit-rating systems generally in vogue where rating is done by superiors are:

(a) Graphic rating scale
(b) Forced distribution
(c) Ranking
(d) Free written
(e) Forced choice
(f) Critical incident

Graphic Rating Scale

Ratings are converted into numerical expressions indicating the ability of each person measured by the qualities deemed most essential. Let us consider the ability to learn new methods:

Ability to Learn

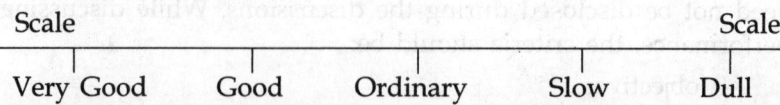

Forced Distribution

Here employees are rated on the basis of a few characteristics such as job performance and promotability. One end of the scale represents the best performance and the other end the poorest job performance. The supervisor is asked to allocate approximately 10 per cent of his men to the best end of the scale, 20 per cent in the next category, 40 per cent in the middle bracket, 20 per cent in the next category and 10 per cent at the other end of the scale. The problem of supervisors using different scales is thus avoided by forced distribution.

Ranking

Persons of similar cadres are ranked in the order of merit. If, for example, there are 8 fitters, the rating could be as under:

Ranking	Fitter No.
1	6
2	3
3	7
4	8
5	5
6	2
7	1
8	4

Free Written

The supervisors are told to write down remarks about the performance and give their own impression as to how good a person is. This may depend upon the writing skills and experience of the supervisor also.

Forced Choice

The rater is required to choose from several sets of adjectives or phrases which best characterise the officer and which are the most descriptive. For example:

(a) Commands respect by his actions
(b) Is cool-headed
(c) Is indifferent
(d) Is overbearing

This is also sometimes called a checklist statement. For example:

Yes	No	Index
A	A	makes frequent mistakes
B	B	respected by subordinates
C	C	cannot follow up assignments
D	D	handles emergency situations well
E	E	lacks confidence

Critical Incident

Factual reporting of good or bad incidents about the persons being rated could be done as follows:

Event	Report
Breakdown in the turbine plant leading to the stoppage of powerhouse.	Was not disturbed. Attended the work in a systematic manner to liquidate the breakdown in a short time. Showed confidence and ability in handling the breakdown.
Labour trouble in the plant.	Was indifferent and did not handle the situation coolly. Owing to his hotheadedness, a crisis was precipitated leading to the stoppage of work.

The yardstick for measuring the performance, future potential, good points, weaknesses, etc. is assuming greater importance and significance with the development of participative management.

The drawbacks of the traditional forms of many annual appraisal systems are:
 (i) they provide little common ground for objectivity.
 (ii) they lack factual discussions between a supervisor and his subordinates.
 (iii) they fail to compare the results achieved with the results expected.

(iv) they provide no specific recommendation for improving performance.
(v) they are taken as a grand annual ritual.
(vi) they are rarely related to salary increases, succession planning, promotion, training needs, etc.

Designing of Appraisal Forms

An organisation should develop different appraisal forms for different categories of employees keeping in view the nature and responsibilities of the job and the performance characteristics. Two specimen forms are given below. The first relates to a service organisation and is meant for evaluating the performance of the staff. Besides identification information, the form lays down the criteria for evaluation and the areas of rating, which are customer service, work quality, knowledge of procedures, accuracy, timeliness, productivity and team work. An employee is given the opportunity to record his comment on the rating if he chooses to. The supervisor and reviewer are required to recommend development needs and plans for every employee. Similarly, the employees are also asked individually what do they propose to develop their potentialities. Second appraisal form is for evaluating the performance of senior executives of a large manufacturing organisation which describes its appraisal scheme as 'Performance Enhancement System'. The form is divided into five parts. Employee data is recorded in part I. Performance of the executive in key result areas specific to the present job – quality, costs, productivity and management – is given in part II. The executive is to be rated on managerial characteristics such as planning, leadership, team building, task orientation, communication, innovation, etc. in part III. The appraisal includes qualitative assessment along with quantitative one on a grading scale. The appraisal committee records post-appraisal review after discussing it with the executive whose brief career plans are also laid down. Part V of the form deals with financial recommendations about increments, promotion, upgradation and pay revision, etc. Both the appraisal forms referred to above are well designed with their rating criteria specifically defined and career plans included as a part of appraisal exercise.

Appraisal Form 1

Staff Performance Evaluation

The Company's success is dependent on collective and individual performances, and we are committed to the principle that employee compensation, recognition and advancement should be based on personal performance.

Identification Information

Employee Name : _____

Job Title : _____ Department : _____

Employed on : _____ Present Position Since: _____

Period of Review : From _____ To _____

Evaluation for : _____

Name & Designation of Supervisor : _____

Name & Designation of Reviewer : _____

> **General instructions for the supervisor:**
> 1. Rate the Performance Standards on pages 225-228 for all staff employees. Obtain the approval of the reviewer, who should be your supervisor.
> 2. Complete the development recommendations on page 228-229 (for supervisory positions only) in a factual and realistic manner.
> 3. The employee, supervisor and reviewer must sign this document at the end of page 229.

Performance Standards Rating

(Fill this section for all employees)

This section focuses on an employee's performance in various functional areas of the job. Rate your employee's effectiveness in each functional area that is a part of his/her job, using the rating scale shown below; and enter the rating in the box provided. Ratings that reflect less than effective performance should always receive comments.

A. EXCEPTIONAL

B. SUPERIOR

C. EFFECTIVE

D. INCOMPLETE

E. UNACCEPTABLE

F. TOO EARLY TO EVALUATE
G. NOT APPLICABLE

CUSTOMER SERVICE RATING [   ]

Ensuring that customer's (internal or external) needs and problems are satisfied.

(THIS RATING PERTAINS TO THOSE EMPLOYEES WHO COME INTO DIRECT CONTACT WITH CUSTOMERS, REGULARLY OR FROM TIME TO TIME)

( ) PROVIDING PERSONAL SERVICE ( ) UNDERSTANDING GUEST NEEDS
( ) HANDLING OF GUEST COMPLAINTS ( ) RESPONSE TO GUEST NEEDS
( ) FOLLOW UP ON GUEST NEEDS

_____
_____

WORK QUALITY RATING [   ]

Producing work of consistent and acceptable quality.

(THIS RATING PERTAINS TO THE EMPLOYEE'S DAY TO DAY DUTIES AS GIVEN IN HIS/HER JOB DESCRIPTION)

( ) OUTPUT OF DAY TO DAY WORK ( ) QUALITY OF WORK
( ) CONSISTENCY

_____
_____

KNOWLEDGE OF PROCEDURES RATING [   ]

Utilising knowledge of work/departmental standards and procedures

(IN THIS RATING THE EMPLOYEE'S WORK SHOULD MEET WITH THE STANDARDS AND FOLLOW THE PROCEDURES DEFINED BY THE MANAGEMENT).

( ) SERVICE STANDARDS ( ) COMPANY VALUES
( ) HOUSE RULES ( ) EMERGENCY PROCEDURES
( ) PRODUCT KNOWLEDGE ( ) DEPARTMENTAL PROCEDURES

_____
_____

ACCURACY RATING

Completing assignments with necessary degree of accuracy and attention to detail.

>(THIS RATING PERTAINS TO SPECIFIC ASSIGNMENTS THAT MAY BE GIVEN TO THE EMPLOYEE FROM TIME TO TIME)

( ) ASSIGNMENTS COMPLETED ( ) COMPLETED ON TIME
( ) WITH ACCEPTABLE ACCURACY

_____
_____

TIMELINESS RATING

Fulfilling duties and completing projects within the required time frame

( ) ABILITY TO PRIORITISE DUTIES
( ) COMPLETING THEM WITHIN SPECIFIED TIME

_____
_____

RESPONSIBILITY RATING

Accepting responsibility for routine duties, and performing functions without repeated prompting from the supervisor.

( ) INITIATIVE ( ) PUNCTUALITY
( ) ATTENDANCE – PLANNED/AUTHORISED LEAVE
( ) ATTENDANCE – DAYS PRESENT (A minimum of 268 days present qualifies as EFFECTIVE rating)

_____
_____

PRODUCTIVITY RATING

The degree to which the employee effectively produces mathematically measurable results.

>(THIS RATING PERTAINS TO THE END RESULTS PRODUCED BY THE EMPLOYEE'S EFFORTS WHICH SHOULD BE MEASURABLE)

( ) OUTPUT MEASURABLE AGAINST THE STANDARDS SET

TEAMWORK RATING

Seeking task information and participation from other members of the department, cooperating and volunteering his/her own knowledge and services to increase productivity and boost morale.

(THIS RATING PERTAINS LARGELY TO THE EMPLOYEE'S PERFORMANCE WITHIN HIS/HER OWN DEPARTMENT)

( ) COOPERATION WITH COLLEAGUES (Within/Inter-Departmental)
( ) PARTICIPATING IN DEPARTMENTAL TASKS
( ) TRAINING/IMPARTING KNOWLEDGE & SKILLS

GENERAL COMMENTS

OVERALL PERFORMANCE EVALUATION (Fill this section for all employees)

What is the overall effectiveness of this individual when performance in all areas of the job is considered? In achieving results, how does this individual compare to other employees in the same profile?

In this section you are asked to make a single rating of the employee's overall job performance. Listed below are the definitions of each of the six levels of performance.

Decide which point on the scale best describes your employee's overall job performance, and clearly enter the rating in the box provided:

1. **EXCEPTIONAL – Performance is truly outstanding**

This category is reserved to single out distinguished performance in all key result areas where objectives are surpassed by a huge margin.

2. **SUPERIOR – Performance consistently exceeds job requirements**

There are no areas where accountability is not fully met, and some where it is significantly exceeded.

3. **EFFECTIVE — Performance is competent and meets job requirements**

Praiseworthy performance, where all objectives are met, or where areas of under-achievement are balanced by areas of superior performance.

4. **INCOMPLETE — Performance does not yet meet all job requirements**

There is room for further learning or improvement before all accountabilities can be met. A remedial (not disciplinary) or supportive action plan will assist in achieving full competence.

5. **UNACCEPTABLE — Performance is unsatisfactory**

Does not meet minimum job requirements; disciplinary or other radical, remedial action is necessary.

6. **TOO EARLY TO EVALUATE — Employee has been in current position six months or less**

Not fully established, and performance assessment is therefore presently inappropriate.

COMMENTS ON OVERALL PERFORMANCE RATING

(A performance rating which exceeds or falls below the EFFECTIVE level requires additional explanation.)

_____
_____
_____
_____

EMPLOYEE REVIEW

Optional comments; if the employee wishes to do so, any comments concerning performance evaluation may be indicated here.

_____
_____
_____
_____

DEVELOPMENT RECOMMENDATIONS (Fill this section for supervisory level employees only)

CURRENT POSITION (To be filled by the employee and supervisor jointly).

In reviewing the year's performance, what kind of training/experience should be provided in order to maintain an effective level of performance?

_____
_____
_____
_____

DEVELOPMENT NEEDS/PLANS (To be filled by the employee and supervisor jointly)

What kind of development, training, or experience needs to be provided to support the employee's career path, and what are the plans for meeting those needs?

_____
_____
_____
_____

EMPLOYEE SELF DEVELOPMENT (To be filled by the employee only)

What actions, education, extra work experience is the employee planning to undertake on his or her own, that will increase his or her potential for growth in the company?

_____
_____
_____
_____

PERFORMANCE EVALUATION DECLARATION

This evaluation has been discussed in person with the employee:

Employee	Supervisor	Reviewer
Date	Date	Date

Appraisal Form 2*

EXECUTIVE PERFORMANCE ENHANCEMENT SYSTEM

PERFORMANCE REVIEW	PART I-NOMINAL DATA		
NAME OF PERSON	DESCRIPTION		
COMPANY/DIVISION/DEPARTMENT/SECTION			
REPORTING TO			
PERIOD UNDER REVIEW	FROM		TO

PART II - PERFORMANCE REVIEW

KEY RESULT AREAS	NOT MET OBJECTIVE POOR 1	MET SOME OBJECTIVE AVERAGE 2	MET MOST OBJECTIVE GOOD 3	MET ALL OBJECTIVE V. GOOD 4	EXCEEDED OBJECTIVE EXCELLENT 5	QUALITATIVE ASSESSMENT
KRAs SPECIFIC TO THE PRESENT JOB						
QUALITY						
COSTS						
PRODUCTIVITY						
MANAGEMENT						

PART III - MANAGERIAL CHARACTERISTICS, STRENGTHS/DEVELOPMENT NEEDS

MANAGERIAL CHARACTERISTICS	POOR 1	AVG. 2	GOOD 3	V. GOOD 4	EX 5	QUALITATIVE ASSESSMENT
PLANNING						
ABILITY TO MOTIVATE						
LEADERSHIP						
CUSTOMER & INTERFACE MANAGEMENT						
TEAM MANAGEMENT						
TASK MANAGEMENT						
TASK ORIENTATION						
SUBORDINATE DEVELOPMENT						
PROFESSIONAL KNOWLEDGE						
COST MANAGEMENT						
COMMUNICATION						
INNOVATION						
QUALITY MANAGEMENT						

APPRAISEE'S RESPONSE TO THE ASSESSMENT (TO BE FILLED IN BY THE APPRAISEE)

APPRAISEE NAME & SIGNATURE	REPORTING OFFICER NAME & SIGNATURE	NAME	SIGNATURE	DATE

* Forms used by an organisation of repute in India.

PART IV - OVERALL ASSESSMENT - CAREER PLAN

OVERALL ASSESSMENT

POOR	AVERAGE	GOOD	V. GOOD	EXCELLENT
1	2	3	4	5

	NAME	SIGNATURE	DATE
REPORTING OFFICER			
REVIEWING OFFICER			

SUMMARY : POST APPRAISAL DISCUSSIONS TO BE FILLED IN BY THE REPORTING OFFICER WITH AN AGREED ACTION PLAN FOR ENHANCED PERFORMANCE

BRIEF CAREER PLAN (1-2 YEARS)

DEVELOPMENT INPUTS PROPOSED (1-2 YEARS)

PART V - FINANCIAL RECOMMENDATIONS

PRESENT POSITION	PROPOSED RECOMMENDATIONS
NAME	NO INCREMENT
AGE	INCREMENT %AMOUNT
DESIGNATION	UPGRADE
DOJ	PROMOTE
CO./DIVN.	REVISED DESIGNATION, IF ANY
DEPTT./SECTION	REVISED BASIC
QUALIFICATION	DEPTT HEAD
EXPERIENCE	NAME
BASIC	SIGNATURE
GRADE	DATE

IF INCUMBENTS POSITION IS TO BE CHANGED, SPECIFY THE FOLLOWING POSITION

LOCATION   FUNCTION

COMPANY/DIVIN./DEPTT./SECTION

APPRAISAL COMMITTEE'S APPROVAL

NAME & SIGNATURE	NAME & SIGNATURE	NAME & SIGNATURE	NAME & SIGNATURE

Non-executive appraisal forms are far simpler to fill and are usually short. However, the broad guidelines are the same as discussed here.

Promotion

Promotion or periodical upgradation motivates people. Such recognition is more of a social need rather than just an increase in salary. It motivates the employee as it adds to his social status and group-relatedness. It fulfils his desire for achieving distinction and the craving for social approval. It is looked at as a reward of demonstrated ability.

Sometimes promotion does bring little perquisites like separate office rooms, reserved parking place with name plates, private secretaries, better office furnishings, etc. and is an added satisfaction. To be effective, perquisites should be carefully graded in increasing scales to match the status symbol and positional placement in the organisational hierarchy.

Promotion also satisfies the hidden ego of a man since his work has been considered important. It satisfies his self-esteem. It has been seen that a frustrated worker who is regarded useless or is written off from the point of view of returns to the company, often improves his productivity and performance on being promoted. His lower output was due to his stagnation. His reservoirs of physical and mental capabilities were either not fully understood or not fully tapped by the employers.

Tom Walthing has mentioned that a good manager at every level tries to identify his successor and coach him for the day he would take over. It is a good policy. However, in practice, it may not always be desirable in a large organisation for each manager to be succeeded by someone from within his own section, department or division. It may be better to have some interchange between parts of an organisation and the outside society so that promotions do not become totally inbred. Infusion of some new blood may even revitalise the working of the organisation.

Every organisation must have a promotion plan. The promotion policy must be concerned with expansion, contraction, change, equal opportunity to all, recruitment and motivation. It clearly impinges on industrial relations.

A well designed promotion plan and structure should give as much attention to people moving sidewards as it does to people moving upwards. Two important factors are often overlooked in the design of a promotion plan. Firstly, the fact that people's attitude changes over time, and secondly, that people who have devoted their time exclusively to their work and specialisation, when pushed up the ladder, can become stale, narrow in their outlook and out of touch with developments outside the sphere of their immediate concern.

Plans for promotion should be conceived to cover the whole of the organsiation. There is nothing more demoralising to the lower-placed staff of an organisation to see whole armies of new men being recruited from outside to fill every senior vacancy or selected band of people getting quick promotions superseding seniors or disregarding their claims.

In medieval times, there was a little problem in planning for promotion as sons succeeded their father. This practice has since become outdated. In certain backwaters of our society it still continues, but it may not continue for long.

Merit vs. Seniority

A company may promote its employees on the basis of merit or seniority or both. Merit promotions serve as an incentive to qualified and hardworking personnel. It distinguishes between good and bad workers on the basis of their contributions to the job, productivity, innovativeness and excellence in their areas of operation. Seniority based promotion rewards the age and length of service, attachment and loyalty to the organisation and long-term commitments. Merit-cum-seniority is preferred over either of the two bases as it rewards both merit as well as seniority. Among the seniors, meritorious ones gain promotion. Management in most organisations prefer merit over seniority, while trade unions oppose it because in their view it makes employees compete with each other and goes against team spirit and trade union solidarity.

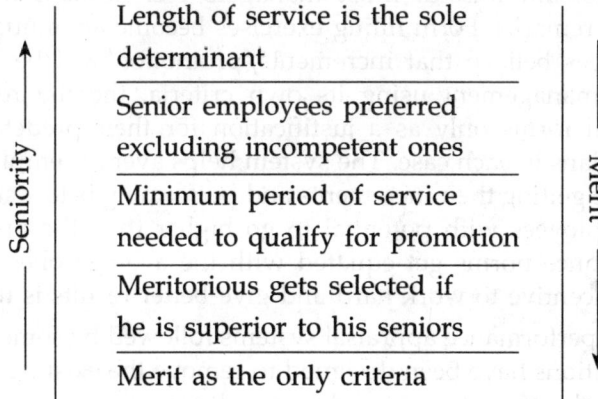

Fig. 11.1: Bases for Promotion

If a promotion policy is not fair, it will have an adverse effect on motivation. Methods that help develop a feeling of fairness include internal advertising of all the jobs in the organisation and no restrictions whatsoever in seeking betterment of careers outside. The system of annual appraisal is another aid to make the promotion system fair.

Promotion policies have a considerable impact on the attitudes of people towards the organisation which they serve. These policies determine whether the top class and bright people would stick to the organisation. They also influence their sense of belonging to the organisation.

Timing is important for promotion. Some larger organisations maintain a short list of those ready for promotion to the next grade. When a vacancy occurs they merely promote the person at the top of the list. Experience shows that delay breeds speculation and strife which is harmful for the individuals as well as the organisation.

Promotions should be earned. These should not be automatic or for considerations other than work and the results achieved, otherwise, as Dr. Laurence J. Peter has put forward, "In a hierarchy, every employee tends to rise to their level of incompetence." This principle can be seen working in many organisations. This happens because of the fact that people are promoted on the basis of their present work, and their potential for managing the new job is not properly evaluated.

Performance Appraisal in Indian Companies

A common complaint against performance appraisal systems in many Indian companies is that good things get said, but bad things remain unsaid. Most managers feel hesitant in giving adverse remarks. Form filling exercises become an annual ritual. Employees believe that increments/promotion will be handled by the management using its own criteria, thereby rendering appraisal forms only as a justification for their predetermined action plans in each case. The system helps average employees to continue getting their increments and performing below standard. The employees with potential to go higher than the prescribed performance norms get equated with the average ones in most cases. Incentive to work hard and give better results is thus lost.

The performance appraisal systems followed by some leading organisations have been designed to remove the existing fallacies and develop a performance-driven culture.

* Performance appraisal at the Essar group is a monthly affair. Appraisers and appraisees meet regularly to ensure that corrections are made instantly.
* Satyam follows a two-dimensional approach. The X axis is focused on asset building like people's capability, innovative ability, etc. while Y axis focuses on the results.
* GE India not only measures the performance of its employees but also the alignment between how the company rates its employees and how it rewards them in supporting the overall goal of business.
* RPG informs its employees when giving increments, the basis of calculating it and also where the employee stands in the rating.
* LG's appraisal system has three broad parameters: performance, attitude and knowledge.
* Johnson and Johnson provides opportunities to its employees, through 27 different parameters (developed by the company's founder), to reflect upon the company's policies, processes, culture and decision-making.
* HDFC encourages feedback through its appraisal system. Employee writes whether his boss listens to him, recognises his contribution and empowers him to work effectively.

PERSPECTIVE | 360 Degree Appraisal -TISCO

The 360 degree appraisal at TISCO has three components:

* There is a self-appraisal portion where one reviews what he has done: what kind of difficulties he encountered in the process, his major achievements and developmental needs.
* Employee's self-appraisal goes to his superior for further assessment which is data-based and objective as it is measured against corporate goals.
* The last portion is a subjective portion where one is assessed on how one has managed his work and achieved results. This assessment is done to disseminate the message that there is a style of management the company believes in, and if the results have been achieved in any other way, it is not as satisfying. Thus, assessment is done against a set of managerial capabilities/traits.

The entire appraisal is an open process. All assessment is shared by the officer concerned and the process is not complete until the officer has signed the last step in the process. Disagreements, if any, must be resolved before the officer signs on the dotted line.

The data generated by the above process is closely linked with several decisions which the management takes later. Major personnel decisions such as rewards, annual increments for promotion or posting, job rotations and other administrative actions are linked to it.

360 Degree Appraisal

Prof. T.V. Rao and his team at IIM-Ahmedabad developed an organisation effectiveness programme in the 1980s which was branded as 360 Degree Appraisal in the US in 1998. The technique is being used in one form or another the world over by larger corporations including many fortune 500 companies. It is a multi-rater appraisal and feedback system. A questionnaire is designed to assess the candidate, and the appraisal is done anonymously by others (peers, immediate supervisor, other managers, internal customers, etc. normally, not less than three) and collected by an external agency, which pools and compiles the information. The objective is to measure behaviour critical to employee performance and provide feedback to the candidate through workshop, boss, and HRD division.

Commitment of top management and an organisational climate receptive to such a system are prerequisites for introducing 360 degree appraisal. The system being sensitive in nature, it may not be acceptable to many in an organisation where there is politics and lack of team spirit. When seniors are assessed by juniors, for instance, the seniors may not be prepared for it.

360 Degree Appraisal is not a mere tool to assess people. Its purpose is to build competence and prepare people for change. It helps in developing an organisational culture which is open and participative where people from all levels including the top are willing to listen, learn and improve. Sample questions from a 360 degree appraisal form for senior executives of an MNC are given below:

* Makes an overall plan covering key aspects of an assignment
* Encourages others to take initiatives and be involved in decisions
* Challenges others constructively
* Integrates information from various sources, interprets it, identifies salient points
* Shows realistic appreciation of the broad business
* Gives feedback securitively and constructively
* Secures effective cross-functional cooperation
* Shows resilience despite setbacks and challenges
* Makes efforts to discover and understand others' views

Aditya Birla Group provides a good example of 360 degree appraisal. The process was started in 1999 when 42 senior managers who directly reported to the Chairman, Kumar Mangalam Birla, rated him on his leadership style, managerial ability and personal traits. The rating showed Birla as a leader empowering his people, delegating well, and a visionary. Some described it as a gimmick by Birla. But only after two months of the exercise, Birla sent a six page letter to all the senior managers assessing his respective role, mentioning areas that required improvement and spelling out his expectations.

Situation Analysis

Martin and George are managers of two production units in the same plant. They have two deputies, Lekha and Prasad, both of whom are considered very efficient. Each has worked for a number of years with his respective manager.

```
        Martin                George
          —                     —

          —                     —
        Lekha                 Prasad
```

Martin was selected for advanced training in the US for one year. The management did not consider Lekha for an officiating promotion and George was given the charge of both the units with two deputies under him, viz. Lekha and Prasad.

The nature of working of Martin and George was entirely different from one another. Their respective deputies had also picked up their working methods.

Soon after the departure of Martin to USA, there were serious differences between George and Lekha; they fell apart. There were two reasons for this:

— Lekha was frustrated as he did not get an officiating promotion to the place left vacant by Martin, and hence, did not extend cooperation to George.

— George started interfering in the day-to-day work of Lekha which the latter did not like. He was also not accustomed to such interference as Martin had given him a lot of freedom in his work.

The differences became so strong that George got Lekha transferred to some other unit. The work of the unit of Lekha further deteriorated but George was adamant not to take him back. He assured the management that he would himself handle this initial setback. Lekha requested that he should be sent back to his original section but his request was turned down by the management.

Soon after Martin returned from the US. On taking over the charge and reviewing the situation, he strongly recommended that Lekha be posted back in his department.

How would you resolve such a situation to the satisfaction of all?

Review Questions

1. What are the objectives of performance appraisal system?
2. What is graphic rating scale? How is it superior to the simple grading system?
3. Distinguish between forced distribution and forced choice as systems of merit rating.
4. Describe the critical incident method of merit rating with a suitable illustration.
5. Between seniority and merit, which criteria would you prefer and why?
6. What are the consequences of an unfair promotion policy?
7. Discuss the merits and demerits of informal promotion.
8. 'A good manager at every level should try to identify his successor and prepare him to take over when the situation arises'. Comment.
9. Suggest a model for succession planning.
10. What is 360 degree appraisal? Discuss its merits and demerits.
11. What are the company practices regarding performance appraisal in India?

Further Readings

1. Roger Bennett: *Managing Personnel and Performances* (Hutchison, London, 1981).
2. R.L. Cardy: *Performance Management: Concepts, Skills and Exercises* (Armonk, New York, 2004).
3. J. Hale: *Strategic Rewards: Keeping Your Best Talent from Walking out the Door* (Compensation and Benefits Management, Vol. 14, pp. 39-50, 1998).
4. Laurie Bassi and Daniel McMurrer: *Maximizing Your Return on People* (HBR, March 2007).
5. Fred Luthans and Suzanne J. Peterson: *360 Degree Feedback with Systematic Coaching: Empirical Analysis Suggests a Winning Combination* (Human Resource Management, Vol. 42, pp. 243-256, 2003).
6. D. McGregor: *An Uneasy Look at Performance Appraisal* (HBR, Vol. 35, pp. 89-94, 1957).

Chapter 12

Training and Development

To develop flexible managers for the future, we should teach them to write poetry, read military history and study weather maps. Writing poetry will teach precision of thought and language, reading military history will teach policy-making (armies have been put into battle with half page operations orders), and studying weather maps will teach decision-making under uncertainty.

– W.J. Reddin

(Business Horizons, Aug. 1974)

Learning Objectives

After reading this chapter you will be able to:

1. Understand the need for training all category of employees from workers to top executives.
2. Elaborate training methods both on the job and off the job.
3. Discuss the role of training division in assessing training needs, developing plans and organising training programmes.

Training is a must for all categories of employees in all establishments. Trained manpower is the biggest asset of an organisation.

Induction

The induction of a new worker is an important aspect of employment. The acceptance of a job implies entrance into a community in which the worker, as a social being, will seek human satisfaction. This satisfaction depends very much upon his being accepted therein.

This is a two-sided process. On the employer's part, the applicant has to be turned into a worker who is satisfied with his job and environment. On the other hand, a worker has numerous questions in his mind. His doubts and fears need to be clarified. To achieve this dual aim, a defined practice based on experience, imagination and sympathy is needed. It is a mistake to leave the worker to know and clear his doubts on the working site. The prospective worker should have required induction when a job is under discussion or soon after his selection.

A worker may first come into contact with the receptionist or employment exchange officer when he calls at the employment office. How well he is received will affect his attitude to his engagement at the time and during the years of his employment. He will appreciate courtesy in manner, reasonable clarity and orderly arrangements throughout.

When he has been engaged, the employee must be clear about when he is to begin work and to whom he has to report. A written form of engagement containing these particulars avoids misunderstanding. A printed statement describing the ways of the firm and the rules governing the work and the workers should be given to him or explained by someone who is conversant with these rules. A brochure setting out the most pertinent work rules and explaining any important points of conduct, especially where personal safety is concerned, may be printed for this purpose.

Training the Workmen

Approach to the Problem

The training of the workers can be viewed from three angles:

(i) It is the follow-up to selection. Selection is only the first stage in fitting the individual into his job. The selector needs to be in touch with the people he has selected. On the one hand, he may check his own techniques and success and, on the other, he may ensure that individuals are rightly placed. Business sense calls for an adequate opportunity to be given to all the suitable persons selected for employment to learn their jobs.

(ii) It is the process of learning applied to the work room. Different people learn in different ways. But learning can never be effective unless carried out in a systematic manner. The training of workers, therefore, in common with all other kinds of teaching, must take into account four factors: (a) the learner, (b) the job to be taught, (c) the trainer, and (d) the methods to be used.

(iii) It is a means adopted for achieving greater competence. The trained worker is on the road to becoming more efficient. Unless an absolute limit of capacity exists, no employee of any grade, whether manual, clerical or executive, can fail to benefit from training programmes.

The problems which arise in the process of training will be revealed in the consideration of these points:

(a) The persons to be trained

The persons to be trained may belong to different age groups having varying capacities to work. They may be young, fresh from school or entering somewhat later into the industry. They may be men or women – single or married – from different walks of life. Some will be suitable only for unskilled work, though a few may be suitable for training in relatively skilled occupations. Workers in these situations present many kinds of human problems. They will react differently to the same methods of instruction and will learn at varying levels. As such, they call for individual treatment from the trainers.

(b) The job to be learned

The jobs may be just as varied as the capacity of the learners. Jobs may be unskilled, semi-skilled, or even relatively skilled. It may be mass production or repetitive work. It may be complicated, or simple and easily learned. But simplicity must not be overstressed, since few establishments keep an individual continuously on one subdivided element and, therefore, instructions must cover the job as a whole. Moreover, a person learns better if his interest has been stimulated by showing him where he fits in the chain of production.

(c) The trainers

Proper training involves competent instructors. The steps necessary to procure competent instructors are:

(i) Selection of persons who know the processes and jobs thoroughly; can express their ideas clearly; can describe movements accurately; and are patient and tactful with slow learners.

(ii) Introduction of these persons to the methods of teaching. This would include a statement of the general laws of learning and common maxims governing good teaching, and at times, detailed methods, for instance, showing how to pack, or to assemble the particular parts of the thing on which they are to work.

(iii) General instructions to the instructors in such matters as the source and supply of materials; the inspection of finished goods; time and motion study; costing and planning; wage calculations or any matter on which questions might be expected from the trainees.

(iv) Clarification of their own views on the human problems of training to bring these views into line with the company's policies.

Methods of Training

Training methods vary from the unorganised system of learning from working colleagues to the more systematic methods of instruction.

(a) Learning by 'Exposure'

This is still the most common method, especially in smaller factories. It is a costly and ineffective system subject to criticism on two grounds:

(i) From the worker standpoint – Proper teaching takes time and will reduce output where trouble is honestly taken in training another.

(ii) From the psychological standpoint – This method may not be unsatisfactory. It is learning by imitation, or more precisely, by 'exposure' to the example of another. Even though it may be a good model, imitation can never be perfect and instruction in such circumstances proceeds by the correction of errors. However, mistakes at times imprint themselves on the memory and, become part of the unconscious, showing themselves in bad working habits. Its eradication takes a long time and makes learning by 'exposure' costly.

(b) Systematic Training – Vestibule School

The main characteristic of the vestibule school is that it is in a separate room which may be part of the workroom but still distinct from it. Its location and set-up give it certain advantages.

(i) The pupils can be brought into the classroom spirit; they will be less distracted, and consequently, the teacher will be able to use his specialised skill more effectively.

(ii) Emphasis can be put on good quality production and attention given to the weak points of the pupil. This can encompass temperamental and other qualities, and the school be made a helpful bridge between the classroom and the factory.

The vestibule school has its drawbacks which must be removed, if it is to be made effective.

- The atmosphere may become unreal, with work being made too simple and difficulties removed too fully.
- Speed may be sacrificed and a tendency to 'slow motion' set up.
- The school may become an end in itself, with the result that pupils experience a sense of shock when they are transferred to the workroom.

These drawbacks, however, will be obviated if certain steps are taken:

— To avoid unreality, the work in which pupils are trained should be production work.

— Some firms insist on quality first and speeding up to the standards later.

— The danger of the school being an end in itself can be removed by arrangements which give it an acknowledged place in the factory organisation.

Training in the Workroom

Training in the workroom takes place under normal conditions of work. It is organised instruction for which generally the foreman is responsible even if he does not teach the workers himself.

The workroom has its disadvantages as a place in which to teach and learn. The distractions of the bench are considerable. Concentration at work is not easy and amidst the prevailing noises, the worker may fail to catch the full meaning of important instructions. The plus point is the environment in which the learner ultimately has to work. His disappointment will, on the whole, be less if he faces the working difficulties during the learning period. Here, the discipline is that of the foreman rather than of the teacher. If the disadvantages of the workroom can be reduced, it can prove better than any other method, for here both speed and quality of workmanship can be acquired.

Learning Curves

Learning curve shows the relationship between performance and training time. Patterns have been devised for many occupations and skills by psychologists in conjunction with teachers. Their major conclusions can be summed up as follows:

(i) All practice curves have a common general form indicating a degree of uniformity in the learning process, whatever the subject.

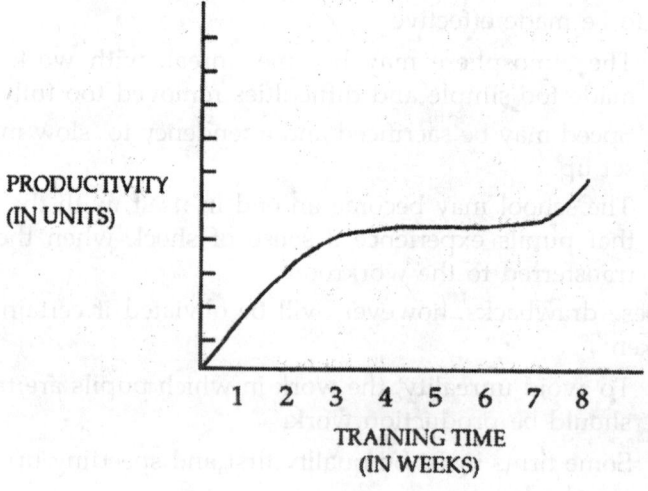

Fig. 12.1: Learning Curves

(ii) Learning starts at a low point, then accelerates rather rapidly but becomes stabilised in a fairly level curve or 'plateau'. This level marks the degree of skills attained in the sense of consistency in producing output right in quality and high in quantity.

(iii) Inability to get off this plateau, broadly speaking, has in the past implied the end of the learning process.

Experience shows that there are conditions which enable trainees to break away from these plateaus and establish higher levels of proficiency. Incentives and hopes of promotion bring dedication or greater concentration and effort which lead to improved attitude towards the job.

Training the Office Staff

Efficiency of an office, whether government or private, depends upon the quality of the staff. While the sense of responsibility and loyalty to an organisation is important, it cannot be a substitute for good knowledge of job techniques and scientific methods of operation. For example, an employee, howsoever loyal and devoted to an organisation, cannot handle the correspondence work effectively if he lacks good expression. Similarly, an employee having years of experience may not be able to use the latest techniques if he is not familiar with them. The administrative offices where, on an average, an employee is paid many times more than a factory worker, can run economically and efficiently only when they are managed properly. Among the four 'Ms' of management – men, money, machine and materials – it is the men who are the most important for offices.

While devising a training programme for office staff, several factors have to be taken into account. Individuals differ in their capacity to work, intelligence and basic aptitudes. The potentiality to grow is also not the same in all employees. Even in the best managed organisations, not all people joining at the level of assistants and clerks will retire as directors or senior executives. The requirements of the office and the role that it plays in the whole business setup are also to be kept in view while training people. Some of the important factors which influence training programmes are:

Age

All men have a similar capacity to grow in age but not with age. Those who adjust themselves to the changes taking place in their environment, equip themselves with the latest knowledge and techniques, and apply their minds for improving their efficiency, rise in life. Not all employees take the initiative to learn continuously and advance. People in the older age group, therefore, need training as much as those in the younger age group. It is necessary to wipe out orthodox practices, procedures and methods in an organisation and introduce new scientific ones.

Training young minds is easy as they have no inhibitions. Old employees do not forget past habits so easily. The training techniques for the two age groups should thus be different.

Academic Qualifications

Men who have acquired knowledge through university and college education cannot be bracketed with those who have not. It is not only a question of faith in the degrees and diplomas of our universities but also a fact that experience is a substitute for academic qualifications only in a limited sense. Trainees are, therefore, to be grouped according to their academic achievements. Sometimes, even among the trainees who hold the same degree, a distinction may be made on the basis of their levels of achievement. A trainee, with a brilliant academic record may be more receptive and may take less time in grooming than one with poor academic records or one who is an easy-going person. In making such distinctions, however, the basic aptitudes and interests of the trainees have to be kept in view.

Aptitude and Interest

Employees differ in their basic interests. Some are very intelligent but not hardworking, while others may be hardworking but lacking in intelligence. It is the job of the trainer to make people feel interested in their work and to improve their knowledge. The likes and dislikes of the trainees for particular jobs, responsibilities etc., cannot be ignored. Some employees like table work, while others may have more interest in liaison, coordination and field work. Moreover, training can remove certain misgivings or orthodox beliefs regarding the nature of a particular job and thus create an interest in the employee. Lack of interest is often due to lack of information.

Job Requirements

An office is primarily a means to attain the objectives of business. It is the nerve centre of modern organisations. There has been a tremendous increase in the volume of office work in recent years because of governmental regulations and publicity work.

The kind of work done in all offices is basically the same, i.e., processing the information for efficient coordination of production, distribution and financing of merchandise or services. This processing of information involves four steps: communication – written and oral; summarising operating results; record keeping, systematising; and cost reduction. The scope of training curriculum is determined, to a certain extent, by job requirements. For better communication, proficiency in a language is a must. Proficiency may be attained through regular courses, guided readings, film shows, writing contests, etc. The organisation may have to build a library of its own. For improving record keeping, training in modern methods of accounting and costing is essential. The efficiency of an employee can also be improved by training him in the modern methods of office communication, set-up and administration. General awareness of the economic and social environments, governmental regulations and technological changes should also be included in the training curriculum for all types of staff.

Company Policy

The company's overall personnel policy regulates the training programme. If the chairman or the board is keen to develop people at different levels of the organisation, and the promotion policy is linked with improvement in qualifications, training programmes are easy to implement.

The facilities that an organisation provides for improving qualifications and attending courses, seminars, buying books and journals, etc. go a long way in creating interest among the employees. An investment in office manpower never goes waste. Even if a well-trained employee leaves an organisation, he carries the goodwill of the organisation and helps build an image for the organisation outside.

Training of Management Trainees

The future of any organisation depends largely upon the availability of the right type of executive personnel at the right time. Well-trained managers are hard to find and business houses cannot always approach the open market for their requirements. They have to develop a cadre of professionally qualified people to man the key posts in future. Moreover, each organisation has its own culture and requires people who not only accept it, but are also acceptable to it. An expanding business organisation with a progressive outlook, therefore, regularly recruits management trainees while smaller organisations do so less frequently, depending on their requirements and resources.

A well planned training programme for management trainees is a must for developing the creative faculties of trainees and orienting them to the practical aspects of administration. The training should start with an orientation programme in which the trainees are introduced as the executives of the organisation and acquainted with its policies and programmes. They are familiarised with the past history of the organisation, its activities, its work and offices, its products and its people. They may be addressed by some of the company executives, and provided with the company's balance sheet and other printed information giving details about the organisation. They may also be sent on visits to different factories and offices of the company. The familiarising programme should be as informal as possible. It is also desirable not to create any false impressions in the minds of the trainees to avoid frustration in the future.

The trainees should be placed on the job after their orientation. Rotational programmes are considered the best for them. They may be placed under the supervision of the heads of selected departments for stipulated periods, so that they can learn the rudiments of the job from the very beginning. It would be desirable not to treat them as 'crown princes' while they are on job training. They can learn something from the man at the lowest ladder also. While at the job, the trainees should be carefully observed and their activities be analysed. Their observation power, the ability to do the job and adjustability are on test. They can also make their contribution to the administration by bringing in new ideas and procedures against the established ones, some of which may have become obsolete. The trainees may also make unbiased comparison of the working of different departments.

During the entire period of training, each trainee may be placed under the care and guidance of one senior level executive. The system of understudy may be adopted for making one executive responsible for the development of one trainee. Even when the trainee will be on the job in other departments, his supervisor will have control on him. This system, however, works well only when really competent people are made supervisors who may compete among themselves in producing the best manager out of the trainees rather than creating their henchmen.

Group discussions, seminars and case sessions are important means of developing the trainees. In group discussions, trainees get an opportunity to improve their power of expression and deliberation and also their knowledge by having a cross-section of opinions on different issues. Their personality also comes into play in such meetings. The trainees may also be sponsored for short-term seminars and courses organised by management institutes so as to gain from the experience of experts in the field of management.

During the entire training, period good reading material should be provided to the trainees. Selected articles on management, technological advancement, industrial, commercial and social problems should be distributed among them from time to time. A reference library should also be built for them.

A system of reward and recognition may also be introduced to motivate trainees. The training period may be reduced in the case of trainees who show an outstanding ability to learn and develop in a short time. Provision of benefits such as housing for trainees may prove to be a strong motivating factor. During group discussions and seminars, the trainees may be asked to preside over the meetings in rotation. The company's regular interview board may allow one of the trainees to sit as an observer. A system of counselling should be built for the trainee whose performance is not up to the mark.

In the organisational hierarchy the number of positions at the top level are limited. At the lower level, the aspirants for middle and higher level positions are many. The middle managers find themselves in a dilemma in a situation like this. Only a few of them get the opportunity to rise to senior positions. Some may manage to retire honourably. The fear of being dismissed looms large on the heads of the remaining. They are supposed to make place for those on the waiting list at the lower level and the new entrants from the outside. Openings outside may not always be very bright for them. What should they do? Who is responsible for all this? What should the organisation do for them? These are some of the problems which have attracted the attention of management scientists in recent times.

Green Stamps for Shelf-sitters

The middle managers whose careers come to a halt are called shelf-sitters. They may become shelf-sitters either because of their incompetence or organisational inability to create further openings for them or both. They are kept on the pay roll because, as Fielden and Common claim, "The vast majority of top executives simply does not have the stomach for casting out the dead wood".

The factors which render shelf-sitters incompetent are mainly physical, mental and social. Most of the middle management positions are occupied by people of the middle age group. They may lack the energy and enthusiasm of young managers. They may lack dynamism also. Their habits, acquired rightly or wrongly, characterise them. In their effort to please bosses or suppress their juniors, they may overact. Family responsibilities and financial burdens may compel them not to take risks and accept challenges. Those who reach middle positions at the fag-end of their career, after having served for the most part of their lives in low positions, are natural shelf-sitters. They deem it an honour to retire on these positions. The bureaucratic organisations, in particular, are full of people in the older age group on middle managerial and administrative posts. They carry the virtue of indecision, red-tapism and strict adherence to certain false notions and principles.

The organisation's inability and incompetence which develops a band of shelf-sitters may be both due to inner constraints and managerial policies. Few organisations can afford to give opportunities to all middle personnel to adorn the top positions. Those who are close to the top bosses go up, while others have to sit on the shelf or go out. Defective manpower planning and recruitment practices are also responsible for the growth of shelf-sitters. Sometimes large organisations create well-paying positions which have little real function and fill real jobs with totally unqualified people. The beneficiaries of the largeness then become the victims of it.

The shelf-sitters can help themselves by creating an environment in which they are considered to be more useful and indispensable. This would require not only up-to-date knowledge in their areas of specialisation, but also better relations with their bosses and subordinates. They have to strengthen their role as an important link in the organisational hierarchy in such a way that the management feels that in throwing them out, the possibility of causing damage to the organisation may increase. Development of professional outlook among managers may also help in containing the problem. Managers should not be frightened of the prospect of changing jobs. The second career may be more enriching and rewarding than the existing one.

The organisation can help considerably in preparing the shelf-sitters for better careers outside. It may introduce a plan under which a manager earns educational credits or 'green stamps' (based on the length of service in lower and middle management), which he can cash in to pay for academic courses that prepare him for better job opportunities outside the organisation. The shelf-sitter should be given an indication in advance that he would not be considered for better positions so that he may use his 'green stamps' to forge a second career and avoid demotion and stagnation. The expenditure on a plan like this would certainly be less than that of retaining the unwanted shelf-sitters. On humanitarian grounds too, it is desirable to equip an employee for a better career outside if there are not enough openings within the organisation.

The 'green stamps' may also reduce the chance of becoming shelf-sitters. Fresh training may change the attitude of the manager, develop his skill and knowledge, and make him useful to the organisation again. Thus, the plan may 'tackle a real problem' and contain a hidden bonus for corporations as well as potential shelf-sitters.

The emphasis of the 'green stamp' plan is on increasing the educational qualifications. The success of the plan, therefore, depends on the availability of educational programmes and job opportunities based on these programmes for middle managers.

Training the Executives

The executives who are responsible for getting things done through the efforts of others need training for several reasons. Majority of them occupy senior positions by virtue of exercising responsibility in less senior roles in the same organisation. By winning the confidence of their superiors on account of hard work and loyalty, many of them may have easy access to higher positions, even though they may be lacking in some of the skills required for such positions. The specialists and technical personnel who rise to executive positions need more general managerial abilities as their specialised knowledge may go out of date.

Executive development programmes vary in content and methodology. Some of these are highly structured, tailor-made and have specific focus, while others are completely unstructured, open and provide behavioural insight. Some prominent ED techniques are discussed below:

In-basket Exercise

The trainee would find a number of letters and documents in his or her drawer/tray and is asked to act upon them as if he or she is actually in the position to deal with them. This exercise is aimed at developing problem-solving skills.

PERSPECTIVE

Talent Acquisition and Retention – TCS

TCS employs people from over 67 different nationalities. The composition of its global workforce shows increasing trend in the number of female employees and foreign nationals across the globe. The company continues to invest in talent development through a stringent academic accreditation programme as well as by providing training, internships and projects to students. As a result of these initiatives, it has become an employer of choice on engineering campuses across India. It launched TCS Ignite in 2007 with a view to make significant strides in the areas of training, digitisation and innovation. Ignite demonstrates the commitment of the company to inclusive growth by hiring 60% first generation graduates. Ignite trainees are encouraged to pursue higher education while working. Initial Learning Programme centres are established at different locations in the country for fresh recruits.

The retention rate of employees in TCS is one of the highest in India. The low attrition rate has been achieved by continuously investing in learning and development programmes for employees, competitive compensation, creating compelling work environment, empowering employees at all levels as well as well-structured reward and recognition mechanism.

Incidence Process

A group of trainees is given an incident with details. They have to formulate issues around which discussions may take place. A short-term decision may be made. Then there can be reexamination of the case and a course of action may be suggested by the group. At the end, the group leader may inform what actually happened in the case – giving opportunity to the trainees to compare their formulations with actual happenings.

Sensitivity Training

Also called 'T' group or laboratory training, it is largely an unstructured group training programme with no leader, no agenda and no stated goals. The objective is to develop interaction. It is mostly used for training senior executives and top personnel. The group consists of eight to twelve persons who have face-to-face interaction. The emphasis is on here and now. Confrontation is allowed without outside intervention. The interactions and experiences serve as the real substance of the learning process, and improve sensitivity and awareness.

Brainstorming

Brainstorming is a group creativity technique designed to generate a large number of ideas for the solution of a problem. This method was popularised in 1953 by Alex Faickney Osborn in a book titled *Applied Imagination*. Osborn proposed that groups could double their creative output with brainstorming.

Brainstorming has become a popular group technique, when applied in a traditional group setting. Because of such problems as distraction, social loafing, evaluation apprehension and production blocking, conventional brainstorming groups are a little more effective than other types of groups but they are actually less effective than individuals working independently. In the *Encyclopedia of Creativity*, Tudor Rickards, in his entry on brainstorming, summarises its controversies and indicates the dangers of conflating productivity in group work with quantity of ideas.

Although traditional brainstorming does not increase the productivity of groups (as measured by the number of ideas generated), it may still provide benefits, such as boosting morale, enhancing work enjoyment, and improving team work. Thus, numerous attempts have been made to improve brainstorming or use more effective variations of the basic technique.

Ground Rules

There are four basic rules of brainstorming. These are intended to reduce social inhibitions among group members, stimulate idea generation, and increase overall creativity of the group.

1. **Focus on quantity:** This rule is a means of enhancing divergent production, aiming to facilitate problem solving through the maxim *quantity breeds quality*. The assumption is that the greater the number of ideas generated, the greater the chance of producing a radical and effective solution.
2. **Withhold criticism:** In brainstorming, criticism of ideas generated should be put 'on hold'. Instead, participants should focus on extending or adding to the ideas, reserving criticism for a later 'critical stage' of the process. By suspending judgement, participants will feel free to generate unusual ideas.
3. **Welcome unusual ideas:** To get a good and long list of ideas, unusual ideas are welcomed. They can be generated by looking from new perspectives and suspending assumptions. New ways of thinking may provide better solutions.
4. **Combine and improve ideas:** Several good ideas may be combined to form a single better idea, as suggested by the slogan '1+1=3'. It is believed to stimulate the building of ideas by a process of association.

Nominal Group Technique

The nominal group technique is a type of brainstorming that encourages all participants to have an equal say in the process. It is also used to generate a ranked list of ideas.

Participants are asked to write their ideas anonymously. Then the moderator collects the ideas and each is voted on by the group. The vote can be as simple as a show of hands in favour of a given idea. This process is called distillation.

After distillation, the top ranked ideas may be sent back to the group or subgroups for further brainstorming. For example, one group may work on the colour of the product, another group may work on the size, and so on. Each group will come back to the whole group for ranking the listed ideas. Sometimes, the ideas that were previously dropped may be brought forward again, once the group has re-evaluated the ideas.

It is important that the facilitator be trained in this process before attempting to work with this technique. The group should be primed and encouraged to embrace the process. Like all team efforts, it may take a few practice sessions to train the team properly before dealing with the important ideas.

Electronic Brainstorming

Electronic brainstorming is a computerised version of the manual brainstorming technique. It is typically supported by an electronic meeting system (EMS) but simpler forms can also be used like e-mail and other browser based systems, or peer-to-peer softwares.

Using an electronic meeting system, participants share a list of ideas over the internet. Ideas are entered independently. Contributions become immediately visible to all and are typically kept anonymous to encourage openness and reduce personal prejudice. Modern EMS also supports asynchronous brainstorming.

Simulations

The trainee may receive information from computer on a specific situation/problem. He would formulate his strategies, feed them to the computer, get reaction, and at the end, check his decision with the computer's result. This exercise is helpful in developing orientation to quantitative techniques.

Role Play

The trainees are asked to enact the roles they may be called upon to play in their jobs. It is suitable where a situation which is similar to the real life position can be provided in training. The trainees get the feel of real life pressures. The method will be effective only when trainees take their roles seriously.

Business Games

The trainees are provided information about different aspects of the working of a company like production, finance, marketing, etc. The groups of trainees are then assigned different roles, e.g. one group may look after production, another group may be concerned with sales and so on. These groups then run the company, take decisions. The results of these decisions are calculated in terms of profitability.

Social Changes

The executive of today is living in a dynamic society. The last few decades have witnessed changes of far-reaching importance in our social and community structure. The contributions of psychologists, sociologists, anthropologists and other social scientists have enriched management science in many ways. Some of the presumptions regarding human nature and the methods of dealing with men have gone out of date. An old fashioned executive may take pride in talking of the good old days when his orders were respected like the command of a military officer and followed unquestioningly and ungrudgingly but the new generation is different. People in industry are better organised today and conscious of their rights and privileges. The officers come from different strata of the society. Senior positions are no longer restricted to the members of a particular class. The changing social structure demands greater awareness on the part of executives.

Identification of Training Needs

It is debatable whether the executive's immediate superior should be in charge of his training needs. The superior's superior may be more suitable to identify such needs because of his position as he may be free from some of the apprehensions which the immediate supervisor may have.

A scientific system of appraising merit is of great help in identifying training needs. The areas of deficiency may be located and it may be ascertained which skills require improvement and in which areas acquisition of new skills and knowledge is essential. A generalist managing a technical section may be better equipped if he acquires some technical knowledge. A highly qualified technical person may lack in some of the important aspects of human relations. An executive may be good at work but poor in communication, while another may be good at communication but poor at execution. A non-financial executive dealing with financial matters may face some difficulties which can be overcome by acquiring basic knowledge of financial management. A controller of stores having no knowledge of modern inventory control methods and techniques may find himself handicapped in dealing with critical issues involving stores.

PERSPECTIVE

Cultural Sensitivity Training At Nike

When Nike's code of conduct was being implemented in Vietnam, it was reported that cultural gap existed between the workers and managers. Specific areas of gap identified were:

* On the most basic level, there were language differences which served to exacerbate other differences.
* The Taiwanese and Korean supervisors managed the Vietnamese workers according to their native standards rather than those in practice in Vietnam. Consequently, the Vietnamese workers were displeased.
* The Vietnamese workers were accustomed to a rural, self-paced agricultural work routine and found it hard to adjust to a regimented factory routine with thousand of workers.
* Vietnamese workers were not very educated and, therefore, were not aware of their basic rights as workers.

The result of cultural gap was expectation gap. Productivity was lower, rate of attrition was high and there were possibilities of abridgement of rights affecting the morale of the workers.

Special human relations and cultural sensitivity programme and an awareness campaign called SHAPE (Safety, Health, Attitude of Management, People Investment and Environment) were launched to fill up the cultural gap.

Role of the Training Division

While it is basically the responsibility of the bosses to identify training needs, a training division can be of great help, both in devising the appraisal system and in locating the areas of deficiency.

Organisation of internal training programmes and sponsoring of outside seminars and courses are the responsibilities of the training division. Internal training should be informal in nature. Executive club/study circles may be formed to have informal gatherings. Experts from the cross-section of society may be invited to address the groups from time to time. Business games, case sessions and film shows may also be organised for the groups. Such meetings may foster better relations among the executives and may be informative and stimulating to them. Providing library facilities and circulating articles on current trends related particularly to management should be the responsibility of the training division.

Seminars and Outside Courses

Executives usually welcome participation in conferences and outside courses for several reasons. They are free from office routine for some time. Their performance is not being watched by their bosses. They get an opportunity to meet their counterparts from other industries and exchange ideas with them. They can participate in the deliberations of the conference/seminar with an open mind. They also get a sense of achievement as participation in an outside course amounts to improvement in their qualifications.

An advanced course/seminar for senior level executives should have the following characteristics:

1. It should be of a short duration, since the executives would be busy with heavy responsibilities, and long-term courses are not likely to attract many.
2. It should be organised at a place fitting the dignity, status and convenience of the executives.
3. It should be drafted in such a way that the executives from different academic backgrounds may find it easy and interesting.
4. It should be drafted with instructional methods including lectures, case sessions, group discussions, business games, selected readings, conferences, project reporting, films and audio-visual aids. Group discussions and case sessions are preferred the most.
5. The faculty should consist of both the professors and the business executives.
6. The number of participants should be limited in order to encourage interpersonal contact between the participants for a smooth running of the course.

Training must be a continuous process. The changes in attitudes, behaviour, leadership style and other individual traits do not come in a day or a week. The desired results in this direction are achieved gradually. The effects of company training programmes and participation in outside courses and seminars are to be judged over a period of time. A regular training programme linked with a scientific system of merit appraisal and counselling goes a long way in improving organisational efficiency.

Situation Analysis

(a) Murty is a senior foreman with high intelligence and unusual technical abilities. For any technical bottleneck, he can use his brain and find a solution. He generally fulfils the production targets assigned to him. However, he antagonises almost everyone he comes across and cannot get along with others. He also has a bad tongue and temper. He has often been reprimanded by his superiors and fellow foremen for his tactlessness, use of inappropriate words and lack of cooperation. Warnings to change his tactics have not brought any improvement and he persists in his actions.

Considering his technical abilities, he is indispensable to the organisation but his group behaviour is very intolerable.

What should be done before he is considered for the post of a senior executive for which he is technically qualified and high up in the seniority list?

(b) A company manufacturing engineering goods is facing the problem of high turnover among qualified engineers. When the first plant was installed ten years back, there were only twelve engineers, out of which two belonged to the owner's family.

Today, the company has on its rolls 50 engineers, besides a number of technicians and skilled personnel. Five out of seven brilliant young men who were recruited from an IIT campus left their jobs within six months of their joining. The chief engineer, who is the owner's nephew, does not trust the new recruits and wants them to work strictly according to the plans and schedules laid down. It is difficult to convince him about the effect of new techniques/processes and designs. Among those who left the company during the last few years, many had the bitter experience of undue interference and bossism and lack of opportunities to show their initiative or skill.

What steps do you suggest to improve company management?

Review Questions

1. 'Training is a must for all categories of employees in an establishment'. Discuss.
2. Why is an induction programme necessary for new employees? How can it be made more effective?
3. What is learning by exposure?
4. Explain the concept of learning curve.
5. Discuss the importance of rotational training programmes.
6. Discuss in brief:

    Sensitivity Training

    In-basket Exercise

    Brainstorming
7. Explain the concept of 'green stamp for shelf-sitters'.
8. Discuss the role of training division in assessing training needs, and designing and implementing training programmes.

Further Readings

1. Alan M. Saks and Robert R. Haccoun: *Performance Management Through Training and Development* (ITP Nelson, Toronto, 2000).
2. N. Clark: *HRD and Challenges of Assessing Learning in the Workplace* (International Journal of Training and Development, Vol. 8, Issue 2, pp. 140-156, 2004).
3. William McGehee and Paul W. Thayer: *Training in Business and Industry* (Wiley and Sons, New York, 1961).
4. William J. Rothwell: *Effective Succession Planning* (Amazon, New York, 2001).
5. J.M. Werner and R.L. DeSimone: *Human Resource Development* (Cengage Learning, New Delhi, 2001).
6. K.N. Wexley and G.P. Latham: *Developing and Training Human Resource in Organizations* (Harper Collins, New York, 1991).
7. Scott I. Tannenbaum and Gary Yuki: *Training and Development in Work Organization* (Annual Review of Psychology, Vol. 43, pp. 399-441, 1992).

Chapter 13

Compensation and Incentives

"...The problem of wage structure with which industrial adjudication is concerned in a modern democratic state involves, in the ultimate analysis, to some extent ethical considerations and progressive social philosophy which have rendered the old doctrine of Laissez Faire obsolete."

– **Supreme Court of India**
(Standard Vacuum Refining Co. of India Ltd. Vs. Its Workmen, 1966)

Learning Objectives

After reading this chapter you will be able to:

1. Critically examine wage theories and concepts that developed as industrial economy flourished.
2. Discuss methods of wage payment and incentive systems.
3. Evaluate company practices with regard to production-linked incentive schemes.

Wage Theories

The remuneration which workmen receive is termed as wages. Economists look upon wages as a payment to one of the factors of production for its contribution to the production process. The first wage theory known as the Subsistence Theory of Wages was developed by the English economist David Ricardo in 1817. According to him, "the natural price of the labour is that price which is necessary to enable the labourers, one with another, to subsist and to perpetuate their race, without either increase or diminution". By adopting the Malthus' principle of population (that population tends to press upon the means of subsistence), Ricardo's theory became an 'iron law' of wages. The workers were not to be paid wages above the 'natural price' so that there was no inducement for them to have more children.

John Stuart Mill put forth another theory in 1848. It was known as the Wage Fund Theory. Mill looked upon wages as a function of capital. According to him, out of each year's production, a certain amount must go for equipment, raw materials and the entrepreneur's profits, the remainder being available for labour. If more were to go to labour, then there would be less to invest. This theory was again harsh to the workers. Its assumption of a fixed stock from which wage payments were to be made was severely criticised.

Karl Marx was the first to develop a theory that asserted the workers' rights in the industrial system. In his view, human effort was the source of all value. Other factors of production only represented the labour that was embodied in them. Employers with greater bargaining power were exploiting the workers by paying them less than the full value of their daily output. Marx apprehended more exploitation of labour by the capitalists to maintain their profits.

In the late nineteenth century, economists came up with yet another theory known as the Marginal Productivity Theory of Wages. John Bates Clark, Alfred Marshall and Prof. Hicks developed this concept. According to this theory, a private businessman in a competitive economy would employ additional labour if the added cost (marginal cost) of the labour was less than the added money returns (marginal revenue) that its hire would generate. The workers would be free to move from lower paying industry to higher paying ones. They would continue to shift until the marginal value product of labour was the same across all industries. This would result in a uniform rate of wages in all industries for a given grade of labour. But this theory is inadequate as it fails to explain the behaviour of wages.

In practice, wage rates are fixed through a process of collective bargaining. Trade unions exert powerful influence on wage fixation. Government intervention is also there in fixing minimum wages. Economists led by Kerr and Ross believe that 'impersonal market forces' are no longer operative in wage determination, having been supplanted by 'conscious human decision'. The economic theory alone cannot explain labour market and wage determination. An interdisciplinary economics is needed to arrive at a realistic and meaningful explanation of wages under collective bargaining.

The wage rate in any industry depends upon a variety of factors. The financial condition of companies and their capacity to pay; wages in other industries in the region; government policy and statutory requirements; the extent of unionisation among workers and the cost of living are important considerations in wage fixation. In underdeveloped economies where unemployment is chronic, industrialists cannot be given the licence to determine wages on the purely economic principles of demand and supply or the marginal productivity of labour. In the Standard Vacuum Refining Company of India Ltd. *vs* Its Workmen (1961), the Supreme Court of India observed that "the doctrine of Laissez Faire is obsolete" and that the requirements of workmen living in a civilised and progressive society should be recognised.

The Minimum Wages Act was passed by the Government of India in 1948 on the ground of protecting labour from sweating and exploitation. The Act makes it obligatory on the part of the government to fix minimum rates of wages in employments specified in the schedule or added to it. The Act is not applied to all the industries indiscriminately. Minimum wages under the Act are recommended by the Wage Fixation Committees appointed by the government mostly in trades or part of the trades in which no arrangements exist for effective regulation of wages by collective agreements or otherwise. In an organised industry, wages are determined industry-wise on regional or national basis through collective bargaining, compulsory adjudication, and voluntary arbitration of wage board recommendations. The wage boards are tripartite bodies meant for formulating industry-wise wage structures on a scientific basis. Separate wage boards for all major industries have been set up in India. Regional considerations do not receive much attention from the all-India boards. The cost of living and the capacity of the industry to pay are the criteria which most of the boards take seriously.

Fair Wage Concept

The recommendations of the Committee on Fair Wages (1949) have exerted considerable influence on the wage fixing authorities in India. The committee has developed three concepts in relation to the level of wages:

(i) the living wage
(ii) the minimum wage
(iii) the fair wage

The living wage should enable the male worker to provide for himself and his family not merely the bare essentials of food, clothing and shelter, but also a measure of frugal comfort, including education for children, protection against ill health, requirements of essential social needs, and a measure of insurance against misfortunes, including old age.

The minimum wage must provide for not merely the bare subsistence but also for the preservation of the efficiency of the worker. For this purpose, minimum wages must also provide for some measure of education, medical requirements and amenities.

While the lower limit of fair wage must obviously be the minimum wage, the upper limit is set by what may broadly be called the capacity of the industry to pay. Between the two limits, the actual wages would depend upon:

— productivity of labour
— prevailing rates of wages in similar occupations
— level of national income and distribution
— position of the industry in the economy of the country

The above concepts received full consideration at the hands of the Supreme Court of India in the case of the Express Group of Newspapers. The policy of the Government of India is to promote fair wages in the organised sector.

Methods of Wage Payment

Wages are paid either on time basis or output basis. Workers prefer time scale wage as it guarantees a fixed income at certain intervals, avoids competition with fellow workers and promotes unionism. In industries where individual contributions cannot be measured precisely and the workmen have no control over the speed, it is the only acceptable method of pay. In jobs where quality considerations are least, the relationship between individual effort and output is measurable and jobs are standardised, the piece rate method of wage payment can be adopted.

The Payment of Wages Act, 1936, specifies the wage period – one month – and the mode of payment – cash. Organisations employing 100 or more persons are required to pay wages to their workmen by the 10th of every month while small organisations are required to pay by the 7th.

Dearness Allowance

The objective of paying dearness allowance to the workers and the salaried employees is to compensate them for increases in the cost of living from time to time. In USA, Canada and several European countries, the collective agreements include 'escalator clauses' which provide for automatic cost of living adjustments. The practice of paying a dearness allowance as distinct from wages is peculiar to India. It is advocated on the ground that the adjustment of wages to increase in prices cannot be bargained for on every occasion. In order to avoid discontent, tension and possible loss in output due to strikes, stoppage of work, etc., the automatic adjustment is to be preferred.

Changes in Wage Structure

Wage structure is not static. It is highly dynamic and has to adapt to the changing conditions. Let us take the example of a large company – the Steel Authority of India – and trace out its policy foundations and changes effected from 1955 onwards.

Earlier, when the Hindustan Steel Limited (HSL) was formed, the Rourkela and Durgapur Steel Plants were its only constituent units. The salaries prevailing at that time in the government departments, government industrial undertakings and steel plants in the private sector were initially considered for evolving the salary and wage structure of the company. Persons who were brought from the private sector steel plants were fitted into the HSL pay scales. Differences in many cases were allowed to continue as special/personal allowance. It came to be known as TISCO allowance.

Subsequently, manpower planning was initiated. It was based on project reports and studies of a high-powered committee (known as the Madiman Committee). Based on the work of this committee, a certain amount of rationalisation was brought in and wage structures were marginally revised.

In 1962, the recommendations of the Second Pay Commission were introduced and pay scales were accordingly revised. It was also decided that for grades up to the post of General Foreman, increments would be given only on 1 January or on

1 July, depending upon their date of promotion or appointment in the particular grade. If the date fell between the beginning of January and the end of June, the increment would be effective on 1 January, and on 1 July for the second half of the year. Executives in higher grades (that is, Rs. 1300-1600/- and above) were allowed increment only after completion of one year and not on 1 January or 1 July.

Later on, with effect from 1st April 1965, the recommendations of the Central Wage Board for Iron and Steel Industry were implemented by the company. This was done in a manner that the pay scales of the employees whose pay did not exceed Rs. 650/- and who were below the grade of Rs. 400-950/- (earlier scale Rs. 350-850/-) were revised in such a way that the employees got the benefit of at least one increment in the authorised scales.

On the basis of the recommendations of the Central Wage Board for Iron and Steel Industry, a fixed DA of Rs. 45/- was declared.

The HSL Wage Rules, 1965, were later framed on the basis of the recommendations of the Central Wage Board of Iron and Steel Industry which envisaged that, for every variation of 2 points in the consumer price index beyond 152 for 1964, there should be a variation of Rs. 1.50/- in the dearness allowance. No downward revision in the dearness allowance was envisaged unless the index fell below 144. The dearness allowance was revised every three months in March, June, September and December on the basis of the All India Consumer Price Index of the previous quarter. This ensured 100 per cent neutralisation in dearness allowance payable to low-paid employees tapering off gradually with the rise in wages.

Such pay scales which were not covered in the recommendations of the Wage Board were later revised, mostly on the basis of the principles contained in the recommendations of the Wage Board.

It was also envisaged, in agreement with the union, that a Plant Level Committee, consisting of union representatives and the employer, should examine the question of pay revision whenever needed if the job content underwent any change. Similarly, a Standing Committee at the company head office level was also envisaged. Since then, the pay scales have been revised many times on this basis. This has helped maintain peaceful working conditions and industrial peace.

The power to revise wage/salary structure vest with the Chairman/Board. The cases are then put up for the approval of the general managers.

Revision or upgrading of pay scales is processed by the personnel department in consultation with the industrial engineering and the finance departments. It is then referred to the head office for further processing. Once it is cleared by the head office, necessary orders for revision or upgrading are issued.

Pay fixation in the grade on promotion or appointment is done by the personnel department in consultation with the finance department.

The responsibility of disbursement of wages in the plants rests with the finance department. The respective heads of the departments are responsible for sending the attendance and other particulars on fixed schedules. Complaints received on wages by the respective personnel officers are cleared promptly in consultation with the finance department.

The final payment of provident fund, gratuity, etc., on resignation, retirement or replacement of employees is also done by the finance department in close consultation with the personnel department within a month.

Earning Progression Analysis

Some companies with well-developed salary systems are now introducing a new approach which gives the individual employees better protection and more scope for initiative via Earning Progression Analysis. This involves an analysis of the various factors which should be taken into account in a pay review, an assessment of them separately as percentage changes, then adding them together to obtain a net overall figure of percentage change. The main factors analysed are:

Cost of Living: Has the cost of living gone up and, if so, by how much?

Merit Rating : Everyone in a supervisory management position is already on an earnings progression curve. If an employee is a potential high player, his salary will rise quite rapidly year by year ana perhaps go on rising throughout his career. One element in determining the rate at which his curve rises is the merit rating he is given at the time of his salary review, as a recognition of his performance in the present job.

Productivity and/or Profitability: Has the business increased in efficiency during the year? Should it pay more or less?

Promotability Rating: Promotability ratings need not be subjective. They can be arithmetically related to the rate at which a manager rises from one job level to the next, where certain facts like time spent on the previous jobs are known.

Benchmark Adjustments: This is the factor which relates earning progression analysis to job evaluation, and is the adjustment made, if any, to bring a person's earnings into the right relationship with the nearest appropriate benchmark.

Incentives

Incentive is an additional compensation for better performance. An organisation may choose a system to reward each individual on the basis of his or her performance or the group of workers as a whole employed in a workshop, department, section or unit. The common individual incentive schemes are:

1. *Piece-Rate System*: Wage is determined by multiplying the number of units produced by the worker with the rate of wage per unit. It is easy to calculate, wage cost is easily predicted and the employee gets the satisfaction of reward based on his personal performance. But the system may result in the speeding up of work while sacrificing quality. It also may create tension at the workplace by promoting unhealthy competition.

2. *Differential Piece Rate*: Earning of an employee depends upon his ability to produce more or less than a standard predetermined output. One who produces less than the fixed standard, gets payment at a lower rate, and one who produces more than the prescribed norms, gets paid at a higher rate. It was devised by Taylor, the father of Scientific Management, to motivate people to achieve or exceed established standards. The method is difficult to implement in cases where the measurement of individual's performance cannot be quantified accurately or where the norms of production cannot be fixed scientifically.

3. *Gantt Bonus Plan*: Worker who does the prescribed level of work in the allotted time or even less, gets wages for the standard time worked, plus bonus which may range from 20% to 50% of the time saved. This scheme guarantees a fixed time rate for all, and the bonus is earned only by those who save time and achieve targets.

4. *Halsey Plan*: Worker gets bonus for 50% of the time saved. The benefit of the other 50% goes to the company. In a straight piece rate, a worker's earning will be much higher.

5. *Emerson Efficiency Plan*: Bonus is payable only for a fairly higher level of performance. Merely crossing the standard does not entitle the person for a better pay.

6. *Commission*: It is a widely used individual incentive system in sales job. It is computed as a percentage of sales in units or rupees. Sales personnel employed by the company may get it in addition to their salary. Sales agents not in permanent employment of the company may get only the commission on sales effected by them.
7. *Special Incentives*: Sales contests, productivity contests, cash your ideas schemes, etc. may be organised to motivate employees.

Individual incentive system is resisted by trade unions because it promotes unnecessary competition among employees and weakens trade union movement. Operational problems such as difficulty in fixing standards, sharing gains of time saved, etc. also make the system vulnerable to criticism. Group incentive schemes have become more popular in recent years. Such schemes provide reward to all employees in a work unit, department, division or organisation. The productivity standards are fixed for departments or divisions and bonus may be paid to all the employees on reaching or exceeding the standards. This promotes team spirit and better coordination at work. Organisation-wide incentive scheme is an extension of group incentive programme. All employees of the company, for instance, may be paid bonus if sales exceed the target fixed by the management.

The group incentive schemes, however, are not a perfect substitute for individual incentives. The connection between individual effort and reward is lost. The scheme may lead to conflict among groups if people in one department get a higher amount of bonus than those in other departments. It may also result in over-emphasising one aspect of the job to the detriment of others. Marketing people may be rewarded on the basis of number of units sold, while production men may get bonus on the basis of reduction in cost and improved productivity. In a period of boom, a little effort by the salesmen may bring far better results and the sales personnel may get a handsome bonus. But if the factors governing reduction of cost are not favourable then production men may not be entitled to a bigger bonus.

A categorical verdict on the suitability of incentive systems is difficult. There have been many occasions where incentive systems have failed to produce any results. Discussion with many company chiefs/directors have revealed three basic reasons for the success of an incentive plan:

- A properly designed plan
- Intelligent administration
- Proper coverage

On the whole, it can be said that the incentive scheme of an organisation and its success depends upon the interaction of various factors, some of which are measurable and some are not. Therefore, some of the simple rules which should govern incentive schemes could be:

(1) Management should recognise that the effectiveness of incentives depends upon the total situation, which includes worker-management confidence, relations with the union, quality of communication and supervision, and the traditions of the industry.

(2) Management should not introduce an incentive system without fully understanding its repercussions. This may require procedures for the participation of employees and negotiations with the union.

(3) Management should not adopt unfair practices. It must avoid actions that look like 'rate-cutting', which is not an easy task in view of the need to improve methods and rates from time to time.

(4) Management should pay in proportion to the output, once the output has risen above the level required for the guaranteed pay. Some of the employees are paid only half of the savings from extra output, but this is no longer acceptable to many unions or employees. Management may still find increased productivity profitable, even if it does not reduce wage costs per unit, for the overhead costs will be spread over a greater output.

(5) Management should train supervisors all the way down the line to understand the incentive system, so that the foremen and the department managers will be able to deal with problems within their own departments.

(6) Great care should be taken in setting the standards to avoid rates that are too low or too high. Without sound standards, it is impossible to have fair incentive rates.

This is not by any means a conclusive list and many more related factors could be added to it. A successful incentive scheme should provide for the best use of manpower; productive facilities; recognition of the needs of employees, the company and, at times, the public too. It should be fair and equitable to all concerned. It should promote good labour relations, reduce personnel problems and encourage initiative. Above all, it should be flexible and strong enough to withstand the test of time.

Incentive Scheme in a Steel Plant

An incentive scheme introduced in one of the largest steel plants in the public sector is discussed below.

The basic features of the scheme are as under:

All personnel whose contribution to production was identifiable and quantifiable were covered under this scheme. This included operation, maintenance, services and general staff of the operation (production) department of the plant. A classification of the bonus to be paid to the personnel was adopted, based on their contribution to the production effort, as indicated on the next page.

Executive Compensation

Company executives are paid proportionally much higher compensation than other category of employees as they are responsible for the overall results. It is based on the presumption that what is in the best interest of the shareholders should also be what brings the greatest reward to the executives. The compensation package at this level is generally linked with organisational performance – profit earned, the rate of return on investment, and the growth of company. Board is the sanctioning authority for deciding the pay packages of senior executives. The final say on pay is of the shareholders who can approve or reject it at the general body meeting.

The size of the compensation package depends upon such factors as:

a) Size of the company: big companies can afford to pay fat salaries

b) Profitability: more profitable the company, higher will be the emoluments

c) Business under control: diversified business may bring better opportunities

d) Company power structure: pay is linked with status in the hierarchy

Compensation package includes both short and long-term benefit. Basic pay, dearness allowance, annual bonus, conveyance, housing and other allowances, cash payments for entertaining guests, festivals and holidays, education of children, etc. are short-term compensation. Long-term compensation includes stock options, insurance cover, retirement benefits, life membership of clubs, loans at concessional rate and other long-term benefits. Perks like free lunch, utilising company facilities for personal use, etc. are the extras linked with status. In case of downsizing and takeovers, companies pay heavy compensation to retiring executives under schemes like 'Golden Handshake', 'Golden Parachute', etc. Statutes in many countries require compulsory disclosure of the emoluments offered to senior executives and fixed ceilings on total remuneration and perks.

Group	Department	Quantum
(a) Production	All major production units such as coke ovens, furnaces, steel melting shop, rolling mills, etc.	100%
(b) Maintenance	All major production units such as coke ovens, sinter plants, blast furnaces, steel melting shop, rolling mills, etc.	90% of the respective departments
(c) Services	All departments under the Chief Mechanical Engineer, Power Engineer, Chief Industrial Engineer, rail transport, research and control laboratory and technical services units.	90% of the arithmetical average of the bonus declared for production groups
(d) General	Time office, stores, plant (vehicles) pool, etc.	50% of the arithmetical average of the bonus declared for production groups

Executive staff up to the level of General Foreman/Senior Executive were covered by this scheme and paid on the basis of percentage bonus declared for their respective departments. Incentive bonus was calculated on a slab system.

Only that output which satisfied the specifications laid down (whether for sale or for reprocessing) was reckoned for the payment of bonus. The targets were generally determined on the basis of the designed capacity of the production units. Incentive earnings were expressed as a percentage of basic pay.

The starting point for bonus for different departments was related to their technical process, the expertise gained in handling the sophisticated equipment and technological interdependence. Here, it was kept at 60% for steel melting shop and the rolling mills, 75% for blast furnaces and 80% for coke ovens, for a bonus earning of 10%.

The rated capacity was, however, uniformly related to a bonus earning of 50% in all cases. The starting point and 50% point (corresponding to rated production) were joined by the accelerating type of curve. The bonus curve was extended on a straight line basis up to 12% for production groups of all departments.

The above scheme was production-oriented. However, it did not take into account many factors like:

(i) Bonus was not related to effort. For the same level of production, everyone got the same bonus, irrespective of their effort.

(ii) The whole department formed one group. This did not provide sufficient motivation to individual sections/groups to improve their productivity.

(iii) Maintenance personnel working in various departments were paid incentives on the basis of 90% of incentive earnings of the production group of respective departments. This did not take into account:
   – maintenance labour utilisation did not take into consideration manning for a particular level of production.
   – equipment availability or maintenance effectiveness.

(iv) Bonus was paid on the basic pay and not on the grade.

(v) Some of the auxiliary departments like foundry and pattern shop, machine shop, steel structural shop, roll turning shop, etc., could have been put into their own group rather than into the services group.

(vi) Supervisory personnel got bonus on the same basis as workers. No emphasis on factors like quality, cost, production, plan fulfilment and the like existed.

The first incentive scheme was later replaced by an improved scheme which was productivity-oriented. The revised scheme was finalised in consultation with the Administrative Staff College of India. The salient features of the revised scheme were as under:

(a) Employees working in different work situations had equal bonus earning opportunities when they completed equivalent amount of work.
(b) It offered greater flexibility to the workmen to fill idle time with available work.
(c) It encouraged productivity. Employees under this scheme could earn more either by producing more or by working with fewer men or by both.
(d) It also encouraged good production, i.e. lowering of rejects and defective output.
(e) It discouraged overtime work and absenteeism.
(f) It offered greater potential for earning for the same performance compared to the earlier incentive scheme.
(g) It made bonus more direct to work and enabled settlement of bonus on a weekly basis.
(h) Bonus was paid on the basis of the grade of an employee.
(i) Bonus was paid for the days actually worked.

The scheme was based on the performance of workmen in small groups. Performance for this purpose depended upon effort and effective production. The performance was measured by the performance index calculated weekly.

The bonus of workmen in each group was related to the performance index of their respective group. The performance index of a group was calculated weekly on the following basis:

$$\text{Performance Index} = \frac{\text{Effective output} \times \text{Job credit per unit of production in man-hours of group}}{\text{Actual man-hours utilised by group during the week} + 1.5 \text{ (Man-hours of attendance on overtime duty over and above the reference duty posts)}} \times 100$$

Job credit meant the credit in man-hours for a particular job per unit of specified effective output, including all the work that is necessary or expedient to attain effective output. It included work content, rests and polity allowances for forced idleness on work and for technological imbalances, etc.

Job credits for different units of output for each group were as follows:

Process Workers

(i) *Direct Workers' Group*: The cycle time for the controlling group was to be derived from the production capacity per shift given in the project report. The stipulated time for capital repairs, scheduled maintenance would not be taken into account in this calculation. A shift would be taken as eight hours.

The cycle time for the controlling group was to be used for other groups in the same department.

The job credit for each group was to be calculated on the basis of controlling cycle time (To), required manpower (Mr) including spell hands and the work content (W), as given below:

Job credits for each group = Mr x To + W/4

(ii) *Indirect Workers' Group*: The standard time for indirect workers group was to be obtained as follows:

Required force for the indirect workers group × Sum of job credits of the direct workers group

Total required force of direct workers group is served by the indirect group.

Maintenance Workers

Since detailed work measurement studies meant considerable time, an interim scheme for maintenance workers was developed relating the maintenance workers directly with the process workers. Each maintenance group was related to one or more process workers group. Job credits for the maintenance activity (JCM) were established by the following formula:

$$JCM = \frac{\text{Job credits for process job}}{\text{Job crew in process job}} \times \text{Job crew for related maintenance activity}$$

Using this formula, job crew for process workers was to be obtained by work measurement. Job crew for the related maintenance activity was to be determined on the basis of work sampling.

Work Content

This was taken to account for the amount of work in man-hours required for carrying out the job at a normal pace of work inclusive of suitable allowance for relaxation, personnel needs, contingencies, etc.

Bonus Rate (Rupees/Day)

The performance index was to be converted into daily bonus rate from a table giving the bonus rate (Rs/day) for different wage scales against different values of performance index and achievement of production rate.

The scheme was applicable to the PI range of 60 to 123. All values of PI below 60 were to be treated as 0 and all values of PI above 123 as 123.

An individual's bonus for a week was to be calculated as:

Settled bonus rate of the group in which an individual works for his wage scale. × Actual attendance of the individual on normal duty in that group for the week.

The monthly bonus was to be the sum of the weekly bonus for the weeks ending in a month and payable at the end of the month.

Applicability

This scheme was applicable to all the workers who were covered under the first incentive scheme introduced in 1961.

An example of the scheme as applicable to the open hearth furnace group of the steel melting shop is given below:

1. Group size : 221 men
2. Unit of output : 100 tonnes of steel
3. Job credit (man-hours per unit of output) : 20 hours per 100 tonnes of steel
4. Actual output during a week (tonnes) : 38,000 tonnes
5. Attendance on normal duty during the week (estimated) : 8,600 hours
6. Attendance on overtime duty during the week (estimated) over and above the reference duty posts : 1,300 hours

7. Performance index = $\dfrac{380 \times 20}{8600 + (1300 \times 1.5)}$

$= \dfrac{7600}{10550} = 72.03\%$

8. Amount payable

For individual in wage scale	Monthly bonus in rupees for 25 days attendance
350-575	165.3
260-395	120.7
168-290	84.2
113-147	52.2

Situation Analysis

(A) A business house has three plants manufacturing different products and registered separately under the Companies Act. While two units are earning profit, one unit is incurring losses for the last few years. The workmen of the losing unit have claimed bonus at par with the employees of the plants earning profit on the plea that all the units are interlinked and managed by the same authorities. The balance sheet and profit and loss account are prepared separately for each organisation. Workers have no complaint against the published accounts.

Discuss the claim of workers of the unit not earning any profit for the payment of bonus.

(B) An electrical supply company has four zonal offices for distribution systems. Technical staff is attached to each zone. At the head of the staff is an assistant engineer. Next to him is a technical superintendent and below him are inspectors.

The technical staff (superintendent and inspectors) in the substations and zonal stations demand that their hours of duty and other conditions of service should be fixed in the same manner as those of the employees working in the power stations which are registered as factories under the Factories Act. On this basis, the superintendent and the inspectors claim overtime which the workmen in the power stations are getting.

Regulations do not provide for the payment of overtime to technical superintendents and inspectors. Substations and zonal stations were not registered as factories as no manufacturing process was carried out there.

Discuss whether the superintendent and the inspectors working in the zonal and substations are entitled to overtime.

Review Questions

1. What is the Iron law of wages? Discuss its relevance to developing economies.
2. What are the factors on which the wage rate in an industry depends?
3. Explain the concept of fair wage. Are our industrial workers getting fair wage?
4. 'Wage structure is not static'. Comment.
5. Explain the concept of 'Earning Progression Analysis'.
6. What are the different incentive methods for individuals and groups?
7. What do you mean by 'job credits'?
8. Discuss merits and demerits of different incentive plans.

Further Readings

1. David W. Belcher: *Wage and Salary Administration* (Prentice Hall, New Jersey, 1962).
2. David Lepak and Mary Gowan: *Human Resource Management* (Pearson Education, 2009).
3. J.D. Dunn and Frank M. Rachel: *Wage and Salary Administration: Total Compensation System* (McGraw-Hill, New York, 1971).
4. Joseph J. Martocchio: *Strategic Compensation: A Human Resource Management Approach* (Prentice Hall, New Jersey, 1971).
5. George T. Milkovich and Jerry M. Newman: *Compensation* (Irwin Homewood, Illinois, 1993).
6. J. Pfeffer: *Six Dangerous Myths about Pay* (HBR, Vol. 76, pp. 108-119, 1998).

Part IV
Managing Industrial Relations

Chapter Structure

Chapter 14. Industrial Disputes and Collective Bargaining

Chapter 15. Working Conditions and Social Security

Chapter 16. Morale and Participative Management

Chapter 14

Industrial Dispute and Collective Bargaining

"In Great Britain, to a somewhat lesser extent in the US and to a remarkably lesser extent in Europe, the relationship between the state, the corporation, and the trade union is an adversary relationship. Japan, more or less uniquely, of all the industrial countries of the world, has not been subject to this adversary relationship. A substantial part of the success of the Japanese economy is the result of a much more effective working relationship between the government, corporations, and trade unions."

— **John Kenneth Galbraith**
(Look, Japan, Dec. 1980)

Learning Objectives

After reading this chapter you will be able to:

1. Understand that trade unionism is the direct result of exploitation of workmen in modern industrial systems.
2. Analyse the causes of industrial disputes and the role of state in bringing about conciliation between employers and employees.
3. Elaborate the methods of settling industrial disputes.

The seeds of conflict in industrial life were sown by the factory system itself in the early phases of its development. The ownership rights were placed in the hands of a privileged few, while the masses were turned into wage earners. The disparity in the income of the two classes was widened to the effect that while the owner class could enjoy all the luxuries and comforts of life by investing the capital only, the labour had to struggle hard for two square meals, living accommodation, social security and the basic amenities of life. The history of industrialisation is replete with instances of inhuman treatment. Trade unionism is the direct result of exploitation of labour by the employers. Governments had to intervene in the matter of industrial relations to safeguard the interests of the labour. In the affluent West, the labour has managed to increase its size of cake considerably, but in the underdeveloped countries, it still has a long way to go. Social scientists look upon industrial conflict as a complex phenomenon. Human nature, social environment, economic forces, technology and the state policy – all play their role in structuring the group interactions between employers and employees.

The nature and pattern of industrial unrest has changed in recent years with globalisation and privatisation of industrial, financial and commercial activities. The number of strikes instigated by labour unrest has been following a declining trend in recent years, however the number of workers involved in strikes has been increasing in India and many other countries. According to ILO, there has been a growing unrest, especially among MNCs, on issues like wage hikes, reinstatement of dismissed workers and demand for recognition of labour unions. The sectors which have seen an upsurge in labour unrest are transport and financial intermediaries.

Trade unionisation has suffered a setback in recent years as companies have started outsourcing on a large scale and employing contract labour with a small number of core workers in their manufacturing plants, and trading and service organisations.

Psychological Causes

There will be no conflict if people have a rational attitude. But in reality conflict cannot be avoided, and employer-employee relations are no exception. Perception differs. The same object is looked upon differently by different people. Higher production, for instance, is beneficial to everybody. But employers would like to limit it to the extent that it maximises their profits, while workers would oppose any speeding up or additional effort for increasing production without corresponding reward.

There are many factors related to perceived differences. Occupation and income, membership of a group, ego, experience and personal motives are some of the important factors. The duties and responsibilities, income level, status in the organisation, ego and personal motives of a manager are different from those of a workman in a factory. The two differ in their perception of issues, situations and persons. A strike, for instance, is looked upon as a coercive tactic by the management, while labour regards it as an instrument to fight injustice and exploitation.

The factors which motivate the managers and the workmen are not always the same. The managers strive for power, status, authority and self-fulfilment. The workmen are more concerned with wages and incentives, work satisfaction, supervision, service conditions, etc. In terms of need hierarchy, the lower level needs, when satisfied to a reasonable degree, do not remain a motivating factor. The higher level needs begin to dominate. Even trade unions in the initial stages are concerned more with the economic benefits and security of their members, but when they grow strong, they fight for prestige issues, right of recognition and participation in management, a share in company profits, etc.

Frustration and aggression are the causes which lead to conflict between two individuals or groups. When negotiations fail, parties resort to direct action. Frustration occurs when the object sought for is not achieved. Aggression is the result of frustration, though in some cases it may be instinctive also. When labour is frustrated, productivity suffers, absenteeism increases and morale goes down. When managers are frustrated, they fail to decide issues and administer company affairs properly. Aggression is reflected in the disciplinary actions taken by the management, and violence by the workers during strikes and work stoppages.

The attitudes of individuals and groups predict their behaviour. In one of the strikes in General Motors, the workers' slogan was: 'A LOOK AT THE BOOK', i.e. wage increase was possible without increase in the price of the car. The management's slogan was: 'A LOOK AT THE BOOK OR A FINGER IN THE PIE', i.e. the object of the union was to get a voice in management. The differences in attitudes led both parties to different tactics and courses of action to meet their goals. Management may adopt the carrot and stick approach, efficiency engineering and patronising one union against another to achieve its own objectives. Trade union may insist on collective bargaining, recognition, feather bedding (resisting change in technology) and clear-cut policies on personnel matters to safeguard the interest of the workers. Managers lock out or workmen go on strike to test one another's strength.

Social Changes

The nineteenth and twentieth centuries have witnessed unprecedented changes in the methods, techniques and scale of production, transportation and communication due to scientific and technological innovations. The social changes, however, lagged behind. The traditions, customs, and beliefs of the people have come in the way of adjusting with the demands of the new environment. When the industrial revolution took place, villages and small-scale industries were uprooted, and the craftsmen were compelled to move to urban areas for jobs in factories where they had no specific roles to play. They became part of a big system and were lost in it. Establishment of an industry required huge sums of capital which only the rich could afford. This widened the gulf between the owner and the working classes. The treatment given to the factory workers was inhuman. Long hours of work, miserable living and working conditions, poor pay, lack of job and social security and exploitation in many other forms led workers to behave irrationally. The logical and rational responses gave way to irrational ones due to social maladjustment.

In developing countries where industrialisation started late, factory labour was drawn basically from the agricultural sector. The pressure of population on land and the lack of employment opportunities in villages forced men and women to move to urban areas in large numbers in search of work. In villages, at their own farms, they had no regulations regarding the hours of work – they had no supervisor and were the masters of their own affairs. In the factory, they became subject to different types of regulations, strict supervision and no ownership rights. Housing, transportation and other amenities being costly and the wages being low made it difficult for the people uprooted from their village homes to settle down in the cities to work. Poor adjustment with the environment resulted in the development of irrational responses which led to conflicts between the workers and their masters.

The growth of unionisation should also be viewed in the context of the wider social change. Workers join unions as they feel that the status and the security that they have lost by leaving their homes could be regained by uniting together and fighting for their rights.

The organised sector also attracts labour from underdeveloped and backward regions. In India, *adivasis* and other communities from remote hill areas and other such regions move to urban centres due to economic compulsions or natural calamities. A large number of such workers get employed in mines and construction of roads, bridges, houses, etc. They become subject to all types of exploitation by the contractors. In big industrial plants, like steel and heavy engineering, they get paid better. In nationalised mines also, the pay and service conditions have improved. Unionisation has provided some strength to these depressed and exploited communities.

The joint Hindu family system and casteism have also been affected by industrial civilisation. The longer a person remains away from home, the weaker his relations with other members of the family become. Urban centres absorb a large number of rural migrants. The caste barriers are broken out of necessity and people organise together for better living and service conditions.

Exploitation and Class Conflict

The eighteenth century economists looked upon labour as a factor of production that was combined by the entrepreneur with other factors of production – land and capital – to produce goods and services for sale. As an input to the production process, labour itself became a commodity to be bought and sold. The price of labour was determined by the market to a point where the supply of a particular type of labour was balanced by the demand for it. A relationship based on pure exchange developed between the employer and the worker. Human considerations and social obligations had no place in this theory. The division of labour was another characteristic of the 'free market' economy. Each person was supposed to specialise and do a defined task. With the emergence of the factory system, village and small-scale industries were uprooted and the surplus labour migrated to industrial centres. The supply of labour was greater than the demand, and hence, labour as a commodity could be purchased at a lower price. The exploitation of labour, therefore, began with the rise of industrial civilisation in the West.

Karl Marx challenged the old economic concepts and raised his voice against the exploitation of labour. He believed in a revolutionary struggle that would replace capitalism with socialism. According to him, a conflict between the capitalists, who own the means of production and distribution, and the workers, who own only their labour power, was inevitable. The profit of the employer was really 'surplus value' that was withheld from the workers. It was unearned by the employees and actually belonged to the labour. He called upon the workers to unite and fight for their rights. Marxism had a wide appeal with the labour force throughout the world. Though not many countries adopted socialism, labour became a force to be reckoned with in the economic and political systems in greater parts of the world.

Sidney and Beatrice Webb of Britain and John R. Commons of USA looked upon the rise of trade unionism as a response to the widening of the product which led to a separation of interests between the workmen and the employers. Workers formed unions for the purpose of maintaining and improving their working conditions, and as a means of protecting themselves from the impact of product market competition. Selig Perlman extended the concept of job-conscious unionism further. He considered the role of unionism was to abolish competition among workers for jobs so that the marginal employer does not set labour standards. Tannenbaum saw unionism as a reaction against automization, and as a means of restructuring a social system for the workers.

Role of the State

The initial attitude of the State towards unions and their activities was unfavourable. The Combination Acts were passed in 1799 and 1800 in England to forbid any union activity. In the USA, the doctrine of criminal conspiracy and restraint of the trade hindered union development. Collective bargaining in the early history of industrialisation was a 'privilege' and not a protected institution.

The State, however, could not avoid its responsibilities towards labour for long. The rise of unionism among workers and the democratic political set-ups forced the governments to intervene in industrial relations matters. England was the first country to pass legislation for the protection of workers. In 1842, the Massachusetts Supreme Judicial Court in the US refused to apply the doctrine of criminal conspiracy to a union that struck to enforce a closed shop. Unionism and collective bargaining were gradually encouraged by legislation in several countries including the USA.

V.V. Giri has summed up the role of different types of State in labour matters as follows:

> "*A welfare State has to treat every worker as a human being with dignity and individuality and not as a mere cog in the big*

complex of industrial production. Increased productivity is the aim of all economies, whether capitalist or socialist. If a capitalist enterprise looks forward to an ever-expanding vista of profits, a socialist State must, in the interest of society, constantly aim at reduced costs without, of course, exploiting the workers engaged in production. Thus, while the human element is relevant to the capitalist system primarily as a means to increased production and profits, it is vital to a socialist system from the point of view of both efficient production and maintaining the position of the worker as a citizen of the State."

John T. Dunlop has elaborated on the role of the State as an agency to set guidelines for job-related labour management relationships. In his view, the specialised government agencies concerned with the workers are part of the total industrial system.

The Dunlop theory is broad-based. The management, the labour and the State play their respective roles in weaving the fabric of industrial relations in different economic and political systems, each with its own values, goals and limitations on account of the ideology followed or resources available.

Systems Approach

J.T. Dunlop has given industrial relations a 'system' treatment, indicating thereby the possibility of differentiating among different relationships based on peculiar socio-economic conditions. According to him, the term 'Industrial Relations' should not be construed as one which denotes the union-management relations operating within the spectrum of industrial relations as a whole, in which there are interactions among other groups also and linkage established with the economic and social systems prevailing in society. Thus,

The full range of complex interactions among the various groups such as workers and managers, workers' trade unions and employers or their organisations, together with those interactions linked with the social system as a whole, and more particularly with the economic system, is referred to as the Industrial Relations system.

The principal groups identifiable in the system and which constitute the structure of industrial relations are as follows:

(1) A hierarchy of employers, managers and their organisations and their representatives or supervisors.

(2) Workers and their organisations and their representatives.

(3) Specialised governmental agencies which are concerned with the workers and their relationships with the employers.

More than the structure of the industrial relations system, the contexts or determinants of the system are of far greater importance. The determinant forces can be grouped as follows:

— The technological context of the society
— The economic or the market constraints which influence the behaviour of the groups
— The power context, i.e. distribution of power among the groups at a particular point of time

Technological Context

It includes:
(i) the characteristics of the workplace, and
(ii) the level of advancement of technology.

The characteristics of the workplace affect the industrial relations climate of an industry, which in turn has an impact on the industrial relations system as a whole. For instance, the mining industry has a different technological context as compared to the manufacturing industries. Mining communities have frequently been isolated from important urban areas and create special problems in human relations.

The advancement of technology affects industrial relations by way of not only disturbing the existing employment patterns but also by determining the size of the workforce employed. Schemes of rationalisation and automations, for instance, are usually resisted by the workers.

Market Context

The market context or the economic factors which greatly influence industrial relations include the competitive position of the industry in the market as also the size of the enterprise, the lower cost and the capacity of the industry to pay, etc. These factors affect the product market, which in turn affects the lower management relationships in the form of rules, rewards, etc. which govern the workplace.

Power Context

The policy of the government, the attitude of the employers, the status of industrial workers, the question of recognition of unions, etc. are all interrelated. The power of the government to direct and control the affairs, the style of management, the degree of unionisation, the extent of membership, political ideologies, etc. exert influence on industrial relations.

The actors in a given context establish rules for workplace and the work community, including those governing the contracts among the industrial relations systems. These rules are broadly grouped into three categories by Dunlop, viz:

(i) the recruitment and commitment of labour force
(ii) compensation and wages
(iii) procedures for the settlement of disputes over the application for the existing complex of rules or new rules

These rules can be expected to be altered as a consequence of changes in the contexts (technological, market or social) and in the relative status of the actors. The actors who set the rules may be workers and their unions constituting one category; employers, managers and their associations having similar interests forming the second category; and government is the third category consisting of civil servants concerned with labour matters.

The rules of the system may be expressed in a variety of forms: the regulations and policies of government hierarchy; the laws of any worker hierarchy; the regulations, decrees, decisions, awards or orders of governmental agencies; collective bargaining agreements; customs and traditions of workplace and work community.

Influence of Industrialising Elite

Three types of industrialising elite are:
— The dynastic feudal elite drawn from landed commercial aristocracy.
— The middle class elite drawn from a minority commercial group which exalts the market.
— The revolutionary intellectual elite.

The industrial relations system of any country depends largely upon the type of industrialising elite found in the country.

The industrial relations system may be designed to be applicable to three broad areas of industrial relations:
— Industrial relations within one enterprise
— Industry or other segments of a country
— Composition of sectors

The multiple usage of the term recognises the possibility of integrating a group of allied systems, say different regional systems into a national system or subdividing it into smaller systems.

The national industrial relations system and particularly the status of the actors in the system are significantly influenced by:
- The period in the world history in which the system was first congealed or drastically reconstructed following a revolution or a war.
- The sequence of social change – the sequence in which the larger community secures independence, and industrialises the course of economic development.

Present Context

A worker of today is not a mere input of production like materials or money or machinery. He is primarily a human being endowed with intelligence and knowledge as also lapses and shortcomings. He is a member of a free society with political leanings. As such, he expects the realisation of his economic, social, political and cultural rights for the free development of his personality and dignity.

An industrial worker today is different from his predecessors. He is better educated, better trained, and more refined in his tastes and outlook. He is also conscious of the law and institutional backups, social, economic and political rights, security of job, union backing, promotion aspirations, etc. His economic demands have increased and he has turned to unions/associations for the fulfilment of these needs.

Managements and managers must, therefore, take note of this awareness on the part of the working class. The traditional style of functioning based on the management attitude of dominating over the subordinates must undergo some change or total transformation. The manager, while interacting with the workers, has to be necessarily more informal, friendly, communicative and participative. Managers must shed their former rigid, legalistic, and formal attitudes of the World War II era. Along with the changes in old ideas, they have to provide a better/safe workplace, machinery for the redressal of grievances, better communication and participation in the decision-making process.

Employees of small, medium and large industries must realise that both capital and labour are partners in the service of the community, which is wedded to certain goals and objectives, and must, therefore, create a climate in which their primary obligations to the industrial community as well as to the society at large can be effectively discharged.

While discussing the 'present context', mention of the public sector is relevant as it has emerged as a major employer.

The government, through its administration of public sector undertakings, democratic machinery, enlightened professional management responsive to the aspiration of workers, wanted to project an image of the model employer. However, it has only been partially successful in this attempt. The man-days lost on account of industrial disputes have been lower in public sector undertakings than in the private sector.

Managers of public sector undertakings in India had to go through difficult times during the first 25 years of their operation because of conflicting ideas. They had to follow governmental procedures and rules of accountability but were expected to deliver performance results comparable to their private sector counterparts. The professional and technical managers were made to work under civil and administrative services and had little or no technical back-up. The vital decision-making process was also remotely controlled. Various responsible sectors in the society tended to treat public sector undertakings as centres for generating employment without having any bearing on labour productivity indices, an instrument for subsidising wages and perquisites, providing accommodation, welfare amenities and medical care on a developed scale, giving total security of service, irrespective of worker performance, without correlating these to the performance and profitability of the unit. Many such shortcomings of the working of public sector undertakings are now in the process of rectification.

There were various factors that marred industrial relations and performance of public sector undertakings. In the private sector, union demands were influenced by the financial and economic health of the unit. Unions knew that higher cost of production and erosion in profits could lead to the closure of the units and may cause loss in employment. No such fear was shown by the unions of public sector undertakings while bargaining.

Public sector undertakings are a fertile ground for trade unions of all hues owing allegiance to various political parties with each politician trying to carve out a position of influence for himself and the trade union owing allegiance to him. Managements are often caught in the crossfire of these trade unions. The overtone of political infighting is imported into the functions of the union. Even simple issues are politicised, negating straightforward solutions.

Even minor issues of public sector undertakings can be taken, magnified and questioned in Parliament, the Committee of the Public Undertakings and the Government Audit, creating a sense of insecurity in the minds of the top executives. This often inhibits their mind from taking forthright and courageous decisions. The avenues open to the private sector for dealing with political pressure are not available to the public sector. While the private sector management can effectively deal with such unions and contain their demands, the managers of public sector undertakings can only take recourse to constitutional and conventional methods open to them.

> **PERSPECTIVE**
>
> **Strike at Maruti**
>
> A section of workers at Maruti's Manesar plant went on strike on 4th June, 2011 afternoon. The striking workers were demanding recognition of a new union – Maruti Suzuki Employees Union (MSEU) – independent of the existing one dominated by the workers of the Gurgaon plant of the company. Besides, they proposed the formation of a governing council comprising workers' representatives from both the plants to deal with issues like negotiating wages. Retaining contract labour from the two new upcoming units inside the Manesar complex was another major demand. The strike was backed by CPI and AICTU whose leader met the Chief Minister of Haryana several times during the strike period to press for workers' demand. The company management refused to recognise and accept any union which had members from outside the plant or had any political affiliation. It sacked 11 workers for instigating the strike and refused to take them back when negotiations started. The company had a history of not reinstating sacked employees. In 2000-2001, the company had sacked hundreds of workers and none of them were taken back. But this time the company management had to yield under pressure from the Haryana Government. The strike ended after 13 days when the company agreed to take back the sacked workers. But the striking workers' main demand of recognising a new union was not accepted. The strike resulted in a loss of Rs. 420 crores or 12600 units of cars. Maruti vendors reported losses of around Rs. 30 crores for each day of the strike.

Diffusion of authority also complicates the industrial relations scene of public sector undertakings. In case of industrial disputes, various agencies of the state and central government are to be involved as per rules. While this concern of the government is legitimate, it leads to the loss of initiative on the part of managers of the public sector. Union leaders take full advantage of the situation and exert pressure on the top executives of the public sector from MPs, ministers and ministries. This has a demoralising effect on the public sector managers.

It is an uphill task to ensure complete identity of approach between the objectives of an enterprise, management policies and practices, government regulations and aspirations, and attitudes of workmen. This is because human beings differ in their social background and traits. In the political framework of democracy, sincere efforts are necessary to understand the dynamics of human behaviour and modulate that behaviour with a view to achieving desired objectives.

Once there is an agreement on this basic approach, many of the inadequacies, deficiencies and aberrations of the existing industrial relations system will disappear. The choice is not between building up a sound base for harmonious industrial relations and not doing anything about it. The proposition is based on the premise that the key personalities responsible for industrial peace or unrest are the workers, employers and the government. Also, there is a need to harmonise the varying interests of the society.

Role of the Management

The genesis of most of our industrial disputes can be traced to the inadequate attention paid to human resource development by many managements. To get the best out of someone, and to provide a creative outlet to his potential, proper policies need to be formulated for right selection, induction, training, promotion, recognition, arousal of his feelings to regard the institution as his own and convincing him that his well-being lies in the well-being and prosperity of the establishment.

The employers and managers would do well to:

(i) know the social changes and new awareness of the working class.

(ii) know the attitude of managers towards their subordinates. In other words, the superior-subordinate relationship must undergo transformation.

(iii) know the fact that investment in creating better working environment, safety, health and welfare amenities are investments in human capital which, if neglected, will result in the alienation of the workforce and, if implemented, will secure better involvement of the workers with the enterprise.

(iv) introduce procedures for removing grievances so that individual or collective grievances do not accumulate to such an explosive point as to create an industrial unrest.

(v) encourage suggestions received from the workers and introduce award schemes for useful suggestions for improving production, quality, maintenance, working environment, equipment availability, methods, administration, efficiency, profitability, safety methods and reducing the incidence of accidents, rejection, rework, downtime, wastage of any kind, etc.

(vi) adopt a constructive and positive attitude at the conference table, before the conciliation officer, the arbitrator and the adjudicator so that the self-respect of the representatives of the workmen is not offended, and management's credibility is established. This will help in issues being resolved in a peaceful and constitutional manner.

(vii) implement the verdicts of the labour courts or industrial tribunals in letter and spirit unless it involves certain fundamental questions of constitutional law which may require further interpretation of a higher court.

(viii) remember that unnecessary or prolonged litigation breeds distrust and does not finally settle any issue in the true sense of the term.

(ix) note that human relations get damaged beyond repair while fighting endless litigations and, therefore, voluntary arbitration for timely settlement of disputes should be adopted.

The role of management, in many cases, has led to serious industrial strife. Multiplicity of unions, coupled with the complexity of deciding the issue of recognition of a majority of unions, has helped the management to play with the unions by either not granting recognition to any union or granting recognition to the union that will toe the management's line of action rather than the one which can actually keep industrial relations and unrest under control.

Even genuine disputes are not settled in a spirit of accommodation but dilatory tactics are employed to keep the settlement in abeyance through various processes of reconciliation, adjudication, appeal to high courts, etc. leading to resentment among workers.

Certain matters like recruitment and promotion policies, placements, special rewards for outstanding performance or suggestions, etc. are decided by the management without taking the union into confidence on the plea that these are management's prerogatives, and this very often leads to frustration among workers and industrial unrest.

Similarly, many managements are totally oblivious to the basic human needs of the workers and their aspirations, their need for security, provision of basic amenities, recognition for good work, etc. leading to a conflicting situation that may cause industrial unrest.

Many managements do not even have proper procedures for the redressal of grievances with the result that minor irritants continue to pile up and vitiate the entire work environment.

When collective bargaining is agreed and resorted to for the settlement of disputes, representatives of the management are not vested with adequate authority to decide on the demands at the bargaining table, making the whole process a farce and bringing out a credibility gap in the minds of the workers.

Along with this, the industry is witnessing a division in the management cadre. Lower and middle class executives are forming their own associations to put forward their demands about salaries, perks, service conditions, etc. This alienation among the executives has come about because of the erosion of relative earnings of the executives as compared to the workers. Whereas the minimum wages of workers have increased some 30 times since the latter half of the 20th century, the wages of class I executives, junior engineers, doctors have not increased even 10 times. Our wage map is so distorted that in some centres a class IV worker in industrial and banking establishments with overtime draws more salary than a deputy collector or a judicial magistrate. This factor has added a new dimension to the industrial relations scene. The management in many industries finds that the traditional support and loyalty from lower and middle class managers are lacking during many critical situations.

At the same time management must refrain from conceding such demands which cannot be supported by the economics of operation because such concessions often lead to chain reactions in other fields.

Responsibility of the State

As stated earlier, the process of industrialisation was started in India in the 19th century by the British where the management was British and the workers were Indians. This left an indelible imprint of colonial overtones on the employer-employee relationships. The earlier labour regulations during World War I, in response to a spate of strikes, were primarily aimed at preventing work stoppages and maintaining industrial law and order. During World War II, ordinances were promulgated under the Defence of India Rules and Essential Services (Maintenance) Ordinance prohibiting strikes and lock-outs. Authority was vested in the government to enforce industrial peace and prohibit workers in essential services from going on strike or leaving employment.

With the attainment of independence, the working class expected that the government would side exclusively with the working classes. However, certain compulsions of the country/government such as:

(i) need for the regulation of economy under the overall framework of five year plans

(ii) directive principles laid in the Constitution for bringing about a welfare State

(iii) the fact that in a developing economy, the government cannot be a silent spectator to the forces that undermine national economy

(iv) irresponsible acts of certain unions with different political affiliations, and exploitation of poverty and lack of education amongst the masses

came in the way of the expectations of the workers.

While the government recognised the right to strike by the unions and the right to lock-out by the employers, it could not allow the national economy to suffer because of the misuse of either of these two rights. The government could not see wildcat strikes, go slow, work to rule, violence by the union and lock-out or closure by the management. The government was aware that harmony in industrial relations was of the utmost importance to the developing economy and, therefore, the government had to use its influence to moderate the actions of either side.

Government has a very onerous responsibility of social and economic development and cannot be a silent spectator where the process of development is being jeopardised by wasteful and protracted labour disputes, disruption of railways, roadways, airways and other vital public services and creation of a poor investment climate as a result of industrial unrest. Government in such conditions has to impose certain restrictions on both the management (in matters of lock-out, closures, lay off, retrenchment, etc.) and the unions (for strikes in essential and public utility services, intimidation, destruction of machinery in the factory, etc.) for larger interests of security, social justice, maintaining essential services and supplies and orderly development of society. In such situations, national interests are at stake due to improper activities of either of the two parties or both, and such activities must be restrained by the government.

Government, therefore, had to provide for conciliation machinery for the settlement of disputes. However, rapid growth of industries and unions on the one hand and extra conciliation duties assigned to totally inadequate conciliation officers on the other, made the conciliatory proceedings unduly prolonged and ineffective.

Yet compulsory adjudication was considered necessary as early trade union movement in the country was weak. It was necessary for the government to intervene and adjudicate to safeguard the interests of the workers. Later when the trade union movement found a firm footing, workers/unions found the process of adjudication a long drawn affair and were reluctant to follow the process.

Rising unemployment and industrial recessions have led to an alarming rise in unsocial activities, extremist politics and violence. Inflation has eroded the wages in real terms. While the volume of wages has gone up, the real wages and purchasing power have either stagnated or gone down. The problem has been further aggravated by the ever-increasing capital investment needed for creating unit production capacity. This has curtailed employment opportunities. Also, unions have been demanding a greater share in the profits.

While, on the one hand, the use of sophisticated technology, automation, computers, high wages of workers, etc. have brought down the quantum of employment, it has, on the other, induced educated youth from politically awakened middle class society (which is extremely sensitive to the issues of wages, aspirations, ambitions, and regard themselves as copartners) to join the industry.

The government, therefore, has to:

— Be very careful in its legislative philosophy if labour legislation is to be used as an instrument for development of industrial peace and production.

— Realise that it is the government policies that determine the quality and speed of industrialisation in the country. Restrictive policies stifle growth.

— Know that labour legislations made so far have been anti-productive and responsible for industrial disputes and conflicts.

— Look into the failure of present dispute settlement machinery to deliver the goods. Extensive changes are needed in its structures, otherwise the situation may go out of hand.

- Ensure that the laws that are enacted do not directly encourage multiplicity and proliferation of trade unions.
- See that managements are not pressurised to concede to ex gratia payments even after the bonus has been settled under the terms of the Bonus Act. There should be no reason why the government should be a party to the violation of a law of which it is the creator.
- Lay down clear norms in the matter of wage policy so that the present distortion in the wage map is corrected. All wage settlements must subserve the national objective of securing high rate of economic growth.
- Stick to the 'no work, no pay' policy when necessary. Wages have to be earned by work. Mere capacity to pay should not result in excessive payment as this will create distortion, and surpluses cannot be used (as they should be) to generate additional employment.
- Make others aware that wage policy should promote and not upset the stability of prices. Competitive prices and modern technology are the main keys to get into the foreign market and earn the much needed foreign exchange.
- Firmly establish the rule of law and respect for the law. Stiff penalties should be imposed for breach of law, violence and destruction of property. Political affiliations should not mean any concessions for violation of law. Discipline has to be inducted in every sphere of national life and the surest way to do this is to enforce the laws of the land.

The Role of Unions

The traditional role of the unions is to protect and promote the interests of their members. No one will contest this if it is not overdone. Perhaps, the time has come when an adjustment in their role is necessary.

Marx called for the overthrowing of capitalist system by an organised workforce. Workers who were degraded to the status of 'wage slaves' could free themselves by forming a political party of their own. The revolutionary character of trade unions was further emphasised by Lenin who believed that if a union becomes reformist, it would seek a better return for labour within the capitalist system itself, without destroying it. Socialist consciousness, thus, aims at revolutionary rather than reformist means. In contrast to this, American pluralists pleaded that trade unions should work for the economic or business interests of the workers. The primary objective of a union should be to gain higher wages and better conditions. The unions are not required to be 'class conscious', but 'wage conscious'. Trade unionists in developing countries, which have gained independence after a long struggle against colonial rulers, are propagating responsible trade unionism. According to Ashok Mehta, trade unions should defer immediate wage gains in the larger interests of the country.

Workers in the organised sector in India (numbering about 25 million) constitute a minority of the total labour force (estimated at 300 million including the rural labour force). Even a small portion of the gains achieved by the organised sector has not trickled down to the majority of the labour force. The net result is that a vast majority of people live below the poverty line.

India's population today is over 100 million. The way to create more employment is to activate the production process and maintain industrial peace. Production must be maintained at any cost. No disruption for any reason should be permitted since the instruments of amicable solutions to industrial conflict are available or can be created. Industries maintain the workers, and workers must, therefore, maintain the industries.

Unions and workers should realise that being employed in itself is a big privilege these days. Many sectors of our industries – airlines, banks and insurance – are comparatively more highly paid, yet in these very sections, demands for increased wages are being pursued so vigorously under the threat of stoppage of work that other needy groups are being ignored.

Trade unions should restore discipline in their rank and file so that disputes are not used as an excuse to start extra industrial problems. Trivial industrial disputes should not be blown out of proportion and made an excuse for general lawlessness, violence, intimidation, damage to property or machinery. It should not be made a matter of everyday life. Many trade unions have adopted norms which cannot stand the test of civilised fair play. Lawlessness is a state of anarchy and anarchy has never promoted growth – social, political or economic. If we can learn one lesson from the Japanese union, it is that prosperity of a nation depends upon the health of farms and factories and this in turn depends upon the attitude of workers and the union. As per the old saying, 'the goose that lays the golden egg should not be killed nor should it be killed to get all the golden eggs at once which are not there'.

A major responsibility of trade unions lies in orienting and modifying their outlook towards industrial development itself. It has to be decided by the union leaders whether the surplus or gains coming out of the industries should be enjoyed only by the workers or should there be a fair share for the management (to be used for the expansion and modernisation of the industry)and for the government for bringing all-round national development inclusive of the weaker section of the population, and opening further avenues for employment.

Another critical area is the unification of the trade union movement. The industry has suffered the maximum owing to a multiplicity of unions and inter-union as well as intra-union rivalry. Multiplicity of unions has given rise to competition in trade unionism. In their bid to attract the workers in the industry, they have failed to realise the disastrous consequences on the industry. Some unions pitch their demands so high that they fail to acknowledge the compulsions of economic growth. Prolonged lock-outs and strikes result in phenomenal loss of production.

Unions should also pay attention to educating their members. An ignorant worker is a liability both to the union and to the management. An informed worker will give better turnover and will also strengthen the base of the trade union movement. He will invoke the concept of loyalty which will stop mass exodus from one union to another when unrealistic demands are made by rival unions.

Unions should not teach the workers to be conscious only of their rights. They should also stress on the obligations of the workers towards maintaining industrial peace, higher production, efficiency and plugging the losses. No fair person will object to a fair share of profits but a serious situation may arise when such payments are out of proportion, and lead to industrial sickness or closure. It would be a classical case of 'fence eating the crops'.

Collective Bargaining

It is a process by which employers and employees (represented by workers' unions) confer in good faith and come to an understanding about the terms and conditions of working and other related aspects. It is of recent origin and is being increasingly made use of since the latter half of the century. It gives an opportunity to both the parties to discuss the matter, its pros and cons, and arrive at a mutual agreement binding upon either side. The basic concept is that labour and management should settle their own problems with or without the intervention of government, as the case may be, in an amicable manner.

Most of the organisations have industrial relations department which handle such work in the initial stages. At later stages, the chief executives get involved in it.

A congenial climate is necessary for collective bargaining. Two conflicting but generally found situations in which collective bargaining takes place are:

Conflict	Harmony
1. Mistrust between employees and union.	Both agree to look into each other's interest.
2. Employees try to destroy the union and the union tries to pressurise the management.	The union understands the position of the management and vice versa. The union accepts the necessity of profit for the employer and the management understands the necessity of the union to maintain its strength, representation, etc.
3. Agreements are often violated on flimsy pretexts. There is a lack of understanding of each other's point of view.	Problems are viewed by either side with an attitude of problem solving.
4. Agreements arrived at, if any, are short-lived. It is more of an armed truce than an agreement.	Agreements arrived at are honoured.
5. Coercive and violent scenes/acts cannot be ruled out.	Even if both parties agree to disagree on certain points and if it is to be referred to the government or any arbitration agency, it is carried out in good spirits.

The problems faced by management during joint negotiations were summarised by Hicks in 1932.

"When a trade union demands an advance in wages, or resists a reduction, it sets before the employer an alternative: either he must pay higher wages than he would have paid on his own initiative... or on the other hand, he must endure the direct loss from the stoppage of work. In either case, he is less well off than he would have been if his men had not combined, but one alternative will generally bring him less cost than the other. If resistance appears less costly than concessions, he will resist. If concessions seem cheaper, he will meet the union's claims."

Phelps Brown says that the employer's attitude will be to *weigh the prospective loss of profit against the cost to him of a strike.*

Magrum states that, *"management's immediate consideration is usually the potential losses from strike compared with the costs of the demanded concessions."*

There is widespread acceptance of the need for management to make cost loss calculations but only very general advice is available on how they should go about it. This is perhaps understandable since the recognition of all possible influences and the assignment of monetary values is by no means a simple exercise. Indeed some regard it as an impossible task, e.g. Boulding states: *"The strike cannot be treated (as the economist would like to treat it) as a rational phenomenon, in which each side nicely calculates the expected benefit of another day's strike and weighs this against an equally nicely calculated loss".*

Theories on Collective Bargaining

Hicks expressed the bargaining situation in the form of two curves having opposite slopes: 'an employer's concession curve' and a 'union's resistance curve' plotted on a graph where the X axis represents 'wage rates'.

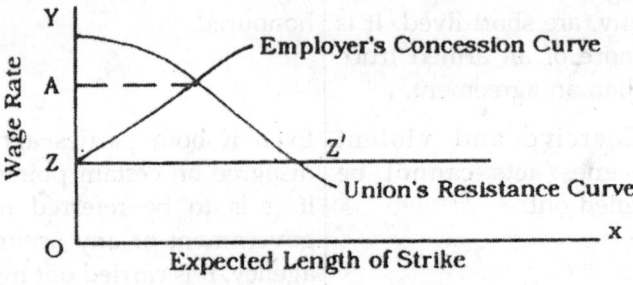

Fig. 14.1

The employer's concession curve relates the wages an employer would be willing to pay to avoid a strike to the expected length of strike. The employer's decision depends upon two factors: wages demanded and expected period of strike.

OZ is the wages the employer is paying at the time of strike. The employer's concession curve eventually becomes horizontal, i.e. at some point, the employer will prefer to go out of business rather than meet a demand in excess of a certain wage. The union's resistance curve shows the wage the union will accept rather than take industrial action, expressed as a function of the expected length of strike. The sacrifice the union is willing to bear (i.e. the length of time they are prepared to maintain industrial action) will vary depending upon the potential gain. The resistance curve also shows that some maximum wage exists beyond which the unions will not contemplate action. At its lower end the union's resistance curve cuts a line Z. This represents the time beyond which the union cannot sustain action whatever is being offered. Between the high and low areas of the curve, the slope is less marked. Hicks feels that very often the resistance curve will be horizontal over a considerable part of its length, since there is some level to which in particular they consider themselves entitled. In order to secure this level, they will stand out for a long while, but they will not be much concerned to raise wages above it.

The employer's concession curve and the union's resistance curve interact at a point P. The corresponding wage OA will be the highest wage the employer is willing to concede. Anything higher will be refused because he expects any strike intended to secure a higher demand will not last long enough to make any immediate concession worthwhile.

The Hicks model has been criticised by theorists because it is not deterministic and we cannot discover what the precise wage will be. The two functions on the graph provide the boundaries within which the solution should be found. However, this was the first model to formally recognise the fundamental significance of time.

There is one weakness of Hicks theory: it tends to minimise the influence of management. Labour leaders attempt to get the best wage they can based on their estimate of the employer's concession curve and their ability to sustain a strike. The union is thus an active element in the process while the employer is largely passive.

In 1950, a bargaining theory of wages involving the costs of agreeing and disagreeing was developed by Chamberlain. This model focuses on the concept of bargaining power which is defined as the ability to secure another's agreement on one's own terms.

Carter and Marshall, in a presentation based on the Chamberlain theory, express the union and management's attitude using the following formulae:

$$\text{Union's bargaining power} = \frac{\text{Cost of disagreeing with employer}}{\text{Cost of agreeing on employer's terms}}$$

$$\text{Employer's bargaining attitude} = \frac{\text{Cost of disagreeing with union}}{\text{Cost of agreeing on union's term}}$$

Attitudes will be favourable towards settlement whenever the functions are equal to or exceed one.

In this model, both parties are seen to be actively engaged in the process of bargaining.

In a more recent article, Nelson places emphasis on initiative by management.

"Management faced with a labour contract negotiation and a strike threat has two basic alternatives: either offer the employees a concession package which will prevent a strike or offer a lower cost package which may result in strike (with the hope that the eventual labour cost savings over terms of the new contract will at least cover the cost of strike)."

Nelson suggests that the management's course of action should be based on an break-even analysis and he produces what he admits to be an overly simplistic model.

Nelson's diagram shows the estimated strike costs and a line representing labour costs saving, i.e. the difference between the anticipated final wage increase and the original demand. The intersection shows the point in time before which a strike is less costly than concession, and after which concession is less damaging than a continuation of the dispute.

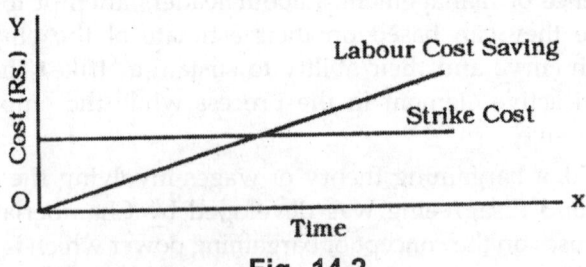

Fig. 14.2

The reasoning behind Nelson's break-even chart is the same as that behind ideas of both Hicks and Chamberlain, but Nelson's model attempts to formulate the decision problem within the framework that is known by both accountants and management.

Giri believed that internal settlement of disputes was eminently preferable to compulsion from outside and that collective bargaining and voluntary arbitration should be encouraged over compulsory arbitration or adjudication.

Giri's View

(1) Compulsory adjudication/arbitration, introduced for the first time as a result of war-time exigencies and continued thereafter as a measure inevitable in a period of economic uncertainty and emergency, has given a great setback to the growth of trade unionism in the country. The spirit of self-confidence and self-reliance engendered by healthy bargaining has given way to the habit of importunity and litigation. In collective bargaining, even though strikes or lock-outs may take place, matters are settled in a spirit of give and take. Neither party entertains a spirit of humiliation or feels the urge for retaliation and revenge. But this is not the case with compulsory arbitration. Where one party has lost and the other has won, the victor and the vanquished get back to their work in sullen and resentful mood towards each other and neither can forget or forgive the other. Such an attitude of suppressed hostility in one party and of unconcealed satisfaction and triumph in the other may lead to transient truce but not lasting peace.

(2) Compulsory arbitration has cut at the very root of trade union organisation. Unity among men, particularly trade unionists, is the direct outcome of necessity. It stands there as a policeman looking out for signs of discontentment, and at the slightest provocation takes the parties to the court for a dose of costly and not wholly satisfying justice. The moment the back of the policeman is turned, the parties grow red in the face with redoubled determination, and the whole cycle of litigation starts all over again, with the proverbial court delays as well as continued rancour and bitterness. Let trade unions become strong and self-reliant and learn to get on without the assistance of policeman. They will then know how to organise themselves.

(3) Compulsion may be inevitable during war or in times of emergency, but it is inappropriate in times of peace as drugging is to health.

(4) In case of public utility services, to begin with, government should have the power to refer all unresolved disputes for compulsory arbitration, and simultaneously, to prohibit strikes or lock-outs because such services cause immediate

and acute suffering to the public. In case of non-public utility services which account for the bulk of commercial and industrial activity, it should be permissible to give full scope for collective bargaining.

Steps in Bargaining

A congenial climate is a basic necessity for collective bargaining which has two principal phases:

(i) negotiations leading to collective agreement

(ii) contract administration and implementation

The former is concerned with initiating and negotiating between the union and the employer regarding existing contracts that were jointly decided earlier, specifying employment conditions and/or the memorandum prepared either by the management or the union and admitted for negotiations.

The latter is concerned with the day-to-day interpretation and application of the principles outlined in the agreement collectively reached between the union and the employer. It requires many clarifications, discussions and coordinated efforts to implement the agreement in its true spirit for success.

No standard procedure exists which can be illustrated in this regard. However, from the experience of the authors, the following guidelines maybe adopted for collective bargaining.

Basis of Negotiation

The basis of negotiation depends on either the charter prepared by the employer or submitted by the union or both as agreed to. Some employers take:

— A passive role to see what the union demands are and then decide the extent to which they can go to accede to the demands or reject them.

— An offensive role whereby they assert their points and take a more active part in the discussions.

In any case, it is better for either party to know in advance the other's viewpoint and demands, prepare an agreed agenda of points and then start the discussions.

Preparation

Both the employer and the union must spend a good deal of time in studying the memorandum before starting discussions. The union may like to take the opinion of their committee members and the employer may like to discuss the points with various heads of departments. Such a practice generally leads to a satisfactory negotiation and avoids too many adjournments for discussions outside the main conference room.

In order to come to a satisfactory agreement, both the employer and the union should go through the following records:

Background Data

- Follow-up points and their status arising from the previous collective agreement and subsequent review meetings held, if any.
- Points of grievance, their status, how the grievances have been handled and the pending unsettled grievances.
- Suggestions received, their processing, implementation of accepted suggestions and rewards given.
- Violation of the agreement earlier reached and whether there has been any third party arbitration arising out of the interpretation or implementation of the contract agreement.
- Amendments needed, if any, to the existing contract agreement.
- Unsettled issues, list of pending issues and write-ups as to how these are to be resolved in the new agreement.
- Economic effects or compulsion of demands, singly or collectively, and the company's ability to meet those demands.
- Justification of demands. Both parties should have related background statistics. Since getting or compiling information in some cases may be time consuming, preparations must start well in advance before starting the negotiations.

It is further suggested that the following background information which may not be directly related but may be useful during negotiations be obtained before starting the discussions:

- Wages and wage surveys
- Amenities and perks given
- Cost of living index of the area
- Balance sheet of the company as published
- Related statistics/reports from various journals
- Factory law, other statutory guidelines and labour relations policies
- Special state/central laws applicable to the industry, if any.

- Rights of management and union under existing law and statutes relating to industrial and labour relations.
- Extent to which rights and prerogatives of the management must be retained.
- Factual data of any problem peculiar to the company supported by charts, graphs and tables for easy transmission and understanding by the other party.

Comparative information/statistics of similar groups of industries along with a comparison of one's own factory may be helpful in justifying a point raised in the discussions.

Outside Counsel

Sometimes when the company does not have experience or service of a professional industrial relations manager, it may be desirable to obtain/hire the services of a competent counsel/professional who is thoroughly informed in the field of industrial relations. However, the responsibility for conducting the negotiations should not be delegated to the legal counsel, irrespective of his competence. The role of the counsel should preferably be limited to giving advice, counselling before, during and after discussions, and in laying down the language of the contract clauses when the proposed agreement is finalised.

Negotiating Committee

Collective bargaining and its outcome agreement are a matter of vital importance for the management. Hence, great care should be exercised by the chief executive in selecting persons for the negotiating committee on behalf of the management. Besides technical members, it must include a senior member of the personnel and industrial relations department thoroughly conversant with company affairs.

If it becomes necessary to hire a legal counsel, he should be thoroughly briefed about all the aspects of the discussions, especially the legal ones. He should be available to the committee before, during and after the negotiations for counselling, if required.

Since collective bargaining acts as a two-way channel to improve employer-employee relationship, the union may bring a group of selected employees along with them for enabling them to see that the negotiations are being conducted in good faith by the management.

At times, owing to special circumstances, it may become necessary to keep the number of negotiating members of both sides small.

Conducting Negotiations

Negotiations should be conducted from the management side by the chief executive, director (personnel) or personnel manager unless special circumstances demand legal counsel or any outside member to conduct the negotiations.

Negotiations should not be continued for too long a time at a stretch. In between, a short recess gives an excellent opportunity for reflection and reconsideration of the stand taken on certain issues.

At times, it may be helpful to give a special break in the negotiations to enable both sides to review and rethink the matter under consideration.

It is necessary that deadlocks be avoided during negotiations; or at least, no efforts be spared in that direction. Reaching a buffer end does not help in solving a problem. Both the management and the union should, therefore, explore the problem from various angles and keep avenues open for reaching desired solutions.

As collective bargaining proceeds, management may give feedback to their senior executives on certain aspects that may be thought desirable and get their views on them; for it is they who would be implementing the decisions and be responsible for the day-to-day industrial relations matter with the employees under their control.

It always helps to take up such points first on which an agreement could be reached easily and the tempo of negotiations built up in an amicable manner rather than starting with points which may lead to a deadlock.

It should be the endeavour of either side to keep the areas of disagreement as small as possible, thereby enlarging the areas of agreement. It may help in reaping the benefits of collective bargaining and cementing good relations between the management and the union.

In case of any proposal or point under dispute which in the opinion of the management is not sound, the management side may clearly explain its repercussions on the company's business. Such objective discussions may clarify the significance of each point and facilitate the meeting of minds.

While negotiating either of the two situations may arise:

Situation I	Situation II
Management puts forward its points first to the union	*Union puts forward its demands first to the management*
It may be remembered that the management has a right to put forward their proposals for negotiation with the union.	The management should give the impression that they are very keen on solving the problems collectively and hence this request.
The management can put counter proposal at any point of time during the negotiations as an evidence of bargaining in good faith.	The management can insist on receiving memorandum of the union in advance and not at the time of the meeting so that it can be studied for fruitful discussions.
Wherever possible, the management should try to take control of the situation by assuming leadership during negotiations and try that their proposal should serve as the basis of negotiations.	Yet it is advisable for the management to request the union to explain each point of their memorandum for better understanding and general exploration of the objectives as well as viewpoints of the union.

In the first discussion of a proposed contract, a general exploration of the viewpoints and objectives of both parties should be explored.

If the proposed contract has been submitted by the union and accepted for discussion, the union representatives may be requested to first explain each point contained therein.

The management may then proceed and try to reveal the unsoundness of any proposal and its adverse repercussions on the company's working. Such type of discussions may clarify the significance of each point and facilitate understanding.

After the union memorandum is taken, it may be helpful for the management (or vice versa) to prepare a checklist and make separate tables for:

- The points that can be accepted as written or proposed.
- The points that are ambiguous or the real intent of which is not clear or has more than one meaning. These may be taken up for clarification during the meeting. The language should be revised so that its meaning and intent is clear.

- The discussion on such points should be deferred so that some thinking can be applied to examine the implications/repercussions of such points.
- The points that can be accepted if amended in a certain manner. The management should be able to present such amendments with facts and reasonable explanation for the changes sought.
- The points that the management cannot accept and clear reasons for the same. Also, the alternatives that the management can suggest for them.

Such checklists will be found helpful during discussions.

Finalising the Contract

Record notes of the discussions held for each session should be kept and preferably be signed by both the parties. They should cover the proceedings faithfully as discussed and correctly record the viewpoints of both sides. This will help both sides to have a record for recapitulation during the finalising of the contract agreement. However, record notes should not be treated as the contract agreement.

A separate contract agreement should be drawn arising out of collective bargaining:

- There should be suitable numbering of the headings, paras, and sub paras. Pages should be numbered and indicate the date, venue, persons present and the signatures of both the parties.
- The terms and conditions agreed should be specific, definite and without ambiguity. It may be remembered that ambiguous clauses are obstacles to good industrial relations as different interpretations of the same clause can be a point for potential dispute.
- The draft of the proposed written agreement should be finally reviewed by the counsel before it is finalised by signature.
- Periodicity of review meetings, composition of the review board, etc. should be agreed and reduced to in writing.

Where the union-management understanding is good, relationship is sound and each party is working in a friendly spirit and is willing to make adjustments in the interest of friendly cooperation, a short document outlining the basic agreement is sufficient. Where such relationship does not exist and both parties are likely to insist on the essentials of the agreement, then a specific and detailed contract is essential.

Administration of the Contract

An agreement arising out of collective bargaining is just the first step and so follow-up action should be planned to effectuate the terms of the agreement.

A major difficulty in implementing the agreement is explaining the new contract agreement to all those concerned who must know and implement it. New provisions of the contract generally require careful explanation.

The contract is to be administered by all those who work under its term. However, the major responsibility of its administration falls on the managers, officers and the members of the union committee as well as the shop representatives. Differences, if any, in the interpretation of any clause should be expeditiously settled between the management and the union. These should not come in the way of effective implementation of the agreement and should not eventually become a source of grievance. The implementation and application of the programme must be developed in the day-to-day operations and relationships.

Adjudication Machinery

When the management and the labour fail to resolve their dispute through a process of collective bargaining or voluntary arbitration, the state intervenes to bring the parties to the negotiating table by starting the conciliation proceedings. If conciliation proceedings also fail, the government may, at its discretion, refer the matter to the labour court or industrial tribunal or national tribunal.

Authorities under the Industrial Disputes Act, 1947

Works Committees

These are to be established in industrial organisations employing 100 or more workers for promoting dialogue between the employer and the workmen. Workers' representatives are to be chosen from among the employees of the organisation.

Conciliation Officers

These are appointed by the government for specified areas/industries for mediating in and promoting settlement of disputes. Conciliation proceedings are compulsory in case of public utilities, and optional in others. Settlements arrived at are binding on the parties. If no settlements are reached, the failure is then reported by the conciliation officer to the government, empowered to refer the dispute to the industrial tribunal for adjudication.

Boards of Conciliation

These are constituted by the government for promoting settlement of disputes, consisting of an independent person, the chairman, and

and two to four members each from the labour and management sides. If arrived at, the settlement is binding on both the parties. If a settlement is not arrived at, the failure is to be reported to the government which may refer the dispute to the labour court or industrial tribunal or national tribunal.

Courts of Enquiry

These are constituted by the government to inquire into any matter relating to industrial disputes. They may consist of one or more independent members, and should submit the report to the government within six months of the commencement of the enquiry.

Labour Courts, Industrial Tribunals, National Tribunals

One or more courts and tribunals are to be constituted by the government. These generally consist of one man whose qualifications as prescribed by the Act include experience in the judiciary. He should, therefore, be a judge of a high court, chairman of a labour appellate, tribunal, etc. Tribunals may be assisted by two persons or assessors representing the parties to the dispute. National tribunals are constituted when disputes involve questions of national importance or relate to establishments in more than one state.

Situation Analysis

A mining company was engaged in raising iron ore and limestone. Limestone was being supplied to a cement plant situated about 20km away and iron ore to an iron smelting plant 30km away.

The company had a fleet of 15 steam locomotives purchased some 30 years ago from the railways. Nine locomotives were used for iron ore circuit; 3 for limestone circuit; 1 used to be under heavy repairs/overhaul and 2 under minor running repairs. Of late, the downtime of locomotives had increased very much and the company was finding it difficult to fulfil the commitments of despatch even though sufficient quantity was being mined or raised.

A committee was appointed by the general manager to look into the despatch failures and suggest ways and means to improve the availability of locomotives so that despatches did not suffer. The incharge of the locomotive department was not included as a member of the committee – it was perhaps thought that he might influence the views of the committee. The committee, after doing some investigations, recommended the addition of two diesel engines to augment the fleet. The argument put forward in favour of the additional diesel engines were:

(i) quicker and better haulage
(ii) 45 minutes for fueling of diesel locomotives per day as against 6 hours for taking coal and water for steam locomotives
(iii) economical to operate
(iv) one man per engine instead of two in steam locomotives (viz. one driver and one fireman)
(v) cleaner working conditions
(vi) less repairs and maintenance problems

The general manager, after weighing the relative advantages, decided to replace the fleet of 15 steam locomotives by diesel engines rather than operating 15 steam locomotives and two diesel locomotives. He did not consider it worthwhile to consult the incharge of the locomotive department in this regard. The replacement was phased at the rate of 3 diesel locomotives per year, i.e. 3 diesel locomotives would be added to the fleet and 3 working steam locomotives would be taken out of circulation and disposed of.

Before the first batch of 3 locomotives arrived, the management decided on a programme to train 12 comparatively younger and educated persons from amongst the drivers. These persons were trained for a period of 6 months each in the operation and maintenance of diesel locomotives. Instruction sheets for diesel locomotives were drawn up by the experts. They were translated into the local language and distributed to each driver. The difficulty of importing spares of diesel locomotives and the care which should be taken in operating these locos were also adequately explained. A higher scale of pay was also given to the diesel loco drivers.

When diesel locomotives were put in services, as per the plan, one driver per loco per shift was placed on duty with one reliever to relieve him every two hours. It was also indicated that no fireman would be retrenched and that they would be provided with alternate jobs.

When the union was informed of the changes, its secretary objected to this arrangement. The drivers too, because of pressure from the union or for some other reasons, refused to go to work.

Even when the management finally yielded to put two men per diesel engine on the previous scale of pay, a technical difficulty arose. The union contended that once a driver had been given a higher scale of pay, he could not be reverted to a lower scale. On the other hand, they demanded that the rest of the drivers should also be upgraded. Ultimately, the management, for the sake of industrial peace, agreed to put this into effect also.

As soon as this was done, all the firemen also wanted a proportional increase. They further wanted that the cabin of the driver of the diesel engine should be expanded to give freedom of movement for two persons. This was difficult to do in the case of small diesel engines that were purchased.

The union gave a strike notice. The management was afraid that if the firemen were given a pay rise, all the other categories would also demand the same. The enlargement of the engine cabin would mean huge capital expenditure, and the foreign experts who had come to commission the engines were opposed to this.

Cancellation of the order for diesel engines was also not possible as firm orders were given. Besides, a period of another year had elapsed in the meantime. Another three diesel locomotives had arrived and work for another three was already in progress at the manufacturer's end.

The management wanted to have a dialogue with the union as they knew that the drivers could dictate their terms and bring the entire operation of the mines to a standstill.

However, the union secretary did not accept the view of the management and insisted on a driver and an assistant driver per loco. His argument was:

  (i) a loco driver cannot work for six hours at a stretch without an assistant driver.
  (ii) for safe driving, it is necessary to have a better view. Two men on two sides can watch both sides of the track and this would lead to safer working conditions.
  (iii) firemen, if not given the position of asst. drivers (as no coal firing is needed in diesel locos), would not get the promotion opportunities due to them.
  (iv) the practice continuing for the last 30 years cannot be changed as this will affect the group relationships.
  (v) sufficient space must be provided for two men to work on each diesel loco cabin. The union is not convinced that one man per diesel loco is workable.

How can we can resolve this situation?

What were the organisational lapses that led to the situation?

Was proper communication lacking between the management and the workers/union?

Was there any technical mistake in giving specifications for diesel locomotives? Or whether the general manager/the committee had erred somewhere and that error had led to this situation?

Review Questions

1. Do you agree with the view that class conflict is inevitable in industrial society?
2. Discuss the causes of industrial disputes in modern society.
3. What role does the State play in promoting industrial harmony?
4. What role do the trade unions and managers play in shaping industrial relations?
5. How do different parties view collective bargaining as a method to resolve conflict?
6. Do you prefer adjudication over collective bargaining?
7. What do you propose to deal with the problems arising out of:

    a) inter-union and intra-union rivalries

    b) secret ballot

    Which method do you recommend and why? If you have an alternative method, you may discuss.
8. What are the problems of collective bargaining? Why in India is it not as popular as in many other industrial countries?

Further Readings

1. John T. Dunlop and J.J. Healy: *Collective Bargaining: Principles and Cases* (Richard Irwin, Illinois, 1955).
2. Arun Monappa: *Industrial Relations* (Tata McGraw-Hill Publishing Co. Ltd., New Delhi, 2000).
3. Sidney and Beatrice Webb: *The History of Trade Unionism* (A.M. Kelley, New York, 1965).
4. P.R.N. Sinha, Indu Bala Sinha and Seema Priyadarshini Shekhar: *Industrial Relations, Trade Unions and Labour Legislation* (Pearson Education, New Delhi, 2006).

5. Nirmal Singh and S.K. Bhatia: *Industrial Relations and Collective Bargaining: Theory and Practice* (Deep and Deep Publications Pvt. Ltd., New Delhi, 2000).
6. J.S. Sondhi and S.P.K. Ahluwalia: *Industrial Relations In India: The Coming Decades* (Sri Ram Centre for Industrial Relations and Human Resource, New Delhi, 1992).
7. Abel K. Ubeku: *Industrial Relations in Developing Countries: The Case of Nigeria* (MacMillan Press, London, 1983).
8. C.S. Venkataratnam: *Globalization and Labour Management Relations – Dynamics of Change* (Response Books, New Delhi, 2001).

Chapter 15

Working Conditions and Social Security

"No human being can be considered apart from his environment, and no human being is independent of his environment, for good or ill, each of us is affected by conditions external to our bodies and then to our minds."

"The environment in which we earn our living can stimulate or depress, help or thwart, determining in some way how we shall react."

— **May Smith**
(Introduction to Industrial Psychology)

Learning Objectives

After reading this chapter you will be able to:

1. Understand how good and safe working conditions lead to better health, higher efforts and productivity.
2. Analyse the causes, symptoms and consequences of fatigue and steps for its prevention.
3. Give a brief account of social security legislation in India.

Good and safe working conditions are conducive to better health, higher efforts and hence, higher productivity.

Safety

A factory should have a full-time safety department to look for unsafe working conditions, publicise safety measures, conduct safety classes, demonstrate the use of safety appliances and stress upon the need for safety. Use of safety helmets should be a must in factories. Similarly, safety belts should invariably be used by workers while working at places with more than normal height, and safety glasses while welding or working in hazardous areas.

Lighting and Ventilation

Many factories have insufficient lighting and ventilation arrangements. This leads to inaccurate work, more rejections and accidents. Sometimes high intensity lights cause strain in the eyes and headaches. Excess humidity leads to perspiration, discomfort and decreased desire for physical efforts. High temperature and very low humidity dries up the mucus membranes resulting in colds and infection. Similarly, dust, toxic gases, fumes etc. are injurious to workers and call for an efficient system of ventilation.

Distractions

Distractions should be minimised. Some common forms of distractions are noise beyond certain limits, moving objects, direct sunlight, welding sparks, etc. These may cause tension and fatigue. A constantly ringing telephone is another source of noise.

Sanitation

Essential facilities such as toilets, drinking water, rest rooms, lockers, canteen, etc. have a bearing on the employees' health and productivity. Some of these factors have now been brought under statutory control and certain minimum facilities have to be provided for.

Fatigue

Fatigue or decreased capacity to work can be caused either due to physiological reasons or the environment/nature of work. It also sometimes occurs due to the monotony of work. Accumulation of wastes like carbon dioxide, lactic acid, etc. in the blood can also cause fatigue. Fatigue can generally be lessened by giving rest periods after certain hours of work. Since fatigue continues to exist as 'a debt to be paid at the compound rate of interest', it is necessary to know its symptoms, causes, effects and measurement to check its growth at the right time.

Symptoms	(i)	ability to command the muscles is weakened
	(ii)	tactile sensibility is lowered
	(iii)	capillaries are relaxed; hence, a flushed face
	(iv)	poor expression, enlarged handwriting and lack in coordination of body movements
Causes	(i)	long hours of work encroaching on the hours of sleep
	(ii)	inadequate lighting, heating and ventilation
	(iii)	faulty machine design
	(iv)	faulty posture
	(v)	personal factors – illness, mental worry. Nine out of ten times fatigue is due to improper home conditions; dissipation; specific disease; irregular hours; undue load of outside activities and other personal worries.
Effects	(i)	less output
	(ii)	lower quality of work
	(iii)	increased possibility of accidents
	(iv)	bad temper
	(v)	spoiled work
Measurement	(i)	rate of labour turnover, extent of absenteeism
	(ii)	spoiled work records
	(iii)	voluntary or spontaneous rest periods taken by employees
	(iv)	analysis of production data, specially towards the end of the day
	(v)	accident records
	(vi)	general attitude of the workers
Preventive Steps	(i)	rest intervals in between work hours/days to be provided adequately; posture changes may help
	(ii)	abundance of well-diffused illumination and ventilation and fresh air
	(iii)	motivating workers
	(iv)	avoiding job monotony
	(v)	keeping workers healthy
	(vi)	educating workers not to carry domestic problems to the factory and vice-versa

Accident Proneness

Some people are more prone to accidents than others in similar environments. Accident frequency tends to decline with increasing age and/or experience. Even job prestige and incentives are found to have some bearing on the rate of accidents.

Accident proneness is defined as a "personal idiosyncrasy predisposing the individual who possesses it in a marked degree to a relatively high accident rate". Many studies have revealed that "industrial workers exposed to equal risks were unequal in their liability to sustain accidents". This unequal liability was a relatively stable phenomenon, manifesting itself in different periods of exposure and in different kinds of accidents. It is a known fact that people who are always stumbling and dropping things, whether they are driving a car, operating a machine or even counting change, get panicky easily. They manifest a sort of disorder in their defence reaction mechanism. However, this theory has been challenged by many. It does not tell the whole story about an accident. A man may be prone to accidents in one work situation but not in others. Similarly, the health, age, strain of work, and psychological and physical environments may play a more important role in determining the occurrence and frequency of accidents than the hypothesis of proneness alone.

It is because of this that some authors believe that the frequency of 'repeater' accidents approximates a pure chance (poisson) distribution.

Age and Experience

The relationship between the age and experience of the worker and his accident frequency has been studied by many psychologists. The younger groups have been found to be more prone to accidents than the older ones, because of their immaturity. Experience makes its contribution towards reduction in the rate of accidents by acquainting the employees with proper work and safety habits. Training in correct work methodology and safety habits also go a long way in reducing accident frequency rates in any job.

Monotony at Work

As stated earlier, in a large number of cases, accidents are caused because of fatigue or monotony at work. While fatigue is usually considered to be the result of physical strain, the psychological factors which may cause it are often ignored. In fact, it has been found that "in nine out of ten cases, fatigue has a story behind it of improper and uncomfortable home situations, mental worries, etc." The monotony also brings fatigue early at work. An uncomfortable psychological environment diverts the attention and reduces the alertness of the mind which may result in accidents.

> **PERSPECTIVE**
>
> ### Major Hazards In Call Centres
>
> The most significant hazards in call centres stem directly from the work organisation performances, management techniques and occupational stress.
>
> #### Manual Tasks
> - Workers are exposed to the risk of muscle or skeletal injury (e.g. sore neck, shoulders, back, wrists and hands) as a result of awkward, static or repetitive working postures
> - Repeated performance of similar work involving same body actions and same muscles being used continuously (e.g. keyboard entry performed each time a phone call is answered).
> - Work area design (e.g. bending, twisting, static postures, effect of lighting, glare).
> - Demand on workers due to increase in the duration of exposure, frequency of task resulting into muscle tension, overexertion, etc.
>
> #### Occupational Stress
> - Workers are unable to satisfactorily adjust to the demands and changes in the work environment, leadership and supervision, role clarity, negative events resulting into going on leave, resigning, seeking medical assistance and compensation.

Discipline and Attitude

The attitude of the workers and/or supervisor may also be responsible for the rate of accidents. Sometimes wilful neglect by the workers may cause an accident. An employee may participate in horseplay with air pressure guns or fail to wear safety clothes, goggles or come for duty under the influence of liquor, etc. Lack of discipline among employees may thus be responsible for certain accidents in the factory. The attitude of the supervisor is a factor to reckon with. The incidence is less in the departments where supervisors have a high sense of safety consciousness and are not only strict in enforcing safety measures but also guide the employees by examples and precepts.

Safety Motivation

The psychological aspects are thus inherent in safety problems which are multidimensional. That some people are more prone to accidents than others, should not be concluded merely on the basis of statistical analysis. The individual should be examined as a whole since the different causes of accidents may combine in different degrees in an individual. Adequate care at the time of selection may help in avoiding accidents in many cases. Persons who are fit for particular jobs emotionally, physically and mentally may be screened at the time of selection itself. Psychologists have devised various tests which help management in choosing the right man for the right job. Employees who have been trained properly on the job are less subject to accidents than those who are poorly trained or untrained. A high sense of safety consciousness among supervisors is also essential for enforcing discipline among workers so that they adhere to the safety rules. Job motivation is another important factor that reduces accident frequency. Safety campaigns; inviting people to give suggestions on safety devices and plans; making them feel important by providing them status and reward which keep their interest in the work alive, are some of the measures which have been found useful in reducing accidents in many factories.

Indian Factories Act, 1948

The Indian Factories Act, 1948, makes it obligatory for the employers to maintain hygienic and safe working conditions inside the factory, regulate the hours of work and take certain welfare measures. The Act applies to all industrial establishments employing ten or more workers where power is used and twenty or more workers in all other cases. It prohibits the employment of children below 14 years of age in any factory. The licensing, registration and prior scrutiny of the factory plans by the factories inspectorate are provided under the Act. The inspector of factories is given powers to ensure that the provisions of the Act are implemented by the employers. The main provisions of the act regarding health, safety, welfare, hours of work, employment of young persons, annual leave, etc. are given below:

Health

Factories should be kept clean and free from effluvia arising from any drain, privy or other nuisance. Effective arrangements for disposal of waste and effluents; ventilation and temperature; exhaust appliances; regulating artificial humidification; avoiding overcrowding; adequate lighting; provision for drinking water (provision for cooling drinking water where 250 or more workers are working); latrines and urinals for male and female workers; and separate provision for spittoons should be made.

Safety

Provisions for fencing of machinery be made; young persons be prohibited to work on dangerous machines; provision for striking gear and devices for cutting off power be made; safeguards be taken in self-acting machines, casing of new machineries; hoist and lifts, lifting machines, chains, ropes and lifting tackles should be of good quality; speed limit be fixed for revolving machinery; proper maintenance of pressure plant floors, stairs and means of access be ensured; protection of eyes and precaution against dangerous fumes;

measures to ensure the prevention of explosion where dust, gas, fumes or vapours are manufactured be taken; precautions against fires, means of exit, safety of buildings and machinery, etc. be taken.

Welfare

Separate washing facilities for males and females; facilities for storing and drying clothing; facilities for sitting, first aid appliances (not less than one for every 150 workers); ambulance room and doctor where 500 or more workers are employed should be made. A canteen should be provided where more than 250 workers are employed; shelter, rest rooms and lunch rooms where more than 150 people are working. Creches should be provided where more than 50 women workers are employed and, welfare officer/officers be appointed where 500 or more workers are employed.

> **PERSPECTIVE**
>
> **Caring For People: Marriott**
>
> As a company, Marriott is over 80 years old, and its founding principle has served it well – if you take care of associates, they will take care of customers. In late 30s, when there was no healthcare coverage for the staff, Marriott had doctors on its roll to care for the people. A culture of empowerment has been nurtured to enable people to develop decision-making ability. The company is in hospitality business which requires employees to give their best at all times – 24x7, 365 days. Consider the employee at the front desk – he or she has to be at the job at 8 a.m. in the morning, or 3 p.m. in the afternoon, or again at 3 a.m. in the morning and has to work at the same level of efficiency.
>
> The culture of empowerment and training facilitates fast track involvement of employees. They get an opportunity to work in a global hospitality association. In a sense, they have a global career.

Working Hours

1. The maximum hours of work for an adult in a week should not exceed 48.
2. A weekly off, either on Sunday or on one of the three days before or after it is a must. A notice to this effect may be put up on the notice board.
3. Maximum hours of work per day should be 9 (may be increased for shift changes).
4. Half an hour rest after 5 hours of work (hours of work without rest may go up to 6 with permission) should be allowed.
5. Working hours cannot be spread for more than 10½ hours during the day.
6. When a worker works for more than 9 hours in a day or 48 hours in a week, he would be entitled to double wages as overtime.

7. Double employment is restricted.
8. Notice of the periods of work should be displayed and a register of adult workers be maintained.
9. Women cannot be employed in night shifts.

Employment of Young Persons

Children below 14 years are not allowed to work in a factory.

Young persons must possess a certificate of fitness. They are not allowed to work in night shifts. Maximum working hours for them are 4½, per day (spread over 5 hours). The period of work for children should be displayed on the notice board and a register of child workers be maintained.

Annual Leave With Wages

After 240 days work during a calendar year, leave entitlement with wages in the next calendar year will be 1 day for every 20 days worked for adults and 1 day for every 15 days of work for young persons. Days of layoff as maternity leave should be treated as earned leave availed not to be deducted from the number of days worked. But no leave would accrue during this period.

Carry forward of annual leave up to 30 days in case of adults and 40 days in the case of a child be allowed. Refused leave may be carried forward to any limit.

A worker should be entitled to proportionate leave with wages if discharged or dismissed before he puts in the qualifying period of service.

Flexible Working Hours

People are accustomed to work for fixed hours in factories and offices. The system has its own virtues. Managers find it easy to supervise and control their staff, plan for production and provide for lighting, heating, catering and other services. But then it has its limitations and creates problems, not only to the employees, but also to the men and women in other walks of life. Fixed hours of work are the main cause of congestion on roads and resultant transport bottlenecks in the cities. Employees' family and social life are affected adversely. At times, they find it difficult to cope with their commitments at work and domestic needs. Inside a factory, disciplinary problems may arise out of late arrivals. Employees also feel the authoritarian touch in the imposition of rigid work hours.

A few companies in Europe have experimented with the concept of flexible time as an alternative to fixed working hours. They divide the working day into two parts: a core time around midday and flexible periods during morning and afternoon, and allow their employees to vary, on individual basis, the times at which to start and finish their work. Thus, an employee is not compelled to start 'on time' and can vary his work timings from day to day. But all employees are required to be present during the core time and work at least for the contracted number of hours per day, per week and per month. These times vary from the industry area to the country. Flexible work hours ranging from one to three hours in the morning form the basic concept of flex time.

German Experiment

The idea of flextime was conceived in 1967 by Herr Hillert, personnel manager of a German aerospace company – Messerschmitt-Bolkow-Blolm. The company with 3,000 employees in administration, research and development, was faced with serious transport problems. Everyday there was a long queue at the main gate and the clocking in points. Similarly, employees eased off work each day a few minutes earlier than scheduled, so that they could lead the queue to clock out. This adversely affected production and the morale of the employees. Herr Hillert introduced flextime known as *Gleitseit* in German as a solution to this vexed problem. The employees were allowed to report for duty any time between 4.00 p.m. and 6.00 p.m. except for a fixed 48 minutes lunch break. They are required to put in their total monthly contractual hours of work. Credit or debit balance to the extent of 10 hours is allowed to be carried forward to the next month. The time of arrival and departure is recorded on punched cards in time clocks placed near the entrance and everyone, from director downwards, has to abide by the rules of the system.

Lufthansa introduced flextime in some of its offices in 1970. Employees were required to be present during the core time which is 9.30 a.m. to 3.30 p.m. In the morning, employees can report any time between 7.00 a.m. and 9.30 a.m. In the afternoon, they can leave at any time between 3.30 p.m. and 7.00 p.m. They have to work for contracted hours during the month. It is estimated that the company has saved about $500,000 per year from gleaming 'lost days and hours' as a result of the scheme.

British Experience

A few British firms have successfully introduced flexible working hours in their administrative offices. Allen and Hanburys Ltd. introduced the scheme in 1970 with flexible hours between 7.00 a.m. and 9.30 a.m. and 4.30 p.m. and 6.30 p.m. Thirteen hundred employees are benefited under the scheme. Pilkington Brothers Introduced flexible hours of work for their employees in service, technology and engineering departments in 1971. London and Manchester Assurance introduced the scheme in 1972 with flexible hours of work between 9.00 a.m. and 10.00 a.m., 12.00 noon and

3.00 p.m., and 4.00 p.m. and 7.00 p.m. The system has proved to be useful and a number of British firms have adopted it for their white collar employees.

The Swiss firm Sandon AG adopted flexible working hours in 1970 at Basel for its 2000 white collar workers. The scheme provided for flexible work hours between 7.00 a.m. and 9.00 a.m., 12.00 noon and 2.00 p.m., and 4.00 p.m. and 7.00 p.m. Several other firms in Europe are bidding farewell to the old system of rigid work hours. The basic features of the schemes adopted by some of the firms are given on the following page.

Five days, forty hours work week is the normal practice with several US companies. Many organisations are now giving option to their employees to adopt 4 days/10 hours per day schedule. A recent research shows that the system is gaining popularity with the employees. A bank in St. Louis has been operating on a 5 days/ 4 days work week option since 1971. Employees can choose to work on either 5 days/8 hours per day or 4 days/10 hours per day schedule. An insurance company in St. Louis introduced a pilot scheme in April 1974. Each employee was allowed to report for duty between 7.00 a.m. and 9.00 a.m. All employees continued to work for 7 hours 45 minutes a day with a lunch break of 45 minutes. The results were quite encouraging in terms of reduction in absenteeism and tardiness, and improvement in the morale of the employees and work performance. The scheme was adopted on a permanent basis in early 1975. More than 2000 companies in the US are now working 4 days/40 hours a week. In Canada, 17% companies have a direct 4/40 routine.

U.S. Practice

Employees welcome flexible hours of work for several reasons:
- The time to start and finish the work can be varied on an individual basis.
- Better balance between work and private life can be maintained.
- Better tuning between work rhythm and workload can be maintained.
- Travel becomes easier as the morning and evening rush can be avoided.
- Informational atmosphere is increased and tension reduced.

Employees' Outlook

The adoption of flextime may result in an improvement in the transport system and balanced growth of cities which may benefit the people at large.

Managerial Problems

The negative aspects of flextime are primarily associated with supervision, production scheduling and maintenance of services and safety. Supervisors look upon it as a 'floating arrangement' and a scheduling headache. Particularly in flow production and process industries, the scope for individual flexible work time is either absent or very much reduced. Workload fluctuations, communication gap and confusion are likely to result in the absence of effective control and supervision in flexible hours. The cost of maintenance of essential services and safety may go up if the office is kept open for longer hours.

Flextime is linked with individual freedom and, therefore, liked by employees. Experiments in different countries confirm the usefulness and desirability of the system for white collar workers in company offices, research and development organisations and government departments. The system may prove beneficial in the metropolitan cities of India and would be worth experimenting.

Social Security

Workers feel insecure for various reasons. Inadequate wages, lay-off and retrenchments, accidents and injuries in the course of employment, occupational diseases, old age, sickness, total or partial disability and maternity are some of the causes of anxiety and fear.

These insecurities can be depicted as:

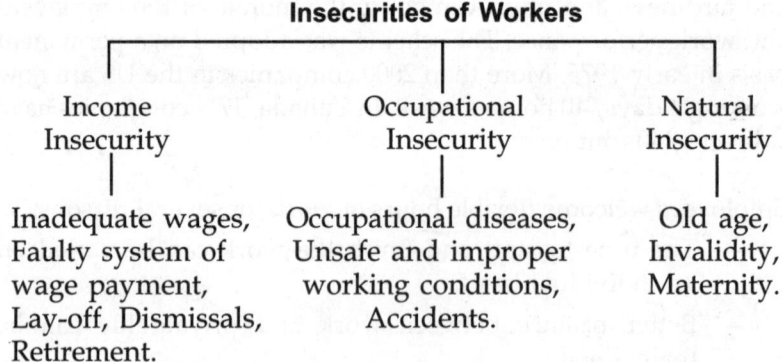

Insecurities of Workers

Income Insecurity	Occupational Insecurity	Natural Insecurity
Inadequate wages, Faulty system of wage payment, Lay-off, Dismissals, Retirement.	Occupational diseases, Unsafe and improper working conditions, Accidents.	Old age, Invalidity, Maternity.

The society and the state are jointly responsible for protecting the workers and their families from insecurities. Social security measures are essential to fight against the giants of *want, disease, squalor, idleness, and ignorance*. Social security should aim at compensation, restoration and prevention.

FLEXIBLE WORKING HOURS
Experiments in Europe

S. No.	Organisation	Year of introduction	No. of employees covered	Core time (fixed hours)	Mid-day break (minutes)	Flexible hours	Maximum credit/debit hours allowed in a month
1.	Messerschemitt-Bolkow-Blohm GmbH (W. Germany)	1967	3000	8.00 a.m. - 4.00 p.m.	48	7.00 a.m. - 8.00 a.m.	10
2.	Sandoz AG (Switzerland)	1970	2000	9.00 a.m. - 12.00 noon 2.00 p.m. - 4.30 p.m.	45	7.00 a.m. - 9.00 a.m. 12.00 noon -2.00 p.m. 4.00 p.m. - 7.00 p.m.	10
3.	Allen & Hansbury Ltd. (England)	1970	1300	9.00 a.m. - 12.00 noon	—	7.00 a.m. - 9.30 a.m. 4.30 p.m. - 6.30 p.m.	5
4.	Bergerat Monnoyeur (France)	—	—	9.15 a.m. - 4.30 p.m.	45	8.00 a.m. - 9.15 a.m. 4.30 p.m. - 7.00 p.m.	—
5.	Lufthansa (W. Germany)	1970	1100	9.30 a.m. - 3.30 p.m.	45	7.00 a.m. - 9.30 a.m. 3.30 p.m. - 7.00 p.m.	—
6.	Pilkington Bros. (England)	1971	—	9.00 a.m. - 12.00 noon 2.00 p.m. - 4.00 p.m.	90	7.00 a.m. - 9.00 a.m. 4.00 p.m. - 7.00 p.m.	—
7.	Wiggins Teape Ltd. (England)	1972	600	10.00 a.m. - 4.00 p.m.	30-60	8.00 a.m. - 10.00 a.m. 4.00 p.m. - 6.00 p.m.	7
8.	London & Manchester Assurance (England)	1972	450	10.00 a.m. - 12.00 noon 3.00 p.m. - 4.00 p.m.	30	5.00 a.m. - 10.00 a.m. 12.00 noon -3.00 p.m. 4.00 p.m. - 7.03 p.m.	—

Social Security Legislations

The State in India has laid down various measures and acts for improvement in social security. The benefits to workers under some of the important enactments are:

1. The Workmen's Compensation Act, 1923

The employer has to pay compensation to the workmen for injury caused in the course of and out of employment. Injuries which are cured in less than three days/caused because of the workmen being drunk or by wilful disobedience, etc. are not to be considered for compensation. Compensation is payable for occupational diseases caused during the course of duties. Cases of fatal/serious injury are to be reported to the concerned authority. Rates of compensation for death, permanent/total disability, etc. are also given in the Act.

2. The Payment of Wages Act, 1936

The wage period should not exceed one month. Wages are to be paid in cash before the expiry of the 7th day in establishments employing less than 1,000 workers and on the 10th in other cases. Discharged workmen are to be paid before the expiry of the second working day; unauthorised deductions from pay are not allowed. Permissible deductions include fines, absence from duty, damage or loss of goods and money, recovery advances, adjustment of over payment, income tax, provident fund, insurance premium and house rent. Fines are not to be charged unless permission is obtained from the government. Fines are to be used only for the welfare of the workers.

3. The Minimum Wages Act, 1948

The appropriate government is authorised to fix the minimum rates of wages of employees in scheduled employments; fix separate minimum rates for time and piece rate workers; periods for cost of living allowance; revise minimum wages; fix hours of work per day (9), a weekly day of rest with pay; overtime wages.

4. The Employees State Insurance Act, 1948

Benefits to workmen:

Sickness benefit: Cash payment, maximum for 56 days – may be extended up to 309 days in case of T.B., leprosy, etc.

Maternity Benefits: Maximum for 12 weeks, not more than 6 weeks can precede confinement.

Disablement Benefits: Periodical payment for employment injury – total or partial.

Dependent Benefits: Periodical payment to dependants in case of death of an employee.

Medical Benefits: Medical care through service system or panel system, E.S.I. hospitals, etc.

Scheme administered by the Employees State Insurance Corporation, employers, employees and the government contribution to the corporation.

Employees drawing emoluments up to Rs. 1,600 per month are entitled to bonus.

5. Payment of Bonus Act, 1965

Qualifying service: 30 days. Minimum bonus: 8.33% of wages. Maximum bonus: 20% of wages. Available surplus is to be calculated after deducting depreciation and taxes from the gross profit. Set-on and set-off allowed up to four years.

Bonus holiday for new establishments: up to 5 years.

Payment of bonus is to be made within eight months of the closing of the accounting year.

The employer is required to pay gratuity to the workman on the termination of his employment/superannuation or retirement or resignation or death or disablement due to accident or disease. Qualifying service for the benefit – 5 years. Only in the case of death, 5 years service is not necessary. Rate of gratuity: 15 days wages for every completed year of service or part thereof.

6. Payment of Gratuity Act, 1972

Amount of gratuity not to exceed 20 months wages.

Forfeiture of gratuity: To the extent of loss or damage to the property of the employer by wilful omission or negligence by the employee when his services are terminated for the same.

(A) A workman loses his right eye due to an injury caused by a spark entering into his eye. A notice is put up in English near the place of work directing the workman to use goggles while at work. The affected workman neither asked for goggles nor had the supervisors supply these to him on their own, though goggles were available in the store. No one warned the worker for working without goggles. The workman claims compensation on the ground that he does not know English. The supervisor says that the workman was aware of the notice and the accident occurred due to his own negligence.

Situation Analysis

Discuss whether the workman will be entitled for compensation under law?

(B) An employee (a minor) of a cotton spinning factory meets with an accident while at work. His thumb, index, middle and ring fingers are chopped off. He claims Rs. 2520/- by way of compensation. His mother, an old lady, enters into a compromise with the management by accepting Rs. 500/- as compensation. The employee feels aggrieved and insists that compensation be paid to him or else he would go to court. Discuss whether the employee will be entitled for full compensation under the law?

(C) A manufacturing company in Bombay has a distribution office in Delhi. A strike takes place in the manufacturing unit on account of which the supply of goods for distribution in Delhi is limited. The management in Delhi decides to lay-off 17 out of 30 employees. There are no certified standing orders or agreement between the management and the employees regarding lay-off. The laid-off employees demand full wages for the period. Discuss the claim of the employees in this regard.

Review Questions

1. Discuss the importance of good and safe working conditions in a factory.
2. What are the causes of industrial fatigue? What measures will you suggest to prevent fatigue at work.
3. What is accident proneness? What measures are needed to prevent accidents at work?
4. Discuss the major provisions of the Factories Act, 1948, regarding working conditions.
5. What are the merits and demerits of flexible working hours?

Further Readings

1. Olga Aikin and Judith Reid: *Employment, Welfare and Safety at Work* (Penguin, Harmondsworth, 1971).
2. D. Gebhardt and C. Crump: *Employee Fitness and Wellness Programme in the Workplace* (American Psychologist, Vol. 45, pp. 262-272, 1990).
3. S. Grebner, N.K. Semmer, L.L. Faso, S. Gut, W. Kalin and A. Ellfering: *Working Conditions, Well Being and Job Related Attitudes Among Call Centre Agents* (European Journal of Work and Organizational Psychology, Vol. 12, pp. 341-365, 2003).
4. R.S. Lazarus: *Psychological Stress and the Coping Process* (McGraw-Hill, New York, 1966).
5. J. Loehr and T. Schwartz: *The Making of A Comporate Athlete* (Harvard Business Review, Vol. 79, pp. 120-129, 2001).
6. S.K. Malik: *Labour Laws* (Allahabad Law Agency, Allahabad, 2005).
7. S. Weiss, J. Fielding and A. Baum: *Health at Work* (Erlbaum, New Jersey, 1990).

Chapter 16

Morale and Participative Management

A Japanese manager conducts the dialogue in circles, widening and narrowing them to correspond to the subordinate's sensitivity to the feedback. He may say, "I would like you to reflect a bit further on your proposal." Translated into Western thought patterns, this sentence would read, "you are dead wrong, and you better come up with a better idea." The first approach allows the subordinate to exist with his pride intact.

— **Richard Tanner Pascale**
(Harvard Business Review, April 1980)

Learning Objectives

After reading this chapter you will be able to:

1. Define morale and analyse the reasons for high or low morale in an organisation.
2. Develop an effective grievance redressal procedure to handle workers' grievances in a timely and effective manner.
3. Discuss the role of joint consultations and workers' participation as congenial to good industrial relations.
4. Discuss the desirability of Employee Stock Option Plans in a developing economy like India.

Building up of Morale

The role of morale was recognised quite early in military organisations where four elements of battle efficiency were recognised: the number of men, arms, regimentation and morale. Of these four, Napolean is said to have attached maximum weightage to morale for winning a battle.

As a result of industrial revolution and growth of large scale industries/business organisations, the concept of morale has been received as a strong driving force. Even though highly intangible and difficult to quantify, morale is a powerful force in an organisation. Workers and groups with high morale are more productive than workers and groups with low morale.

Morale can be termed as a mental condition of an individual or groups that decides their attitudes and limits the degree to which they accept leadership or responsibility. Sometimes an individual may have poor personal morale and yet, as a member of a group, he may have a high morale.

Measuring morale occasionally, and continuously keeping up with the process of morale building, in other words, the process of integrating interests, are the important tasks of leadership. Good morale is ultimately the result of successful leadership.

Morale can be measured directly or indirectly. Direct measures include discussions, attitude surveys, interviews and observations. Indirect measures include analysis of grievance cases, personnel turnover, accidents, absenteeism, breakdowns, etc.

The results of surveys serve a very useful purpose. They bring to light the areas of weak spots, training needs, grievances, weak policies of the management and so on. The very fact that the management is seeking the opinion of employees, often improves the existing morale.

This determines the acceptance of leadership. An industrial society can be overthrown if there is destruction of the morale of its industrial population. On the other hand, a high morale can lead to:

(i) willing cooperation

(ii) loyalty and a sense of belonging to the organisation

(iii) immediate awareness and equitable adjustments of conflicts as they develop

(iv) justice and equitable distribution of rewards, i.e. promotions, logical dues, facilities, etc.
(v) provision of values, both tangible and intangible, that are desired by the collectives in adequate and proper amounts.
(vi) cutting down red-tapism to the minimum, employer-employee meetings, training, education and indoctrination.
(vii) satisfactory and safe work environment.

The scale of morale is somewhat subjective. However, it can be graded into a few levels such as:

Employees of all ranks show great interest in work and the organisation. Subordinates rate leadership high and cooperate promptly. Grievances and fights between personnel are few and far between. Disciplinary actions are rare. There is a high sense of belonging among the employees.	*High Morale*
Cooperation is satisfactory. There are no serious cases of indiscipline. There is evidence of some liking for the job and leadership. The organisation is regarded as a good place to work by the employees. There is no strong feeling that people are not getting their rightful dues.	*Satisfactory Morale*
There is dislike for executive leadership. Executives and employees have no confidence in the decision or the integrity and ability of the top management. Employees feel that a few selected hands are enjoying the privileges of the company and good/loyal employees are getting a raw deal. There is a feeling among the employees that they cannot get their rightful dues without coercing the management, and that at a good man is not prospering because he is not a 'yes man' of the management.	*Low Morale*

To keep the morale of employees at a satisfactory level, it is necessary that the top management should know the factors that stimulate or depress morale. A judicious use of these factors helps in keeping fluctuations in the level of morale under control.

A simplified questionnaire which can be used to assess the morale of executives is shown here to illustrate the point.

SIMPLIFIED QUESTIONNAIRE – MORALE OF EXECUTIVES

Sl. No.	Questions	Response		
		Yes	Sometimes	No
1.	Do you think that the management is fair in its dealings with the executives?			
2.	Do you feel that the executives have a pride of place in the organisation?			
3.	Do you feel that the management is fair with the executives in matters of pay scales and perks?			
4.	Do you feel that deputation for training is generally done impartially in your organisation?			
5.	Do you feel that you have the management support when you take some emergency decisions depending on the exigency of a situation?			
6.	Do you feel that your present reporting and status are justified in keeping with your attainments?			
7.	Do you have access to your works manager and chief executives for your personal matters of importance?			
8.	Do you feel that the management is giving you sufficient opportunity for career growth?			
9.	Do the promotions go to the deserving people in all fairness after giving due weightage to qualifications, experience and competence?			
10.	Do you feel that good work is recognised by the management and duly rewarded?			
11.	Do you feel that the management is following a rational promotion policy?			
12.	Do you feel satisfied with your reportability and responsibility?			
13.	Do you feel that you are utilising your knowledge and ability in your job?			

14. Do you feel that you have been given adequate authority/power to handle your workers?
15. Do you feel that there is proper motivation for putting your best efforts in your assignment?
16. Does the management feel that the executives should be successful leaders of their subordinates?
17. Do you feel that your boss is competent enough to guide your activities?
18. Is intentional bypassing of the immediate officers discouraged by your superiors?
19. Do you feel that executives in middle management are given a chance to participate in vital decision-making?
20. Do you feel that there is no communication gap in your organisation?
21. Do you feel that the management considers your grievances and suggestions seriously?
22. Do you feel that your boss is encouraging you for better work and is not in the habit of finding faults in your work?
23. Do you feel that you should stick to your present organisation and should not join elsewhere to better your prospects?
24. Do you feel a sense of belonging to the company?
25. Do you feel that your family will be well protected by the company and given all the help in rehabilitating themselves in case of your permanent disablement or death while on duty?

Note : Here the questionnaire (which is meant to be indicative only) has been worded in a manner to facilitate analysis and direct measurement. The rating could be done as follows:

Average number of affirmatives	Rating
20 & above	Very High Morale
16 to 20	Good Morale
11 to 15	Average Morale
10 & below	Low Morale

It is important that sample size and random distribution of questionnaires should be ensured. A fair cross-section should be covered without any bias.

For purposes of score, 'sometimes' can be considered as 50% 'Yes' and 50% 'No'.

There should not be any rigidity about the rating scale. It should be flexible. There could even be separate weightage or marks for different questions if the specialists so feel. This should be decided upon after proper discussion.

There is another style of designing questionnaires where the questions are mixed up and couched in words in a manner that sometimes 'yes' and 'no' convey the same meaning. It is a way of knowing how sincerely a questionnaire has been answered.

Removal of Grievance

No system, however meticulously designed for a group, can take care of all the needs and aspirations of its members. The problem becomes more complex with large organisations where the possibility of communication gap or failure widens.

Grievances and complaints of employees are indicative of employer-employee relations in an organisation. These are primary manifestations of workers' dissatisfaction against working conditions, terms of employment, management failures, etc. which, if not attended to in time, may create explosive situations.

Absence of grievance in an organisation is not necessarily a healthy sign. It is more likely that repressive measures are working in the organisation as a result of which freedom of expression, showing dissatisfaction with the decision of superiors do not exist. It may also be an indicator of a suppressive environment which may be charged with emotions and may explode with far-reaching consequences.

A time-bound effective grievance redressal procedure provides a formalised channel for seeking redressal of such grievances, and obviating the need for resorting to agitational approach. A grievance procedure is therefore a formal system of steps through which a dissatisfied employee can take his complaints to various levels of the management for redressal.

There are three objectives behind setting up a grievance procedure. These are:
(i) to settle the grievance of the employees in the shortest possible time, and
(ii) at the lowest possible level of authority;
(iii) the system should provide for various stages so that the aggrieved employee can seek redressal even from the highest authority.

For this, let us see as to how a grievance arises? It arises when an employee feels that some sort of injustice has been done to him or he has been treated differently. It may be a case of:
— Promotions and seniority
— Amenities/working conditions
— Disciplinary sections/fines/recoveries
— Terms of employment
— Compensation
— Transfer
— Leave
— Victimisation/managerial failures
— Payments and miscellaneous other matters

except for those that are directly related to the formulation of management policies.

Disposal of Grievance

An effective way of quick and rightful disposal of a grievance is the institution of a 2 or 3-tier grievance procedure.

The mechanism on which a 3-tier grievance procedure works in a large industrial undertaking is discussed below:

Tier-I

A plant is divided into suitable administrative zones. An aggrieved employee discusses his grievance with the labour officer of the zone. In case he is not satisfied with the explanation of the labour officer, he puts his grievance before the personnel officer of the department, in writing. The grievance application is submitted in a prescribed format called STAGE-I form.

The personnel officer examines the grievance on the basis of available facts/records and the prescribed rules of the company.

If the grievance is found tenable, action is initiated at his level to redress it within a week.

Tier-II

In case an employee either does not get a reply to his Stage-I grievance within 10 days or is not satisfied with the reply given to him, he puts in a Stage-II grievance to his head of department in the prescribed form.

The head of the department examines the case carefully with the assistance of his personnel officer. In case he finds it tenable, suitable action for its redressal is taken by him within the framework of the authority delegated to him.

Tier-III

If either no reply to his Stage-II grievance is received within 15 days or he is still not satisfied with the reply given to him, the employee can submit his grievance at Stage-III directly to the secretary of the grievance committee constituted by the management for this purpose.

The secretary of the committee calls for the relevant records and comments of the concerned departments and, after careful examination, puts up the case before the grievance committee.

The secretary can settle certain types of Stage-II grievances relating to the grant of contributory provident fund loan, correction of CPF account, non-payment of dues, etc. at his level. He immediately takes up the matter with the concerned authorities directly and tries to settle it without waiting for their clearance with the grievance committee.

In case the matter recorded in the grievance application is not clear, either the concerned employee is called by the secretary for further information or preliminary reports on such cases are called for from the concerned departments.

Grievances relating to promotions and major punishments can, however, be taken up within 30 days from the date of issue of the promotion orders directly at Stage-III level, without necessarily exhausting Stage-I and II levels.

The above measures obviously help in settling such cases expeditiously at the lower levels.

The Constitution of the Grievance Committee

A. *Operation Department*   *Generally filled by*
1. Chairman : Works Manager
2. Representative of the Personnel Manager : Not below the rank of Asst. Personnel Manager
3. Representative of the Financial Adviser : Not below the rank of Dy. Financial Adviser
4. Two representatives of the recognised union.
5. Secretary, Grievance Committee : No. 2, i.e. Assistant Personnel Manager

B. *Administrative Departments*
1. Chairman: Personnel Manager or Finance Adviser
2. Representative of either Personnel Manager or Financial Adviser (If the Personnel Manager presides, there will be no other representative from the personnel department; similarly, if the Financial Adviser presides, there will be no other representative from the finance department).
3. Two representatives of the recognised union.
4. Secretary, Grievance Committee

C. *Construction Department*
1. Chairman : Project Manager or Chief Engineer (Construction)
2. Representative of the Personnel Manager : Not below the rank of Asst. Personnel Manager
3. Representative of the Financial Adviser : Not below the rank of Dy. Financial Adviser
4. Two representatives of the recognised union
5. Secretary, Grievance Committee

In the meeting of the Grievance Committee, all facts and relevant records are presented for examination by the members of the committee. Thereafter, the committee tries, as a whole, to decide the case unanimously. However, when no unanimous agreement is recorded, the dissenting views are recorded and a detailed note of dissent is obtained from the dissenting member or members. Such cases of dissent are later submitted to the General Manager/Managing Director for his final decision, along with the original records and relevant facts. Dissent cases are generally few if the case is decided on merit and not on personalities.

After the finalisation of the minutes of the committee, the decision is communicated to the department concerned and also to the aggrieved employee by the Secretary of the committee.

Revision Petition

If the worker still does not feel satisfied with the decision of the Grievance Committee, he can submit his revision petition to the General Manager within 10 days of the date of receipt of the decision. The revision petition is also examined by an independent officer. It is generally the Vigilance Officer or any other officer nominated by the General Manager.

Even the Personnel Manager looks into such cases personally and only then is the case submitted to the General Manager for his decision. His decision, which is final, is communicated to the applicant by an officer other than the Secretary of the Grievance Committee. The decision of the General Manager is required to be communicated to the aggrieved within 30 days of the receipt of his revision petition.

An employee may seek the assistance of a recognised union in presenting or discussing the case at any stage or even at the stage of revision petition/appeal.

Some of the salient features of the system are:

(i) Grievances pertaining to policy matters, such as grant of incentive bonus to non-entitled categories; revision/upgrading of scales or posts; applicability of different service rules; fixation/revision of line of promotion; cases pending before the courts; promotion cases from non-executive to executive cadre, etc. are not considered by the Grievance Committee.

(ii) Unanimous recommendations of the committee are normally implemented by the management if not arrived at. If a unanimous decision is not arrived at, the General Manager's decision is final.

(iii) When a grievance is pending for decision before the Grievance Committee, the worker is not normally expected to resort to conciliation/adjudication.

(iv) Faithful compliance of such a procedure as laid above leads to industrial harmony.

Grievance Application

First Stage

To
    Personnel Officer

From

Name :
Ticket no. :
Designation :
Department :
Section :
Nature of grievance
and reasons in brief :

                                    Signature of employee
                                              Date:

(For office use)

Grievance no. and date
Whether interviewed
the employee :
Results of enquiry :
Signature with date   Personnel Officer   Aggrieved Employee
of communication and
receipt

Second Stage

To
    Head of the Department

From

Name :
Ticket No. :
Designation :
Department :
Section :
Reasons for appeal :

                                    Signature of employee
                                              Date:

(For use in office)

Grievance number
and date :

Whether interviewed
the employee :

Results of enquiry :

Signature with date : (Head of the Dept.) (Aggrieved employee)
of communication and
receipt

Grievance Application

Third Stage

To
    The Secretary
    Grievance Committee

From

Name :
Ticket no. :
Designation :
Department :
Section :
Reasons for appeal :

                              Signature of employee
                                              Date:

(For use in office)

Grievance no. & date :

Results of grievance :
    Stage-I
    Stage-II

Decision of the
Grievance Committee :

Signature with date : (Secretary)   (Aggrieved employee)
of communication and
receipt

Counselling

Counselling also helps in improving discipline which is necessary to maintain orderliness. Problems like late coming, disobedience, wilful absenteeism, drunkenness while on duty can be rectified by:

(i) private counselling/advising the employee to change his habits.

(ii) verbal counsel by explaining the consequences of failure to heed the advice being rendered.

(iii) counselling in writing and issuing warnings asking him to explain his conduct.

Lay-off, downgradation or discharge of employees should not be hurriedly exercised without building up a case even if it is within the competence area of the manager.

Sometimes an employee, because of reasons such as family difficulties, health, financial imbalance, social commitments, housing etc. may be tense and not able to concentrate on his work.

He may feel greatly relieved if there is some superior in whom he can confide or whose advice he can seek. The counsellor should be a person who is trained to listen, counsel and report the facts to the management without either embarrassing the employee or making a commitment to him. Sometimes little help or coordination enables him to get over the situation or his confused way of thinking. He may feel grateful and regain his failing interest in the work.

Such counsel may not always bring good results. Sometimes it may result in an adverse decision, depending on how the counsellor handles the situation.

An employee may be subjected to many outside and inside forces stimulating or vitiating his mental condition or working efforts. Some typical negative forces are:

— Mental condition arising out of failure to achieve some desired/coveted aim, loss of a family member, housing, etc.

— Defeatist attitude arising out of his failure at work, love, home life (affecting his attitude towards work).

— Physical condition causing temporary setbacks, or aging or some emotional instability.

— Change of interest leading to wishful thinking, desire for change and so on.

Some of the corrective measures that may emerge from counselling are:

— Self-realisation of the forces acting on the individual.

— Change in work and habits.

— Outlets for repressed desires.

In case the immediate supervisor has the calibre to handle such cases, he should do so himself, or the Personnel Manager or his assistants can play this role more effectively.

Suggestion System

The suggestion system can pay back the company in many ways for the time and effort spent in its operation. Many companies have set up suggestion systems and give handsome rewards when the suggestions are accepted.

The plan is generally operated as under:

- A senior officer is designated as the chairman of the suggestion system. A committee is set up by him to scrutinise the suggestions received. The committee, constituted after careful consideration, includes personnel from various disciplines.

- A comprehensive suggestion system is drawn up, and approval of the management is obtained and published. It is given wide publicity. The system covers all aspects of the scheme.

- Decisions are taken very promptly as delay lowers the effectiveness of the system. When suggestions are turned down or not accepted, the secretary of the suggestion scheme normally explains the reasons for it to the suggester and thanks him for his initiative.

- Awards are given wide publicity. The recipient of an award may be photographed with the chairman of the committee. An annual bulletin on the suggestion scheme should be published in which such photographs can be included.

- Suggestion boxes are set up at various points in the factory. They should be distinctly different from a letter box in appearance. They should be cleared once in a week. The day is generally fixed and printed on the suggestion box.

- Some establishments keep the suggestion form anonymous. Awards are scrutinised by suggestion numbers. It is only after a decision has been taken that the person holding the token is asked to disclose his identity. In some cases, names and other details of the suggester are kept in a sealed envelope along with the suggestions form. It is opened only after a decision has been taken. This is done to keep the system free from the effects of personal bias.

A suggestion system format of a public sector company is given below to show how it operates.

Suggestion Scheme

Suggested name   Personal No.
Father's name   Designation
Department   Section
Main features of the scheme :
(Give details of suggestion
sketch/drawing, etc.)

How do you assess that it will contribute to efficiency/cost-saving/or any other improvement? If economic results are anticipated, please give calculations.

                         Full signature of the suggester
Date

To be filled in triplicate. First copy to the Head of the Department. Second copy to be given to the Secretary of Suggestion Scheme and the third copy to be retained as office copy by the suggester.

     (Please use a separate sheet if space is insufficient)

              Not to be Filled by the Suggester

Date of receipt: Put up for examination on:
Decision of the committee:
Remarks/approval of the Secretary/
Chairman of Suggestion Committee:
Result communicated to the suggester on:

                               Secretary,
                           Suggestion Scheme

Workers' Participation in Management

The gulf between the manager and the managed can be reduced considerably if the two sit together across the table frequently to discuss problems of mutual interest. A scheme of workers' participation in management is desirable for every organisation since:

- It involves the workers in company affairs directly and hence creates better awareness of its problems.
- It creates a sense of responsibility as the decisions in joint committees may be taken with the consent of both the parties.

- Managers are in a better position to deal with administrative problems, particularly those relating to labour matters as they may get firsthand information from the union representatives in the joint committees.
- Workers can easily understand management's take on various issues in the course of deliberations in these committees.

Different countries have different workers' participation in management programmes. In England, formation of joint councils is not obligatory but a good number of companies have joint councils which deal mainly with labour matters and make suitable recommendations for consideration of the top management. In Yugoslavia, a unique system described as auto-management is practised. A workers' council makes important decisions regarding company plans, allocation of resources, distribution of profits, etc. In USA, the most widely known approach to participation is the Scanlon plan which provides for the joint labour-management councils to solicit employee suggestions, and how efficiency could be increased, production cost reduced and waste eliminated. In France, every organisation where more than 50 workers are employed has a legally backed comite d'enterprise. Worker members are elected to this committee which deals with such matters as working rules, codes of discipline, employment, training, etc. In the Federal Republic of Germany, the works councils are legally obligatory in every enterprise. German unions attach great importance to the principle of co-determination. The council can insist on co-determination on such matters as the period of the working day, the time and method of paying wages, holidays, social welfare provisions, housing, etc.

In India, formation of joint committees is promoted both by legislation and tripartite conventions. The Industrial Disputes Act, 1947, provides for compulsory formation of works committees in all industrial units employing 100 or more workers. The formation of other committees, such as the Production Committee, Safety Committee, House Allotment Committee, etc., has been encouraged by the Indian Labour Conference on a voluntary basis. In a few undertakings, both in the private and public sectors, the scheme has been successfully introduced. The Tata Iron & Steel Company (TISCO) workers' participation was introduced as early as 1946, though in a limited way, through plant joint committees. At present, they have joint committees at different levels. At works level, there are such committees as Plant Works Committee, Joint Rates Committee, Job Evaluation Committee and House Allotment,

Medical Fitness, Central Canteen Management, Safety Appliances, Suggestion Box Committees, etc. At the department level, there are joint Departmental Councils to advise on production matters, discipline, cost control, etc. At the company level, there is a Joint Works Council to study operational results, production problems and methods to improve, supervise the works of joint committees at lower levels, follow up the implementation of the recommendations made and refer important issues to the Joint Consultative Council of Management which is the apex body to advise on matters concerning production, welfare, economic and financial issues placed by the management before it, and for the implementation of recommendations.

> BHEL, a public sector undertaking, has a successful scheme of workers' participation. At work place, Shop Councils with 12 representatives each from workers and management sides are formed to deal with the problems related to production, absenteeism, safety, physical environment, etc. At plant level, there is a Plant Council consisting of 12 members each from both sides to deal with plant level problems of production, employee benefits, incentives, safety, etc. At the corporate level, there are three committees – Production Liaison Conference, Specialised Committees and Joint Committee. The Production Liaison Conference, with top union officer and Director of the plant along with a few representatives from both sides, discuss records and plans related to production, sales, overtime, etc. Specialised committees, consisting of officers of central trade union and Director Personnel and other representatives, deal with the subjects delegated from joint committees and other items as judged necessary by the union and management. Joint Committees at the apex, consisting of union officers from different trade unions on the basis of their following, Chief Managing Director and all full time Directors, relevant General Managers and Personnel Heads, deliberate on policies and plans relating to employee benefit and services, workers' participation at various levels and specialised subjects. The details of the scheme are given in the Worker's Participation Chart.

> The Bhilai Steel Plant, a unit under the Steel Authority of India, provides another good example of participative management with bipartite committees functioning in such diversified areas as production, safety, welfare, grievances, merit rating, canteen, education, medical, accommodation, sports and culture, environmental hygiene, social security, collective bargaining, etc. The functioning composition and frequency of the meetings of their committees are given in the Bhilai Steel Plant Chart.

Labour Union's View

One section of the trade union leaders believes that there can be no common platform unless ownership management and control all come in the community's hand and the private sector is wiped out. Some of the leaders in the class believe that if workers join managers over a cup of tea for cooperation, they become a party to exploit their own brethren. The managers, according to them, want neither to share power nor divulge information and data which may be necessary to arrive at correct decisions. The workers' representatives who are normally less qualified than managers may be easily misled. Workers, according to them, are primarily concerned with their work, and living and working conditions. If managers ask for participation, it is either with an ulterior motive of weakening the workers' union or selling the management's point through better public relations with the trade union.

Another section of the trade union leaders perceives things in a different manner. Although they are not satisfied with the outcome of the joint councils/committees, they do not discard the theory altogether. They do want the foundation to be laid down before trying to build up a tall superstructure. They look upon the failure of participation schemes on two counts: firstly, the employers are not enlightened, and they lack a sense of responsibility towards the society and the workers and, secondly, the workers are disunited and there is no planning in trade unions. They also recognise that the trade unions are leader-based. There is a need for workers' participation in trade unions as much as it is in the industry. For managers also, they suggest that the owners should give them chances of better participation in management as it is not unusual for managers to sometimes come to know of the decisions of the top bosses only through union leaders.

A common reason for the failure of participation schemes, according to many trade union leaders, is the limited approach to the whole issue. The scheme is confined to productivity and production, but when workers see the management purchasing stores, raw materials and machinery at inflated prices and selling finished products at throw-away prices in concert with suppliers and purchasers, they become disgusted and feel that their sacrifices have been frittered away by corruption. The gains are shared by the owners, managers and technicians in the form of high salaries, perks and commissions.

Worker Participation
Union Management Consultation at BHEL

Type	Subjects for Consultations		Major Participants
Corporate Level			
Joint Committees	— Policies and plans for production, quality of production, sales and equipments. — Policies and plans for employee benefits and services.	Union	: The Union Officers having 10 % following including corresponding representative to Central Trade Union Organisation of INTUC, AITUC, CITU, BMS in proportion to the following of their affiliates in different units.
	— Policies for workers participation at various levels.	Management	: CMD, all the other full time Directors and relevant GGMS and Personnel Heads.
	— Specialised subjects to be dealt with the Joint Committee	Union	: Offices of Central Trade Union and of BHEL Union.
Specialised Committees	— Subjects delegated from Joint Committee. — Other items as judged necessary by Union and Management.	Management	: Directors (P), relevant GGMs, GMs and Personnel Heads.
Production Liaison Conference	— Records and plans related to production, sales and exports.	Union	: Top Officer incharge and relevant representative.
	— Records and plans related to overtime.	Management	: Director incharge and relevant managers.
Plant Level	— Plant level business, production programmes, targets and productivity manning and workload, work organisation, work planning, work process, etc.	Union	: Not more than 12 representatives of the workers as nominated by the Unions and the Central organisations to whom they are affiliated in the same proportion as they are represented in the apex level Joint Committee.
Plant Council	— Plant level employee benefits and services. — Urgent consultation items at plant level. — Problems emanating from shop council which have been unsolved — Development of skills and abilities of the employees. — Payment of rewards under suggestion scheme to workers. — General health-welfare and safety measures.	Management	: There will be a Co-Chairman nominated by the worker members of the Council. : Equal number of representatives from the Management GM (Operations) shall be the Chairman of the Council. Other members, Head (Production), Head (Personnel), Head (Finance), Head (Engineering), Head (Materials), 2 representatives from Executives, 2 representatives from Supervisors and 2 from Chairman of the Shop Councils.

Worker Participation
Union Management Consultation at BHEL

Type	Subjects for Consultations		Major Participants
Work Place Level Shop Council	— Problems related to work methods, production programmes and targets, productivity issues and issues such as raw material planning, on the job training, etc. — Improvement of production, productivity, efficiency including elimination of wastage and optimum utilisation of machine capacity and manpower. — Absenteeism in the shop and remedial measures. — Safety measures in the shop. — Physical environment/working conditions. — Identification of specific areas of low productivity and suggestions for correction. — Any matters referred to by the Plant Council.	Union Management	: Not more than 12 representatives of the workers from the specific function, product, process, physical location or in combination of these. Nomination from participative union in the same proportion as in apex level Joint Committee. Co-Chairman as nominated by the workers representatives. : Equal number of representatives of the Management. Head of Department/Shop will be the Chairman. 1 representative from sr. management level, 1 representative from middle management level, 1 from junior management level and 2 representatives from supervisory group will be other members.

FUNCTIONING, COMPOSITION AND FREQUENCY OF MEETINGS OF BIPARTITE COMMITTEES IN BHILAI STEEL PLANT

Grouping	Type of Committees		Composition	Frequency of meeting	Mode of Union Representation	Main objectives
	Area	Name				
WORK TECHNOLOGY RELATED	PRODUCTION	1. Central Production Committee	Mgt. 10 Union 10	Quarterly	Nomination	Sets and reviews production targets. Seeks to enhance productivity through proper and effective utilisation. Reviews and takes measures for controlling overtime and absenteeism. Reviews cost data and suggests cost reduction methods.
		2. Departmental Production Committee	Mgt. 10 Union 10	Monthly	-do-	
	SAFETY	1. General Safety Committee	Mgt. 5 Union 5	Monthly	-do-	Formulation and review of safety policies. Supervision of safety education and safety compliance. Promotion of safety measures and safety consciousness.
		2. Departmental Safety Committee	Mgt. 5 Union 5	Monthly	-do-	
EMPLOYEE WELFARE	WELFARE	1. Joint Committee	Mgt. 5 Union 5	Monthly	-do-	Considers and reviews general welfare of employees.
		2. Zonal Welfare Committee	Mgt. 5-7 Union 5-7	Monthly	-do-	Considers ways and means for improving facilities and services. Evolves training and development policies.
		3. Departmental Welfare Committee	Mgt. 5-7 Union 5-7	Monthly	-do-	Considers and settles grievances.

(Contd...)

FUNCTIONING, COMPOSITION AND FREQUENCY OF MEETINGS OF BIPARTITE COMMITTEES IN BHILAI STEEL PLANT

Grouping	Type of Committees		Composition	Frequency of meeting	Mode of Union Representation	Main objectives
	Area	Name				
GRIEVANCES		1. Grievance Supervisory Board	Mgt. 4 Union 2	Quarterly	-do-	To supervise the working of grievance redressal system.
		2. Grievance Committees	Mgt. 4 Union 2	Monthly	-do-	Timely redressal of grievances.
		3. Stage-II grievances	—	—	—	Participation and settlement of stage-2 grievances with Heads of Departments
MERIT-RATING		1. Merit-rating Review Committee	Mgt. 3 Union 1	Half-yearly	-do-	To review merit-rating of employees.
CANTEENS		1. Central Canteen Committee	Mgt. 2 Union 2	Quarterly	-do-	Inspection and review of functioning of canteens.
		2. Departmental Canteen Committee	Mgt. 1 Union 6-7	Once in two months	By election	Running and managing of Departmental Canteens.
EDUCATION		1. Education Advisory Committee	Mgt. 5 Union 2 Others 2	Half-yearly	Nomination	Evolve, improve systems and policy of education administration.
		2. School Welfare Committee	Mgt. 5 Teachers 4	Monthly	-do-	Proper communication between management and teachers in matters relating to their welfare.

(Contd...)

FUNCTIONING, COMPOSITION AND FREQUENCY OF MEETINGS OF BIPARTITE COMMITTEES IN BHILAI STEEL PLANT

Grouping	Type of Committees		Composition	Frequency of meeting	Mode of Union Representation	Main objectives
	Area	Name				
	MEDICAL	1. Medical Advisory Committee	Mgt. 5 Union 1	Monthly	-do-	Suggests improvements in medical services.
	ACCOMODATION	1. Accommodation Advisory Committee	Mgt. 7 Union 1	Half-yearly	-do-	To lay down guidelines and review of policies with respect to allotment of shops and quarters.
SOCIAL AND ENVIRONMENTAL	SPORTS & CULTURE	1. Sports & Recreation Council	Mgt. 5 Union 1	Once in 2 months	-do-	To lay down policy guidelines and review its implementation regarding the organisation of cultural and welfare activities in the Steel Township.
		2. Zonal Recreation Committees	Mgt. 5 Union 5	As and when required	-do-	To organise sports and cultural events on zonal level.
		3. Ispat Clubs	Mgt. 2 Union 5	Once in 2 months	-do-	To organise sports, cultural and community service in respective sections of the township.
	ENVIRONMENTAL HYGIENE	Advisory committee for Environmental Hygiene	Mgt. 2 Union 1	Quarterly	-do-	To consider matters relating to environmental hygiene and recommend measures to tackle them.

(Contd...)

FUNCTIONING, COMPOSITION AND FREQUENCY OF MEETINGS OF BIPARTITE COMMITTEES IN BHILAI STEEL PLANT

Grouping	Type of Committees		Composition	Frequency of meeting	Mode of Union Representation	Main objectives
	Area	Name				
	COMMUNITY WELFARE	Camp Welfare Committee	Mgt. 3 Union 1	As and when required	-do-	To lay down guidelines for the rehabilitation of the evicted persons.
	SOCIAL SECURITY	S.E.W.A.	Mgt. 5 Union 4	Monthly	By election	To provide cash assistance to the families of deceased and disabled employees.
COLLECTIVE BARGAINING/ PRODUCTIVITY	WAGE SCALE DETERMINATION	1. Committee on Wage Differentials	Mgt. 2 Union 1	Quarterly	Nomination	Determination of wage scales through accepted evaluation manual.
	COLLECTIVE BARGAINING	1. Plant level Committee	Not fixed	Once in a fortnight	-do-	Collective bargaining on matters relating to service conditions of employees and other matters connected to industrial disputes.
		2. Zonal Committee	Not Fixed	Monthly	-do-	
		3. Department Level Committee	Not fixed	Monthly	-do-	

Manager's Perception

As a privileged class, some managers seem to be afraid of losing their power with the installation of joint councils. They dislike this baby (of joint participation) right from its birth. They are not happy if it grows as it snatches more and more butter of their share. They are also unhappy if it dies as the blame may come directly on them. They do relish if it is weak and would not mind paying for its treatment. The infighting among workers does not affect their health. If one union says that workers' representatives should be nominated and another wants them to be elected, a safe course for them will be to let the two have a tug of war and trial of strength first. They will normally agree with the winner.

Managers also want to maintain privacy as far as important issues like wages, service conditions and perquisites to workers are concerned. They would not permit these matters to be dragged on to the platform where they are sitting face to face with the workers. There are very few organisations which allow joint councils to deliberate on collective bargaining issues. They want workers to sit like well behaved boys. Discipline and decorum are the words which are more appropriate in their terminology than thumping on the desk and rebuking one another. But the other party may not be as well-dressed and educated and 'sophisticated' as they want it to be.

Managers also want the other party to rely on the information given. They want their published accounts, for instance, to be accepted as they are. Any attempt to disturb the window dressing is intolerable. One way communication is the best communication of many of them.

Then there is the vital question of status. In one case, the joint council was working successfully for quite some time. The chairman of the company himself used to preside over the meetings. But one fine afternoon he decided that some junior chap should be entrusted with this work. He stopped attending the meetings and started sending the junior official. The other party felt aggrieved and boycotted the meetings. Better counsel did not prevail on the members of the council and it ultimately broke down.

Experience in India shows that a scheme of workers' participation can be successful only when:
— Trade unions are strong and well organised. There is no multiplicity of unions at the plant level and the selection/nomination of workers' representatives for joint committees is done through a democratic process.

- Employers' attitude is favourable to the formation of joint bodies. They are willing to sit together, understand the problems of labour and give their due share to them.
- A helping hand is extended by the government machinery. It need not necessarily be through legislation. Motivating the two parties to come together to a common platform may be helpful in creating a healthy environment.

Workers' Share in Capital

Workers' participation in equity capital is desirable for several reasons. It promotes an identity of interests and understanding between labour and management. When the organisation is sound and its shares are at a premium, workers may like to invest in the company. Their small savings may bring them on the list of owners. After retiring from services also, they may enjoy the fruits of their investment. It may also be a hedge against inflation. The company gains because the cost of raising funds through sale of shares to workers is low compared to other sources. Workers may put in their best at work as now they have a stake in the organisation when their hard-earned money is invested in it.

Big business corporations in USA have taken a lead in popularising the 'Employees Stock Purchase Plans. The General Motors Corporation, Sears, Roebuck & Co., Dow Chemical Company; and the American Telephone and Telegraph Company etc. have introduced such plans successfully. The financial strength and the image of large organisations attract employees to subscribe to their equity capital.

The employees stock purchase plans in US corporations have taken a number of forms. An organisation may create a trust fund and contribute to it along with its employees. Shares are purchased out of the fund so accumulated from time to time. Some corporations provide loan facilities to their employees for subscribing to the share capital. The loan is recovered in installments from the salary of the employees. Monthly investment plans are introduced by many organisations. These plans provide for monthly deductions from the payroll of the employee and authorise a stock exchange broker to purchase the company's stock on the open market. The full shares and fractional shares are allotted to each employee's account on the basis of his contribution.

PERSPECTIVE

Employee Stock Ownership Plan In Anderson & Associates Inc.

What is an ESOP :	An ESOP or Stock Ownership Plan is a plan designed to enable each eligible employee to have a share in the ownership of our company.
Why does A & A have an ESOP :	The ESOP has allowed stocks to be distributed broadly at no financial sacrifice to either the company or the employee owners. This establishes a stable, long-term ownership transition plan which is vital to our kind of professional organisation.
Who pays for ESOP :	The ESOP account is funded through annual contributions from Anderson & Associates. Employees pay nothing. These contributions are distributed in the form of company stock, cash or other assets held in the ESOP trust. The amount of ESOP contribution in a given year is decided by the Board of Directors and is dependent on a number of factors, the primary one being profitability.
What is in it for A & A :	Finances – Our ESOPs can help create financial resources and opportunities which will enhance our success. Quality – Since the daily efforts our employees make are the biggest factor in our company's success, nothing is more important than providing an incentive to do the best job possible.
What is in it for our employees :	Each year A & A will put in a share in the contributions. The holdings of ESOP are held in trust and administered by Anderson & Associates. As the company grows and progresses, the value of your stock should grow right along with it. As your years of service increase, so should your share of stock in our company.
What is in it for our clients and business partners :	Because we, the employees, own a part of the company, every action and decision made directly affects us. The employee owner concept greatly benefits our clients and business partners because the quality of service, the level of productivity and attitude in general are improved.

The movement towards privatisation has given boost to ESOPs in different countries. Under Margaret Thatcher's privatisation programmes in the U.K., employees were given opportunity to buy shares of public sector companies being privatised at a discount. Employees were offered some free shares (subject to a 2 year holding requirement), priority in allocation of shares, a discount of 10% on purchase of shares and the opportunity to buy shares on matching basis (buy one, get one free). Tax benefits to ESOPs included corporate tax deduction for principal and interest payment on ESOP loans and deferred capital gains taxes for sale of stocks. In France, profit shares are distributed to individual employees on the basis of salary or salary plus length of service. The profit sharing pool on an average amounts to 10% of profits. Tax and social security concessions are available to both the sponsoring corporation and the employer if receipt of share is deferred for a minimum of three to five year holding period. Over 5 million French employees are covered by 16000 of these schemes. In Canada, the government of British Columbia has developed the 'Employee Share Ownership Programme' under the Employee Investment Act to encourage employees to make equity investments in companies for the purpose of job creation, job protection and participation in business ownership.

In South America, Chile developed a strategy for 'labour capitalism'. Workers were offered 5-10 of privatised company's shares at discount price. They were allowed to borrow up to 50% of their severance pay to buy the shares. With no cash outlay, the employees could get shares below the market price. In 15 privatised companies, workers got significant levels of ownership. In Slovakia, employee participation in ownership takes two forms: employees can buy shares in their own companies on favourable terms requiring 10-15% deposit with 10-15 year repayment terms at low interest rates or management buyouts with no special incentives.

In Russia, privatisation gave a boost to employee ownership, making it a country to have the largest number of employee owners of approximately 12000 medium and large scale enterprises privatised after 1992, about two thirds of which were majority owned by their employees following privatisation. Workers were given some shares free and were provided significant purchase discount. Managers were also given the option to buy before opening the sale of shares to the public. The level of ownership, however, went down after the first round of sale of shares when the workers started selling shares to outside investors.

In China, workers in large factories were given shares under 'social ownership' schemes. Many of the village enterprises have been given to the workers. Hungary followed the US pattern. The privatisation legislation gave strong preference to the use of leveraged ESOPs allowing purchase of company shares spread over a 15 year period, with an optional 3 year grace period of interest payments only. Loans up to 85% value of shares could be obtained from the banks. Tax benefit up to 20% of pretax profit of ESOP companies to repay debt or fund ESOP was allowed. In Egypt, Employee Shareholder Associations (ESAs) acquire shares on behalf of employees where privatisation takes place. Some of the associations own majority stake and some the controlling blocks. There are over 150 ESAs.

ESOPs in India

An experiment on full ownership by workers was made in India in Kamani Tube, a sinking firm which was revived by the sacrifices made by workers who took over the company by putting in their PF, gratuity, etc. Government and other financial institutions provided help and appointed their nominees on the board of directors along with one director from workers' side. Employees agreed for a wage freeze @ 75% of what they were getting in 1985 for ten years, no overtime wages, no strikes and no demands. Six hundred out of a total of seven hundred forty six workers joined the cooperative to run the factory.

Some public enterprises have introduced ESOPs, but the schemes are not that popular. Steel Authority of India offered 200 shares to each of its employees in March 1994. Employees who were on the rolls since April 1992 were entitled to buy shares under the scheme from their own resources. Shares were offered on a premium.

There was no serious attempt by the government to promote ESOPs till 1999. Sachchar Committee recommended the employee ownership scheme as early as 1977 by reserving 10-15% of new shares to be called workers' shares, exclusively for the employees, and asked for the amendment of section 81 of Companies Act and also proposed loan facilities for the workers to buy shares. But recommendations never saw the light of the day.

In 1999, Securities and Exchange Board of India (SEBI) issued some guidelines for setting up of ESOPs. It did attract some companies to come forward with ownership schemes for their employees. But the environment in the country is not yet favourable for such schemes. Workers and trade unions are sceptical about the schemes as there is no surety that there would be adequate return on shares in the future. The volatile stock market going down for quite some time has added fuel to the fire. Even the software companies' shares have lost their attraction.

The need to have some guidelines for developing ESOPs made the government to circulate the 'Stock Option Guidelines, 2000' including Employee Stock Purchase Plan, Employee Stock Option Plan, Employee Stock Purchase Schemes and Stock Appreciation Rights with the objective of issuing shares to a company's employees directly by the company or its holding company or by its promoters, or indirectly through a trust constituted for the purpose. While developing ESOP the companies are required to specify:

i) The number of shares that may be issued under a stock based incentive plan.

ii) The class of employees that would be entitled to participate in the plan or scheme.

iii) The pricing formula on the basis of which shares would be allotted to the employees, not being below the face value of shares in any case.

iv) The number of options to be issued to each employee and the value to which such stock can be prescribed along with the prescribed time for 'grant' or 'exercise' of the option.

v) The manner of obtaining the approval of shareholders.

vi) The lock-in period of such shares from the date of option or vesting of offer or exercise under such scheme or plan to the point of granting of such shares, as the case may be.

vii) If shares are unlisted, the basis of valuation of shares would be submitted to the Chief Commissioner of income tax holding jurisdiction of the company.

viii) The conditions relating to restriction on non-transferability of such shares.

ix) The conditions contained in the written document shall not be changed after the effective date of the scheme or plan.

The guidelines require listing of shares under ESOP in a recognised stock exchange in India or abroad, submission of complete details of the scheme to the Chief Commissioner of income tax having jurisdiction of the company within six months of the issue of guidelines or the effective date of plan, whichever is later.

> **PERSPECTIVE**
>
> **EMPLOYEE STOCK OPTION SCHEME: ICICI BANK**
>
> In fiscal 2000, ICICI Bank instituted an Employee Stock Option Scheme (ESOS) to enable the employees and Directors of ICICI Bank and its subsidiaries. As per the ESOS as amended from time to time, the maximum number of options granted to any employee/Director in a year is limited to 0.05% of ICICI Bank's issued equity shares at the time of the grant, and the aggregate of all such options is limited to 5% of ICICI Bank's issued equity shares on the date of the grant (equivalent to 55.7 million shares at April 25, 2009).
>
> Options granted for fiscal 2003 and earlier years vest in a graded manner over a three-year period, with 20%, 30% and 50% of the grants vesting in each year, commencing not earlier than 12 months from the date of grant. Options granted for fiscal 2004 to 2008 vest in a graded manner over a four-year period, with 20%, 20%, 30% and 30% of the grants vesting in each year, commencing not earlier than 12 months from the date of grant.
>
> Options can be exercised within 10 years from the date of grant or five years from the date of vesting, whichever is later. The price of the options granted prior to June 30, 2003 is the closing market price on the stock exchange, which recorded the highest trading volume on the date of grant. The price for options granted on or after June 30, 2003 till July 21, 2004 is equal to the average of the high and low market price of the equity shares in the two week period preceding the date of grant of the options, on the stock exchange which recorded the highest trading volume during the two week period. The price for options granted on or after July 22, 2004 is equal to the closing price on the stock exchange which recorded the highest trading volume preceding the date of grant of options. The above pricing is in line with the SEBI guidelines, as amended from time to time.
>
> On the basis of the recommendation of the Board's Governance & Remuneration Committee, the Board at its Meeting held on April 25, 2009 approved a grant of approximately 1.7 million options for fiscal 2009 to eligible employees. Each option confers on the employee a right to apply for one equity share of face value of Rs. 10 of ICICI Bank at Rs. 434.10, which was the closing price on the stock exchange, which recorded the highest trading volume in ICICI Bank shares on April 24, 2009. These options would vest over a five year period, with 20%, 20%, 30% and 30% respectively of the grant vesting each year commencing from the end of the second year from the date of the grant. No options have been granted to whole time Directors for fiscal 2009.

Profit Sharing Schemes

The main value of successful profit sharing", says I.L.O. "seems to lie in the contributions they may make towards a spirit of collaboration and a sense of partnership between employers and workers."

In the UK and the USA, profit-sharing plans have been in existence for many years though on a limited scale. Individual units have their own plans which are formulated on the basis of the agreements between labour and management. The sharing of gains takes different forms in different companies. Some organisations make cash payments at the end of a specified period while others make deferred payments by investing workers' share in P.F. and annuity, etc. Payment of profit in the form of shares is also not uncommon. The number of workers covered by profit-sharing schemes is, however, not very large in these countries. The scheme is not compulsory. The trade unions view the profit plans more as a fringe benefit than sharing the gains. They would not like to weaken their bargaining strength by accepting profits as a substitute for wage increases.

The statutory profit-sharing schemes have been introduced in some Latin American and Asian countries. The trade unions in the developing countries are not as strong as in the advanced industrial nations of Europe and America. They seek interference of the state in securing a part of the profit for them statutorily. It adds to their income and also provides them with a lump sum amount to meet certain expenses. In India, workers insist on the distribution of bonus at annual festivals such as Durga Puja or Diwali. While deferred distribution plans are popular in the affluent countries, in India the payment of bonus is mostly preferred in cash by the workers.

The practice of paying bonus started in India during the First World War. The 'war bonus' benefited the textile workers in the Bombay and Ahmedabad regions. The rate of bonus was 35% in 1918. When the war was over and profitability declined in the textile industry, workers continued getting bonus though at a reduced rate. During the Second World War, the demand for bonus was made by workers in all major industries as the companies were earning huge profits. The Bombay Mill Owners' Association decided to declare 12½% bonus. Judicial decisions went mostly in favour of workers rights to get bonus when companies earned profit. A committee on profit-sharing was appointed by the Government of India in 1948. The committee felt that profit-sharing could be viewed from three different angles:

(i) as an incentive to production

(ii) as a method of securing industrial peace

(iii) as a step towards the participation of labour in management

The committee considered the first two points and concluded that the indirect effects on production would be sufficiently tangible to make an experiment in profit-sharing worthwhile. On the third point, the committee did not make any observation since it was outside its purview. The committee recommended the introduction of profit-sharing scheme in selected industries on an experimental basis. The committee's recommendations, however, did not find favour with the government. In 1961, the Government of India appointed a Bonus Commission. The Commission recommended that 60% of the available surplus should be allocated for distribution as bonus. A minimum bonus equivalent to 4% of the total basic wages and dearness allowance during the year or Rs. 40, whichever is higher, should be paid to each worker. The maximum bonus should be equivalent to 20% of the total basic wages and dearness allowance paid during the year. Employees drawing a total basic pay and dearness allowance up to Rs. 1600 per month should be entitled to bonus with the provision that the quantum of bonus payable to employees drawing a total basic pay and dearness allowance of over Rs. 750 per month shall be limited to what it would be if their pay and dearness allowance together amounted to only Rs. 750 per month. The available surplus for the purpose of bonus was to be determined by deducting from gross profits: depreciation; income tax and super tax; and returns on paid-up capital and reserves. The computation and payment of bonus should be unit wise. The major recommendations of the Bonus Commission were accepted by the Government of India. The Payment of Bonus Ordinance was issued on 19 May, 1965. In September 1965, the Payment of Bonus Act was passed by the Indian Parliament replacing the ordinance.

The statutory payment of bonus, however, has not served the purpose for which profit-sharing schemes were introduced. Far from improving industrial relations, bonus has been the most frequent source of unrest in India. The number of days lost due to bonus disputes has increased during the last few years. Workers have been asking for higher wage rate than the prescribed minimum in the Act. There have been disputes on computation of the available surplus. Certain categories of employees who were excluded from the purview of the Act, such as those employed in non-competitive public sector undertakings have agitated for extending the scope of the Act to make them entitled to bonus.

In developing economies, there is a wide gap between the current wage and the fair wage. Workers look upon the statutory bonus as a part of their wages rather than an incentive for increasing productivity. If provisions for compulsory payment of bonus have not paved the way for improving labour-management relations, one does not have to go far to seek the answer. The continued rise in prices, poor living and working conditions, lack of social security, mismanagement of certain industries and the inter-union rivalry are the primary reasons of discontentment among the working class in the country.

Situation Analysis

A managing director of a profit making steel plant, with which he has been associated since the stage when he was an executive trainee, is not much interested in spending money on the welfare of his employees. He feels pay, working conditions, benefits, etc. are well above average.

He has decided to make a museum of miniature sized working models of the plants and a coloured film about the company of which he is the chief at a cost of about Rs. 7 million. It is not going to have many viewers but he somehow manages to get his ideas passed for implementation owing to his strong convictions. He feels this would revive the prestige of the company.

The chiefs of other departments are not too happy about it but do not wish to say anything to displease the managing director. However, middle management officers start grumbling.

The education officer feels that his request for a petty sum for expanding the school has been turned down. Medical officers feel that a sum of one million asked for improving the medical facilities and improving upon dental as well as mental units have unnecessarily been deferred. Plant managers feel that too much fuss is created when few extra hands are asked to cope up with the increasing workload. Training facilities and tours are being curtailed. Labour leaders are sceptical that workers are being harassed by denying them overtime hours and so on.

How do you account for the decision of the managing director and justify the grumbling of other departmental heads?

Review Questions

1. Define morale. How will you measure morale of employees in an organisation?
2. Suggest an effective procedure for handling workers' grievances in a large organisation.
3. How does counselling help in maintaining discipline?
4. Is worker's participation in management necessary for high morale and productivity?
5. What are ESOPs? Give a brief account of ESOPs in the US and India.
6. Has legislation on bonus achieved its objectives? What types of bonus schemes are effective?

Further Readings

1. *Worker's Participation in Decision-Making Within Undertaking: Summary of Discussions of a Symposium on Workers' Participation Within Undertakings* (Labor Management Relations series, ILO office, Geveva, 1974).
2. Md. Khalid and Md. Shahid: *Globalization and Workers' Participation in Management* (Raj Publications, 2010)
3. Lorne C. Plunkett and Robert Fournier: *Participative Management: Implementing Empowerment* (Wiley, New York, 1991)
4. Ruddar Datt (Ed.): *Workers' Participation and Ownership* (Pragati Publications, New Delhi, 1999)
5. O. Sharma and M. Mustafa: *Workers' Participation In Management*, (Deep and Deep Publications, New Delhi, 1998)
6. P. Venkatraman: *Worker's Participation in Management* (APH Publishing Corporation, 2007).

Part V

Technology and HR

Chapter Structure

Chapter 17. Technology and HR

Chapter 17

Technology and HR

"Although it is hard to find a manager who would not agree that productivity is a problem, it is harder to find one who agrees that it is his problem."

– John Stewart

Learning Objectives

After reading this chapter you will be able to:

1. Understand that technology has contributed greatly to the growth of human civilisation.
2. Realise that the adoption of new technology at plant level needs a leadership with clear goals and commitment.
3. Suggest productivity improvement measures at work.

Some managers believe that output is given by machines and it is the modernity of machines that governs productivity, while others feel that it is the man behind those machines that governs productivity. The others feel that productivity is primarily an attitude of the mind; a welcome change for the better, a willingness to accept and explore scope for improvement making optimum use of available resources and keeping rejections to the minimum. It is the man who creates and drives the machines. Man is intelligent and creative but slow, whereas a machine is uncreative but fast. Both must work in harmony and in unison to supplement the efforts of each other in order to maximise productivity.

Technology and Man

One way to look upon the growth of human civilisation is to consider the technology used by man in different stages of growth. Historically, man has passed through four broad eras: hunting, agricultural, handicraft and industrial. In hunting era, he invented fire by rubbing stones and prepared pointed tools made of stone to kill animals for his food. In agricultural era, he made ploughs and a variety of tools made of wood and metals to grow food from earth. In handicrafts era, he developed technology to produce a variety of goods for his consumption. The tools and techniques were primitive and the scale of operation was small. Craftsmanship was more important than the tools and techniques. Industrial era began with the invention of steam engine in 1786. Machines began to replace men. Early machines were large in size, heavy in weight and consumed bulk energy. They were heavily dependent on man for feeding, control and regulations. Man, according to Karl Marx, supplemented without loss whatever human faculties the machine lacked, whatever imperfections hampered the machine in satisfaction of its needs. If machine lacked eyes, man had to see for it, if it was without legs, man had to walk for it and if it needed arms, man had to pull, drag and lift for it. Machines gradually became less dependent on the man with every advancement in automation. They are now smaller in size, consume less energy and produce more. Computers have brought a virtual revolution in the world of industry. The RISC based computers, for instance, can display full motion videos from various sources, including images sent over telephone lines. The user will have to simply tell it to scan distant database for information.

The technology developed in industrial era brought prosperity as well as miseries for mankind. The positive aspects of this technology were the increased productivity per man, ease in operations, better engines and safety, increase in skill requirements, large scale production and rise in income and standards of living. The means of transport and communication developed and the flow of goods and services was made possible at low cost and less time.

But the process of industrialisation proved to be very painful. Large number of people were dislocated and compelled to leave their villages and small towns to work and lead difficult life in industrial towns, particularly in the initial stages. The jobs were routinised, and individual initiative was lost in the wake of standardisation, set work procedures and techniques. Working population was deprived of ownership rights. Work became external to workers and it was no more voluntary. Workers found themselves powerless and their jobs meaningless. Society was divided into the haves and have-nots. The alienation of workers resulted into the growth of trade unions, labour management conflicts, strikes, work stoppage and other forms of unrest and tension. The tension and conflicts which arose in industrial society were analysed in different manners by specialists and scholars of different disciplines. The sociologists, described it as maladjustment between the old and the new order, the irrational responses having taken over logical responses due to the miseries of the transition period. People uprooted from houses, farms and small factories were forced to work in cities for others, for the jobs which did not require their contribution in terms of skill or craftsmanship and the fruits of which were not theirs. Low wages, poor and unsafe working and living conditions continued for quite some time. The psychologists felt that the situation had become critical due to differing perceptions and motivations. The workers perceived that owners and managers were engaged in maximising profits which were largely their contribution, the latter thought that the trade unions wanted to increase their share of the cake, productivity was the result of capital – financial resources, technology and machines. Management authority concentrated in very few hands deprived people working in the organisations of safety, affiliation recognition and self-fulfilment needs. Economists analysed the situation in terms of class conflict. Marx and his followers blamed capitalist system for all the evils of industrial society. The surplus value theory was propagated to prove the naked exploitation of labour by capitalists/management.

The man-machine adjustment process has been long drawn and painful. Different remedies were suggested by experts from different fields. Sociologists and psychologists wanted better social cohesion and group functioning, and reward and recognition and improved interpersonal relations. Economists talked of equity in distribution, and change in ownership patterns. Technologists emphasised on improvement of machine design, better utilisation of time, better work method, and techniques. The founding fathers of management evolved general principles and scientific methods to deal with the problem. Division of work, departmentalisation, scalar principle, team work, discipline, etc. were considered necessary. Time and motion study, individual incentive linked wages, proper selection and training of workers were emphasised for improved performance and job satisfaction. Management experts have been experimenting with various methods to make the jobs more pleasant and reduce the rigour of machine. These include change as a regular part of job to avoid boredom and fatigue, job enlargement and enrichment, opportunity to act and decide independently or in small groups, innovate and show ingenuity, freedom of movement and flexibility in operations, balanced mental and physical efforts to accomplish the job, attractive work environment, feedback about performance and share in the gains. The opposition to introduction of advanced technology, new machines and tools has been reduced with the gains appearing on the surface. Most developed countries have advanced technology and least troubled industrial relations, while less developed countries have less developed technology and poor industrial relations. Marx criticised capitalist system for alienating workers, but the standard of living which the market economies offered to workers has been much higher than the socialist system which is now almost wiped out from Eastern Europe and Russia.

In East, Japan has shown an entirely new path – involving people at work not only in the process of production, but also in redesignating machines and equipment, improving processes, systems and procedures of work, deciding about materials and other inputs. The quality circle movement that started in Japan in 1960s proved to be a curtain raiser in this context. The movement emphasised a bottom-up approach to management – solutions to problems must come from people who face it. Quality circles aim at not only improving the quality of products, but building a 'happy bright workplace worthwhile to live in and display human capabilities fully'. Advanced management techniques like JIT and zero inventory have further contributed to increased efficiency in operations and more savings in cost. The stress on social equality at work in the form of common uniform, common canteen, common medical and other facilities and uniform rules for attendance, leave, etc. have further facilitated the adjustment process at work. The new approach emphasises on machine for workers instead of workers for machine.

The adoption of new technology at plant level needs a leadership with clear goals and commitment. The management has to first determine the specific goals which they desire to achieve through new machines and processes. The goals may be specified in terms of production targets; economy in operation; time-saving, delivery at time; reduction in repair, maintenance costs, direct labour and overheads, and raw material waste and rejections; integration of design and decision support system; increase in drafting and design productivity; improvement in overall productivity and benefit to the people who would operate it. In the absence of clear goals, achievements may fall short of expectations and the blame may come on those who champion the cause of introducing new technology. The support of top leadership is essential. If they back out, the scheme may flop; if they show reluctance, problems may arise in implementation. The technology champions must take them in confidence first before going for the project. It is also necessary to keep workers and supervisory personnel informed. Their cooperation cannot be taken for granted unless they perceive the desirability of introducing new machines and new methods. The resistance to new technology comes because of the fear of anticipated difficulties in operations, higher demands in terms of skill, knowledge and techniques, and lack of confidence in people who are to use it. People must be prepared for change which new technology demands. The results of most surveys and research studies show that human resource is the key to the success of new technology in any organisation.

Traditionally, human resource managers are not involved in technology management. They have been considered generalists, suffering from 'technemia' – inadequate technological sophistication. Their role has been confined to planning, procurement, placement, appraisal and training of people, discipline and industrial relations. They are not consulted in matters like choosing a new technology, equipment and processes and anticipating the response of the people who would operate it. Financial and technical aspects are looked into more carefully by the management than the human resource. The non-HRM priorities, however, prove to be very costly at times when investment in new plants and machines do not give desired results due to workers' opposition. Human resource managers can play an important role in management technology when various options in technology come for consideration. They can assist in examining the human part of it – the skill requirements of different types of plants, the cost of procuring people with such skills, if not available within, the time required to train and prepare them, etc. They may also draw the blueprint for organisational changes which may be required for a particular type of technology. For instance, when skill requirement goes up considerably and the number of personnel required is reduced, a flat structure instead of vertical one may be needed. Once the decision about new technology is taken, HRMs have to initiate the process for manpower planning, procurement and development and make available the required personnel according to the time schedule so as to avoid any commissioning of the project due to scarcity of staff. They have to ensure quality and quantity of human resource needed. At the implementation stage, their role is crucial. They have to motivate the teams placed on the jobs with changed technology to achieve the goals set by the management, effectively control the turnover, absenteeism, grievances and obstruction to work and see that the system of reward and recognitions works effectively. They may also contribute to the functioning of interdepartmental steering committees or other bodies which may be set up to coordinate the activities, iron out differences, anticipate problems and ensure smooth functioning of the new plants and machines. New technology may disturb the power bases of old guards, bring new faces on the scene and result into new alignments in the organisation. Human resource managers may be called for to organise OD programmes to prepare senior executives for change before it is resisted.

The lesson that most organisations have learnt in the process of managing technology is that the human resource issues must be examined before and not after new technology adoption. The fear from new technology is certainly less marked today than it was in the past. The acceptance of new machines and new processes is facilitated if people are convinced about the benefits to the organisation and to them. The 'technological imperatives' have given way to 'technological options', making it necessary for management to involve managers from the so called non-technical departments in decisions concerning selection, adoption and implementation of new technology. The human resource managers can play an important role in deciding about the options and preparing people to accept and implement new technology.

Productivity Improvement

It is an established fact that increased productivity means:
- Reduction in the prices of services and goods produced; higher possibility of exports and foreign exchange earnings.
- Higher turnover of goods as low prices trigger demand.

- Higher profits for the organisation.
- Increase in the earnings of the employees and higher employment opportunities.
- Improved economic conditions and enhancement of national wealth as well as per capita income.
- Rise in the standard of living and quality of living.

Productivity is the key to prosperity and workers have a role to play in increasing productivity.

Factors of Productivity

If we accept productivity as an attitude of the mind, it is essential that we continuously strive for excellence and make constant efforts for improvement in:

- Human relations and working environment
- Psychological need identification
- Capacity utilisation
- Gainful use of materials
- Quality improvements, cutting down rejections and rework
- Maintenance and tooling
- Layouts and handling methods
- Design and technology
- Modernisation needs
- Planning, scheduling and follow-up
- Systems and procedures
- Long-term strategy and action plans
- Better management of all available inputs, and qualitative and quantitative increase of outputs
- Developing team spirit and collective efforts

If we analyse all the above mentioned aspects in depth, it becomes clear that human resources (or what we call workers, supervisors and officers) can play an important role in increasing productivity by playing their parts. They have to:

- Recognise the needs, importance and urgency for productivity increase.
- Adopt a fair and strong trade union to safeguard rights and be conscious of their responsibilities.
- Avoid wastage of time, money, machine hours, man-hours, materials, energy or waste of any kind and strive for high efficiency at work.

– Readily accept proposals for training, changes for betterment in methods of work, modernisation to meet technological changes as well as spread this message to their colleagues who are unaware of these.

> **PERSPECTIVE**
>
> **Technology Upgradation – BHEL**
>
> Intensive in-house efforts have enabled Bharat Heavy Electricals Ltd. to meet the expectations of its customers worldwide. Its corporate R&D Division is well established. Recently, it has set up Centres of Excellence for Simulators, Computational Fluid Dynamics, Machine Dynamics and Nanotechnology. The Company is already operating specialised institutes namely, Welding Research Institute, Ceramic Technological Institute, Centre For Electric Traction and Hydro-Lab and Pollution Control Research Institute.
>
> BHEL has developed several state of the art products, such as nanofluids, catalytic combustor, 260 MW steam turbine for combined cycle power plants and other innovative products in the area of power, locomotion and nuclear energy.
>
> To stay as a world-class total solution provider, upgradation has been done in technology for control and instrumentation of power plants. It is said to be the first in the world to have developed 80 MVAR controlled Reactor to improve power transfer capability of high voltage transmission systems.
>
> Employees have played an important role in all technology up gradation programms of the company.

Measures of Productivity

The contributions of different factors of production individually and collectively can be measured by the formuale given below:

(A) *Labour*

* Value added per employee (Rs.) $= \dfrac{\text{Value added per annum}}{\text{Total no. of employees}}$

* Manpower Productivity (Rs.) $= \dfrac{\text{Output of goods \& services}}{\text{Total persons employed}}$

* Labour Productivity (Rs.) $= \dfrac{\text{Production Value}}{\text{No. of man-hours spent}}$

* Worker Performance Ratio $= \dfrac{\text{Standard time needed for the total work done in a year}}{\text{Actual time taken for doing the work during the year}}$

* Machine Performance % $= \dfrac{\text{Total standard machine time for work done during the year}}{\text{Actual Machine time taken to do the work during the year}}$

* Machine Productivity (per hour) (Rs.) $= \dfrac{\text{Output of goods \& services}}{\text{Machine hours used}}$

(B) *Capital*

* Labour Profit Productivity Ratio $= \dfrac{\text{Profit}}{\text{Wages Paid}}$

* Capital Turnover Ratio $= \dfrac{\text{Production Value}}{\text{Investment}}$

(C) *Material*

* Material Productivity Ratio $= \dfrac{\text{Output of goods \& services per annum}}{\text{Value of material used per annum}}$

* Material Utilisation Ratio $= \dfrac{\text{Material usefully utilised}}{\text{Total material used}}$

* Inventory Turnover Ratio $= \dfrac{\text{Sale value per annum}}{\text{Average inventory value}}$

(D) Energy

* Useful Energy Utilisation % = $\dfrac{\text{Total energy used}}{\text{Total energy purchased}} \times 100$

* Energy Productivity (Rs.) = $\dfrac{\text{Production value of goods \& services}}{\text{Cost of energy dissipated}}$

(E) Overall

* Overall Productivity Ratio = $\dfrac{\text{Total output of all goods and services}}{\text{Total input cost of all products}}$

* Capacity Utilisation % = $\dfrac{\text{Operating capacity}}{\text{Installed capacity}} \times 100$

* Productivity Ratio = $\dfrac{\text{Value Added}}{\text{Conversion cost}}$

Value added is generally taken as value of output of goods and services *less* value of purchases *less* excise duty.

Conversion cost is generally taken as labour cost *plus* equipment cost *plus* overhead cost.

Why Low Productivity

Like illness in the human body, there are many causes for low productivity in an organisation. Some of these are:

— Low morale of workers
— Absence of managerial controls
— Idle machines
— Low level of output
— Outdated, old and obsolete machines
— Slow work, pace
— Frequent machine breakdowns
— Improper machine loading and scheduling
— Missing production schedules and delivery dates
— Frequent shortage of materials
— Excess inventory holdings
— Crowding and confusion in material handling

- Poor quality of finished goods
- Large reworks, higher in-process inventory and large accumulation of work
- Poor house-keeping
- High cost and low profits
- Wastage of energy

Any of these systems alone or in combination can bring down productive efficiency.

Role of the Management in Increasing Productivity

Conscious efforts have to be made for improvement in productivity. In a majority of Indian industrial undertakings, there is vast scope for improving upon various conventional management functions, such as:

- Design and layout
- Production planning
- Scheduling and control
- Materials management and handling
- Financial management and control
- Office systems and procedures
- Loss prevention and safety
- Maintenance management
- Personnel management
- Harmonious industrial relations, grievance handling, suggestion and reward scheme, etc.

After having explored all the possibilities of improvement in the above functions, it is worthwhile to further organise higher productivity achievement through concerted drive.

Organising For Productivity

As stated earlier, a productivity drive by itself cannot lead an organisation to higher productivity. This urge has to be accepted by all employees. Then only will human efforts aim towards excellence. Once the employees accept the organisational goals, they will be self-motivated to achieve excellence. They would ensure that it does not remain a one time activity but be a continuous on-going process. Thus, higher productivity will be attained. It is also a collective effort and cannot be left in the hands of a selected few. In industry it is necessary to continue the drive for higher productivity so that the gains once achieved are retained and not lost.

The plan generally drawn and followed to achieve higher productivity is given below:

- A programme is drawn for creating an awareness in the employees at all levels regarding the need for increasing productivity. This is done through publicity, posters, group

- meetings, formation of suitable committees in various departments and a sincere dialogue with the labour unions to win them over to the idea of increasing productivity.
- Organising brain-storming sessions. Best ideas on any problem are generated when they are perceived from all angles by a group of people from various connected disciplines.
- Organising training programmes at various levels for educating employees on concepts of productivity.
- Selection of good projects for study and appointing project study teams with a project leader for each study. These groups should preferably be multidisciplinary in nature.
- Formation of quality circles in major departments that can isolate problems and suggest their ideas through written reports for bringing about improvements.
- Inducing employees to form more and more of quality circles in each area of work so that productivity improvements become a voluntary culture, and ideas for improvement are identified on a continuous basis. Nobody knows the work better than the people doing it. The larger the involvement, the more the generation of ideas.
- Monitoring effectively for early completion of identified productivity projects.
- Follow-up and implementation of approved suggestions for bringing about an improvement.
- Developing a system of recognition and rewards.
- Evolving a scheme to rationally share the fruits of higher productivity.
- Sustaining the enthusiasm at work.

Motivation For Productivity

A principal factor underlying lower productivity is decline in motivation and commitment to quality work on the part of a significant number of people. It has been seen that behavioural modification of employees is a positive way towards motivating people to higher productivity. A behaviour which is positively rewarded tends to repeat the performance.

What could, therefore, be the possible reasons for this decline in motivation and what could be the ways to motivate employees towards productivity improvement? There has been a significant change in the attitude of people towards work. There has admittedly been some change in the old order/ value of being taught to work hard to achieve success. The change has not occurred overnight but has been brought about by a variety of economic, social and political factors. Relative increases in income have had some effect on the concern for work. There has also been an emergence of psychology of entitlement of certain rights and privileges.

Motivation can be 'intrinsic' or extrinsic in nature:

Intrinsic : It refers to psychological support like encouraging or helping in analysing the problems; being available for discussions when needed by the group; giving guidance; holding review meetings; giving directions for the future, etc. These give a sense of meaning and satisfaction.

Extrinsic : Extrinsic awards come from outside and are more concrete in form. Examples are:

— Favourable appraisal reports
— Monetary awards
    * Lump sum
    * Token awards
    * Increments
— Status improvement
    * Promotion
    * Making group leaders for projects
    * Membership symbols and badges
    * Special awards
— Company recognition
    * Publicity through newsletters, magazines
    * Publication of photographs
    * Praising in specially called meetings
    * Nomination to external seminars, etc.

Many advocate negative action or reinforcement for bringing the sleeping members of the organisation within the productivity net. The methods adopted for this are either implicit or explicit.

Implicit negative reinforcements for persons not engaged in productivity movement are done by non-recognition, playing down his/her achievements or playing up the performance of others with whom he/she is compared.

Explicit negative reinforcements can be through criticism, reprimand, holding pay rise, promotion, etc.

However, the authors do not recommend negative reinforcements. Their experience has been that negative reinforcements create hostility and management is often termed unfair. They do not see the linkage between their behaviours and negative reinforcements. They feel incidents are being blown out of proportion. Negative reinforcements may also lead people to correct themselves but may not result in voluntary acceptance of the set goals. One can take a horse to the pond but cannot make it drink water.

Similarly, a word of caution for reward also. This should not be overdone. As far as possible, rewards have to be intrinsic and not extrinsic. Where extrinsic rewards are given, these should better be in the nature of a token and not on a too liberal scale. Extrinsic awards tend to put the loci of motivation outside the man rather than it being within himself.

Productivity Centres and Coordinators

Many employees have good ideas and they are very energetic about them initially. However, the ideas die down because of complicated formal procedures of suggestion schemes, difficulties associated in writing them down, taking them to the appropriate authority and getting a feedback on their suggestions.

In order to encourage ideas emanating from even grassroot levels, many organisations have a centrally located booth or counter, in important areas of activity, where a project coordinator is stationed to:

(i) receive the suggestions;

(ii) help the soggester to formulate his ideas;

(iii) encourage him to make a written report with the help of a project coordinator;

(iv) give periodical feedback about the status of his project;

(v) explain to the soggester (in case his ideas are not workable for any reason) or give him the refinements needed to implement his suggestion; and

(vi) organise a workshop/seminar to exploit the ideas/ suggestions received.

It is the responsibility of the project coordinator to coordinate, organise, catalyse and conduct productivity improvement programmes in his department and submit periodical reports to his general manager. It is his function to:

— Plan and organise awareness programmes and training programmes on productivity for his employees.

— Follow up suggestions on productivity improvement.

- Convert the ideas into productivity improvement projects and initiate detailed studies through the task force constituted for this purpose.
- Monitor the progress of project studies.
- Collect, compile and statistically analyse the data and help in writing the project reports.
- Arrange meetings, workshops for discussing the project reports in depth with reference to the problem, its magnitude, suggestions offered to liquidate the problem, advantages likely to be gained, etc.
- If necessary, to authorise the task force for an extended study and to lay down guidelines for the same.
- Refer financial decisions and policy matters to the appropriate level and follow these up.

In short, the project coordinator works as a consultant and guide for all productivity matters.

Quality Circles

Organisation of quality circles at work has proved to be a boon in Japan and other industrialised countries in raising productivity and quality of the goods and services. A quality circle is a small group of employees doing similar work who come together voluntarily to identify work-related problems, investigate causes thereof in a systematic way and recommend solutions. Workers forming a quality circle choose a leader from amongst themselves. The QC is based upon the recognition of the value of a workman as a human being, as someone who willingly activates on his job his wisdom, intelligence, experience, attitudes and feelings – not just his hands, feet and muscles. It recognises that the workmen are endowed with intelligence and imagination and being the real doers, they are the experts on the intricacies and hidden potentials of their jobs. They can make valuable suggestions on matters related to machine design, work process, raw material use, improvement in product quality and reduction in cost. The basic objectives of QC, according to Prof. Ishikawa are:

(i) to contribute to the improvement and development of the enterprise.
(ii) to respect humanity and build a happy organisation meaningful to work in.
(iii) to display human capabilities fully and eventually draw infinite possibilities.

(iv) to provide job involvement, motivation and opportunities to employees for problem-solving and decision-making by promoting teamwork and cooperation.

(v) to enhance communication within an organisation and develop closer management-employee relationship.

(vi) to enhance the quality of an organisation's products and services.

The QC is advantageous to the workers as it makes the job more enjoyable. It generates self respect and promotes fellowship and team spirit. It is useful to management since it helps in improving quality and productivity, reducing cost, innovating new techniques and processes, and creating congenial work atmosphere. The QC movement involves people at all levels in the organisation. The top management sets the rules and regulations guiding QC and motivates people encouraging and rewarding their participation. The middle managers work as facilitators: helping in collecting information and data, using problem-solving techniques, guiding and training members and interacting with the steering committee of higher management. The QC leader who is the member of the team is usually a front line supervisor. He has to coordinate, motivate and guide his team. The circle members are the workmen responsible for producing or performing the jobs assigned to them by the supervisor. As the quality circle philosophy aims at building up the morale of the employees, talents and innovative skills, the leader and the members of the group are given training to start with. Senior officers of the company may be nominated to act as facilitators to coordinate the activities and ensure implementation of the recommendations of quality circle. The success of quality circles largely depends upon the attitude of managers. When managers only talk about the theory 'Y' and work according to the theory X, quality circle philosophy will not thrive as it relies on increased satisfaction from involvement in decision-making and the opportunity to satisfy a higher order hierarchy of needs which are possible only when the members in the circle enjoy trust and confidence of authorities.

Sharing Productivity Gains

Many public and private sector undertakings have taken the productivity drive enthusiastically. The situation on the economic front (be it labour wages or product prices) is forcing many enterprises to compulsorily think in terms of productivity drives in their units. If the efforts continue, there will be more and more of productivity awareness and it will lead to higher income or gains (both tangible and intangible). Once there are gains, the methods of dispersal or reinvestment of gains assume importance.

Whatever may be the mode, a part of the gains will come back to the employees. The mode of the comeback has risen manifold. At times, it has become the bone of contention between the employers and the employees. The mode of disbursement among the employees has led to industrial troubles too.

Some researchers have shown that in the Indian context, rise in salary alone does not help. Employees become well off but the standard of living or quality of life of their family members do not improve because the community in which they live remains backward in terms of community facilities, social education, etc. It has been seen that even where a worker's monthly wage has increased from Rs. 300/- to Rs. 1500/- his family life has not shown any appreciable improvement in real terms. In some cases, higher monetary gains to uneducated workers have brought some social problems also.

Some enlightened employers and employee unions have realised this and do not favour higher individual earnings beyond a certain level in view of such consequences. They feel that, besides the increase in employees' earnings, the community at large should also share the gains of productivity. Many enterprises, therefore, are not willing to give away all the employees' share of gains to the employees as increase in wages but keep a part of it for financing community welfare and development schemes. They feel that in the background of social change that is continually taking place, the productivity movement has to recognise the behaviour pattern of the human element, its linkage with the environment and quality of life rather than reinvestments only for the factors of production.

A general model showing gain sharing and a format for planning annual productivity welfare plans are shown at the next page.

The possible avenues for sharing the gains of productivity could be many. Some possible ways by which the gains could be shared by the collective or the community to improve the way of living are indicated here:

— Educational facilities and scholarships for employees and their children in deserving cases. Job-oriented training programmes.
— Vocational training for family members of the weaker sections and widows of employees.
— Uniforms for school-going children. Subsidised course books, exercise books, stationery, etc.

Managing Human Resource

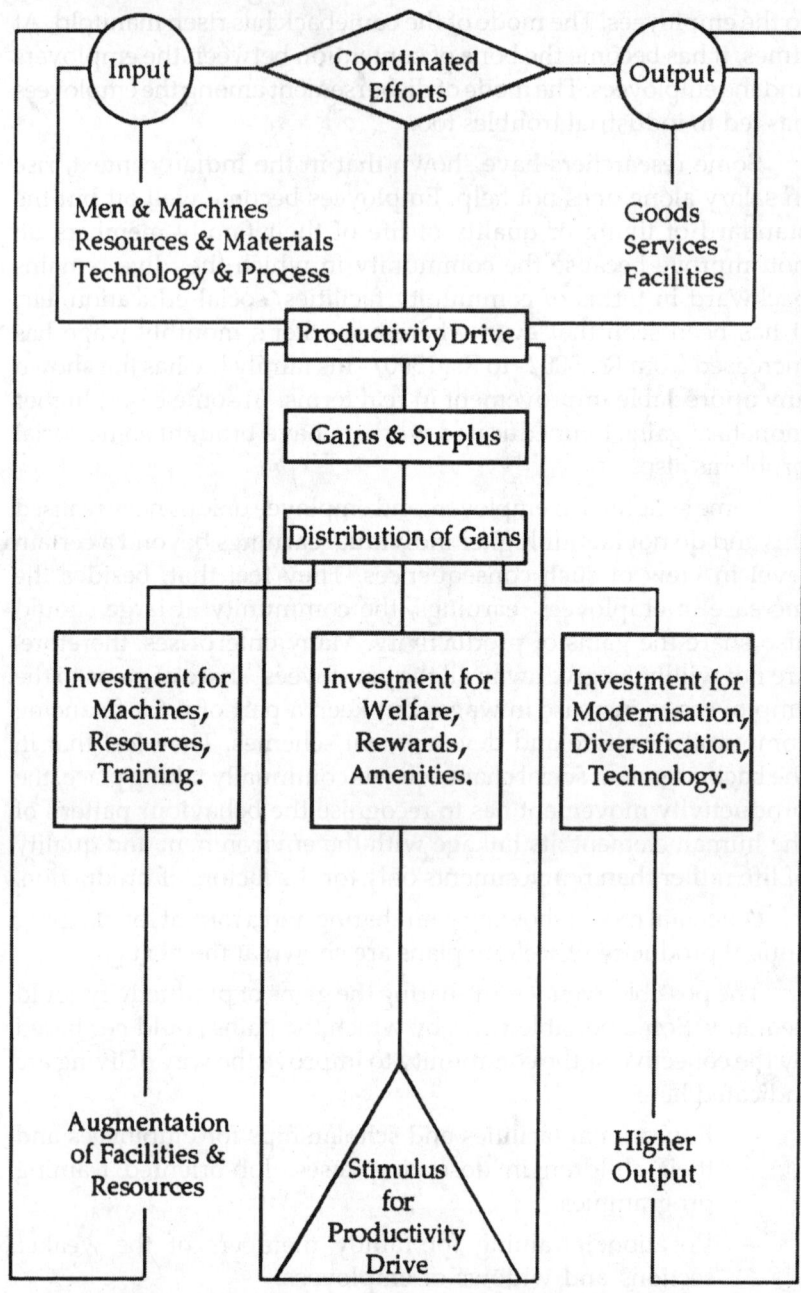

Fig. 17.1: Productivity Gain Sharing Model.

ANNUAL PRODUCTIVITY AND WELFARE PLAN
(Year ———)

Activity No.	Projects & action points	BENEFITS					SCHEDULE	TASK FORCE	
		Tangible		Intangible		Months	Project Leader	Supporting Groups & Sections
		Planned	Actual	Planned	Actual	1 2 3 4 5 6 7 8 9 10 11 12		

- Medical facilities, community health centres, public hygiene programmes, mobile dispensary, ambulances, school health services, training in first aid, etc.
- Community clubs, recreation centres with TV and Radio, libraries, reading rooms, playing fields, screening good and educational films, etc.
- Help in starting cooperative ventures for housing, canteens, general stores by giving soft loans.
- Dairy, poultry farming, cattle farming, etc.
- Developing halls for the pursuit of artistic talents, for use during weddings or other community functions.
- Transit hostels and holiday homes in important tourist resorts.
- Development of housing colonies, roads, drinking water supplies.
- Providing transport services and extending soft loans for purchase of transport vehicles.
- Subsidised meals and special food for persons working in health hazardous areas.
- Increasing the sense of belonging by giving employment to employees' children.
- Providing missing township amenities in employees' colonies.
- Giving special aids and vocational training to handicapped employees and handicapped members of the employees' families.

Many such examples can be cited or thought of. The main aim is to provide greater satisfaction to the community as a whole and invest in their general well-being. It is also important that the *inter-se* priorities for such community schemes and welfare development projects should be examined and prepared by a competent board and adequate budgets provided.

Situation Analysis

Nandan was assigned the responsibility of a productivity coordinator in his company because of his industrial engineering background. He was to report directly to the general manager in this regard.

He was very enthusiastic about his new assignment and felt that he would be able to draw the attention of the management towards improvements that could be effected and his importance in the company would go up.

He read the available literature on productivity improvement, studied the quality circle movement in Japan and similar work being done in other industrial undertakings both in the public and the private sectors. He completed all the rehearsals that were needed for starting the productivity drive, identified some areas for study, formed several task forces to complete those special assignments and started directing them.

Kulkarni was the task force leader of one such group which had taken up the assignment of reducing the consumption of grinding wheels. After a few months of study, Kulkarni came out with his report. His suggestions were workable and their implementation would have resulted in some saving in the consumption of grinding wheels. The report projected a substantial saving in monetary terms per 10,000 grinding wheels consumed.

The project coordinator organised a workshop to discuss the report, arranged publicity, (made publication) in departmental journals, got Kulkarni a cash reward and a certificate of merit, recommended him for out-of-turn promotion and additional increments. In short, he made Kulkarni a hero in the organisation. He did not consider it worthwhile to get the report examined by the finance department for its claims of savings, and the consumption figures of grinding wheels from the works department (which was only about 150 a year), and other personal traits of Kulkarni from the personnel department.

At the time of annual promotion in the new year, the name of Kulkarni did not figure in the list of promotees as his confidential reports for the past two years were not satisfactory. Some of the entries were:

— His conduct in the department was deplorable.
— At times, he came in the workshop drunk and misbehaved with his colleagues/supervisors under the influence of alcohol.
— He was often missing from his place of work under the pretext of being on union duty (being a shop representative in the union committee) of looking into the complaints of the workers.

His immediate superior had recommended his demotion and transfer to a non-production department.

Kulkarni immediately filed a petition through the union that his case for promotion had been overlooked in spite of his excellent performance.

When the matter was discussed in the room of the Personnel Manager:

- The Plant Manager mentioned about the bad personal traits of Kulkarni and his spending excessive time investigating the so-called complaints of the workers, resulting in substantial loss of production.
- The Union Secretary recalled the good work done by him, and the glorification and publicity given by the management for his inventive mind.
- The Union Secretary further stated that there was no evidence on record of Kulkarni being frequently absent from his place of work. He also claimed that Kulkarni was not informed in writing and that his supervisors were jealous of him. Besides, he was authorised to look into the complaints of his workers as he was their elected leader.

There was no meeting point between the two parties and even the Personnel Manager could not resolve the dispute. The matter was, therefore, referred to the General Manager.

Suppose you are the General Manager. How would you resolve this dispute to the satisfaction of both the parties?

(i) How would you proceed in the matter?

(ii) What were the lapses of the management, the project coordinator and Kulkarni that led to such a situation?

(iii) How did the communication gap arise between the project coordinator, the plant manager and the union?

(iv) Who had erred in this situation and why?

(v) What are your suggestions to prevent recurrence of such situations in future?

(vi) State your approach to the problem as an arbitrator.

Review Questions

1. Discuss the linkages between human resources and productivity in an organisation.
2. 'Human resource issues must be examined before and not after new technology adoption.' Comment.
3. Discuss the factors which lead to increased productivity.
4. How should a productivity drive be organised?
5. 'Group motivation is the key to improving productivity.' Discuss.
6. How should productivity gains be shared?

7. How is productivity measured? Why are productivity indices important?
8. Draw a productivity gain sharing model.
9. 'Human resource is the key to the success of new technology'. Discuss.
10. Comment on the following report of TCS:

TCS established the first software R&D centre in Pune, India, in 1981 called the Tata Research Design and Development Centre, mindful of the importance of research to ensure sustained market leadership. Over the last two and a half decades, R&D has evolved in TCS in line with the environment and market conditions with renewed customer focus. As on March 31, 2009, TCS had established 20 R&D Innovation Labs with specific focus on technologies and verticals. The Company has also established 46 Centers of Excellence (CoEs) in all areas of information technology and business services as well as on partner products. This ensures all our offerings incorporate the latest products and services capabilities from the Company and its alliance partners, and allows us to build new skill sets among the employee base.

The network of TCS Innovation Labs work on research themes ranging from Operational Efficiency, Business Agility and Simplification, to Customer Experience, Ubiquity and Enterprise Security. They also explore new areas like Green IT and emerging technologies like Cloud Computing and the evolution of the internet beyond Web 2.0. The Innovation labs work closely with the TCS business units and customers across a well-defined set of innovation horizons.

Tools and Frameworks: The Company continues to invest in technology products, frameworks and tools to assist customers to achieve significantly higher operational efficiency and realise time, cost and energy benefits at maximum Return on Investment (RoI). These are based on leading edge technologies and address both IT and business requirements of the customers. Company has invented and developed a number of products, frameworks and productivity tools in the following areas:

* Software Engineering tools for development, testing, migration, re-engineering, and performance management
* Infrastructure Management tools for relating systems information to business events, simplification of servers, network and storage, measurement and

optimisation of 'Data Center' power, and high-performance computing applications

* Domain-specific frameworks and components for customer analytics, authentication and security, market understanding, risk and compliance, optimisation, visualisation and modeling, 'Business Process', management tools for task automation, workflow, applications integration and knowledge capture

* Knowledge management tools using social networking techniques, information extraction and text mining and Web 2.0.

These tools and frameworks are built and supported by TCS Innovation labs working closely with the technology excellence group and the domain teams from different business units.

Intellectual Property (IP) and Patents: We have defined an IP strategy with a view to building an effective portfolio for future monetisation, collaboration and risk mitigation.

The total number of granted patents is 42. In addition, TCS has over 150 patents pending in multiple jurisdictions, including 58 filed in 2008-09.

TCS Intellectual Property – Patents Filed and Granted

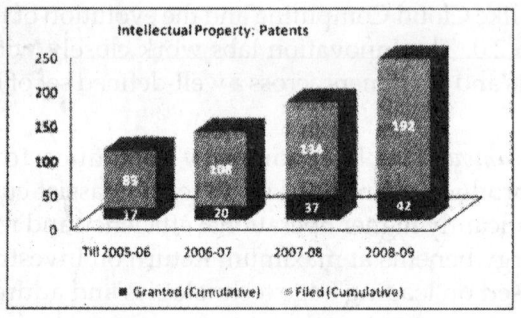

R&D talent pool: Our R&D organisation has grown to over 500 people. We have more than doubled the number of PhDs in TCS R&D to over 50 and have attracted top talent from notable universities from across the globe. A large number of lateral hires from Indian and overseas institutions were inducted into the R&D groups in FY09 and 17 global university academic alliances were put in place.

Human Resources: The Company continued to invest in human resource development. The total number of employees including those in the subsidiaries as on March 31, 2009 was 143,761 (111,407 as on March 31, 2008).

Of these 143,761 employees at the end of fiscal 2009, 17,611 were the employees of the Company's subsidiaries like CMC, WTI, TCS e-Serve Limited, Diligenta and others. The number of non-Indian nationals in the TCS global workforce was 11,484 (previous year – 10,005). Our overseas delivery centers have 4,795 employees.

According to Company estimates, TCS was the biggest recruiter in the private sector globally. The Company had a gross addition (including Indian subsidiaries) of 48,595 (previous year – 35,672) employees and a net addition of 32,354 (previous year – 22,116) employees. This included over 12,500 people as a result of the Citigroup BPO acquisition as well as over 750 people insourced from customer organisations.

Growing Talent Base: Gross and Net Employee Addition in Last 3 Years

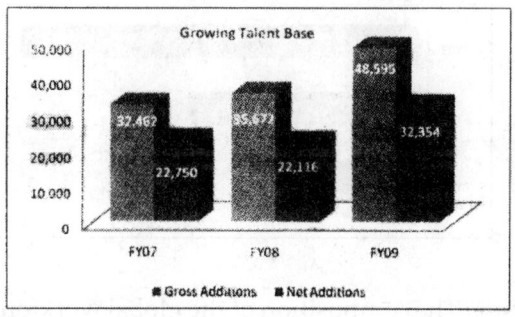

Talent Retention: The attrition rate of 11.4% (previous year – 12.6%) in fiscal 2009 is the lowest in the industry. This low attrition rate has been achieved by continuously investing in learning and development programs for employees, competitive compensation, creating a compelling work environment, empowering employees at all levels as well as a well-structured reward and recognition mechanism.

Attrition Rate for Last Twelve Months

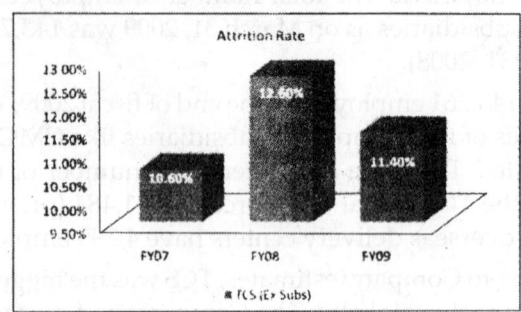

Even though the Company has added 84,267 employees to its rolls in the last two years, 54% of the Company's associates have more than 3 years work experience.

TCS Employees with More than 3 Years Experience in the Last Three Years

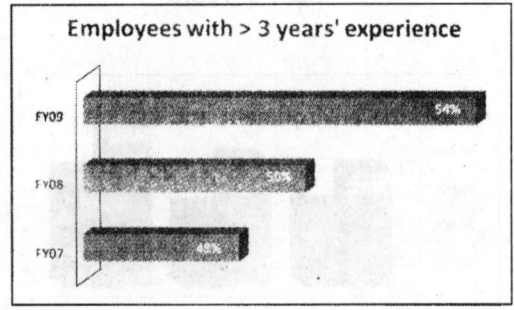

Talent Diversity: The composition of the global workforce continues to show increasing trends in the number of female employees and foreign nationals from countries across the globe. As on March 31,2009, women constituted 30% of the Company's workforce (28% as on March 31, 2008). The Company employed persons from 67 different nationalities. There were net additions of 147 non-Indian nationals during the year. TCS is focused on adding to its global knowledge workforce and integrating these professionals into its workforce.

Technology and HR

Diversity: Increase in Women Employees in Last 3 Years

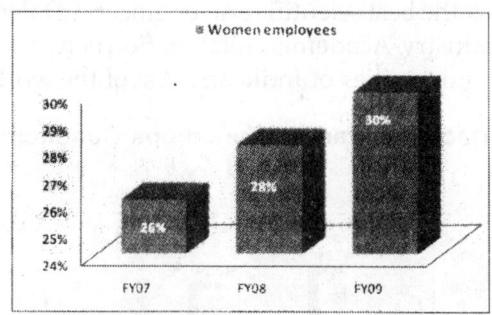

Diversity: Increase in Non-Indian Nationals in Last 3 Years

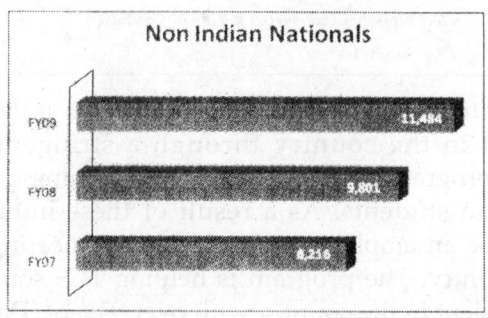

Diversity: Global Workforce of 67 Nationalities

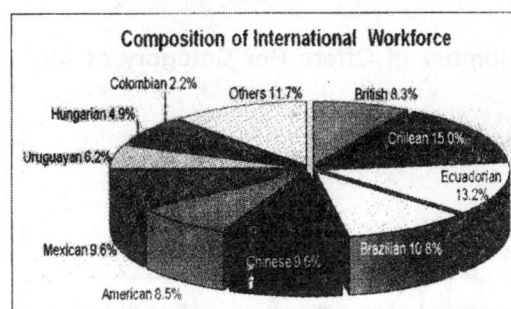

Academic Program: Continuous interaction with universities and other educational institutions remains a central plank of TCS' strategy to attract the best scientific and engineering talent. TCS has also set-up an Industry-Academia collaboration network with some of the foremost universities of India and rest of the world.

Academic Interface Program – Workshops Conducted, Faculty Trained

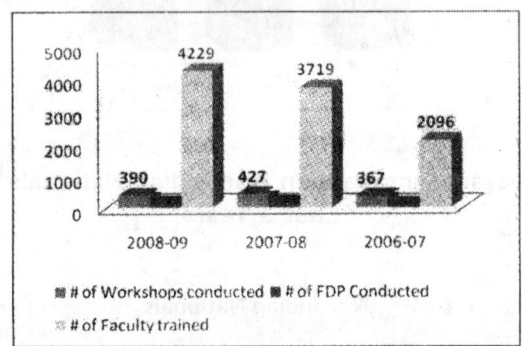

Talent Acquisition: The Company continues to invest in talent development in the country through a stringent academic accreditation program as well as by providing training, internships and projects to students. As a result of these initiatives, TCS continues to be an employer of choice on engineering campuses across the country. The program is helping TCS source the best engineering talent in the country with over 95% of 'Day 1'slots on technical campuses in 2008-09, up from 94% in 2006-07.

For 2009-10, the Company has made 24,885 campus offers. The trainees will join in a staggered manner during the financial year 2009-10.

Number of Offers Per Category of City

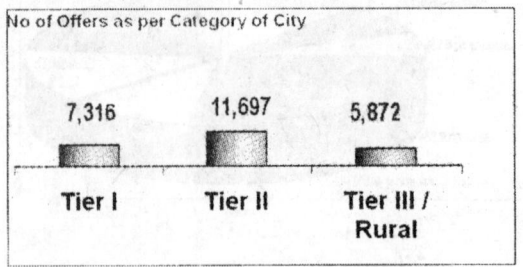

Academic Interface Program – Number of TCS Accredited Academic Institutes

Accreditation of Technical Institutes

Fiscal 2009	Fiscal 2008	Fiscal 2007
309	274	250

Experienced Professionals Recruitment Funnel

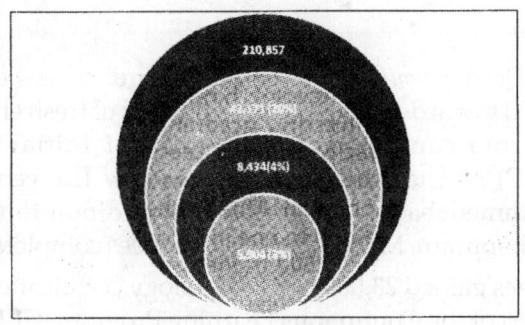

Inclusive Talent Development: TCS Ignite

Launched in 2007, Ignite continues to make significant strides in the areas of training, digitisation and innovation. Ignite also demonstrates the commitment of the organisation to inclusive growth by hiring 60% first generation graduates.

946 science graduates from nearly 500 colleges across the country and from Nepal and Bhutan were trained and fully deployed in FY08-09. Since the inception of the program, the total number of graduates trained and deployed is 2,517. The project leader community rated deployability of Ignite trainees as very high.

Ignite trainees are encouraged to pursue higher education while working. For example, for a MCA degree program at Sastra University in Tamil Nadu, students are given credits for their training in TCS and by completing the remaining credits, they are awarded an MCA degree. Around 1000 Ignite trainees have enrolled for this program. The top 1% of Ignite trainees enroll for a challenging MSc Computer Science program at the Chennai Mathematical Institute.

Number of Students Hired through TCS Ignite

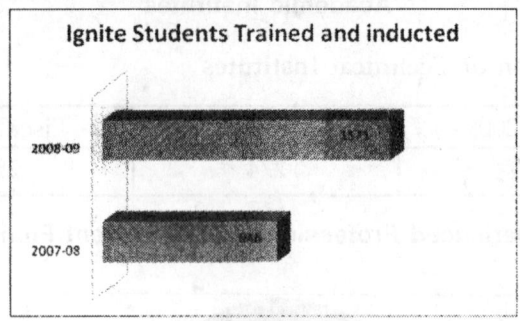

Learning and Development: As the recruitment mix of new employees became biased towards hiring greater numbers of fresh engineering graduates from campuses, the capacity of Initial Learning Program (ILP) had to be increased. Two new ILP centers were opened in Ahmedabad and Guwahati, in addition to the one in Thiruvananthapuram. More than 19,500 trainees completed the ILP.

Our employees gained 23,000 new technology certifications during 2008-09 as part of the Continuous Learning Program (CLP) in FY09. The e-Learning coverage increased to 32% of the total learning days with modules in Portuguese, Mandarin and Spanish rolled out. A new version of Competency Management System (iCALMS) and a Learning Planning System have been implemented to increase the automation of L&D Processes. (Annual Report of TCS 2008-09)

Further Readings

1. L. Adams: *Securing Your HRIS in a Micro-Computer Environment* (HR Magazine, February, p. 56-61, 1992).
2. Renae Broderick and W. John: *The Evolution of Computer Use in Human Resource Management: Interviews with Ten Leaders* (Human Resource Management, Vol. 30, Issue 4, p. 485-508, 1991).
3. D. Mankin, T. Bikson, B. Gutek and C. Stasz: *Managing Technological Change: The Process is Key* (Datamation, Vol. 34, p. 69-80, 1998).
4. D.L. Nelson: *Individual Adjustment to Information Driver Technologies: A Critical Review* (MIS Quarterly, Vol. 14, p. 79-98, 1990).
5. J.A. Senn: *Information Systems in Management* (Wadsworth, Belmont, 1990).
6. B.F. Skinner: *Science and Human Behavior* (Free Press, New York, 1953).
7. S. Zuboff: *In the Age of the Smart Machine: The Future of Work and Power* (Basic Books, New York, 1988).

Part VI

Contemporary Issues in HRM

Chapter Structure

Chapter 18. HR Outsourcing

Chapter 19. Downsizing and Restructuring

Chapter 20. Employee Empowerment

Chapter 21. HRM in Transnational Corporations

Chapter 18

HR Outsourcing

"Outsourcing is a journey of two organisations seeking jointly to overcome predictable challenges."

– **William B. Bierce**

Learning Objectives

After reading this chapter you will be able to:

1. Understand that a decision to outsource is vital these days as it affects operational efficiency, cost, quality and overall performance of business.
2. Explain outsourcing models and the steps needed to build 'intelligent outsourcing'.
3. Locate major areas for HR BPO.

Outsourcing non-core functions of business has been practiced since ages. In recent years, outsourcing as a strategy to divert business processes has become popular with the growth of IT Industry. Most IT managers, says Scott Kirkwood of International Work Approach Service Inc. approach outsource functions in the same way that a house owner would hire a plumber to fix a leaking pipe. However, the decision to outsource is not as simple as this. Outsourcing may affect operational efficiency, cost, quality and overall performance of business.

HR outsourcing is a form of business process outsourcing where an employer hires the services of an outside agency to perform HR functions fully or partially. In most cases, outsourcing is practised partially, i.e. delegating some functions to an outside agency and retaining the functions which the existing staff can do economically and efficiently. In the IT industry, talent shortage leads many companies to outsource staffing functions in a big way.

Reasons for Outsourcing

Outsourcing is resorted to for strategic, organisational, financial and cost considerations. Strategic management aims at value addition, time and cost saving and optimum utilisation of resources. Work may be assigned to an outside agency having specific expertise, latest technology and processes to achieve the above objectives. Organisational factors include shifting to core operations, downsizing, removing red-tapism and bureaucracy. Financial considerations include diverting resources to more profitable operations and ventures. Cost considerations are based on the premise that the outside agency will have the economy of scale as it would be providing similar services to other firms also and would have developed standards and efficient procedures that would save time by speeding up the process.

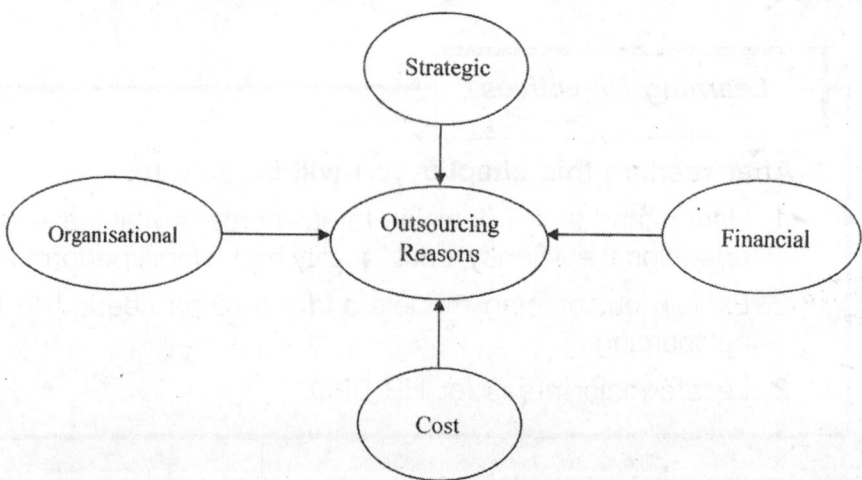

> **PERSPECTIVE**
>
> **Business Process Outsourcing – TCS**
>
> TCS BPO is structured and positioned to deliver services in the customer's business hours by efficiently leveraging TCS GNDM model for delivery of services to global customers. It is uniquely positioned due to its global reach and delivery capabilities which leverages TCS centres in Latin America, Eastern Europe and China. The company acquired the captive BPO operations unit of the Citi group and this unit has been renamed as TCS e-Service Limited. With this acquisition, TCS is well positioned to meet end to end IT BPO requirements of financial services customers.
>
> The company offers value-added transaction processing services to its customers in industry verticals like Banking, Insurance, Telecom, Pharma, Travel and Transportation, and Retail. Knowledge services focus on areas like clinical trials, pharma co-vigilance, market research and retail solutions.

Outsourcing Models

The traditional outsourcing models are:
 (i) Transactional Outsourcing
 (ii) Operational Outsourcing
 (iii) Utility Outsourcing

Companies resort to outsourcing for handling high volume recurring tasks such as payroll transactions, recruitment and selection. Transactional model aims at saving cost and time in the performance of non-core business activities.

Operational outsourcing involves diverting a given operation in a process to an outside vendor such as inviting applications and submitting the list of eligible candidates who may be called for interview by the company. The process should be defined clearly to match the services required.

Utility outsourcing model is used to meet the specific skill requirements of the company such as experienced professionals and specialised staff. Recruitment of project staff will also come under this category. This provides flexibility and reduced length of commitment as the staff may be taken on project basis.

Intelligent Outsourcing

Scott Kirkwood suggests a model which he calls intelligent outsourcing. He lists five major steps in building such a model:

* *Service Discovery*: Identifying the actual services required and their interface to business.
* *Maturity Baseline*: Measuring the current capabilities, gaps and weaknesses to ensure quality service of the vendor.

* *Process and Governance Design*: Detailed interface and measurement plans – whether vendor has developed the process which suits the company
* *Contract*: Securing SLA (Service Level Agreement) based on the governance model – operational interaction and process management and penalty in case of default.
* *Implementation*: Putting the entire action plan into motion. It may require performing the existing functions according to a new model/process, stabilisation efforts to correct complications in the process and accelerating capability improvement.

The above model was developed primarily for the IT industry, but it may be applied to other industries as well. This model helps in clarifying the goals of outsourcing by clearly defining the services required, judging the capacity of the service supplier, developing a governance plan which may include infrastructure development also, entering into service level agreement which matches company practices with service provider, and implementing the plan to achieve the objectives, both short-term and long-term. Intelligent outsourcing should result in focusing the internal efforts on company's core business, reducing time and cost of operation of the functions/processes outsourced and ensuring quality services.

BPO Portal

Advancement in technology will facilitate event-driven administrative transactions like recruitment, promotion, etc. Many jobs currently handled by people may be done by technology. For example, there can be an HR Portal like an ATM machine where an employee may initiate all transactions based on the event happening to him such as on getting promotion, pay roll process may be initiated.

HR Outsourcing Decisions

HR outsourcing is practiced in functions like recruitment and selection, making payrolls, designing and administering employee benefit programmes/incentives, employer communication network, training and development, personnel database management and research, benchmarking studies and statutory compliances. Scope of HR outsourcing has widened in recent years. JP Morgan has identified 10 major areas for HR BPO as given in the chart below:

Scope of HR BPO

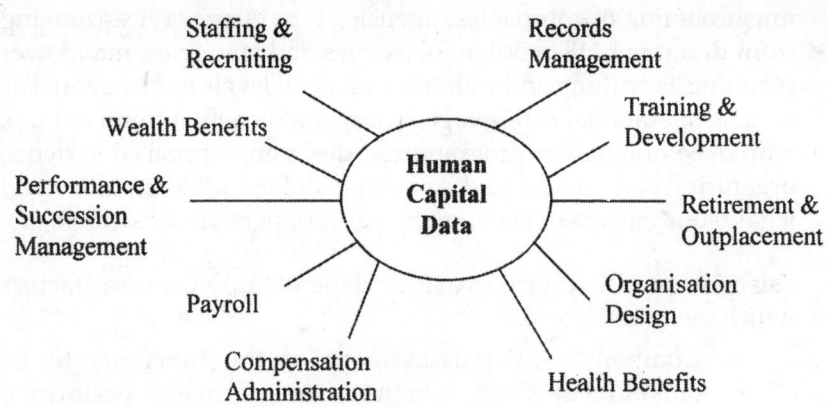

Sources : JP Morgan Chart May 1, 2003

Brian S. Sommer includes the capabilities which can further be added to JP Morgan's Chart of HR BPO:
* Travel and entertainment expense processing
* Workforce analysis
* Tax planning
* 360 degree feedback
* Human capital alignment
* Employee relationship management
* Contingent labour contracting
* Employment and education verification
* Work-life and EAP facilities
* Internet-enabled employee self-service applications
* Union support
* Compensation analysis
* HR employment advertisements/job boards.

Brian also differentiates HR BPO from HR limited function processing. BPO deals are not sales but transfers of people, processes, responsibilities and technology to a third party. HR BPO is the promise of new capabilities, new service levels, new processes, etc.

HR outsourcing is passing though a transition period. Earlier, organisations in the government and public sector were hesitant to outsource personnel functions, but the scenario has now changed. User acceptance is much wider today which is reflected in the mushrooming of companies/agencies providing services ranging from designing HR mission, objectives and strategies, manpower planning, recruiting and training staff at all levels to managerial as well as operational staff, wage, salary and benefit administration, employee orientation programmes, designing appraisal systems, organising conferences and seminars, looking after statutory and legal requirements of client organisations, personnel research, etc.

Selecting the Service Provider

Selection of HR service provider depends upon several factors which include:

— Company's own assessment of the functions to be outsourced. Core functions are normally performed internally. It is like a 'make or buy decision'. Unless the benefits of outsourcing weigh far more than doing the job internally, outsourcing is a redundant idea.

— Availability and credibility of firms which can provide required services economically, effectively and in time.

— Capability of the firm to outsource entire processes or several related processes.

— Size of the service provider matters. BPO business is largely concentrated in the hands of big firms. In 2005, the revenue generated by the large firms in India was more than that of the 100 next listed IT companies.

— Long-term provider viability, commitment and breadth and depth of the provider's solution set.

— Providing R&D effort; capability to generate new processes/improve existing ones.

— Size of the firm desirous of outsourcing affects the choice of service provider. Very small firms may not able to afford a full-fledged HR division. Very big firms would like to outsource to concentrate on their core business. But companies with a well observed hiring process and known for being an employer of choice hardly benefit by outsourcing HR functions.

Selection of an agency/company to perform outsourcing functions is not easy. Some services are standardised which can be availed of easily, while others may be organisation-specific which need infrastructure and specialised staff on the part of the agency to be chosen. The agency must have expertise, experience and qualified staff to serve the client. It should also have established credibility. At times, confidentiality is an important requisite in service. Whether the firm offering services can be relied or not is to be assured before the contract is given. Agency's capability to provide services at a competitive cost by ensuring quality and timely performance has to be ascertained before entering into an agreement. What companies are looking for today is not only a service provider, but a partner who can work with them and also manage future requirements which cannot be predicted today.

Offshore Outsourcing

In offshore outsourcing, the outside firm providing services is not physically present at the client location, but interacts with the client through telephone, fax, e-mail, online chats, video conferencing, etc. India, according to a World Bank study, is the number one choice of US companies as compared to other Asian counterparts for offshore outsourcing services. As per Gartner's analysis, India is in a position to soak up to more than half of the world's offshore BPO. India is in this advantageous position because of the following factors:

- Vast English-speaking population
- Low labour cost (almost 1/10 of the developed countries)
- Young generation's liking for computer education
- Expertise developed by the Indian IT Industry in services like health, education, tourism, banking, finance, etc.
- Time differential between US and India, enabling Indian BPO firms to provide twenty-four hours round the clock service.
- Incentives provided by the government like tax holidays for BPO till 2010.
- Reliable, dedicated and qualified manpower.

The areas of operation which provide tremendous opportunities for BPO are customer services, payment services, HR, content development and data processing. HR outsourcing from India accounts for 14-15% of total offshore BPO.

The challenges which Indian offshore BPO firms are facing are both at micro and macro levels. Even though the world economy is globalising fast, developed countries are not willing to provide level playing fields in BPO. They have their own apprehensions on certain counts such as employment, confidentiality, service delivery, etc. Internal weaknesses at firm level in the form of poor infrastructure, lack of qualified manpower, absence of standards and norms, low wage structure, etc. affect working efficiency and quality of the services rendered. The major challenges of offshore outsourcing for Indian service providers are as under:

* Anti-outsourcing campaigns in Europe and the USA due to the fear of loss of jobs for locals.
* Less developed telecom services as compared to the West.
* Service delivery norms not fixed.
* Visa regulations and tax structures vary from country to country.
* Law and order situation critical in some countries due to terrorism and poor governance.
* Wide variations in the wage structure and employment policies of different countries.
* Intense competition between developing countries to procure offshore BPO business.

BPO has developed in recent years as more and more firms have realised that focusing on core business pays – 'Do what you do best and leave everything else to BPO'. Cost being the key driver in a competitive era, firms outsource functions/processes to benefit from the economy of scale and expertise of outsourcing agencies. The trend is likely to continue in future as well.

However, BPO is not a panacea. Many firms, big and small, consider HRM as a whole to be a core function. At HRO World Europe Conference in Brussels (2006), Uniliver group's senior Vice-President for Global HR transactions said that Uniliver did not want the company to outsource its HR. There are many other ways to transform HR.

Review Questions

1. 'Outsourcing as a strategy to divert business processes has become popular with the growth of IT industry'. Discuss.
2. Why companies outsource HR requirements?
3. Discuss outsourcing models. What is 'Intelligent Outsourcing'?
4. Discuss the scope of HR BPO. Is HR outsourcing passing through a transition period?
5. What precautions are needed in selecting service providers?
6. Discuss the importance of offshore outsourcing. What gives India an edge over other countries in offshore BPO?

Further Readings

1. Stewart Clements: *Outsourcing as a Catalyst for Transformation* (Indian Management, Vol. 43, Issue 3, pp. 64-68, March 2004).
2. Anthony Di Romualdo: *Implementing Offshoring Strategically* (E-Business, Vol. 6, Issue 5, pp. 39-42, May 2005).
3. Arun Jetmalani: *Coming of Age: How TCS Yurned into India's Largest BPO Player* (Economic Times, Oct. 23, 2005).
4. Luther, C.T. Sam: *Relevant Costs for Outsourcing Decisions* (Management Accountant, Vol. 39, Issue 12, pp. 964-67, Dec. 2004).
5. Dr. S. Nakkiran and D. John Franklin (eds.): *Business Process Outsourcing (BPO): Concept, Current Trends, Management, Future Challenges* (Deep & Deep Publications Pvt. Ltd., New Delhi, 2005).
6. A.P. Nair: *The Many Hues of Outsourcing* (E-business, Vol. 5, Issue 1, Jan. 2004).
7. Prakash Gurbaxani: *The BPO Industry in India* (E-Business, Vol. 5, Issue 1, pp. 7-15, Jan. 2004).
8. K. Ramchandran: *BPO: Emerging Scenario and Strategic options for Its Enabled Services* (Vikalpa, Vol. 29, Issue 1, pp. 49-62, Jan-March 2004).
9. Brian S. Sommer: *Smart HR-BPO* (E-business, Vol. 5, Issue 8, pp. 43-56, Aug 2004).
10. M. Yalamanchi: *Sacrificial HR Strategy in Call Centers* (E-Business, Vol. 1, pp. 72-79, Jan. 2004).

Chapter 19

Downsizing and Restructuring

Then, in the 1980's, came the paroxysm of downsizing, and the very nature of the corporation was thrown into doubt. In what began almost as a fad and quickly matured into an unshakable habit, companies were 'restructuring,' 'reengineering,' and generally cutting as many jobs as possible, white collar as well as blue . . . The New York Times captured the new corporate order succintly in 1987, reporting that it 'eschews loyalty to workers, products, corporate structures, businesses, factories, communities, even the nation. All such allegiances are viewed as expendable under the new rules. With survival at stake, only market leadership, strong profits and a high stock price can be allowed to matter'.

– **Barbara Ehrenreich,**
(Bright-sided: How the Relentless Promotion of Positive Thinking has Undermined America)

Learning Objectives

After reading this chapter you will be able to:

1. Understand the rationale behind downsizing and restructuring decisions.
2. Analyse its impact on retrenched employees and also on those who survive such operations.
3. Suggest restructuring plans beneficial to the organisation by minimising the pain of downsizing of the workforce.

The move to downsize the staff began in 1990s to conserve resources and cut expenses because markets were becoming highly competitive world over. This was the decade in which many countries started liberalising and privatising their economies. Foreign firms got entry into domestic markets making it competitive, specially in consumer goods which were in short supply in closed economies and underdeveloped economies. Cost control measures were taken by many corporations to have an edge in international markets. Domestic companies also needed to reduce costs because of the entry of foreign firms offering goods at a lower price. Employees were the first victims of the cutback in expenses. In capitalist countries, the process was smooth as laws favoured employers. In countries where labour is well protected by law, the process has been slower. In India, for instance, lay-off and retrenchments are not easy. Big corporations as well as small entrepreneurs have been demanding relaxations in rules in this regard.

Defining Downsizing

Kim Cameron defines downsizing as a set of activities undertaken on the part of management, and designed to improve organisational efficiency, productivity and/or competitiveness. It represents "a strategy implemented by managers that affects the size of firm's workforce, the costs and the work processes."

The above definition emphasises three main strategies in downsizing work processes.

Some companies describe their downsizing effort as rightsizing and restructuring, but the end result in most cases is pruning of employees – reducing workforce. Such restructuring is not needed in all cases. Its no exaggeration to say that in the garb of restructuring, downsizing is forced in many organisations. It has become a rule rather than an exception.

Downsizing may be needed at times when company is heading towards bankruptcy. Also when mergers and acquisitions take place, some staff may become surplus due to the restructuring of organisation. In such cases, it might be a better idea to consolidate some of the functions in one department which were earlier being handled by different departments.

Downsizing is also resorted to when companies decide to shift from permanent jobs to flexible work arrangements by outsourcing and/or employing part-time staff to do the jobs earlier being performed by regular staff. Organisations faced with a situation of 'shelf sitters' or 'dead wood' staff may also resort to downsizing.

New technology may also force organisations to downsize. Computers, for instance, have changed the look of offices world over – lesser number of people are now handling the jobs earlier performed by large numbers. It has also resulted in reducing the layers of hierarchy.

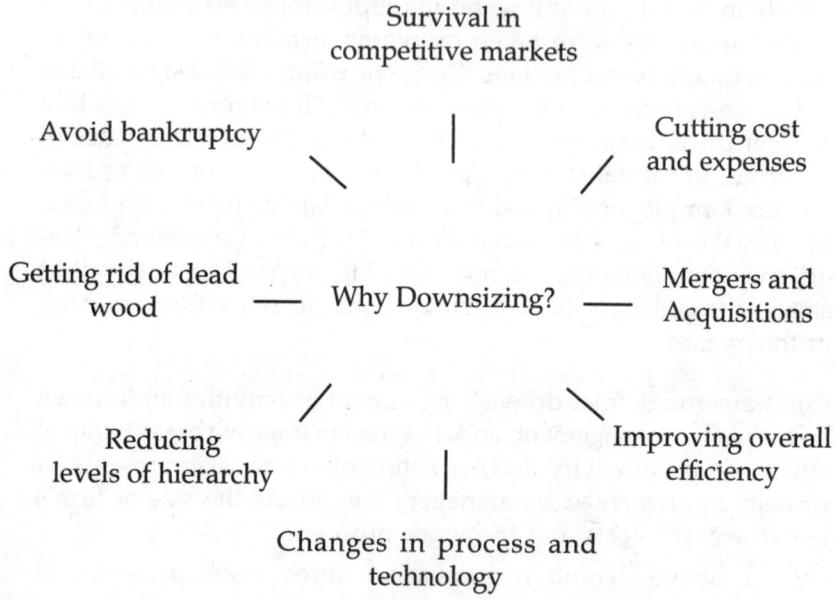

Fig: 19.1 : Reasons for Downsizing

Downsizing decisions are not easy for any organisation. It has a human side, too. People who have given their 'soul' to the organisation, have been loyal to it and contributed to its growth, get depressed mentally and physically when shunted out.

Impact on Employees

Employees suffer the most from downsizing, losing their means of livelihood for no fault of their own. Companies become bankrupt because of mismanagement. Mergers and acquisitions take place as a result of decisions by the controlling authorities of the company. The workforce employed has practically no say in such decisions. Only in cases where the company suffers losses due to trade union activities – strikes, work stoppages, slowdowns, violence – workers may be blamed. Research studies in different countries have shown serious adverse effects on the health, physical as well as mental, of the employees who are shown the door. Besides the loss of regular income, psychological distress is also painful. Work-related injury, accidents, occupational diseases and cardiovascular diseases may occur if job security is threatened. Family life is disturbed with the loss of means of living. In countries where there is no in-built social security system, the impact on workforce is even more severe. This is the situation in most developing and underdeveloped countries which provide large markets to the corporations of the West.

The survivors of downsizing also suffer from uncertainty, fear of loss of job in future, pressure of accepting charges at work, shifting to unwanted locations and distasteful jobs under compulsion. A change in the perception of surviving employees is witnessed in most organisations when downsizing takes place. Work-related stress, mental stress and low morale are the results of uncertainty. In many cases, management's decision to pick and choose, retain or retrench may be seen as unfair and undue exercise of authority. In such circumstances, productivity may go down due to anxiety, resentment, even cynicism and anger. Industrial relations may get a beating once the sword of downsizing appears in an organisation.

Financial performance may also be not up to the expectations of the management which goes for downsizing. In a study by Fortune 100 best companies, it was found that firms engaging in lay-offs continued to perform much more poorly than organisations not laying people off. In some corporations, the gain from downsizing has been a short-term phenomenon only. Long-term gains in most cases have been due to changes in technology, work processes and management techniques. Downsizing may not contribute a major share to such exercises if the chances of relocation and adjustment are possible by improving skills and empowering employees.

Legal Protection

In some countries, workers are protected against undue and unwanted downsizing by law. In Australia, for instance, Federal, State and Territory Occupational Health and Safety legislation imposes obligation on employers who initiate downsizing/restructuring in relation to risk assessment, consultation with employees' representatives, and introduction of appropriate measures to manage any significant hazards, including psychological hazards also.

Labour legislation in India makes it obligatory on the part of the employers to give one month's notice to workers giving reasons for retrenchment, and an intimation to the labour department of the region. 'Last come, first go' is the principle which management has to follow in retrenching workers with compensation at the rate of 15 days' wages for every completed year of service to the workman being retrenched.

Restructuring Plan

Downsizing and restructuring should be well planned. Company should decide the number of jobs which need to be curtailed, number of employees to be retrenched and the time period for implementing the plan to meet the objectives of restructuring. Employees must be informed about the rationale for management action in advance. It should not come as a shock to the people effected. Reemployment or replacement programmes, if possible, should be chalked out and employees taken into confidence. In case company decides for early or voluntary retirement, the amount of compensation should be decided and employees informed accordingly. Some corporations assist employees in outplacement, arrange training programmes for skill upgradation and provide financial help for resettlement. Legal consequences of retrenchment and the cost of compensation should be carefully examined before making the final decision of downsizing. Long-term gains and losses should form the basis of any good restructuring programme. It may be easy to downsize but difficult to find the quality of manpower lost by actions taken in a hurry.

AMACOM cautioned managements in the early nineties not to rush with downsizing without proper planning and necessary preparations. The main message is summarised as under:

1. There is no quick fix; overnight changes do not tend to last; gimmicky approaches to organisational change can hurt more than they can help.
2. Build, don't destroy; plan restructuring around sources of future competitive advantage, not just the elimination of today's internal problems.
3. Manage staff like a business, control the size and scope of overhead functions by creating an internal market place for their services.
4. Flatten the pyramid, not the head count; focus on minimising the number of management levels between the chief executive and first line supervisor.
5. Avoid lay-offs by managing people's flow, give attention to tactics such as targeted incentives for resignation, reemployment and redeployment programmes, conversion of full-time to part-time and contractor filled positions.
6. Anticipate downsizing's downside.
7. Stay streamlined, eliminate the root cause of bureaucracy and corporate culture based on mistrust.
8. Start before you have to, act on your schedule, not the one dictated by an aggressive competitor or junk bond fuel reader.

Downsizing With Golden Handshake

Downsizing with attractive compensation packages has not been very successful in India. When the scheme was initiated a few years back, it was received with enthusiasm, but the euphoria soon died. In majority cases, unskilled, semi-skilled and low-paid office employees who opted for the scheme, realised their folly soon enough, as alternate jobs were difficult to find and the money received as compensation was spent soon. In most cases, only the employees approaching retirement age benefited. Sitting at home at an early age is a social stigma and also demoralising. Psychological and behavioural aspects are no less important than financial incentives. McGregor's theory Y which states that work is as important as play or sleep is validated in such circumstances.

Downsizing and restructuring are management decisions. HR division has to implement it keeping in view the human side of the enterprise. On the one hand, it has to assist and advise operational departments to maximise productivity through human resource, maintain inventory of people and retain qualified manpower, on the other hand, it has to communicate effectively with the effected employees both before and at the time of retrenchment and provide necessary counselling, training, reemployment, outplacement, if possible, and payment of compensation in time.

Situation Analysis

Software major Wipro restructured its organisation to turn a leaner, meaner self in the backdrop of emerging opportunities, growing competition and slower show in recent years. The Bangalore-based giant consolidated its business segments (verticals), rejigged its service line and introduced country-specific marketing plans with a customer-centric focus.

The new initiatives make the organisation's several business unit heads report directly to the new CEO who took charge recently. The company has been lagging behind its major industrial rivals for sometime. The decision to restructure the organisation was taken to have the right structure and right people on board. Business divisions were consolidated into six from the earlier nine which include energy and utilities, finance solutions, media and telecom, pharmaceuticals and healthcare, manufacturing and hi-tech and retail, and transportation.

The changes aim to drive higher agility and customer centricity apart from reducing organisational complexities, thereby driving better accountability. Country-focused structure will be evolved to manage emerging markets.

Comment on the necessity of lean structure and its likely impact on company employees.

Review Questions

1. Define downsizing and explain the reasons for restructuring and downsizing.
2. 'Employees suffer the most from downsizing.' Comment.
3. What is the impact of downsizing on survivors? What can be done by the organisation to keep up their morale?
4. 'Downsizing and restructuring should be well planned.' Comment.
5. Comment on the message of AMACOM to managements going for downsizing.
6. Why downsizing experiments even with handsome compensation packages fail to give desired results?

Further Readings

1. Robert M. Tomasko: *Downsizing: Reshaping the Corporation for the Future* (AMACOM, 1990).
2. K.S. Cameron: *Strategies for Successful Downsizing* (Human Resource Management, Vol. 33, pp. 189-211, 1994).
3. W. Cascio, C.E. Young and J.R. Morris: *Financial Consequences of Employment-Change Decisions In Major U.S. Corporations* (Academy of Management Journal, Vol. 40, pp. 1175-1189, 1997)
4. H. Lam and Y. Reshef: *Are Quality Improvement and Downsizing Compatible? A Human Resource Perspective* (Relations Industrielles, Vol. 54, pp. 727-747, 1999).
5. Kenneth Paul De Meuse and Mitchell Lee Marks: *Resizing the Organization: Managing Layoffs, Divestitures, and Closings* (Pfeiffer, 2003)
6. William J. Baumol, Alan S. Blinder and Edward N. Wolff: *Downsizing in America: Reality, Causes, and Consequences* (Russel Sage Foundation, New York, 2003)

Chapter 20

Employee Empowerment

"Empowerment is not giving power to people, but releasing the power people already have."

– Ken Blanchard

Learning Objectives

After reading this chapter you will be able to:

1. Understand the need to empower employees with authority to take decisions independently.
2. Analyse management techniques to empower employees.
3. Elaborate Kaizen and five 'S' approach to improve organisational effectiveness with employee's involvement.

Organisations are no longer a one way sheet. Independent entrepreneurship and initiative are needed at every level of the organisation. Hierarchal structure is giving way to flat organisations, specially in knowledge-based industries. Employees need to be provided with resources and technical know how in an environment which permits them to take decisions quickly and act in time. Boon and Kurtz (1998) define employee empowerment as 'enlargement of employee jobs to make decisions about their work without supervisory approval while still creating value for customers.' Delery and Doty (1996) consider it 'a process of multiplying power or greater autonomy in an organisation.'

Empowerment involves encouraging employees to take active role in organisational work, involve themselves by taking responsibility and enable and empower them with authority to take decisions.

Empowerment plans should include sharing of information on company's goals and objectives, trust building through team work, providing support system to enable employees to take challenges at job, performance evaluation and feedback system, skill building and developing leadership qualities. All members need to be empowered in an organisation. Power should not be looked as a zero-sum game – one person's gain as loss of another – but as empowering all to achieve organisational goals.

Levels of Empowerment

Empowerment begins by capacity building – enabling people to shoulder higher responsibility and challenges at work and involving them in creative pursuits. Suggestion schemes, formal and informal training, team building exercises, and rewards and incentives enable people to take initiative.

At the grass-root level, employees need to be involved in operative decisions and encouraged to suggest better methods of work and techniques. Their ideas should be implemented if found useful and suitably rewarded. Supervision is also crucial at this stage. The role of supervisor should be helping and problem solving rather than instructing.

At the middle management level, opportunities should be created to show excellence as at this level there may be uncertainties about future in the minds of some employees. Opportunities at higher level may be limited. Those with potential should be trained and encouraged to shoulder higher responsibilities and rewarded suitably. Job enrichment may be a potential tool to empower employees at this level.

At higher level management, decision-making process should aim at autonomy. There are organisations where manager's participation in management is low. Most decisions are made by a few people at the top where power is concentrated. Accountability of managers can be improved by empowering them with authority to decide and show results.

Empowerment at all levels need information sharing, exchange of ideas, involvement in the change process, creating confidence, delegating and trusting, sharing the value system, effective supervision and leadership change in power structures whenever necessary.

Fig: 20.1 Empowering People at Work

The basic assumption of empowerment emanates from the thinking that people have a wealth of knowledge, motivation and energy. Only a part of this is utilised at work. Management has to create an environment in which people are willing to give their best.

Women constitute half of the world population, but a majority of them world over are engaged in the informal work sector. In large parts of the world, they are confined to home, looking after family, kitchen and low-paid occupations. In politics, administration and management, and professions like engineering medical, legal, etc.

Empowerment of Women

their participation is still limited. This is not because women are inferior to men in terms of knowledge, initiative and energy to do higher level jobs. Cultural and social stigmas, customs and traditions have confined them to home and low level jobs. Wherever women get an opportunity, they show excellence in diverse fields. In recent years, education and constitutional guarantee of equal opportunity have helped women in many countries to come up on the front in industry and other professions where they have excelled. A Fortune 500 study (2008) found that big corporations with more women directors had significantly higher financial returns, including 53% higher return on equity, 24% higher return on sales and 67% higher return on invested capital.

Empowerment of women for higher administrative and managerial jobs require change in the attitudes of men holding senior positions, attitude of women themselves towards their capacity and ability to do jobs involving higher responsibility, and suitable working and service conditions for women which may reduce the conflicts in office. Organisations should provide training for new skills and higher managerial assignments to women, encourage them to participate in decision-marking and reward them for showing excellence without discrimination.

Kaizen To Empower

Kaizen means 'improvement' involving everyone in the organisation – managers as well as workers. It has two major components – maintenance and improvement. Current managerial and technological standards should be maintained and continuously improved. It requires flow of ideas, even day-to-day small ideas, adapting to changes in techniques and methods that are more productive, and their implementation within realistic and practical constraints and opportunities. The processes involved should result in eliminating or reducing waste, and providing benchmarks for efficient functioning. The steps involved in Kaizen process are:

1. Identification of problems – waste or opportunity – to improve upon them.
2. Developing an idea to discuss it with the supervisor.
3. Review of the idea by the supervisor and encouraging the employee to act without losing time.
4. Implementation of the employees's idea and taking leadership if it involves big change.
5. Working in a way that other employees may also understand it.

6. Sharing the idea with other employees who can also use it and encouraging them to implement it.

Kaizen requires company leadership to engage itself with its people with the same level of intensity and seriousness as it does with capital investment and business strategy.

Five 'S' Approach to Empowerment at Work Place

The 5 Ss refers to five Japanese principles for managing work place and improving efficiency. These are:

Seiri (Soft) : Things should be done in a proper order, unnecessary items should be eliminated and the strictly minimum should be kept at the work place.

Seiton (Set in order) : Procedure for cleaning should be developed, things should be kept where they are needed – a place for every thing and every thing in its place. Locations should be properly designed with numbers, colour-coding, etc.

Seiso (Shine) : Procedure for cleaning should be specified, work place should be thoroughly cleaned.

Seiketsu (Standardise) : Best practices should be standardised and equipment and work place should be maintained in the best possible manner.

Sitsuke (Sustain) : Practices should be scrutinised regularly, wrong ones should be exposed, learning and use of correct practices should be ensured.

Canon, which is one of the pioneering organisations using five 'S' approach, even asks its foremen to set aside some time to do nothing but think about improvement in the workshop.

PERSPECTIVE

Engaging People – Tata Group

The Tata Group encourages its employees to buy into the global vision. The vision should not be too generic and nor should it be too codified. It should ideally be crafted in the form of a compelling story in which individuals can write themselves as 'heroes' and 'heroines'. Engaging people is considered important. The critical challenge for a global company leadership is to engage itself with its people with the same level of intensity and seriousness as it does with capital investment or business strategy.

Situation Analysis

You And Microsoft
Microsoft India has identified eight critical needs that employees value and has integrated these in its program to motivate them.

Making A Difference Through Work
Asking people whether they are making a difference through their work, accountability and performance, which are critical elements.

Recognition
Both monetary and non-monetary rewards are given to recognise the contribution of employees. Architects of Excellence Awards, for instance, are given to individual engineers and teams, who go an extra mile to facilitate optimum use of technology and customer satisfaction.

Career Growth
Six business divisions – research, development, testing, consulting, sales and marketing, and support – provide vertical as well as lateral avenues of growth by facilitating movement of people. Employees are constantly mentored by seniors from across the globe.

Fun At Work
Fun@work includes rock bands, stage shows, cricket tournaments, painting competitions, adventure tours and family days. These are organised regularly for all the categories of employees without regard to hierarchy. The company has collaborated with another company to train people for various fun activities. Fun activities aim at improving morale, reducing work-related stress, boosting productivity and promoting creative-thinking.

Environment
Work environment is pleasant with excellent infrastructure, virtual recreational space, rooms for relaxation and flexible dress code.

Care
Medical benefits, employee assistance programmes such as tuition assistance, opportunities to pursue higher education while at work are provided to all employees.

Technology
Employees get an opportunity to work on the latest cutting-edge technology. Product development teams are created for innovating and creating new products.

Money
Flexible pay ensures compensation comparable to the best in the industry.

Review Questions

1. Define empowerment. Is it the same as motivating people?
2. What are the different levels of empowerment? What measures at each level help in empowering people?
3. What are the steps involved in Kaizen process? Why is it necessary for company leadership to engage itself with its people?
4. Explain the 5 'S' approach to work place management and efficiency improvement.
5. What steps will you suggest to empower women in an organisation?
6. "In traditional organisations, managers function as the hub of information. In empowered organisations, information flows in many directions. Managers need to be able to create structures of coordination so that decisions made by individual staff members do not adversely affect the work of others." Comment on the above observation of Robert Bacal, author of *Performance Management*.
7. In a case reported in *The Public Sector Innovative Journal*, it was observed that a company delegated management power to the front line staff without any employee request or agreement. In a non-unionised environment, employees were offered the opportunity to share profit, to set salaries, to be involved in recruiting managers and front line staff and to control financial resources. The highest amount of resistance came from the middle and senior managers, some of whom lost their jobs as a result of the changes. But the company continued to grow after this.
Discuss the desirability of introducing such schemes.

Further Readings

1. Conrad Lashley: *Empowerment: HR Strategies for Service Excellence*, (Butterworth-Heinemann, 2001).
2. Ken, Blanchard, John, P. Carbos, and Alan Randelf, Berrett Koehler Publishers, San Francisco, 2001).
3. Kenneth L. Murell and Mimi Meredith: *Empowering Employees* (McGraw-Hill, 2000).
4. Thomas A. Potterfield: *Democracy and the Ideology in Workplace*, (Greenwood Publishing Co. New York, 1999).
5. K.W. Thomas and B.A. Velthouse: *Cognitive Elements of Emporwerment: An Interpretive Model of Intrinsic Task Motivation* (Academy of Management Review, Vol. 15, Issue 4, pp. 666-668, 1990).
6. William Byham: *Zapp! The Lightning of Empowerment: How to Improve Productivity, Quality and Employee Satisfaction* (Ballantine Books, New York, 1997).

21

HRM in Transnational Corporations

The excellent companies have a deeply ingrained philosophy that says in effect: "Respect the individual", "Make people winners", "Let them stand out", and "Treat people as adults."

– **Thomas J. Peters and Robert H. Waterman, Jr.**
(In Search of Excellence: Lessons from America's Best Run Companies)

Learning Objectives

After reading this chapter you will be able to:

1. Understand the role of global, country and functional managers when it comes to managing multinational business.
2. Analysis career opportunities and threats for global managers.
3. Elaborate company approaches and HR management practices of TNCs.

Transnational corporations today are the powerhouses of generating wealth, technology and talent. Many of them wield more economic power than the nation-state in which they operate. In an emerging global market, they have assumed the roles of producers and suppliers of the most sophisticated capital and consumer goods, financial and banking services, transport, communication, insurance and a wide variety of services across the globe. Many of them are household names in developed as well as developing countries. These corporations are instrumental in breaking economic boundaries among nations. A passage from Walter Wriston's *Risk and Other Four Letter Words* aptly describes the role of these corporations in international business:

"Natural gas, owned by Indonesia's oil agency, Pertamina, flows out of a well discovered by Royal Dutch Shell into a liquidation plant designed by French engineers and a Korean construction company. The liquefied gas is located onto US flag tanks, built in US yards after a Norwegian design. The ship shuttles to Japan and delivers the liquid gas to a Japanese public utility that powers an electronic factory making television sets that are shipped aboard a Hong Kong-owned container ship to California for sale to American farmers in Louisiana who grow rice that is sold to Indonesia and shipped there aboard Greek bulk carriers. All of the various facilities, ships, products and services involved in the complex series of events are financed by US, European and Japanese commercial banks..."

Transnational corporations need highly qualified people to manage their enterprises. These people come from different countries with different economic, social and cultural backgrounds. These corporations have generally three layers of managers: global, country and functional.

Global Managers

The global managers, located mostly at the head office or the key offices, are the strategists, problem solvers and crisis handlers. They perceive opportunities, calculate risk, decide to invest or divest, diversify or concentrate and control business at the global level. They are concerned with the development of global products, global information flow, global negotiations, global efficiency and competitiveness. They operate in an environment which is ever changing, challenging and difficult.

Country Managers

The country managers are located at the national headquarters and manufacturing plants or business centres. They are required to assess local potentialities, local needs and aspirations, and provide localness in product's look, brand projection and promotion. They are the local resource builders and team leaders. They run a foreign enterprise within the framework of the political, social and economic environment of a country. They have to implement the policies framed at the headquarters, but they do contribute to such policies by providing their own assessment of situations and opportunities.

Functional Managers

The functional managers are located at manufacturing sites and business places with specific responsibilities in such areas as production, R&D, finance, personnel distribution and product promotion, advertising and sales management. They provide supporting role to the country managers. Their role as innovators and in-cross pollinators has become very important in recent years. It has resulted into the upgradation of local labs into global centres of technical excellence in some transnationals. The functional managers operate in a given environment and are required to contribute to global efficiency and competitiveness. Senior functional experts in most organisations act as 'linchpins' connecting their areas of specialisation across frontiers with other sister organisations. In some cases, however, functional departments are used as 'a warehouse for corporate misfits' or the 'graveyard for managerial has-beens'.

Qualities of Overseas Managers

Transnational corporations require people of high calibre. It is not always easy to locate and attract such people. There is a truth in the statement of one of the former chairmen of Unilever, Floris Maljers, that the biggest constraint in most globalisation efforts is not unreliable or inadequate sources of capital but limitation in human resources. The world market today is characterised by intense competition, technological revolution, consumer sovereignty and environmental constraints. It is the human resource which provides an edge to the organisation in such a complex environment.

The qualities which are needed in managers working overseas include technical competence and leadership abilities; knowledge of foreign language, culture, customs and traditions; rules and regulations; and willingness to adapt to a new environment. A supporting wife, willing to suffer inconveniences initially in a new place and a different social order, may be of great help. In a survey of a large number of American executives working abroad, this fact of adaptability by family was found to be the most crucial to the success of executives.

Transnational corporations are managed professionally. Managers recruited must be highly qualified personnel who are flexible, deployable, multi-skilled, multi-disciplinary and cross-cultural.

Overseas Managers: Background for Success

Background	Percentage
Wife and family adaptability	20
Leadership ability	19
Knowledge of job	14
Knowledge of language	13
Well educated	13
Respect for laws and people of host country	12
Previous overseas experience	4
Desire to serve overseas	4
Miscellaneous	1
Total	100

(Based on a survey of American Executives abroad by Gonzalez and Negandhi)

Career Opportunities and Threats

Managers in global companies have immense opportunities to rise. They have challenging jobs where they can show their metal. They are to work in a cross-cultural setting which makes them learn new languages, mix up with people of diverse cultures, develop their human relations skill and leadership qualities. They can excel as planners, strategists, architects and builders of new units in an unfamiliar environment and get recognition. A managerial job, however, is not a bed of roses. There are threats in the environment. One's wife and children may not adapt easily to the new environment. The husband being terribly busy in office may make the wife feel lonely and isolated. It may take time to socialise in the new environment. Schooling may not be of the same standard as in the home country. Language barriers may further increase the isolation of the family. Problems relating to housing, repatriation, personal insecurity and political risks have to be faced. There is also the fear of losing hold in the head office of the mother company. As postings overseas are normally transferable, after returning back the employee may find that juniors working there have surpassed him and occupied positions which may be difficult to get. The constraints of environment may affect efficiency and performance initially. The first assignment abroad may be difficult, but adaptability develops while working in the new environment and gradually makes the person a global manager.

> **PERSPECTIVE**
>
> **T-type People – Toyota**
>
> *Toyota develops T-type people.*
>
> The vertical stroke of the T stands for the fact that employees must intensify or deepen what they do, and the horizontal stroke indicates that they must learn their jobs.
>
> Creating T-type personnel is a time-consuming process. However, in many countries outside Japan its tough to employ people for a long-term. Toyota's experience has shown that the moment they start operations, turnover begins. Earlier, the company transmitted the Toyota way of working through the mother plant system, whereby a Japanese plant served as the parent of each new overseas plant set up by it. That Japanese plant was responsible for training people in the overseas plant and instilling the Toyota way in them. Because of the rate at which the company is growing overseas, it has done away with the old practice. It now sends people from Japan, coordinators, to instil company's philosophy and concepts in the overseas companies. When a new company is established, the coordinator serves as a teacher, or sensei, for its employees. After some years, a second generation coordinator will serve as an adviser rather than a coach. The coordinators are critical to train people in the Toyota way.

Career Overseas

(Opportunities and Threats)

Opportunities	Threats
Job challenges	Loneliness and homesickness for wife and children
Promotion prospects	Schooling for children
Recognition	Housing problems
Higher emoluments	Language barriers
Learning new languages	Repatriation problems
Mixing with people of different cultures	Personal insecurity
Improvements in technical competence, interpersonal skills and leadership qualities	Political risks and uncertainties, losing seniority in the hierarchy of home office
Increased adaptability to new environments	Stress of new environment affecting performance in initial stages

Employment Policy

Managers may be recruited from home country only, or from home country and host country or even from a third country. There are four major approaches to the employment policy of transnational corporations: ethnocentric, geocentric, regeocentric and polycentric. Ethnocentric policy leads to the recruitment of managers for all senior positions from the home country only. This helps in planning, controlling and creating a distinct culture for the organisation; but when carried to the extreme, it results in discrimination against host country managers who become second-rate citizens. Geocentric approach is based on the philosophy that the best people should be recruited from the world over. No discrimination in matters of promotion, compensation and status is practised. The polycentric approach delegates most of the powers to host country units so that qualified local personnel may be recruited and trained. This helps in identifying local talents who may prove to be an asset to the organisation due to their acquaintance with local language, local laws, customs and habits of people. But carried too forward, this policy may result in alleviating the host country units from home country. The regeocentric approach produces recruitment within a specified region which may consist of several units in a continent or subcontinent. Most companies follow a mix of these approaches.

Approaches to HRM in TNCs

Ethnocentric

An enterprise prefers to recruit managers from home country, rewards them more handsomely, offers them better terms of employment and perks, provides them better opportunities to rise in the organisation, gives them more power and authority and treats them as superior to the host country nationals.

Geocentric

The best available brains are taken from wherever available – home country or host country. Compensation policy is the same for all, no discrimination is practised in terms of employment, perks and benefits, promotions/transfers to higher positions, delegation of authority and status in organisation. Even a host country manager may rise to the top in the company.

Polycentric

A policy of recruiting local managers for local units is favoured. Knowledge of local culture, language and environment is preferred. Local managers enjoy a certain degree of authority and autonomy in managing their business. Employment, compensation, promotion and transfer policies, and service conditions are decided in terms of the needs of the local units. The head office exercises overall control. Upward movement in units located outside the host country is possible only on exceptional merits.

Regeocentric

Managers from the region are preferred, e.g. an American company may prefer Europeans for its offices in Europe, Asians in Asia, etc. The service conditions, compensation, promotion and transfer policies may be uniform for all managers in the same region, transfer or upward movement to other regions possible in selected cases. A decentralised set-up is gradually emerging. While the recruitment for key positions at the head office and abroad are largely done in the country of origin of the corporation, country and functional managers are getting recruited locally. Many transnationals have management trainee schemes. Young recruits are trained for global responsibilities. The brighter ones are picked up for trans-border assignments at a young age. Functional executives with outstanding performance also get into the global net sooner rather than later. Some companies draw from a pool of trained people in selected countries. Cummins, for instance, has set up its highly skilled Indian Engineering Group as a worldwide drafting resource.

> **PERSPECTIVE**
>
> **'Mc Job' Perception**
>
> In 1991, Douglas Copland coined the word 'Mc Job' in his best seller *'Generation X: Tales from An Accelerated Culture'*. He defined Mc Job as 'a low paying, low prestige, low dignity, low benefit, no future job in the service sector'.
>
> By 2003, the term 'Mc Job' had become acceptable, distorting company image and adversely affecting restaurant employment.
>
> The reaction from McDonald's was strong. It described the term 'Mc Job' inaccurate and a slap on the face of 12 million men and women who were working in the restaurant industry. A media campaign was launched to debunk the Mc Job stereotypes. A series of advertisements were released highlighting the benefits of a Mc Job, each ending with the tagline 'Not Bad For Mc Job'.
>
> McDonald's campaign featured the likes of Olympic gold medalist Carl Lewis, Japanese artist Shguru Otake and late night television shows hosting award winning artists and singers. The campaign was intended to inspire the existing employees, attract new ones and convince customers that if you begin a career at McDonald's, the sky is the limit.

Supply Constraints

The emigration policy of most developed countries being highly restrictive, the inflow of human resource from outside is limited. The problem is further complicated by reluctance on the part of many professional spouses to give up their jobs. There are differences in schooling and education patterns of different countries, and also differences in the quality of life, which is poor, particularly in less developed countries which are the greener pastures for transnationals. The growth of unconventional areas like services, and the employee's preference for small companies to occupy the highest seat at a relatively young age instead of waiting in the hierarchy in a large organisation are other reasons for the restricted flow of qualified personnel to transnational corporations. The tough supply position in some cases has even led to a strategy of deploying consultants and investors rather than general management and technical personnel for local operations in different countries.

In Europe, many transnationals prefer Europeans only. This policy will be further strengthened by the 'Social Charter' of EEC which also calls for the transnationalisation of procedures in human resource management and directives on working hours, formation of a European Works Council of community scale undertakings, tighter control on collective redundancies, mutual recognition of vocational qualifications, improvement in national and cross-border training programmes, etc. It is not yet certain whether EEC social charter will also lead to a uniform pay across Europe. The subsidiaries of European transnationals outside Europe will also be affected by the social charter. Some European companies are in no mood to promote local culture in their subsidiaries outside Europe. They prefer sending their experts to manage and promote the national culture of parent organisation. But some have chosen the other way. BP, for instance, has recently established a new European finance centre in Brussels with 40 staff belonging to 13 different nationalities from BP finance centres throughout the world.

Japanese TNCs' Practices

The Japanese transnationals outside Japan follow the basic principles of lifetime employment and seniority wage system in modified forms. In host countries, companies recruit local people for operative and technical jobs. For managerial positions, it is a mix of executives from the parent organisation and local talents. Long-term employment policy is followed by most organisations. Seniority-based promotion is not the rule. In many organisations, promotions are awarded on merit. Performance appraisal system of Western style is being increasingly used by them which is against the principle of collective functioning at home. But one thing is common to all Japanese transnationals – the single status system. Employees are provided common uniform and common facilities like canteen, parking, etc. Every effort is made to minimise the barriers between management and employees. Everyone has to record time, and has the same sick pay and entitlement for medical treatment. Morning exercise is done in most organisations.

Training and Career Planning

The development of human resource through training, career planning and participation in decision-making process is high on the agenda of all transnationals. The strategy of development may consist of 5 Ts: Talent identification, Training, Transfers, Tracking the career and Team building. These corporations are constantly looking for high calibre people in areas of their interest, both from within and without. Talents from outside are identified and attracted to join on handsome pay and perks, and those from inside are given recognition by better status, higher responsibilities and emoluments. A corporation's ability to attract talents worldwide and develop and retain them is the clearest indicator of its being a transnational. It is no surprise that some of the top scientists, engineers and experts in various fields are on the rolls of transnational corporations.

Training in most corporations starts from the day an employee joins the organisation. Most Japanese companies abroad, for instance, have a systematic induction programme for new recruits. The programme includes Japan familiarisation courses to help employees understand Japanese customs and way of life, in addition to information about the company rules and regulations on attendance and punctuality, good housekeeping, quality, etc. European and American transnationals also have a tradition of systematic induction of new employees. Training programmes for transnational managers aim at developing four basic skills: effectiveness skills, coping skills, survival skills and problem-solving skills. Effectiveness skills are developed to enable them to fit in a different set of relations with subordinates, business associates and customers, as well as in dealings with regulatory political and market environment. Coping skills are developed to enable them to adjust in environments and cultures alien to them and their families. The survival skills training is given to those who are sent on short-term assignments, for example, technical experts sent for installing a new plant abroad. The trainees are acquainted with the uniqueness of the culture of the place of their temporary posting. Problem-solving skills are developed in trainees keeping in view the nature of assignments and the type of issues which may come up in the country of posting. In addition to the above, regular training and executive development programmes are organised for management and technical personnel in most corporations. The techniques used in such programmes are case sessions, sensitivity lab, role playing, business games, brainstorming sessions, etc. Such programmes aim at sharpening behavioural skills and decision-making and problem-solving abilities. Training programmes for updating functional managers are also organised regularly by company managements. Technicians and skilled personnel from subsidiaries are sent for training to production centres and training institutes abroad. Most Japanese companies send selected technical personnel from their subsidiaries to Japan for intensive training in their manufacturing plants. The Japanese transnationals have systematic predeparture preparations. Normally, a year before departure the person starts getting information about the culture, customs and ways of doing business in the country for which he is destined. He is also given language training. When he arrives at the new place, he gets a mentor who is responsible for helping him with any problem. Efforts are made to reduce alienation in the new environment. Assignment abroad is treated as an integral part of the job and rewarded accordingly.

Executive Transfers

Executive transfers are a common phenomena in transnationals. Some organisations in the West provide services to spouses, offer dislocation allowance, subsidy to study abroad and displacement service allowance to make international deployment less painful and more attractive. Continuous performance appraisal and tracking the career of executives are also taken seriously by most transnationals. Unilever, for instance, has a clear policy of recruiting from across the globe, rotating managers through various jobs and moving them around the world, preparing career blueprints and appraising performance systematically and tracking careers of promising executives over a number of years before giving them senior responsibilities. The company maintains four development lists to indicate the level of each manager and also his or her potential. A special committee, consisting of two chairmen, tracks the career of those who qualify to be in the Al list. Unilever's HRD policy has paid rich dividends. It is one of the first transnationals to have a strong pool of specialised yet interdependent senior managers, drawn from its diverse organisations.

Team Work

The ability to develop a team, lead it and work with it is one of the key skills of transnational managers. Unlike a local organisation where the workplace may consist of people with similar social and cultural backgrounds, multinational managers have to organise people of diverse nationalities, languages, customs and lifestyles. The managers who are able to go beyond personal inhibitions and hierarchical barriers, and build communication network with their counterparts in different countries are likely to be more successful. A classic case on the point is of Wahid Zaki of Proctor and Gamble. Zaki disapproved of his company' high-walled organisation structure which isolated and insulated the technical development carried out in each subsidiary lab. He is accredited with forming European Technical Teams and running a series of conferences, in which like-minded experts from different countries could exchange their findings, and build an information network to coordinate their efforts on the problems they were working on. It was this team which developed the liquid detergent which had a triumphant roll out in several countries with brand names Liquid Tide in the USA, Liquid Cheer in Japan and Liquid Ariel in Europe and Asia. The Japanese transnationals are known for creating confidence in their employees by giving them a role in decision-making. The Komatsu factory at Birtlay, in the north-east England, for example, has a provision for 'Advisory Council' to provide a forum for the active involvement of the employees and the union in regular discussions on the progress of the company. The first pay review of Komatsu took place in 1987. The council was presented with information on the progress of the company in its first year and on movement in the cost of living and comparable earnings. On the basis of this information, the council recommended 5% increase in wages. Management accepted the recommendation. There was no separate negotiation for pay increase with the union. It was considered to be a matter to be worked out 'in house'. In a survey of Japanese companies in Hong Kong, it was found that the highest emphasis was on group harmony, democratic and participative management, and decision-making by consensus. Out of the ten unique features of Japanese management, the above three qualified for the first three positions; job rotation, welfare, promotion, etc. scored low.

Managerial Remuneration

Managers are the most scarce and costly resource in the competitive world of today. Transnational corporations having production, business or service centres in different parts of the world, find it difficult to have a uniform policy of pay, perks and incentives for their managers. The level of hardships at jobs in different locations may not be the same. The cost of index differs from one country to another. The quality of life varies from one city to another. When a person takes an overseas assignment, he may have to maintain two establishments, one at home and the other in the host country. If the wife joins him and leaves her job, there is a loss of income to the family. Food of the type desired may not be available. Schools may be very costly. The employee expects to be compensated for such hardships in his overseas assignment. There is a practice of giving hardship allowance in some companies. Most organisations compensate employees for the cost of living. The UN index is used for this purpose. Employees are also compensated for currency fluctuations and inflation rates. A balance-sheet approach is followed by some corporations. It takes the existing pay as the base and adds overseas allowance to it. The pay packet includes cost of living allowance, conditions of living allowance and residence allowance keeping in view the situation at the location of posting. Deductions from salary are made on account of taxes, pensionary and statutory benefits as per the rules. In many organisations, salary to managers recruited from overseas is paid partly in home currency and partly in host country currency, if the two are different. Employees prefer payment in hard currencies as it ensures stability and convertability. In some jobs, like construction, executives are paid a high salary for a fixed term as their services may be dispensed with after the job is over.

Transnational corporations realise the importance of locating competent people, developing and motivating them for challenging assignments in an environment full of uncertainties and complexities. Though there is no uniform pattern of human resource management and development, a few common features are discernible. There is a recognition of merit. Transnationals are opening their doors to talented people from diverse nationalities. Sons of the soil are finding place in local units managed by transnationals. The opportunities are available not only for operating personnel but for managerial and technical personnel as well. Top positions in most organisations are held by executives belonging to the countries of origin of the corporations. Management development is given a high priority by most transnationals. A very systematic career planning, appraisal, training and promotion system exists. With globalisation of economies, the need for cross-pollinating the best ideas and practices in management is growing. Transnational corporations can play an important role in preparing the managers of tomorrow.

Situation Analysis

The HR manager of a German subsidiary in India is happy with the kind of work she is doing and the company she is a part of. She describes how respectfully people react when they are told who the employer is. The company's brand is one of the best in the market, expensive but superb in quality, manufactured with the most advanced technology. The company has a long tradition of manufacturing in Germany in a highly competitive environment.

A big motivating factor for the staff is the cheerful environment of the organisation. Colleagues are friendly and there is mingling in the group, so nobody feels isolated. Taking lunch together, utilising spare time in indoor games and outings after work is a good way of blowing off some steam in an organisation which has long working hours. When it comes to performance, the company makes its people walk on a tight rope. Anything that can damage company's name and brand is taken seriously. Hierarchy is to be respected. Heads of sub-divisions meet every week to coordinate their efforts and review progress while in monthly meetings important decisions are taken. The HR manager participates in these meetings where everyone is treated equal.

The communication between officers and the staff in the local unit is described as more open and friendly than it is in Germany where corporate environment is more hierarchical as experienced by the HR manager in her visits to the head office.

How does environment inside the organisation motivate people?

Review Questions

1. Discuss the responsibilities of global managers and the qualities needed in them to manage TNCs.
2. What are the career opportunities and threats for overseas managers?
3. Discuss the employment policy of TNCs.
4. What are the approaches to HRM in TNCs?
5. How the HRM practices of Japanese companies differ from those of the US and European TNCs.
6. Discuss the specific features of the remuneration policy of TNCs.

Further Readings

1. C.A. Bartlett and S. Ghoshal: *Managing Across Borders: The Transnational Solution* (Harvard Business School Press, Boston, 1989).
2. John B. Cullen: *Multinational Management: A Strategic Approach* (Thompson, 1999).
3. S. Davala: *Labour Strategies in Multinational Corporations in India* (E.S. Friedrick, New Delhi, 1995).
4. Bill Davidson and Jose de la Torre: *Managing the Global Corporation: Cases in Strategy and Management* (McGraw-Hill, New York, 1989).
5. Peter J. Dowling and Denice E. Welch: *International Human Resource Management: Managing People in a Multinational Context* (Cengage Learning, New Delhi, 1999).

6. P. Joynt and Bob Morton (Ed.): *The Global HR Manager: Creating The Seamless Organization* (Jaico Publishing House, Bombay, 2005).
7. R. Schuler, S. Jackson and Y. Luo: *Managing Human Resources in Cross Border Alliances* (Routledge, London, 2003).
8. R.L. Tun: *Selection and Training Procedure for Overseas Assignments* (California Journal of Human Resource, Vol. 40, Issue 1, pp. 68-78, 1984).

STERLING BOOKS ON ECONOMICS, COMMERCE & MANAGEMENT

HUMAN RESOURCE MANAGEMENT:
A Contemporary Text
Fourth Revised Edition
Bhaskar Chatterjee

Contents: Evolution and Emergence • HRM and the Business Organisation • Human Resource Planning • Recruitment, Screening and Selection • Training and Development • Job Analysis and Design • Performance Appraisal • The Japanese Approach • Organisation Structure • Organisation Design • Organisation Culture • Leadership • Change Management, Suggested Readings, • Index

• 2009 • ISBN 978 81 207 4474 5 * 6.75 x 9.75 • 358 pp • ₹ 350

BEST BUSINESS PRACTICES FOR GLOBAL COMPETITIVENESS
Prashant Salwan

Contents: Best Practice in Business – Prashant Salwan
Section A-Information and Communication Technologies
E-commerce—An Introduction to the Concept – Sandhir Sharma and Gulshan Bansal • Playing Leapfrog: Using Strengths in ICT to Energise the Manufacturing Sector in India – Komolica Peres • Achieving Best Practice in Business and Closing the Marketing Gap – Prashant Salwan *Section B-Strategic Tools for Enhancing Performance:* A Strategic Tool for Enhancing Performance—the Balanced Scorecard – V.K. Gupta • Government to Citizen Relationships, Gyandoot—Tales and Travails—A Three-Year E-Governance Experience – Sanjay Dubey • Enterprise Resource Planning – Anand Kr Tiwari *Section C-Outsourcing*: Outsourcing – S. Venkat • Operational Issues in Outsourcing – S. Venkat • Annexures • *Glossary* • Index • *About the Contributors*

2007 • ISBN 978 81 207 3464 7 • 6.75x9.5" • 296 pp • ₹ 400

OFFICE MANAGEMENT AND COMMERCIAL CORRESPONDENCE
Revised & Enlarged Edition
R C Bhatia

Contents: Office Forms and Stationery • Office Records and Filing Management • Indexing • Office Machines and Equipments • Duplicating and Typing • Inward and Outward Mail • Commercial Correspondence • Letters of Enquiry & Quotations • Letters of Order • Letters of Acceptance and Cancellation • Trade Reference Letters • Letters Regarding Complaints, Claims and their Adjustments • Dunning Letters or Collection Letters • Follow-up Letters • Letters Regarding Agency • Correspondence with Banks • Letters Regarding Insurance • Letters Regarding Credit and Introduction • Sales Letters • An Application for the Job • Official Correspondence • Correspondence with Shareholders • Important Terms Used in Offices • Question Papers • *Index*

2011 • ISBN 978 81 207 2483 9 • 5.5x8.5" • 352 pp • ₹ 150

ENVIRONMENTAL ECONOMICS
Revised and Enlarged Edition
Karpagam M

Contents: Section I: Theory and Concepts • Section II: Environmental Problems • Section III: Economic Growth, Environment and Sustainable Development • Section IV: Policy Measures • Section V: Benefit Cost Analysis • Section VI: International Environmental Problems • Section VII: Environmental Problems in Developed and Developing Nations • Basic Terms • Bibliography • Index

2011 • ISBN 978 81 207 2146 3 • 5.5x8.5" • 376 pp • ₹ 175

STRATEGIC MANAGEMENT
An Assessment
Biswanath Ghosh

Contents: Introduction: An Overview • Company's Mission, Vision, Objectives and Goals, and 7-S Framework • Assessing the External Environment • Competitive Strategy: Industry Analysis • Internal Analysis of the Firm • Framework for Analysing Competition: Competitive Advantage of a Firm • Strategy and Structure, Leadership and Culture • Strategic Choice • Strategic Control • Formulating Long-term Objectives and Grand Strategies • Growth Strategies: Intensification, Diversification, Mergers & Acquisitions and Divestment • Turnaround Management • Strategic Change Management • Strategic Time Management • Social Responsibilities and Business • Organisational Culture and Strategy • Strategy and Social Audit • Environment Audit • Learning Curve for Strategic Market Planning • Financial Strategy • Human Resource Strategy • Marketing Strategies • Pricing Strategies • Advertising Strategy • Supply Chain Management • Strategy and Corporate Evolution in the Indian Context • Strategic Management in an International Firm • Bibliography

2007 • ISBN 978 81 207 2702 1 • 5.5x8.5" • 432 pp • ₹ 190

STATISTICAL METHODS
Concept, Application and Computation
Y.P. Aggarwal

Contents: The Study of Statistics • Frequency Distribution and their Graphic Representation • Measures of Central Tendency • Measures of Variability • Measures of Relative Standing • Probability, Binomial Distribution and Normal Distribution • Correlational Techniques • The Significance of mean and other Statistics • The Significance of Difference between means and other Statistics • The Chi-Square Tests and other Non-Parametric Methods • The Analysis of Variance, Anova • The Analysis of Covariance Ancova • Reliability and Validity of Test Scores • Regression and Predication • Tests of Assumptions • Some other Multivariate Methods • An Introductory Note of Second Generation of Multivariate Analysis • Additional Experience for Post Test • Index

2012 • ISBN 978 81 207 2002 2 • 5.5x8.5" • 412 pp • ₹ 225

For further information contact:
mail@sterlingpublishers.com • www.sterlingpublishers.com